Ada 95
The craft of object-oriented programming

John English

University of Brighton

Prentice Hall

London   New York   Toronto   Sydney   Tokyo   Singapore
Madrid   Mexico City   Munich

First published 1997 by
Prentice Hall Europe
Campus 400, Maylands Avenue
Hemel Hempstead
Hertfordshire HP2 7EZ
A division of
Simon & Schuster International Group

Printed and bound in Great Britain by
Hartnolls Limited, Bodmin, Cornwall

Library of Congress Cataloging-in-Publication Data

English, John, 1956–
    Ada 95 : the craft of object-oriented programming / John English.
      p.   cm.
    Includes index.
    ISBN 0–13–230350–7 (alk. paper)
    1. Object-oriented programming (Computer science)   2. Ada
(Computer program language)   I. Title.
QA76.64.E54   1996
005.13'3–dc20   96–18696
                                   CIP

British Library Cataloguing in Publication Data

A catalogue record for this book is available from
the British Library

ISBN 0–13–230350–7

---

1 2 3 4 5   01 00 99 98 97

To Jan and Vivian,
for being so patient with me.

Contents

Preface

The word 'craft' in the title of this book has been chosen deliberately. There have been books published with titles such as 'The Art' or 'The Science' of programming, but I feel that neither of these titles is really appropriate for a textbook like this. In Art, you have a blank canvas and are free to express yourself as the spirit moves you in order to produce Beauty; in Science, you are constrained by 'the laws of physics' to produce Truth. A **craft**, on the other hand, is less free than Art but less constrained than Science. Truth and Beauty are both involved in the process, but Art provides a blank canvas which is rarely found in real-life programming. There is almost always some previous system which has to be conformed to: an existing database or file format, or the peculiarities of a particular operating system. Science searches for Truth, but there is little truth in most programs; only fairly trivial programs are susceptible to correctness proofs at present. Most programs are unwieldy beasts, made like Frankenstein's monster from leftover fragments of previous generations of programs, and neither Art nor Science takes account of this.

Craft skills are concerned with making the best out of available resources. If you are given some wood and asked to make a piece of furniture from it, you have to work within the confines of what that wood will allow. If the wood is knotty at a particular place, you may have to revise your initial plans in order to work around the knots, or you may have to discard some of the wood and find some more which matches the piece you've been given. Craftsmanship is concerned with the ability to work around problems like this. In programming, you are rarely presented with a clean sheet and invited to design the next world-beating program; you are usually presented with an existing program and a list of problems to be resolved. How you choose to solve those problems is a measure of your craftsmanship. The existing program will undoubtedly be full of 'knots' which you have to work around. A good craftsman will be able to produce an elegant result from a knotty problem. 'Elegant' is often treated as a synonym for 'artistic'; I feel that the word 'crafty' is, in its original sense, a more accurate translation.

Craftsmanship depends on having a good set of tools to hand. In the realm of programming, the tools are techniques, algorithms, ways of doing things, ways of approaching particular types of problem, and of course programming languages which support those approaches. Object-oriented programming is the latest addition to the craftsman-programmer's toolkit. It is not an ultimate solution in the Scientific sense of ensuring that programs which use it will be guaranteed to be correct; it is not an Artistic solution that frees you from the need to fit in with what already exists. It is a Crafty solution that allows you to design things in such a way that when they are broken you will be able to take them apart and fix them, and when they need extending you will be able to add on the extra features with a minimum of effort.

How this book is organised

Many programming textbooks that I've seen concentrate on teaching the features of a particular language, and use numerous small 'blank canvas' examples to illustrate those features. What seems to be ignored all too often are the real-life situations where the problems deal with an existing legacy of programs or data which must be maintained and modified in some way. What I've tried to do in this book is to concentrate on a relatively small number of examples which are capable of improvement and to refine them throughout the book. The result is that the order of topics is primarily example driven; new topics are introduced by adding extra 'bells and whistles' to existing examples. The examples start with the traditional 'Hello world' program and gradually get more and more elaborate, culminating in two reasonably sized examples: an electronic diary and a spreadsheet. Although these are only about a thousand lines of code each in their final versions, they nevertheless show the sort of maintenance problems that arise in 'real world' applications and illustrate how careful design can alleviate such problems.

The book is in three parts. The first part deals with the fundamentals of Ada programming: how to do input and output, how **if** statements and loops work, what procedures, functions and packages are all about, how to define your own data types, how to handle exceptions. At this stage the examples are necessarily tiny; although I deal with program design in chapter 3 when I reach the first example large enough that design merits a separate discussion, the next few chapters concentrate more on introducing the building blocks of Ada using variations on earlier examples. Instructors should of course continue to emphasise the design techniques I've introduced when students are expected to develop new programs as exercises. At the end of the first part, an electronic appointments diary provides a larger example which merits a chapter entirely devoted to design and debugging, although at this stage the design is deliberately naïve.

By the end of the first part, the reader will have been presented with two examples which will be carried further in the next two parts: an electronic appointments diary and a simple desk calculator. These next two parts concentrate on introducing maintenance problems and introducing new approaches and techniques for dealing with these problems. In my experience the real problems of programming only become apparent when you have to maintain an existing legacy of code, and you only learn to design programs so that they are capable of being maintained in the future when you yourself have been on the receiving end of maintenance problems.

The second part deals with abstract data types; it begins by taking the example from the end of the first part and proposing some possible maintenance scenarios. I use these as an excuse for revising the designs I've already proposed in the first part. The early chapters in the second part deal with improving the appointments diary from chapter 8, while the last chapter returns to the calculator example from the first part. Some new implementation techniques are introduced: linked lists, generics, opaque types and recursion are all investigated. The effort involved in dealing with the proposed maintenance scenarios should reveal what a mess poor programming practices can get you into, and should hopefully provide an incentive to master ways of designing programs so that this sort of effort will be minimised if you ever have to make maintenance changes to programs that you write.

The third and final part is concerned with using the object-oriented programming features of Ada 95 to develop extensible programs. The features of Ada described here provide the essential difference between Ada 83 and Ada 95. This part considers maintenance scenarios which affect not just the (re)implementation of existing features but also the capacity of the current design to accommodate new requirements. What happens when you want your existing appointments diary to cope with different types of appointment? What if at some future date you want to incorporate a new type of appointment into your existing systems? What if you want to extend your existing calculator to cope with the extra requirements of a spreadsheet? What if you want a spreadsheet that updates itself in real time? These are the sort of maintenance problems that arise most commonly in the real world; implementation is irrelevant to users, but the ability to add new features is crucial. And it is up to the craftsman-programmer to reach into his or her toolbox and to craft a solution with the tools available; the final part of this book shows how it's possible.

In my opinion, the best way to learn any programming language is to use it to do something that interests you. I first learnt to program because I was interested in John Conway's 'Game of Life' which was popular in the early 1970s, and I wanted something that would let me find out the eventual fate of the R-pentomino. I never succeeded in this because I got sidetracked into programming as an end in itself! Electronic diaries and spreadsheets should be familiar enough applications to all readers, and I hope that this will make them reasonably interesting. They're large enough to be challenging, but not so large as to require a book twice the size of this one. Adopting a project of a similar size (e.g. a text editor) and working on it in parallel with studying this book is the best way I can think of to become a good Ada programmer. Consider the traps and pitfalls I introduce in my examples and think about similar traps and pitfalls that might befall you in your own programs. Practice makes perfect, after all.

Who this book is for

I've aimed this book squarely at the beginning programmer learning Ada 95 as a first language, mainly because Ada is becoming one of the most popular languages used in introductory programming courses. I teach one of these myself. If you're an experienced programmer you might find the going a bit slow in the first couple of chapters, but Ada is sufficiently different from most other languages that it's worth reading these chapters anyway just in case you miss something important. If you're an experienced programmer it won't take you long to get through them. At the end of the book there is also a glossary and a set of appendices for reference; the final version of the packages developed in the text is also included as an appendix. You can get the full set of examples from the website for this book (*http://www.comp.it.brighton.ac.uk/je/adacraft*) or by anonymous FTP from *ftp://ftp.brighton.ac.uk/pub/je/adacraft*. They've been tested using the GNAT compiler, which is also freely available by anonymous FTP from New York University (see chapter 20 for details).

Since I'm assuming that the average reader has no previous Ada experience, I've completely ignored Ada 83. Mentioning Ada 83 in a book for someone with no prior knowledge who wants to learn Ada 95 would just be confusing. This leaves readers who are experienced Ada 83 programmers in a delicate position; the temptation will be to say 'oh yeah, I know this stuff!' and to skip to the next chapter. If you're in this situation, be warned that there are lots of new things in Ada 95 that weren't in Ada 83. I've included a summary of the syntax of Ada as an appendix which also includes references to the chapters where each feature of the language is covered; readers with a knowledge of Ada 83 can use this to locate information about new features of Ada 95. However, you may well find that by skipping chapters to get to the 'interesting' bits you will miss the descriptions of some of the underlying features, in which case you'll have to go back for another look at the bits you skipped over the first time. Also, since the examples are built up a little bit at a time, you'll sometimes find you need to go back a few chapters to look at the early stages of the examples.

Ada is a big language. I can't make any claims that this book provides a complete coverage of the language; the closest you'll get to a complete coverage is the Annotated Reference Manual. I can, however, guarantee that this book is easier to read than the Annotated Reference Manual! The examples in this book have been carefully chosen to allow me to use them to introduce most of the features of Ada. The topics I've omitted are by and large minor details; the final chapter of the book tells you what I've left out and why, and it points you towards several different sources of information if you want to find out about the things I didn't tell you. Despite the omissions, I hope you will find this an interesting, informative and enjoyable book.

Brighton   John English
October 1995   (email: je@brighton.ac.uk)

Part One

Fundamentals

This part introduces you to the basic structure of Ada programs. I use a handful of small examples to illustrate how programs are structured and the way that fundamental statements can be put together to process data. Much of the work in many Ada programs can be done by reusing existing program components, so I use the standard packages that Ada implementations always provide wherever I can. This allows me to use the examples to illustrate the statements that you have to use to bind these building blocks together into a working program.

CHAPTER 1

Programming concepts

*A journey of a thousand miles
must begin with a single step.*
— Proverb

1.1 What is a program?

A program is typically defined as a sequence of instructions for a computer to carry out in order to do a particular job, but this is perhaps a rather simplistic definition. You can also look at it another way and say that a program is a model of some aspect of the real world which you can use to mimic the behaviour of the real world. The more accurate the model is the better the results you can expect to get. For example, a program to calculate a company's payroll is modelling aspects of the real world such as income tax legislation. A program to forecast the weather is modelling atmospheric conditions such as temperature, pressure and humidity. And a program such as the word processor I'm using to write this book is modelling things like letters, words, lines and paragraphs. Inside the computer all these things are represented as patterns of 0s and 1s but programs manipulate them in such a way as to make these patterns behave like the things they are supposed to represent. A program is not just a sequence of instructions; instead, it models **objects** in the real world in such a way as to mimic the behaviour you would expect from those objects as they interact in the real world. This is the basis of the **object-oriented** approach to programming, where the program is regarded as a collection of interacting objects rather than just a featureless sequence of instructions..

In this book you're going to learn how to write programs in Ada, a general purpose programming language originally commissioned by the US Department of Defense. The first standard for the Ada language was finalised in 1983 and was later revised to produce a new updated standard in 1995. The earlier version is now known as Ada 83 and the later version (the one covered in this book) as Ada 95. Ada programs use a somewhat stilted kind of formal English in order to specify the operations you want the computer to perform. You provide some **declarations** which specify the objects that the program is going to deal with. You also provide a sequence of **statements** specifying the actions you want performed on those objects and the computer will perform them in order, one after the other. A set of declarations together with a sequence of statements like this makes up a **procedure** which you invent a name for. For example, you might write a procedure which clears the screen and call it Clear_Screen.

Computers do not understand Ada directly; the text of your procedure (the **source code**) must first of all be translated (**compiled**) into an internal form by an Ada **compiler**. The compiler protects you against your own stupidity by detecting a lot of common errors such as those which arise from typing mistakes, and these must be corrected before you can go any further. Once a procedure has been compiled successfully it is added to your **program library**. Whenever you want to perform that sequence of statements you can just refer to the procedure by the name you've given it. For example, you might write another procedure which needs to clear the screen before displaying something on it. All it would have to do would be to call on the services of the existing Clear_Screen procedure. This means that you don't have to rewrite things you've already written, which reduces the amount of work you have to do both in writing the programs and in testing them to make sure they work properly. You can also make use of procedures written by other people without having to know all the details of how they work.

The next step for turning your procedure from a **library unit** into a working program is to **link** it (also referred to as **building** or **binding** it). This combines it with any other library units it refers to. In addition to any library units you may have written, the Ada language specification defines a number of standard library units that all Ada systems must provide (e.g. operations like input and output) and it is quite likely that your procedure will have used one or more of these, either directly or indirectly. The linker takes your procedure, any library units it refers to, any others that they refer to and so on, and binds them all together into a single **executable program** which you can then run.

Of course it is quite possible (almost inevitable, as you will discover!) that the program won't work the way you expected; the compiler isn't omniscient, so the fact that your program compiled successfully just means that it's a valid Ada program. It doesn't guarantee that it's the particular Ada program you expected it to be, and it's up to you to test it thoroughly to make sure it behaves the way you intended it to. You might hope for a program which displays a five times table but end up with a program that displays the number 5 over and over again, in which case it's back to the drawing board: you'll need to track down the errors (known as **bugs** in the trade), correct them, recompile, relink, and try again.

Writing a program which produces the right answers from sensible input is only part of the story. You also need to make sure that it still behaves sensibly with nonsensical input. For example, the program might expect you to type in a number; what happens if you type in your name instead? If the program responds with an error message, ignores the erroneous input and carries on working, fine. If the program **crashes** (i.e. halts unexpectedly), this is not so good. You may never get the result that the program is supposed to produce. Even worse, the program might get stuck in an **infinite loop** where it just ends up doing the same thing over and over again until it is forcibly halted.

1.2 Readability, maintainability, portability and reusability

Writing a program which does what it's supposed to do is only part of the story. Once you've got the program working someone will usually think of some extra feature that would be incredibly useful or some improvement to what it already does that will make it easier to use. These sorts of changes come under the heading of program **maintenance**. Most real-world programs are hundreds of thousands of lines long and will be in use for about five years before being replaced. Over a five year period, maintenance will typically cost about four times as much as developing the original program and will involve writing as many lines of code as there were in the original, either as additions to or replacements for lines in the original. More programmers are employed maintaining existing code than writing new code. How easy is it going to be to make maintenance changes to your program? What if it's someone else who has to make the changes rather than you, the original author?

Obviously readability is a major factor in determining how easy it is to maintain a program. You need to be able to read and understand what the program does in order to change it. As I said earlier, Ada programs are written using a somewhat stilted formal English. Writing a program is in many ways just like writing an essay. It can be well-presented and well-structured or it can be a tangled rambling mess. If you want other people to be able to understand what it's all about (or even yourself in six months' time!) you need to make an effort to present the program so that its structure and meaning is easy to understand. If you don't, you'll end up thinking 'what on earth does this bit do?' and wasting a lot of time trying to understand what's going on.

Maintainability is a measure of how easy it is to change a program. Ideally a single change should involve changing just one part of the program. If you have to alter several parts of the program to effect the change there's a risk that you'll forget to change some of them or that you'll make a mistake in some places but not in others. For example, consider a payroll program that can handle up to 100 employees. If the number of employees expands, the program will need changing to handle (say) 200 employees. If there is a single line in the program that says that the number of employees is 100 and the rest of the program refers to 'the number of employees' rather than using the number 100 then there will be no problem. If, however, the value 100 appears as a 'magic number' throughout the program, every single occurrence of 100 will need changing to 200. The chances of missing one are fairly high. Worse, some places where 100 is used might be involved in calculating percentages, or it might refer to the number of pennies in a pound, and we might accidentally end up with 200 pence to the pound or percentages calculated wrongly. And what about the places where the magic number 99 appears? Should 99 be changed to 199 throughout, or rather, to 'the number of employees − 1'?

Another situation that arises quite often is the need to make the program work on several different systems. A program should ideally be **portable** from one system to another; all you do is recompile it and, hey presto, it works! Unfortunately life is rarely that simple; there are usually differences from one system to another such as the size of the largest possible number that can be handled or the capabilities of the display screen. Although you can avoid assuming that your program is running on a system which has particular characteristics it will sometimes be impossible to eliminate system-specific dependencies. About the only thing you'll be able to to do in such situations is to gather together all the system-specific parts of the program so that it's easy to locate them and change them.

After writing a few programs you normally discover that a lot of the time you're doing the same old thing that you did before, at least in places. Input and output; sorting collections of data into order; trying to find things in a collection; there are dozens of common features shared by different programs. After a while a sensation of *déjà vu* comes upon you and you realise you've done it all before. The second time you do it better and/or faster than the first time. The third time you do it better and/or faster than the second. The fourth time you start yawning. How easy is it to reuse what you've already written and rewritten? Ada provides some mechanisms which allow you to write software which is flexible enough that you can reuse it fairly easily in a variety of different situations. Learning to make the most of these mechanisms is always useful but it becomes a necessity as soon as programs start to go above a few thousand lines of code in size.

1.3   Specifications and implementations

Ada's reuse mechanisms are based on separating **specifications** from **implementations**. All you need to use an existing procedure is a specification which gives its name and describes what it does; you don't need to know anything about the implementation, i.e. how it works. This is a bit like driving a car; you don't need to know how an engine or a gearbox works in order to drive, you just have to know what the various controls do. You can take the analogy further: the people who build the car don't need to know how to manufacture the individual components like pistons and fuel pumps that go into it. They just need to know how to assemble these components to produce the car as a finished product. One of the most important aspects of becoming a proficient Ada programmer is learning what components are already available and how to assemble them to provide larger components or finished products.

This separation also enhances maintainability and portability. As long as all you rely on when you use something is a specification of *what* it does, it is easy to change *how* it does it. This can be done behind the scenes with no visible effects other than the need to take any existing programs which rely on the specification and relink them so that they use the new implementation. Portability is also aided by the fact that you can say 'this procedure clears the screen' as a specification but then provide different implementations for different systems with different types of screen.

1.4   Abstract data types

It is quite common for collections of related procedures to be useful in a wide variety of situations. To avoid programmers having to reinvent the wheel every time they sit down to write a program, a collection of related procedures, data type declarations and the like can be put together into a **package** and added to the library as a single unit. This is useful for defining classes of objects as described earlier. For example, packs of playing cards are a class of objects which could be defined by a package. The package could contain some declarations for data types like Card and Pack together with a set of procedures defining the things you can reasonably expect to do with a pack of cards (shuffle the pack, deal a card, replace a card at the bottom of the pack, and so on). If you hide the implementation details such as the internal representation of a card or a pack of cards, users are only able to do things that are provided for in the package specification and things which you would not reasonably expect them to be able to do (such as manufacturing extra aces at will or dealing cards from the bottom of the pack) are prohibited.

What you end up with is an **abstract data type**. Abstract data types provide no information about their internal implementation; instead, all you know is the set of permissible values of the type and the operations that can be performed on them. This is just like the way that numbers are handled in a computer. You don't usually have access to the internal representation of numbers in the computer's memory; all you know about is the visible representation of numbers like 3.1416 and the fact that you can perform operations like addition and subtraction on them. Ada packages provide the mechanism by which programmers can define their own abstract data types.

1.5 Generics

One of the things that hinders reuse in most programming languages is that **algorithms** (methods of solving a problem) are usually intertwined with the type of data that they deal with. For example, a procedure which sorts a list of numbers into ascending order will normally need changing if you want to sort a list of names instead. Even if the changes are straightforward, this means that the source code for the procedure must be available for it to be changed. Commercially available software is not generally supplied in source form so that trade secrets can be preserved and copyright enforced, so this can mean reinventing the wheel yet again.

Ada allows you to separate algorithms from the data they deal with by allowing you to write **generic** library units. For example, in order to sort a collection of data all you really need to know is how to compare data items with each other to discover if they need reordering and how to move them to the correct position in the collection if they are out of order. The same algorithm can be used regardless of whether you're sorting numbers or names as long as these conditions are met. Ada allows you to write a generic sorting procedure which, given a data type which satisfies the requirements of the algorithm, will sort a collection of items of that type. All you have to do to be able to use it to sort items of a particular type is to specify the item type to be used and the method for comparing two items. You can use the same algorithm over and over again for different types of data without the need to modify it in any way.

1.6 Inheritance and polymorphism

Another obstacle to reuse and maintenance is when you have some existing code that almost but not quite meets your requirements. The ideal solution is to use the existing code but extend it and modify its behaviour where necessary to fit your requirements. For example, you might want a program which can deal with different types of bank accounts such as current accounts and savings accounts. Using conventional programming techniques it will need major surgery whenever a new type of bank account is introduced that behaves slightly differently from other account types, such as an interest-bearing bank account. Object-oriented programming introduces the notion of **inheritance** to overcome this problem. Using inheritance all you have to do is to say that this new type of bank account is the same as that old type of account but with the following differences. The new bank account **inherits** all the characteristics of the existing account type, modifying or extending those characteristics where necessary. A minimum of new code needs to be written, which speeds up development and simplifies testing and debugging.

A related problem is dealing with those situations where the different types of account behave differently. Normally this involves checking the type of account at each point in the program where different behaviour is possible and then choosing the behaviour appropriate to that account type. A new account type will therefore involve a number of modifications at different places in the program with the associated risk of missing a change or changing something incorrectly. Inheritance guarantees that all bank accounts will share certain common characteristics such as the ability to deposit and withdraw money. New types of bank account will either inherit the existing behaviour or provide a replacement for it. In either case it will still be possible to perform those operations. **Polymorphism** reflects the ability to provide different implementations of the same operation for different types and to select the correct behaviour automatically for the actual type of object being dealt with. Rather than seeing a program as a set of procedures which manipulate data, you can look at it as a set of objects which you can ask to perform particular operations. Each object responds to a request to perform a particular operation by executing the version of the operation which is appropriate for it. You don't have to check what type of account you're dealing with when you say 'deposit some money'; instead, you tell the account that you want to deposit some money and it does it in the way that's appropriate for the type of account that it is. As a result, you won't need to change any existing code when you introduce a new type of account.

CHAPTER 2

Fundamentals of Ada

What one fool can do, another can.
— Silvanus P. Thompson, *Calculus Made Easy*

2.1 Hello, world!

In this chapter we're going to look at some of the fundamentals of the Ada language, beginning with a classic example: a program to display the message 'Hello world!' on the screen. This is not the most exciting program in the world, but it's a good starting point because it's simple and because it lets you learn how to use a text editor to type in a program, how to compile and link it to produce an executable program, and how to run the executable program once you've done that.

This is what the 'Hello world' program looks like in Ada:

```
------------------------------------------------------------
--
--    Program: Hello
--    Purpose: Display the message "Hello world!".
--    Author:  John English (je@brighton.ac.uk)
--
------------------------------------------------------------

with Ada.Text_IO;                              -- 1
procedure Hello is                             -- 2
begin                                          -- 3
   Ada.Text_IO.Put ("Hello world!");           -- 4
   Ada.Text_IO.New_Line;                       -- 5
end Hello;                                      -- 6
```

⇒ *Type in this program and then compile it and run it to ensure that you can successfully edit, compile and run programs on your system.*

The output of this program should look like this:

```
Hello world!
```

The first few lines of the program are **comments** which are ignored by the compiler. You can use comments to add extra descriptive details for the benefit of human readers of the program. A comment begins with a pair of hyphens; when the compiler sees a pair of hyphens it simply ignores the rest of that line. The comments at the beginning are used to explain the purpose of the program as well as who wrote it and when. The other program lines have comments at the end; as in this example, I'll occasionally use comments to number particular lines so I can refer you to them as I explain what they mean. Programs should always give explanations of what they do, usually as comments; however, I don't use many comments in this book because the explanations are in the text.

An Ada program consists of a **procedure** defining a sequence of actions to be carried out. In this case there are two actions which are defined by the **statements** on the lines numbered 4 and 5; line 4 will display the message 'Hello world!' and line 5 will start a new line on the screen.

2.2   Names in Ada

Line 2 tells the compiler that you're defining a procedure called Hello, and the name is repeated at the end of the procedure (line 6) so you can see what line 6 is the end of, as well as allowing the compiler to check that you haven't made any mistakes typing the name. The name Hello has been chosen to tell us something about what it's supposed to do, but you could call it almost anything else instead. However, calling it X or Aardvark wouldn't be particularly useful. You should always choose sensible names for things to make your programs more readable; one of the objectives of writing a program is to produce something which other people can read and understand. A working program which no-one can understand is not a lot of use as it'll be impossible to modify it later to add extra features.

Names in Ada can be any sequence of letters and digits starting with a letter. You can also use underline characters within a name to break it up into words, as in the names Text_IO and New_Line. Anything else (such as a hyphen or a space) is illegal and the compiler will complain if you try to use anything like that in a name. Names like Ada.Text_IO might make you think that full stops are allowed as well, but this is actually the two names Ada and Text_IO joined together, and similarly Ada.Text_IO.Put is a combination of the three names Ada, Text_IO and Put. Some words like *with*, *procedure*, *is*, *begin* and *end* are part of the language. These are known as **reserved words** and can't be used as names. Table 2.1 gives a complete listing of the reserved words in Ada.

The compiler doesn't care if you write names in capitals, lower case or a mixture of the two. As far as the compiler is concerned, *Hello* and *HELLO* and *hello* and *heLLO* are all just different ways of writing the same word. I've adopted a standard convention in this book, which is that reserved words are always written in lower case (like *procedure* and *begin*) and all other names are capitalised (like *Hello* and *New_Line*). You should use the same convention as it makes programs easier to read. One thing you need to be careful

Table 2.1

Ada reserved words			
abort	else	new	return
abs	elsif	not	reverse
abstract	end	null	
accept	entry		select
access	exception		separate
aliased	exit	of	subtype
all		or	
and	for	others	tagged
array	function	out	task
at			terminate
	generic	package	then
begin	goto	pragma	type
body		private	
	if	procedure	
case	in	protected	until
constant	is		use
		raise	
declare		range	when
delay	limited	record	while
delta	loop	rem	with
digits		renames	
do	mod	requeue	xor

about is mixing letters and digits. The name *HELL0* (hell-zero) is not the same as *HELLO* although it looks very similar; as far as the compiler is concerned, the letter O and the digit 0 are completely unrelated. This is one very good reason to avoid using capital letters throughout; it's easy to see that *Hello* and *Hell0* aren't the same, and since names can't start with a digit the compiler will complain if you try to start a name with a zero instead of an O.

2.3 Program layout

Procedure definitions have the following general form:

```
procedure X is
   -- declarations go here
begin
   -- statements go here
end X;
```

where X is the name of the procedure and the comments mark the places where the declarations and statements which make up the complete procedure should go. Declarations will be described later. You can see this general framework on lines 2, 3 and 6 of the 'Hello world' program, although there are no declarations between *is* and *begin* in this particular case. Lines 4 and 5 have been indented slightly to show that they are enclosed within the *begin ... end* part of the procedure definition. Although the compiler doesn't insist on this, consistent use of indentation improves readability. In this book I follow a standard convention for laying out Ada programs and you should follow this standard in your own programs. There are also programs available called **source code reformatters** or **prettyprinters** which will lay out the text of a program in the standard manner. If you have something like this to hand you should use it to ensure your programs are laid out properly. However, you are at liberty to rewrite the program like this:

```
with ada.text_io;procedure hello is begin ada.text_io.
put("Hello world!");ada.text_io.new_line;end hello;
```

and the compiler won't complain (although human readers undoubtedly will!). The compiler will, however, complain by reporting a **syntax error** if the words and punctuation making up the program are not in the correct order. Correct spelling and punctuation are essential if you want the compiler to be able to compile your program successfully; it won't compile a program containing any error, however trivial it may be. You have to say what you mean and mean what you say in Ada. Appendix A contains a summary of the syntax of Ada for use as a quick reference if you have trouble remembering any of the details.

⇒ *Introduce a few syntax errors into your copy of the 'Hello world' program; miss out a semicolon somewhere or spell something wrongly and see what your compiler says about it. Find out what the error messages mean.*

Notice that each part of the program ends with a semicolon. Lines 1, 4, 5 and 6 each have a semicolon at the end. Lines 2 and 3 don't because they are not complete in themselves; they are parts of the procedure definition which has a semicolon at its very end on line 6. This is a general rule in Ada; each *complete* construct ends with a semicolon.

2.4 Context clauses

The only line I haven't explained yet is line 1. Line 1 is a **context clause** which says that the procedure Hello which follows it will use a **package** called Ada.Text_IO. A package is a collection of related declarations which can be used in any program which needs them. Most of the facilities of Ada are provided by packages rather than being built into the structure of the language itself. For example, the language itself doesn't provide any facilities for displaying text on the screen. However, Ada.Text_IO is a standard package provided with all Ada compilers which gives you a set of procedures for text input and output (I/O). In particular, there are procedures called Put and New_Line which we want to use in our program. Since they are taken from the package Ada.Text_IO, we have to use a **fully qualified name** which qualifies the procedure name by specifying the name of the package which contains the procedure as well as the name of the procedure itself, so that on lines 4 and 5 we have to refer to the procedures we want to use by their full names, Ada.Text_IO.Put and Ada.Text_IO.New_Line. The dots are used to signify selection; Ada.Text_IO.Put is the fully qualified name of the procedure Put defined in the package Text_IO which is in turn part of a package called Ada.

The procedures in Text_IO are defined just like the procedure Hello which makes up the main program; they each specify a sequence of actions for the computer to perform in order to display text on the screen or start a new line on the screen. So when we run this program, line 4 is executed; this is a **procedure call** which causes the procedure Put from Text_IO to be executed. The statements making up the procedure Put will be executed in sequence, and when we have finished executing them we'll go back to the main program and execute line 5. The statements making up the procedure New_Line in Text_IO get executed as a result, and we then return to line 6, which is the end of the program.

For the sake of convenience, you can add a **use** clause at the beginning of the program. If you insert the line:

```
use Ada.Text_IO;
```

between lines 1 and 2 (after the **with** clause) or between lines 2 and 3 (in the declaration section between **is** and **begin**) then the effect is as if all the names from Ada.Text_IO have been declared inside your procedure and you can just refer to Put and New_Line instead of Ada.Text_IO.Put and Ada.Text_IO.New_Line. This is what the program ends up looking like:

```
with Ada.Text_IO;
use  Ada.Text_IO;
procedure Hello is
begin
  Put ("Hello world!");
  New_Line;
end Hello;
```

However, if you use a name that is very similar to one of the names in Ada.Text_IO you might end up referring to the wrong thing as a result of a simple typing error. It also becomes unclear where a name is defined, particularly if you are using a lot of different packages. It is generally a good idea to employ **use** clauses fairly sparingly for these reasons.

Packages are not the only things you can access using context clauses; anything in your Ada library can be accessed in exactly the same way. So, having compiled the procedure Hello, it can be used as a component of a larger program like this:

```
with Hello;   -- refers to compiled version of Hello in library
procedure Hello_3 is
begin
  Hello;
  Hello;
  Hello;
end Hello_3;
```

This calls Hello three times (hence the name Hello_3) and so it will display 'Hello world!' three times on three separate lines. The output of this program should look like this:

```
Hello world!
Hello world!
Hello world!
```

It gives the same effect as if we had written the statements making up the procedure Hello three times over, like this:

```
with Ada.Text_IO;
use  Ada.Text_IO;
procedure Hello_3 is
begin
  Put ("Hello world!");   -- first call to Hello
  New_Line;
  Put ("Hello world!");   -- second call to Hello
  New_Line;
  Put ("Hello world!");   -- third call to Hello
  New_Line;
end Hello_3;
```

Notice that the original version of Hello_3 only uses a **with** clause to access Hello; it doesn't need to reference Ada.Text_IO since it doesn't use Put or New_Line or anything else from Text_IO. When you create a main program from Hello_3, the linker retrieves the compiled code for Hello. Since Hello references Ada.Text_IO, the linker then retrieves the compiled code for Text_IO; this process continues until everything referenced by any of the components that the linker deals with has been added to the final program. Also, there is no **use** clause for Hello, since it's a procedure rather than a package and so doesn't contain any subcomponents that we can refer to.

2.5   Strings

Unlike New_Line, Put requires us to supply it with some extra information (a **parameter**), namely the text to be displayed on the screen. Parameters to procedures are specified in parentheses after the procedure name; in this case the only parameter is the message 'Hello world!' enclosed in double quotes. A sequence of characters enclosed in quotes like this is known as a **string**. Strings are one of the standard data types that all Ada implementations provide. Note that the quotes are not part of the string itself and will not be displayed; they are there to tell the compiler where the string begins and ends. If you wanted to display the quotes as well, you might think that this would do the trick:

```
Put ("" Hello world!"");
```

⇒   *Try this and see what your compiler says about it.*

If you try this, you will discover that the compiler won't accept it. The reason is that it sees the first two quotes as marking the start and end of a string which is zero characters long (a **null string**) and it then expects the closing parenthesis of the parameter list (or one or two other possible continuations). When it sees the word Hello after the null string, it doesn't know what's going on and will complain about it. What you have to do to display a quote mark as part of a string is to write two consecutive quotes, so that the correct version of the line above would be:

```
Put ("""Hello world!""");
```

The first quote marks the start of the string; the next two translate into a quote which is a part of the string; the two after the exclamation mark translate into yet another quote which is part of the string, and the next one marks the end of the string. This looks messy but it's necessary, although fortunately the need to do this doesn't often occur in practice.

2.6   A simple calculator

Here's a slightly larger program which reads in two integers that the user types at the keyboard (e.g. 123 and 456) and displays their sum:

```
with Ada.Text_IO, Ada.Integer_Text_IO;      -- 1
use  Ada.Text_IO, Ada.Integer_Text_IO;      -- 2
procedure Sum is
   First, Second : Integer;                  -- 3
begin
   Put ("Enter two integers: ");             -- 4
   Get (First);                              -- 5
   Get (Second);                             -- 6
   Put ("The sum is");                       -- 7
   Put (First + Second);                     -- 8
   New_Line;                                 -- 9
end Sum;
```

Lines 4 to 9 are the statements which specify what the program will do. The program begins by displaying a **prompt** (line 4) so that anyone using the program knows what they should type in. Whenever you want the user to supply any input you should always display a prompt. There is nothing more frustrating than a blank screen with the cursor flashing expectantly at you and no instructions!

The next step is to read in the values that the user types at the keyboard. We need to be able to refer to these later on in the program, so we need to save them somewhere in memory and give them names to refer to them by. Line 3 declares two **variables** called First and Second to store the numbers in. Variables are declared between the word **is** and the word **begin** in a procedure. All variables must be declared before they can be used. We have to tell the compiler the name of the variable so that it will recognise it when it sees it. If we don't it will report an error when it sees the name First or Second on lines 5, 6 and 8.

We must also tell the compiler what sort of data First and Second are going to hold so that it knows how much space in memory to allocate for them and what operations we are allowed to perform on them. Ada provides a standard data type called Integer to hold integer values, so we declare First and Second to be of type Integer. Note that we don't know what the value of First or Second will be at this point in the program; declaring a variable simply reserves some space in memory but doesn't set it to any particular value. The value is said to be **undefined** meaning that the language doesn't define what it will be. The variable may or may not hold a valid value; it needs setting to a valid value of the appropriate type before you try to access it. If you want to, you can set a variable to a specific value when you declare it:

```
First, Second : Integer := 123;
```

This reserves space for the two variables and sets each of them to a value of 123. If you wanted different values for the two variables, you'd have to use two declarations:

```
First  : Integer := 123;
Second : Integer := 456;
```

What we want to do in this case is to read values typed in by the user into the variables. In order to do this, we need to use another package. There is a standard package to handle the input and output of integers called Ada.Integer_Text_IO, so the context clauses on lines 1 and 2 specify both Ada.Text_IO and Ada.Integer_Text_IO (Ada.Text_IO is still required to allow us to display strings and start new lines). The procedure Get used on lines 5 and 6 is one of the ones provided by Ada.Integer_Text_IO; it reads a number from the keyboard and stores it in the variable whose name is given as its parameter. The effect of lines 5 and 6 will be to read two numbers typed at the keyboard and store them in the variables First and Second. You can then get at the stored value by referring to the variable by name. You have to separate the two integers with one or more spaces when you type them in, e.g. 123 456; if you just type 123456 without any separating spaces, Get will just think it's all one number. Alternatively you can start a new line after typing in the first number; a line break is just as good as a space for separating the two integers. If you don't type in integer values as requested, the program will halt immediately and display an error message.

⇒ *Try typing something which isn't an integer (e.g. XYZZY) and see what error message the program produces. What happens if you type in the first number correctly and the second one incorrectly?*

Finally, lines 7, 8 and 9 display the result. Line 7 displays a string, and line 8 will display the integer result. If you run the program and type in the values 123 and 456, this is what you'll see on the screen:

```
Enter two integers: 123 456
The sum is      579
```

Lines 7 and 9 use the version of Put defined in Ada.Text_IO for displaying strings, while line 8 uses the version of Put defined in Ada.Integer_Text_IO for displaying integers. The compiler is able to distinguish between the two different usages of the name Put simply by looking at the type of value supplied as a parameter; if it's a string we must be referring to Ada.Text_IO.Put which requires a string as a parameter, whereas if it's an integer we must be referring to Ada.Integer_Text_IO.Put which requires an integer as its parameter. This is handy, since otherwise every single procedure would have to be given a different name (e.g. Put_String and Put_Integer) which would mean having much more to remember.

The parameter to Put on line 8 is an integer **expression**, i.e. a set of values being combined in some way to produce a new value. In this case the values that were stored in the variables First and Second by the calls to the Get procedure on lines 5 and 6 are added together using '+' to produce another integer value. Since the compiler has been told that First and Second are integers, it knows that '+' is a legitimate operation and that the result will be another integer. This result is then passed directly to Put as the value to be displayed. A full set of arithmetic operations is provided in Ada; subtraction is symbolised by '−', multiplication by '*' (since '×' would look like the name 'X') and division by '/'. There are also a few others which will be discussed in chapter 5.

2.7 Procedure specifications

One of the most important aspects of learning to program in Ada is knowing how to find out what facilities the packages available to you provide. If you don't know what's available, you might end up wasting a lot of time trying to solve a problem for which a ready-made solution already exists. This means that you need to be able to read and understand the specification of packages like Ada.Text_IO. Ada.Text_IO contains a set of declarations for the procedures and other things it provides; a complete listing of Ada.Text_IO is provided in Appendix B. This is what the declaration for Put in Ada.Text_IO looks like:

```
procedure Put (Item : in String);
```

Note that this is only a **specification** of the procedure; the implementation details between **is** and **end** have been omitted. The implementation is kept in a separate **package body** which will already have been compiled and added to your program library, so you don't get to see it. You don't need to; all you need to know is what the specification tells you, namely that there is a procedure called Put which takes one parameter called Item. The parameter must be a String; the reserved word **in** indicates that Item is an input to Put. The value you supply for Item will be copied into Put so that Put can display it on the screen.

You can also use the parameter name when you call the procedure, like this:

```
Put (Item => "Hello world!");
```

This can be very useful when a procedure requires several different parameters; it helps to make it clear what the parameters are for.

There are actually several procedures in Text_IO called Put, but they all have different parameter specifications; the compiler can work out which one you're referring to by looking at the type of parameter you supply in the procedure call. This is known as **overloading**; a procedure name is 'overloaded' with more than one meaning.

The specification for New_Line looks like this:

```
procedure New_Line (Spacing : in Positive_Count := 1);
```

As you can see, New_Line has a parameter called Spacing. The parameter must be a value between 1 and some upper limit whose exact value may vary from one system to another (it's **implementation defined**). This is specified by the type Positive_Count, which is also defined in Text_IO. To find the exact range of values for Positive_Count, look in the Text_IO package provided with your compiler.

We didn't have to supply a parameter to New_Line when we called it earlier; the ':= 1' in the specification is a **default value** which will be used if we don't supply a value for Spacing. We could have called New_Line like this:

```
New_Line (Spacing => 1);
```

and the effect would have been exactly the same. If we want to start two new lines in quick succession (i.e. leave a blank line on the screen) we could call New_Line like this:

```
New_Line (2);              -- start a new line twice, or...
New_Line (Spacing => 2);   -- ...the same thing
```

If you look at the specification of Ada.Text_IO you will also discover the following procedure specification:

```
procedure Put_Line (Item : in String);
```

Put_Line is the same as Put except that it starts a new line after displaying the string supplied as its parameter; in other words, Put_Line is the same as Put followed by New_Line. This means that you could rewrite the 'Hello world' program like this:

```
with Ada.Text_IO;  use Ada.Text_IO;
procedure Hello is
begin
   Put_Line ("Hello world!");
end Hello;
```

Input and output of integers is a bit more elaborate than it is for strings. The declaration of Put in Ada.Integer_Text_IO looks like this:

```
procedure Put (Item  : in Integer;
               Width : in Field        := Default_Width;
               Base  : in Number_Base  := Default_Base);
```

What this means is that there are two extra parameters called Width and Base which can be used when displaying integers. Field and Number_Base are just the names of some more data types defined in Integer_Text_IO. The Width parameter must be a value between 0 and some maximum value which varies from compiler to compiler (it's also implementation defined); it determines the number of characters which will be displayed. The default is large enough to accommodate the largest possible value for an Integer (typically either six or 11 characters wide); this means that small integers will be displayed with some blank space in front. By specifying some other value you can get exactly the width you want; if the number is too big for the width you specify it will take up as much space as necessary to display its value with no leading spaces. In particular, specifying 'Width=>1' will always display an integer with no extra spaces. Here are some examples:

```
Put (1234);                -- displays "        1234"
                           -- (with leading spaces)
Put (1234, Width=>1);      -- displays "1234"
                           -- (no leading spaces)
Put (1234, Width=>5);      -- displays " 1234"
                           -- (five characters wide)
```

Base is a value between 2 and 16 which specifies the number base to use for displaying the value, so that 'Base=>2' specifies binary output and 'Base=>16' specifies hexadecimal. The default value (called Default_Base) is defined to be 10, i.e. values will be displayed in decimal unless you specify otherwise.

```
Put (29);                  -- displays "          29" (decimal)
Put (29, Base=>2);         -- displays " 2#11101#" (binary)
```

format output

```
Put (29, Base=>16);    -- displays "      16#1D#" (hexadecimal)
Put (29, Base=>5);     -- displays "      5#104#" (base 5)
```

Note that non-decimal numbers are displayed as **based** numbers, i.e. the base followed by the value enclosed in hash marks (# .. #).

Here are some examples which use Width and Base together:

```
Put (1234, Width=>1, Base=>2);    -- minimum width binary value
Put (1234, Base=>2, Width=>1);    -- the same
Put (1234, 1, 2);                 -- the same
```

Note that you can specify parameters in any order if you use their names; the compiler is smart enough to know what order they should go in and deal with them appropriately. You don't have to use their names (as shown in the last example above), but if you don't you must specify the values in the correct order; it's often easier and more readable to specify them by name.

The specification for Get in Integer_Text_IO looks like this:

```
procedure Get (Item  : out Integer;
               Width : in  Field := 0);
```

This tells us that Get has a parameter called Item which is an output from the procedure (as specified by **out**); you have to supply an Integer variable to store the output in when you call Get. You have to supply a variable name for an **out** parameter so the procedure can store the output it produces in it. Input parameters don't suffer from this restriction; any value of the correct type can be provided for an input parameter (e.g. the value of the expression First + Second on line 8 of the Sum program). Get also has an optional parameter called Width; a value other than zero specifies the exact number of characters to be read (although if there aren't enough characters on the line it will just read up to the end of the current line).

Procedures are covered in more detail later, but as you will have gathered by now, procedures and packages play a fairly central role in writing Ada programs. Don't worry about the details too much for now; it helps to be able to look at procedure specifications in packages and work out how to use them, but the nitty-gritty details involved in writing this sort of thing can wait until chapter 4.

Exercises

2.1   Ada compilers only allow a limited range of integers; nine or ten digits is typically the most you can expect the compiler to handle. If you exceed the maximum value it can handle, the program will halt with an error message. Find out what the largest integer is that your system can handle by typing in larger and larger values for the Sum program until you get an error.

2.2 Write a program which uses Put_Line to display your initials in giant letters on the screen using asterisks, something like this:

```
* * * * * * * * * *    * * * * * * *
         *            *
         *            *
         *            * * * * * *
         *            *
 *       *            *
  * * * *             * * * * * * * *
```

2.3 Modify the Sum program to display the difference, product and quotient of the two numbers you type in as well as the sum. Think of a sensible name for the modified program instead of Sum.

2.4 Write a program which reads in three integers representing the length, width and height of a box in centimetres and displays the volume and the surface area of the box. Be sure to check your results are correct. For example, a box whose size is 1cm × 2cm × 3cm has a volume of 6 cm^3 and a surface area of 22 cm^2.

CHAPTER 3

Statements

The statements was interesting, but tough.
— Mark Twain, *The Adventures of Huckleberry Finn*

3.1 If statements

Let's try a slightly more elaborate example than the ones we've seen so far. This one asks the user whether it's morning or afternoon and then replies 'Good morning' or 'Good afternoon' as appropriate. Here's what it looks like:

```
with Ada.Text_IO;    use Ada.Text_IO;
procedure Greetings is
   Answer : Character;                              --  1
begin
   Put ("Is it morning (m) or afternoon (a)? ");    --  2
   Get (Answer);                                    --  3
   if Answer = 'm' then                             --  4
      Put_Line ("Good morning!");                   --  5
   else                                             --  6
      Put_Line ("Good afternoon!");                 --  7
   end if;                                          --  8
end Greetings;                                       --  9
```

Line 1 declares a variable called Answer to hold the answer that the user types in response to the question asked on line 2. The answer will be a single character ('m' or 'a'), so I've declared it to be a variable of type Character, which is another standard data type. Character variables are capable of holding a single character. The answer is read in using a version of Get defined in Ada.Text_IO which has an output parameter of type Character.

Lines 4 through 8 are an **if** statement which allows us to choose between two alternative courses of action. Like a procedure definition it is a compound construction with a semicolon at the very end of it on line 8 and no semicolons on either line 4 or 6. Compound constructions like this always end with '**end** whatever-it-is' in Ada, so that 'procedure X' ends with 'end X' and 'if' ends with 'end if'. The statements on lines 5 and 7 are indented to make it visually obvious that they are enclosed by the **if** statement.

23

When the **if** statement is executed, the condition after the word **if** is tested and, if it is true, the statements between **then** and **else** are executed, which in this case is the single statement on line 5. If the condition is false, the statements between **else** and **end if** (in this case the single statement on line 7) will be executed. The effect is that if the value of Answer is the letter *m*, the message 'Good morning!' is displayed, otherwise the message 'Good afternoon!' is displayed. Once the **if** statement has been executed (i.e. either line 5 or line 7 has been executed), execution continues with whatever follows the **if** statement. In this case it is line 9, which is the end of the program.

Note that you have to use single quote marks to enclose characters; *'m'* is the letter *m* as a value of type Character, whereas *"m"* is a string which is one character in length. The compiler takes this apparently trivial difference quite seriously, since the particular style of quote is used to distinguish values of type Character from values of type String, which in turn determines what operations can legitimately be performed on them.

⇒   *Try using double quotes instead of single quotes ("m" instead of 'm') and see what your compiler says about it.*

In its present form the program doesn't quite do what we really want. If you type anything other than the letter *m* the program will respond with a cheery 'Good afternoon!'. Ideally we would like to check that the answer is in fact an *a* if it is not an *m* and display a less cheery error message if it isn't. We can do this by using another **if** statement instead of the existing line 7:

```
if Answer = 'a' then
   Put_Line ("Good afternoon!");
else
   Put_Line ("Please type 'm' or 'a'!");
end if;
```

The complete **if** statement starting at line 4 now looks like this:

```
if Answer = 'm' then
   Put_Line ("Good morning!");
else
   if Answer = 'a' then
      Put_Line ("Good afternoon!");
   else
      Put_Line ("Please type 'm' or 'a'!");
   end if;
end if;
```

This shows that the statements contained within an **if** statement can be any statements at all, including further **if** statements. Note that each **if** statement has its own corresponding **end if**. If you have a lot of **if** statements nested inside one another you can end up with an awful lot of **end if**s, as well as indentation problems as the **if** statements are going to be indented further and further to the right. To get around this, we can write the **if** statement above a different way:

```
if Answer = 'm' then
   Put_Line ("Good morning!");
elsif Answer = 'a' then
   Put_Line ("Good afternoon!");
else
   Put_Line ("Please type 'm' or 'a'!");
end if;
```

The reserved word **elsif** allows you to specify a secondary condition as part of the same **if** statement. Since it's all a single **if** statement now, only a single **end if** is required at the very end and there is no problem with indentation. You can have as many **elsif** parts in an **if** statement as you want, but there can only ever be one **else** part which must come at the very end and is only executed if *all* the conditions specified after **if** and **elsif** are false. You can also leave out the **else** part completely if you don't want to do anything when the conditions you specify are all false.

Note the missing 'e' in **elsif**! A common beginner's mistake is to spell it **elseif**, but the spelling was deliberately chosen so that if the words **else** and **if** accidentally get run together as **elseif** as a result of missing out the space between the two words, the compiler will immediately spot it as an error.

3.2   Assignment statements

At the moment you have to type in the letter *m* or *a* in lower case in response to the prompt. If you type in a capital *M* instead, the program will respond 'Please type 'm' or 'a'!'. We can modify the program to test for upper case letters and convert them to the lower case equivalents by adding an extra **if** statement:

```
with Ada.Text_IO;
use  Ada.Text_IO;
procedure Greetings is
   Answer : Character;
begin
   Put ("Is it morning (m) or afternoon (a)? ");
   Get (Answer);
   if Answer = 'M' then                            --  1
      Answer := 'm';                               --  2
   elsif Answer = 'A' then                         --  3
      Answer := 'a';                               --  4
   end if;                                         --  5
```

```
   if Answer = 'm' then
      Put_Line ("Good morning!");
   elsif Answer = 'a' then
      Put_Line ("Good afternoon!");
   else
      Put_Line ("Please type 'm' or 'a'!");
   end if;
end Greetings;
```

The **if** statement on lines 1 to 5 checks for the letter *M* or *A* and changes the value of Answer to *m* or *a* as appropriate. It does this by **assigning** a new value to Answer on lines 2 and 4. The **assignment statement**

```
Answer := 'm';
```

stores the letter *m* into the variable Answer, replacing the existing value of Answer. The symbol ':=' is usually pronounced 'becomes', so we can read this statement as 'Answer becomes *m*'. You must give a variable name on the left of ':=', but you can have any expression you like on the right hand side as long as it produces a value of the correct type when it's evaluated.

Note that there is no **else** part in this **if** statement. If Answer is the letter *M*, line 2 is executed; if it is the letter *A*, line 4 is executed; and if it is anything else, we don't do anything. As I mentioned earlier, leaving out the **else** part of an **if** statement simply means that you do nothing if none of the conditions specified after **if** and **elsif** are true.

3.3   Compound conditions

There is another way to do the same thing. We can eliminate the extra **if** statement and alter the second one to test if Answer is either an *M* or an *m* as follows:

```
if Answer = 'm' or Answer = 'M' then
   Put_Line ("Good morning!");
elsif Answer = 'a' or Answer = 'A' then
   Put_Line ("Good afternoon!");
else
   Put_Line ("Please type 'm' or 'a'!");
end if;
```

The first line of this revised **if** statement checks if Answer is an *m* and also checks if it is an *M*. If either condition is true the message 'Good morning!' is displayed.

The **or** operator allows us to combine more than one condition into a single compound condition which is true if either or both of the subconditions are true. It is tempting to try to write the first line of the **if** statement as follows:

```
if Answer = 'm' or 'M' then ...
```

but the compiler will complain if you do.

⇒   *Try this and see what sort of error your compiler reports.*

The reason is that **or** requires something which evaluates to either true or false (a **Boolean expression**) on both its left and its right hand sides. Boolean is another one of Ada's built-in types, and is named after the English logician George Boole who first formalised the notion of an algebra of truth values. The '=' operator compares two values of the same type and produces a Boolean result (true or false) so all will be well as long as you use an expression of the form 'A = B' on both sides of the **or** operator. The condition above has a Boolean expression on its left but a value of type Character on its right, so the compiler will be justifiably sceptical about it. Ada compilers are very strict about type-checking since confusion about types generally indicates muddled thinking on the part of the programmer; the Ada view of data types will be explored in more detail later on.

(3.4) The case statement

When there are a lot of alternative values of the same variable to be dealt with, it's generally more convenient to use a **case** statement than an **if** statement. Here's how the previous program could be rewritten using a **case** statement:

```
with Ada.Text_IO;
use  Ada.Text_IO;
procedure Greetings is
   Answer : Character;
begin
   Put ("Is it morning (m) or afternoon (a)? ");
   Get (Answer);
   case Answer is
      when 'M' | 'm' =>                                 -- 1
         Put_Line ("Good morning!");
      when 'A' | 'a' =>                                 -- 2
         Put_Line ("Good afternoon!");
      when others    =>                                 -- 3
         Put_Line ("Please type 'm' or 'a'!");
   end case;
end Greetings;
```

Depending on the value of Answer, one of the three alternatives of the **case** statement will be executed. The vertical bar 'I' can be read as meaning 'or' so that choice 1 will be executed if the value of Answer is *M* or *m* and choice 2 will be executed if the value of

Answer is *A* or *a*. Choice 3 (**others**) is executed if all else fails. The **others** choice must be the last one and is equivalent to the **else** part of an **if** statement. It is only executed if none of the other choices apply. A **case** statement must have a choice for every possible value of the controlling expression between **case** and **is**, so an **others** clause is usually necessary.

3.5   Range tests

In situations where you want any one of a consecutive range of values to select a particular choice, you can specify a range of values in a **case** statement using '..' to indicate the extent of the range. For example, if you wanted to test if Answer was a letter you could do it like this:

```
case Answer is
   when 'A' .. 'Z' | 'a' .. 'z' =>
     Put_Line ("It's a letter!");
   when others =>
     Put_Line ("It's not a letter!");
end case;
```

This says that if the value of Answer is in the range *A* to *Z* or the range *a* to *z*, the message 'It's a letter!' will be displayed. If it isn't, the message 'It's not a letter!' will be displayed instead.

You can also test if a value is in a particular range using the operators **in** and **not in**. The **case** statement above could be rewritten as an **if** statement like this:

```
if Answer in 'A' .. 'Z' or Answer in 'a' .. 'z' then
   Put_Line ("It's a letter!");
else
   Put_Line ("It's not a letter!");
end if;
```

Not in is the opposite of **in**:

```
if Answer not in 'A' .. 'Z' then
   Put_Line ("It's not a capital letter!");
end if;
```

3.6   The null statement

Case statements must cover all the possible values of the expression between **case** and **is**. This means that there has usually to be a **when others** clause, but sometimes you don't want to do anything if the value doesn't match any of the other selections. The solution is to use the **null statement**:

```
when others =>
  null;                  -- do nothing
```

The **null** statement is provided for situations like this one where you have to say something but don't want to do anything. A **null** statement has no effect at all except to keep the compiler happy by telling it that you really *do* want to do nothing and that you haven't just forgotten something by accident.

3.7 Loops

At the moment you only get one chance to answer the question that the program asks. It would be nicer if you were given more than one attempt. Here is a program that does that:

```
with Ada.Text_IO;
use  Ada.Text_IO;
procedure Greetings is
  Answer : Character;
begin
  loop                                              -- 1
    Put ("Is it morning (m) or afternoon (a)? ");
    Get (Answer);
    if Answer = 'm' or Answer = 'M' then
      Put_Line ("Good morning!");
      exit;                                         -- 2
    elsif Answer = 'a' or Answer = 'A' then
      Put_Line ("Good afternoon!");
      exit;                                         -- 3
    else
      Put_Line ("You must type m or a!");
    end if;
  end loop;                                         -- 4
end Greetings;                                       -- 5
```

This program contains a **loop** statement which starts at line 1 and ends at line 4. Again, it's a compound statement; it starts with **loop** on line 1 and ends with **end loop** and a semicolon on line 4. The sequence of statements it encloses will be repeated over and over again when it's executed. It will only stop repeating when you execute one of the **exit** statements on lines 2 and 3. The **exit** statement terminates the loop and execution of the program continues at the point after **end loop**. In this case it is line 5, the end of the program.

⇒   *Compile and run this program and then type something like XYZZY in response to the prompt. What happens, and why?*

Quite a lot of the time you want to exit from a loop when a particular condition becomes true. You could do this using an **if** statement:

```
if This_Is_True then
   exit;
end if;
```

but it's a common enough requirement that Ada provides a special form of the **exit** statement:

```
exit when This_Is_True;
```

Here's another way of writing the same program as before which illustrates the use of an **exit when** statement:

```
with Ada.Text_IO;
use  Ada.Text_IO;
procedure Greetings is
   Answer : Character;
begin
   loop
      Put ("Is it morning (m) or afternoon (a)? ");
      Get (Answer);
      exit when Answer = 'm' or Answer = 'M'
             or Answer = 'a' or Answer = 'A';
      Put_Line ("You must type m or a!");
   end loop;
   if Answer = 'm' or Answer = 'M' then              -- 1
      Put_Line ("Good morning!");
   else
      Put_Line ("Good afternoon!");
   end if;
end Greetings;
```

The previous version displayed the message 'Good morning!' or 'Good afternoon!' from within the loop; here, the loop just checks whether the answer is valid. As soon as it is valid, the **exit** statement terminates the loop and execution continues at the next statement, namely the **if** statement at line 1 which is now responsible for displaying 'Good morning!' or 'Good afternoon!'. By the time we get to line 1, we know that Answer is either an *m* or an *a* in either upper or lower case and so the **if** statement only has to test if it's an *m* or an *M*; if it isn't it must be an *a* or an *A*.

⇒ *Apart from anything else, this shows you that there is more than one way to solve a particular problem. Can you think of any other ways of solving it?*

In many cases the **exit** statement is the first statement in a loop; you will often want to test that everything's all right before you do anything else:

```
loop
   exit when End_Of_File;   -- i.e. when there is no more input
   -- get some input and process it
end loop;
```

This is a common enough situation that there's a special form of the **loop** statement to cater for it:

```
while not End_Of_File loop   -- i.e. when there is more input
   -- get some input and process it
end loop;
```

The operator **not** inverts the sense of a condition; if a condition X is True then **not** X is False and vice versa. Note that the condition in a **while** loop tells you when to repeat the loop whereas the condition in an **exit when** statement tells you when to exit from it, so a loop that begins 'exit when X' gets rewritten as 'while not X loop ...'.

Another common requirement is to repeat a loop a fixed number of times. This is a frequent enough situation that Ada provides another form of the **loop** statement to handle it (a **for loop**). Here's an example which displays a line of 20 asterisks:

```
for N in 1..20 loop
   Put ("*");
end loop;
```

The range 1..20 specifies how many times the loop will be executed. The **control variable** N will take on successive values from 1 to 20 each time around the loop (i.e. in this case, it will always give the number of times the loop has executed so far). N doesn't need to be declared elsewhere; it is automatically declared by its appearance in the loop heading. **For** loops are dealt with in more detail in chapter 6.

You are also allowed to name loops by attaching **labels** to them:

```
Main_Loop:
   loop
      ...
   end loop Main_Loop;
```

The label is a name followed by a colon immediately before the **loop** statement. Note that if you use a loop label, the name must be repeated after **end loop** as in the example above.

The main reason for providing a loop label is so that you can specify which loop an **exit** statement should exit from. This allows you to exit several loops at once:

```
Outer: loop
    Inner: loop
        ...
        exit Outer when Finished;        -- 1
    end loop Inner;
end loop Outer;                          -- 2
```

The **exit** statement at line 1 will exit from both the inner and outer loops, and execution will continue at line 2 (after the end of the outer loop). This is something which is rarely required in practice; if it does seem to be necessary, it's worth having a good think about your design since there are usually better ways to achieve the same effect.

3.8   The calculator program revisited

Armed with all this extra knowledge about Ada we are now in a position to improve somewhat on the calculator program from the previous chapter. It can be rewritten to accept expressions like '123+456' or '32–5' and display the answer. This is simply a matter of reading an integer, a character and another integer, and then performing the appropriate operation depending on the character between the two integers:

```
with Ada.Text_IO, Ada.Integer_Text_IO;
use  Ada.Text_IO, Ada.Integer_Text_IO;
procedure Calculator is
   First, Second : Integer;
   Operator      : Character;
begin
   Put ("Enter an expression: ");
   Get (First);
   Get (Operator);
   Get (Second);

   case Operator is
     when '+' =>
       Put (First + Second, Width => 1);
     when '-' =>
       Put (First - Second, Width => 1);
     when '*' =>
       Put (First * Second, Width => 1);
     when '/' =>
       Put (First / Second, Width => 1);
```

```
     when others =>
        Put ("Invalid operator '");
        Put (Operator);
        Put ("'");
   end case;
   New_Line;
end Calculator;
```

One problem with this is that the operator is taken to be the first character after the first integer, which doesn't allow for any separating spaces. The integers can be preceded by spaces because of the way that Get works for integers, so that '123+ 456' will be accepted but '123 + 456' won't be. The answer is to use a loop to skip spaces between the first integer and the operator:

```
Get (First);
loop
   Get (Operator);
   exit when Operator /= ' ';
end loop;
Get (Second);
```

The operator '/=' means 'not equal to', so the **exit** statement will be executed when Operator is not equal to a space. This means that as long as it *is* a space, we'll go round the loop and get another character, thus ignoring all spaces.

An even better idea is to extend the program further so that it can read expressions involving more than one operator, e.g. '1+2+3'. This will involve reading the first integer and making it the result, then reading successive pairs of operators and integers and adding them (or whatever) to the result. This will give a strictly left-to-right evaluation, so that '1+2*3' will come out as 9 rather than 7 as you might expect; in a later chapter I will show you how to deal with issues like doing multiplication and division before addition and subtraction. To simplify matters I will require the user to type in a full stop to terminate the expression.

This is a slightly larger program than the previous ones; rather than just showing you the complete program I'm going to take you through a step-by-step design process. Reading and understanding the programs I've shown you so far is important for getting to grips with the facilities that Ada provides, but at some point you have to start writing your own programs and for this you need some tips on how to get started. A lot of people find it easy to understand a program once it's been written but find it hard to know where to start if they have to write it themselves.

In general you can break any programming problem down into three main components: some initialisation to get things ready at the beginning, followed by the main processing involved, followed by some finishing off at the end. In this case the initialisation will involve displaying a prompt and reading an arithmetic expression, the main processing will involve evaluating the expression that the user has typed in, and the finishing off at the end might just involve displaying the result. We'll need an integer variable for the result to be displayed. This gives the following as a first stab at the program:

```
with Ada.Text_IO, Ada.Integer_Text_IO;
use  Ada.Text_IO, Ada.Integer_Text_IO;
procedure Calculator is
   Result : Integer;
begin
   Put ("Enter an expression: ");
   -- process the expression typed in by the user
   Put (Result, Width => 1);
   New_Line;
end Calculator;
```

The next thing to do is to decide how to break down the main processing. A good way to start is to consider the structure of the input that the program will be expected to deal with. Here are some samples of the input I'd expect this program to accept:

```
2.
2+2.
2+2*2.
2+2*2-2.
```

What we have here is an integer followed by any number (zero or more) of arithmetic operators each of which is followed by an integer, followed finally by a full stop. An old programming rule of thumb says that the structure of a program tends to reflect the structure of its input; in this case we'll need to read the first number, then repeatedly process operators and the numbers which follow them until we reach a full stop. So this gives us a sequence of two steps: read the first number and then process the rest of the expression. In the case where there are no operator/integer pairs after the first number, the result will be the first number. This leads to the conclusion that the first number should just be read into the variable Result:

```
with Ada.Text_IO, Ada.Integer_Text_IO;
use  Ada.Text_IO, Ada.Integer_Text_IO;
procedure Calculator is
   Result : Integer;
begin
   Put ("Enter an expression: ");
   Get (Result);
   -- repeatedly process operator/integer pairs (if any)
   Put (Result, Width => 1);
   New_Line;
end Calculator;
```

Processing operator/integer pairs is a repetitive activity, so we'll need a **loop** statement. With any loop you need to ask yourself when the loop will terminate; in this case it is when the final full stop is read, or when something unexpected is read (which should be reported as an error). The result won't need to be displayed if an error occurs, so we can display it when the full stop is encountered, rather than at the end of the program as I've got it above. This can be done by moving the call to Put into the loop and following it by an **exit** statement.

Inside the loop we'll need to read the next character, which should be either an operator or the terminating full stop, so we'll need a character variable (which I'll call Operator) to store it in:

```
with Ada.Text_IO, Ada.Integer_Text_IO;
use  Ada.Text_IO, Ada.Integer_Text_IO;
procedure Calculator is
   Result   : Integer;
   Operator : Character;
begin
   Put ("Enter an expression: ");
   Get (Result);
   loop
     Get (Operator);
     if Operator = '.' then
       -- display result and exit from the loop
       Put (Result, Width => 1);
       exit;
     else
       -- process the rest of an operator/integer pair
     end if;
   end loop;
   -- the call to Put has now been moved into the loop
   New_Line;
end Calculator;
```

As in the previous program we'll want to ignore spaces before the operator; to do that, I'll just use the code which I showed you earlier without any further comment:

```
with Ada.Text_IO, Ada.Integer_Text_IO;
use  Ada.Text_IO, Ada.Integer_Text_IO;
procedure Calculator is
   Result   : Integer;
   Operator : Character;
begin
   Put ("Enter an expression: ");
   Get (Result);
```

```
loop
  loop
    Get (Operator);
    exit when Operator /= ' ';
  end loop;

  if Operator = '.' then
    Put (Result, Width => 1);
    exit;
  else
    -- process the rest of an operator/integer pair
  end if;
end loop;

New_Line;
end Calculator;
```

Processing the rest of the operator/integer pair involves reading the integer (which means we need another Integer variable) and then applying the operator to the result so far and the integer that we've just read:

```
with Ada.Text_IO, Ada.Integer_Text_IO;
use  Ada.Text_IO, Ada.Integer_Text_IO;
procedure Calculator is
  Result   : Integer;
  Operator : Character;
  Operand  : Integer;
begin
  Put ("Enter an expression: ");
  Get (Result);

  loop
    loop
      Get (Operator);
      exit when Operator /= ' ';
    end loop;

    if Operator = '.' then
      Put (Result, Width => 1);
      exit;
    else
      Get (Operand);
      -- apply the operator to Result and Operand
    end if;
```

```
      end loop;
   New_Line;
end Calculator;
```

Applying the operator involves a choice between a number of alternatives: if it's an addition operator we want to add the numbers together, if it's a multiplication operator we want to multiply them, and so on. Since we have a choice between several alternatives we have to use either an **if** statement or a **case** statement. As you saw earlier, a **case** statement is a convenient solution in this case where all the choices depend on a particular value, in this case the value of Operator. The first number is in Result and the second is in Operand, so we'll need to evaluate Result+Operand, Result–Operand or whatever. This will give us a new result which needs to be stored in Result so that it's ready to be displayed when we get to the end of the program, so we need each choice to be an assignment statement along the lines of:

```
Result := Result + Operand;
```

Note that the old value of Result is used on the right hand side of ':=' to calculate the new value of Result. The right hand side of the assignment is evaluated by adding the old value of Result to Operand; this value is then stored in Result, replacing the old value. This idiom is commonly used to add 1 to the existing value of a variable, like this:

```
Result := Result + 1;    -- add 1 to Result
```

A **when others** choice will be needed in the **case** statement to cope with the fact that Operator might be any Character value, not just one of the four operators we're looking for. The good news is that the compiler would complain if we forgot this little detail. If we get to the **when others** choice it means there's an error in the input. An appropriate response to this is to display an error message and get out of the loop with an **exit** statement. So here at last is the final program:

```
with Ada.Text_IO, Ada.Integer_Text_IO;
use  Ada.Text_IO, Ada.Integer_Text_IO;
procedure Calculator is
   Result   : Integer;
   Operator : Character;
   Operand  : Integer;
begin
   Put ("Enter an expression: ");
   Get (Result);                              --  1
   loop                                       --  2
     loop                                     --  3
       Get (Operator);
       exit when Operator /= ' ';
```

```
      end loop;

      if Operator = '.' then            -- 4
         Put (Result, Width => 1);      -- 5
         exit;                          -- 6
      else
         Get (Operand);                 -- 7
         case Operator is
           when '+' =>
              Result := Result + Operand;   -- 8
           when '-' =>
              Result := Result - Operand;
           when '*' =>
              Result := Result * Operand;   -- 9
           when '/' =>
              Result := Result / Operand;
           when others =>
              Put ("Invalid operator '");    -- 10
              Put (Operator);
              Put ("'");
              exit;                          -- 11
         end case;
      end if;

   end loop;
   New_Line;
end Calculator;
```

If you type '1+2*3.' in response to the prompt, what will happen is that line 1 will read the value 1 into Result. Line 2 is the start of the main loop; the first thing inside this loop is another loop (line 3) to skip over any spaces in front of the operator character. We will end up at line 4 with Operator holding the character '+'. Lines 5 and 6 will display the result and exit the main loop when Operator is a full stop, but we haven't got to that stage yet. So line 7 will read the value 2 into Operand, and then the **case** statement will execute line 8 based on the value of Operator. Line 8 calculates the value Result+Operand (i.e. 1+2) and stores the result (i.e. 3) in Result. The upshot of this is that Result has been altered from 1 to 3.

After line 8 has been executed we go round the main loop a second time. Operator ends up holding the character '*' and Operand ends up holding the value 3. The **case** statement executes line 9, which multiplies Result (3) by Operand (also 3) to give a new value of 9 for Result. Around the loop again, and Operator ends up holding a full stop at line 4. The result (9) is then displayed by line 5 before exiting from the main loop at line 6.

If an invalid operator character is typed in (e.g. '1&2.') the section of the **case** statement at line 10 gets executed, which displays an error message. Line 11 then exits from the main loop. Notice how important it is to think about what can possibly go wrong and to deal with it in a sensible way; it's easy to write a program that gives the right answer for valid input, but it's much harder to write a program that can cope sensibly with bad input as well.

3.9 Exception handling

Of course, the program is still not completely bulletproof. If you type gibberish like XYZZY at the point where the program expects an integer, the program will halt with an error message. If you're unlucky it will just say something like 'unhandled exception'; some compilers are more helpful, and will also tell you that the error was an exception called Data_Error, and possibly tell you which line of the program you were at when it happened. A Data_Error means that the input is in the wrong format; another common one is Constraint_Error, which you'll get if you go outside the range of values allowed for Integer on your system (try 1000000*1000000*1000000, which will almost certainly be too big to handle).

A properly designed program should be able to cope with any input at all, not just correct input. To manage this we need to trap Constraint_Error and Data_Error exceptions and deal with them sensibly. Ada allows us to provide **exception handlers** to specify what happens if an exception occurs. This is a topic I'll return to in more detail later, but it's worth a brief introduction before we go any further so that you'll be able to start making the programs you write more robust.

You can put an exception handler into any block of statements enclosed by **begin** and **end**, e.g. a procedure body:

```
procedure X is
begin
    -- your code goes here as usual
exception
    when Some_Exception =>
        Do_This;
end X;
```

where Some_Exception is the name of an exception you want to handle and Do_This is the action you want to take. The action can be any sequence of statements; it can be a **null** statement which does nothing, which will have the effect of ignoring the exception, or it can be something more elaborate. In this case a sensible action might be to print out an error message when a Constraint_Error or a Data_Error occurs. Here's how to do it:

```
procedure Calculator is
   Result   : Integer;
   Operator : Character;
   Operand  : Integer;
```

```
begin
  Put ("Enter an expression: ");
  ... code to process the expression as before

exception
  when Constraint_Error =>
    Put_Line ("Value out of range");
  when Data_Error =>
    Put_Line ("Error in input -- integer expected");
end Calculator;
```

The exception handler section goes at the very end; it's ignored if there aren't any errors. If a Constraint_Error or a Data_Error is reported (or **raised**, to use the correct terminology), you immediately end up at the appropriate exception handler and do what it says. Once you've done this, you're at the end of the procedure and the program terminates.

If you want the program to give the user another chance rather than terminating you need to be a bit more subtle. Here's how you can safely read a value into an Integer variable called X:

```
loop
  begin
    Put ("Enter an integer: ");                            -- 1
    Get (X);                                               -- 2
    exit;                                                  -- 3
  exception
    when Constraint_Error | Data_Error =>
      Put_Line ("Error in input -- please try again.");    -- 4
      Skip_Line;                                           -- 5
  end;
end loop;                                                  -- 6
```

Note that you can't put an exception handler directly between **loop** and **end loop**; you have to put **begin** and **end** around the section that you want to provide exception handling for, and then put the exception handler section immediately before **end**. This is the only case in Ada where **end** is not followed by something to say what it is the end of.

What happens here is that line 1 displays a prompt and line 2 attempts to read an integer. If an exception is raised by Get, you won't get to line 3; instead, you'll be whisked off to line 4 which displays an error message. Line 5 calls a procedure Skip_Line from Ada.Text_IO to ignore the rest of the current line of input so the user will have to type another line. If you don't call Skip_Line after a Data_Error you'll just end up reading the same bad data from the current line (which won't have been read since it wasn't valid).

⇒   *Try leaving out the call to Skip_Line and see what happens.*

After this you'll be at line 6, the end of the loop, so you'll go around and redisplay the prompt and get another line of input. When the user types in a valid value for X you'll carry on past line 2 to line 3, which will exit from the loop.

Note also that you can handle several exceptions with a single handler by separating them by a vertical bar ('|') in the same way as you would specify multiple choices in a **case** statement. Also as in a **case** statement, you can provide a 'catch-all' handler by specifying **when others**:

```
exception
  when others =>
    Do_Something;      -- handle every exception the same way
```

As in a **case** statement, **when others** must come last if you have more than one exception handler. It handles any exceptions not dealt with by the other handlers. If you use it as the only handler it will deal with any exception that occurs. I don't recommend using **when others** unless you really need to; it might disguise any real errors in your program due to undiscovered bugs which would otherwise be reported as unhandled exceptions.

If you want an exception to be handled in different ways in different places, you need to enclose each such place in a **begin** ... **end** block. For example, if you have two assignment statements which could each raise a Constraint_Error:

```
A := A ** 2;      -- might raise Constraint_Error
B := B ** 2;      -- might raise Constraint_Error
```

you could enclose each one in a separate block with its own handler like this:

```
begin
  A := A ** 2;      -- might raise Constraint_Error
exception
  when Constraint_Error =>
    Put_Line ("Assignment to A failed");
end;

begin
  B := B ** 2;      -- might raise Constraint_Error
exception
  when Constraint_Error =>
    Put_Line ("Assignment to B failed");
end;
```

Exercises

3.1 Modify the Greetings program to say 'Good evening!' in the evenings as well.

3.2   Modify the calculator program so that after evaluating an expression it asks the user if he or she wants to evaluate another expression. If the answer is 'y' or 'Y' (yes), evaluate another expression; if it's 'n' or 'N' (no) exit from the program.

3.3   Write a program which asks the user to pick an animal from a list that you display (cat, dog, elephant or giraffe) and then asks 'Is it a household pet?' to distinguish cats and dogs from elephants and giraffes. If the user says it's a household pet, ask if it purrs; if not, ask if it has a long neck. Finally, tell the user which animal you think was chosen. Try extending the program to include a few more animals.

3.4   Write a program to count the number of vowels (A, E, I, O or U) in its input. Allow the user to type in a sequence of characters (as many as they like) ending with a full stop and then display the number of occurrences of each vowel as well as a grand total. This will involve using a set of integer variables which are set to zero at the start of the program. You will then need to add 1 to the appropriate variable whenever a vowel is typed in. Ignore case distinctions, so that 'a' is treated as meaning the same as 'A'.

CHAPTER 4

Procedures, functions and packages

All are but parts of one stupendous whole.
— Alexander Pope, An Essay on Man

4.1 Zeller's Congruence

It's time to move on to another example, this time to find out what day of the week it is for a given date. We'll take a date expressed as three integers (day, month and year) and figure out what day it falls on by using a wonderful formula called Zeller's Congruence. To do this, we need to read in the three integers, evaluate Zeller's Congruence, and report the result. Here's a first stab at the program:

```
with Ada.Text_IO, Ada.Integer_Text_IO;
use  Ada.Text_IO, Ada.Integer_Text_IO;
procedure Weekday is
   Day    : Integer;
   Month  : Integer;
   Year   : Integer;
   Result : Integer;
begin
   Put ("Enter a date: ");
   Get (Day);
   Get (Month);
   Get (Year);
   -- Apply Zeller's Congruence
   Put (Result);
end Weekday;
```

⇒ *Note that I use the British format for dates throughout this book (day, month, year). If you find this confusing, reorder the calls to Get to read dates in the format you're used to (e.g. month, day, year for American readers).*

For the sake of simplicity I'll assume for now that the user will always type in a valid date. Let's see how Zeller's Congruence works first. Here's the formula:

```
Day = ((26M-2)/10 + D + Y + Y/4 + C/4 - 2C) mod 7
```

Here M is the number of the month, D is the day, Y is the last two digits of the year number and C is the century (the first two digits of the year number). Integer division is used, so that 19/4 = 4 rather than 4.75. The **mod** operation gives the remainder of an integer division, in this case the remainder from dividing by 7, i.e. a value between 0 and 6. Things are made slightly more complicated by the fact that the months have to be numbered starting with March as month 1; January and February are treated as months 11 and 12 of the *previous* year. We therefore need to adjust the month and year like this:

```
if Month < 3 then
   Year := Year - 1;      -- subtract 1 from year number
   Month := Month + 10;     -- convert 1 and 2 to 11 and 12
else
   Month := Month - 2;    -- subtract 2 from month number
end if;
```

The result of the formula is a number between 0 and 6, where 0 means Sunday and 6 means Saturday. Let's see how this works using January 25th 1956 as an example. The value of D is 25 and C is 19. January 1956 counts as month 11 of 1955, so M is 11 and Y is 55. This gives us:

```
Day = ((26M-2)/10 + D + Y + Y/4 + C/4 - 2C) mod 7
    = ((26*11-2)/10 + 25 + 55 + 55/4 + 19/4 - 2*19) mod 7
    = (284/10 + 25 + 55 + 13 + 4 - 38) mod 7
    = (28 + 25 + 55 + 13 + 4 - 38) mod 7
    = 87 mod 7
    = 3 (Wednesday).
```

It will help to introduce an extra variable for the value C since it's used twice in the formula above. Here's the latest version of the program:

```
with Ada.Text_IO, Ada.Integer_Text_IO;
use  Ada.Text_IO, Ada.Integer_Text_IO;
procedure Weekday is
   Day     : Integer;
   Month   : Integer;
   Year    : Integer;
   Century : Integer;
begin
   Put ("Enter a date: ");
   Get (Day);
   Get (Month);
   Get (Year);
```

```
      if Month < 3 then
        Year  := Year - 1;
        Month := Month + 10;
      else
        Month := Month - 2;
      end if;
      Century := Year / 100;    -- first two digits of Year
      Year := Year mod 100;     -- last two digits of Year
      Put (((26*Month - 2)/10 + Day + Year + Year/4 +
            Century/4 - 2*Century) mod 7);
   end Weekday;
```

The Ada version of Zeller's Congruence is practically identical to the original except that the single-letter variable names in the original have been replaced by longer names. Also, all multiplication operators must be specified explicitly; while the original formula had 26M in it, a direct Ada equivalent would have to be 26*M. The order of operations is the same as in ordinary algebra; multiplication and divisions are done before additions and subtractions, with parentheses being used to alter the order of evaluation where necessary.

The other thing to notice is that the value of Century is calculated after the **if** statement. This is because the **if** statement might change the value of Year; January 2000 is treated as being month 11 of 1999, so the value for Century will be 19 until March 2000. Likewise Year only gets trimmed to its last two digits after the first two digits have been extracted into Century. The order of events is quite important here.

4.2 Declaring procedures

Zeller's Congruence is clearly the sort of thing that could be useful in a number of different programs. It would therefore be a good idea to make it into a separate procedure which could be called from any program which needs to use it. Procedures are also a good way of breaking long programs up into manageable chunks; as a general rule of thumb, any procedure that won't fit on a single printed page is probably too long to read and understand easily and you should consider breaking it up into smaller procedures.

The first thing to do is to decide what inputs it requires and what outputs it produces. There are three inputs: the day, the month and the year. There is a single output, which is a value between 0 and 6. This is enough information to produce a procedure specification:

```
procedure Day_Of (Day, Month, Year : in Integer;
                  Result : out Integer);
```

What we have here is the specification for a procedure called Day_Of (since Zeller would be a bit cryptic) which has four parameters. Three of them (Day, Month and Year) are Integer inputs, and the fourth (Result) is an Integer output. Designing a specification is always a good way to start writing a procedure, but what we actually need here is a procedure body (i.e. including the implementation details between **is** and **end**) rather than just a specification: specifications are generally only used in connection with packages. Writing the body is fairly straightforward; the necessary code can be extracted from the previous program:

```
procedure Day_Of (Day, Month, Year : in Integer;
                    Result : out Integer) is
  M : Integer := Month;
  Y : Integer := Year;
  C : Integer;
begin
  if M < 3 then
    Y := Y - 1;
    M := M + 10;
  else
    M := M - 2;
  end if;

  C := Y / 100;      -- first two digits of Year
  Y := Y mod 100;    -- last two digits of Year
  Result := ((26*M - 2)/10 + Day + Y + Y/4 + C/4 - 2*C) mod 7;
end Day_Of;
```

Notice that the parameter declarations look just like variable declarations, and that they can in fact be treated as if they were variables inside the procedure body. When the procedure is called, the actual values specified for the input parameters are copied into the corresponding parameter 'variables' in the procedure. The procedure body is then executed, and it can make use of the input parameters just as if they were ordinary variables except that it can't alter them. Since procedures can't alter the value of **in** parameters, we need to copy Month and Year into ordinary variables that can be altered. Output parameters behave just like uninitialised variables; you have to set them to some value before you can use them. At the end of the procedure, the values of the output parameter 'variables' will be copied into the variables which were used for the output parameters in the procedure call. In this case, the value of Result will be copied into the variable which was supplied for the Result parameter.

As well as **in** and **out**, we can specify parameters as **in out** meaning that they act as both inputs and outputs. Like an **out** parameter you have to supply a variable name for an **in out** parameter when you call the procedure so that the procedure has somewhere to store its output; the difference is that the original value of the variable before the procedure call is passed into the procedure as an input. Inside a procedure, an **out** parameter behaves like an uninitialised variable (you don't get the original value of the variable supplied when the procedure is called) but an **in out** parameter behaves like an initialised variable; it is initialised to the value of the variable supplied as the actual parameter when the procedure is called.

Here's how you could call the procedure to find out the day of the week for January 25th 1956 and put the result in a variable called R:

```
Day_Of (25, 1, 1956, R);
```

This will copy the values 25, 1 and 1956 into the three input parameters Day, Month and Year and then execute the procedure. At the end of the procedure the value of the output parameter Result will be copied into the variable R.

You could also use the parameter names in the procedure call for the sake of readability:

```
Day_Of (Day => 25, Month => 1, Year => 1956, Result => R);
```

or if you wanted to you could use a mixture of the two styles:

```
Day_Of (25, 1, Year => 1956, Result => R);
```

If you mix the two styles in this way the named parameters must come after any without names. One of the advantages of using named parameters is that you can specify them in any order and the compiler will be able to arrange them into the correct order automatically:

```
Day_Of (Result => R, Month => 1, Day => 25, Year => 1956);
```

4.3 Declaring functions

Using a procedure in this case means that two steps are needed to display the procedure's result. Here's what we have to do:

```
Day_Of (Day, Month, Year, R);
Put (R);
```

We call Day_Of and put its result in a variable R. Then we have to pass R as a parameter to Put. Two statements are needed, not to mention the extra intermediate variable R. An alternative solution would be to define Day_Of as a **function**. A function is just like a procedure except that it evaluates to a result that can be used as part of an expression; for example, a function call could be used as the value for an input parameter in a procedure call (or a call to another function), or as part of an expression on the right hand side of an assignment statement. A function is restricted to producing a single result, and only **in** parameters are allowed. Functions and procedures are collectively referred to as **subprograms**.

Since there is a single result produced by the Day_Of procedure it would be easy to turn it into a function. This would allow us to write something like this:

```
Put ( Day_Of(Day, Month, Year) );
```

where the result of the function call is used directly as the parameter to Put. This eliminates the extra statement and the extra variable.

Here's how you could rewrite the procedure specification above as a function specification:

```
function Day_Of (Day, Month, Year : Integer) return Integer;
```

Instead of an 'out Integer' parameter to store the result in, you specify 'return Integer' after the parameter list to show that the function returns an Integer as its result. Note that you only have to say 'Integer' instead of 'in Integer' in the function parameter declaration, since you aren't allowed **out** or **in out** parameters to functions. Only **in** parameters are allowed, and as a consequence you don't need to specify **in**.

Here's how the function would be implemented:

```
function Day_Of (Day, Month, Year : Integer) return Integer is
   M : Integer := Month;
   Y : Integer := Year;
   C : Integer;
begin
   if M < 3 then
      Y := Y - 1;
      M := M + 10;
   else
      M := M - 2;
   end if;
   C := Y / 100;      -- first two digits of Year
   Y := Y mod 100;    -- last two digits of Year
   return ((26*M - 2)/10 + Day + Y + Y/4 + C/4 - 2*C) mod 7;
end Day_Of;
```

The **return** statement specifies an expression whose value is the value to be returned as the result of the function. When you execute a **return** statement, you evaluate the expression and then immediately exit the function. For example, if you called the function like this:

```
I := Day_Of (X, Y, Z);
```

the values of X, Y and Z would be copied into the parameters Day, Month and Year. The body of the function would then be executed up to the **return** statement; the value of the expression in the **return** statement would then be returned from the function and assigned to the variable I.

There is also a form of **return** statement for use in procedures:

```
return;
```

All this does is to exit immediately from the procedure it is used in and return to the point where the procedure was called from.

4.4 Scope and lifetime

Now all we have to do is to integrate this function into the program. There are several ways to do this. The first is to put the function declaration directly into the declaration part of the main program:

```
with Ada.Text_IO, Ada.Integer_Text_IO;
use  Ada.Text_IO, Ada.Integer_Text_IO;
procedure Weekday is
   Day, Month, Year : Integer;                         -- 1
   function Day_Of (Day, Month, Year : Integer)
                     return Integer is                 -- 2
     D : Integer := Day;                               -- 3
     M : Integer := Month;
     Y : Integer := Year;
     C : Integer;
   begin
     if M < 3 then
       Y := Y - 1;
       M := M + 10;
     else
       M := M - 2;
     end if;
     C := Y / 100;     -- first two digits of Year
     Y := Y mod 100;   -- last two digits of Year
     return ((26*M - 2)/10 + D + Y + Y/4 + C/4 - 2*C) mod 7;
   end Day_Of;                                         -- 4

begin     -- main program
  Put ("Enter a date: ");
  Get (Day);
  Get (Month);
  Get (Year);
  Put ( Day_Of(Day,Month,Year) );                      -- 5
end Weekday;
```

At this point it is worth mentioning something about the declarations of the variables inside the Day_Of function. When a variable declaration is executed (or **elaborated**, to use the correct technical term) some space in memory is reserved for that variable and initialised if the declaration specifies an initial value. The variable exists until the end of the **begin** ... **end** block which follows it, and the space allocated to it is then reclaimed so that it can be used elsewhere if necessary. This means that when Day_Of is called at line 5 the variable D inside Day_Of is created when the declaration at line 3 is elaborated. D is then destroyed at the end of Day_Of (line 4) before returning to line 5. The region from the declaration to the end of the block it is defined in is known as the **scope** of the variable. Since the variable only exists inside its scope, it cannot be accessed from elsewhere (i.e. from another subprogram) since it might not exist at the time; thus D cannot be accessed from the main program since it only exists during the call to Day_Of at line 5. In other words, variables declared in a subprogram are **local** to that subprogram and are only accessible from inside that subprogram since this is the only time their existence is guaranteed. Parameters are treated the same way; they are effectively local variables which are created during the subprogram call and destroyed when the call is complete.

Variables in different scopes can have the same name as each other; this means that you don't have to worry about avoiding names which are used in other subprograms. Thus there is no confusion about using Day as the name of a variable at line 1 and as the name of a parameter at line 2; the variable called Day at line 1 is local to the main program while the parameter called Day at line 2 is local to Day_Of. When you refer to a name, the most local object of that name is accessed, so that the version of Day being referred to at line 3 is the parameter declared at line 2 whereas the version referred to in line 5 is the variable declared at line 1.

Each time a subprogram is called, the local variables it declares are created. This means that each variable will be reinitialised every time the subprogram is called if its declaration specifies an initial value; if not its value will be unpredictable. There is no guarantee that a particular variable will be allocated the same space in memory each time the subprogram is called, so there is no way of knowing what the contents of the variable will be unless the declaration explicitly specifies an initial value. In particular, variables do not retain their values from one subprogram call to the next. D, M and Y will be initialised every time Day_Of is called; C will always start off with an unpredictable value. If you do want to retain a value from one call to the next, you have to use a variable declared in the surrounding scope. In this case a variable declared in the main program before Day_Of could be used to hold a value from one call of Day_Of to the next since its scope would be that of the main program; since that scope includes Day_Of it would be accessible inside Day_Of but it would not be destroyed until the end of the main program was reached.

Locality of variables is useful for isolating errors; if during debugging you found that the value of C was wrong you would know that the fault lay somewhere inside Day_Of, since this is the only place where C is accessible. It would be perfectly possible to declare C in the main program instead of inside Day_Of (it would still be accessible inside Day_Of) but you would have to look at the main program as well as Day_Of if its value was found to be incorrect during debugging since its scope would be the whole main program. It would also be wasteful of memory, since space would be allocated for C even when it wasn't being used. The moral of the story is that variables should always be made as local as possible. If you want to, you can localise declarations even further than the subprogram level by using a **declare** block:

```
declare
   -- declarations local to the declare block
begin
   -- statements using the local declarations
end;        -- declarations go out of scope here
```

If you want to, you can also put an exception handler in a **declare** block like the one above:

```
declare
   -- declarations local to the declare block
begin
   -- statements using the local declarations
exception
   -- exception handlers for the statements above
end;        -- declarations go out of scope here
```

Although you may not have realised this, you met **declare** blocks for the first time at the end of the last chapter in connection with exception handling inside loops. The reason you might not have noticed is that the declaration section (everything before **begin**) was omitted, which is what you have to do if you don't want any declarations. If there are declarations between **declare** and **begin**, they are local to the block. They are created when their declarations are elaborated, they are destroyed at the end of the block, and they are only accessible within the block. As an example, here's a version of Day_Of where a **declare** block is used to localise the declaration of C:

```
function Day_Of (Day, Month, Year : Integer) return Integer is
   M : Integer := Month;
   Y : Integer := Year;
begin
   if M < 3 then
      Y := Y - 1;
      M := M + 10;
   else
      M := M - 2;
   end if;
   declare
      C : Integer := Y / 100;                          -- 1
   begin
      Y := Y mod 100;
```

```
    return ((26*M - 2)/10 + Day + Y + Y/4 + C/4 - 2*C) mod 7;
  end;                                              -- 2
end Day_Of;                                         -- 3
```

C is not created until line 1 and destroyed at line 2, whereas **M** and **Y** are created at the start of the function and destroyed at line 3.

4.5 Separate compilation

There are several disadvantages to implementing the function inside the main program as described above. One disadvantage is that it makes the program harder to read; the body of the main program is right down at the end and is swamped by the declarations which precede it. Also, if you needed to make a change to Day_Of you would have to recompile the whole thing, not just the function. These problems are easy enough to resolve; Ada allows us to take embedded procedures and functions from a declaration section and compile them separately. All we have to do is to declare the function as being **separate**. The main program ends up looking like this:

```
with Ada.Text_IO, Ada.Integer_Text_IO;
use  Ada.Text_IO, Ada.Integer_Text_IO;
procedure Weekday is
   Day, Month, Year : Integer;

   function Day_Of (Day, Month, Year : Integer) return Integer
      is separate;
begin
   Put ("Enter a date: ");
   Get (Day);
   Get (Month);
   Get (Year);
   Put ( Day_Of (Day,Month,Year) );
end Weekday;
```

This is a lot clearer. The function is then put in a separate file, compiled separately and linked with the main program. We have to tell the compiler where the function came from by including the line 'separate (Weekday)' at the beginning:

```
separate (Weekday)
function Day_Of (Day, Month, Year : Integer) return Integer is
   D : Integer := Day;
   M : Integer := Month;
   Y : Integer := Year;
   C : Integer;
```

```
begin
   if M < 3 then
      Y := Y - 1;
      M := M + 10;
   else
      M := M - 2;
   end if;
   C := Y / 100;      -- first two digits of Year
   Y := Y mod 100;    -- last two digits of Year
   return ((26*M - 2)/10 + D + Y + Y/4 + C/4 - 2*C) mod 7;
end Day_Of;
```

This tells the compiler that function Day_Of is a function declared as being separate inside Weekday. The effect is identical to the original version with the function embedded in the declaration section of the main program (in particular, it is still within the scope of the main program), but the main program is now less cluttered and if you have to make any changes to Day_Of, a sensible compiler will only require you to recompile the file containing Day_Of and then relink the main program. The main program shouldn't need recompiling if it hasn't been changed. If the main program changes you'll still have to recompile both the main program and Day_Of in case the changes to the main program had some effect on Day_Of (such as a change to the function declaration).

4.6 Subprograms as library units

A problem with both approaches described above is that Day_Of is declared as being local to Weekday, which means it can't be accessed from anywhere outside Weekday. This means that it can't be used by another program without physically duplicating the code for it. Also, Day_Of is able to access anything which is declared before it in the declaration section of Weekday. This means that a **coupling** exists between Day_Of and Weekday. Any sort of coupling should be avoided if components are going to be reusable; they should be able to be used anywhere, not just in a particular environment.

To get around these problems we could just compile Day_Of as an independent **library unit** in its own right, just like the procedure Hello which was used as a component of the program Hello_3 in chapter 2. When Day_Of is compiled it gets added to the library and it is then available for use as a component in a larger program. This is only possible if it doesn't rely on anything which is not a standard built-in part of the language or else provided in a package such as Text_IO that can be accessed using a **with** clause. In other words, it is restricted to accessing the same things as the main program is. In this case the function doesn't rely on anything external so there's no problem:

```
function Day_Of (Day, Month, Year : Integer) return Integer is
   D : Integer := Day;
   M : Integer := Month;
```

```
      Y : Integer := Year;
      C : Integer;
   begin
     if M < 3 then
        Y := Y - 1;
        M := M + 10;
     else
        M := M - 2;
     end if;

     C := Y / 100;      -- first two digits of Year
     Y := Y mod 100;    -- last two digits of Year
     return ((26*M - 2)/10 + D + Y + Y/4 + C/4 - 2*C) mod 7;
   end Day_Of;
```

Now we have to specify in the main program that Day_Of is a library unit that we want to refer to, so we need to name it in a **with** clause:

```
with Ada.Text_IO, Ada.Integer_Text_IO, Day_Of;
use  Ada.Text_IO, Ada.Integer_Text_IO;
procedure Weekday is
   Day, Month, Year : Integer;
begin
   Put ("Enter a date: ");
   Get (Day);
   Get (Month);
   Get (Year);
   Put ( Day_Of (Day, Month, Year) );
end Weekday;
```

4.7 Packages

At the moment the program doesn't check if the date that the user types in is valid. It's easy enough to write a function to do this:

```
function Valid (Day, Month, Year : Integer) return Boolean is
begin
   if Year < 1901 or Year > 2099 or Day < 1 then
      return False;
   else
      case Month is
         when 1 | 3 | 5 | 7 | 8 | 10 | 12 =>   -- 31 day months
            return Day <= 31;
```

```
      when 4 | 6 | 9 | 11 =>           -- 30 day months
         return Day <= 30;
      when 2 =>                        -- February; 28 or 29 days
         if Year mod 4 = 0 then
            return Day <= 29;
         else
            return Day <= 28;
         end if;
      when others =>                   -- invalid month
         return False;
      end case;
   end if;
end Valid;
```

The function returns a Boolean result (True or False). It checks that the year is between 1901 and 2099 and that the day is not zero or less; it then uses a **case** statement to distinguish between the various lengths of month and checks that the day is not greater than the last day of the month. Note that the test for leap years (Year mod 4 = 0) is only adequate when Year is guaranteed to be between 1901 and 2099; it would be better to generalise it in case the range allowed for Year ever changes.

⇒ *Modify the condition for leap years so that it works if the range allowed for Year ever changes. A year is a leap year if it is divisible by 4 but not by 100, or if it is divisible by 400 (so 2000 is a leap year but 1900 and 2100 aren't).*

Each branch of the **case** statement returns a Boolean result, usually the result of comparing Day with the last day of the month. For example, 'Day <= 31' is a Boolean expression which will give a result of True if the day is 31 or less and False otherwise; the function just returns the result of the expression directly. The function can be used as the condition part of an **if** statement (which must evaluate to a Boolean value):

```
if Valid (D,M,Y) then
   -- do this if Valid returns True
else
   -- do this if Valid returns False
end if;
```

This function is fairly closely related to the Day_Of function; there are probably dozens of date-related functions we could dream up. It would make sense to gather these functions together into a **package** rather than having a library full of functions with no apparent relationship to each other.

Another advantage of using a package is to avoid 'namespace pollution'. Library units must have unique names, so the more procedures and functions we put in our library the more restricted the choice of names becomes. It is far easier to ensure that names are unique if collections of procedures and functions can be entered into the library under a single package name. Also, as you'll see later, you can minimise the number of unique names even further by using **child packages**.

The first step is to generate a **package specification**. This needs to contain declarations for everything we want users of the package to be able to access: variables, subprograms, whatever. In the case of subprograms, we only provide specifications in the package specification; the actual code for subprograms goes into a separate **package body**. Here's a first stab at the specification of a package to contain the Day_Of and Valid functions:

```
package Dates is
   function Day_Of (Day, Month, Year : Integer) return Integer;
   function Valid  (Day, Month, Year : Integer) return Boolean;
end Dates;
```

The package specification goes in a file by itself and must be compiled and added to the library. Next we produce a package body to provide the implementation of the two functions. The package body has the same name as the package specification; the only difference is that it begins with the words 'package body' rather than just 'package':

```
package body Dates is
   function Day_Of (Day, Month, Year : Integer)
                           return Integer is
      D : Integer := Day;
      M : Integer := Month;
      Y : Integer := Year;
      C : Integer;
   begin
      if M < 3 then
         Y := Y - 1;
         M := M + 10;
      else
         M := M - 2;
      end if;
      C := Y / 100;     -- first two digits of Year
      Y := Y mod 100;   -- last two digits of Year
      return (((26*M - 2)/10 + D + Y + Y/4 + C/4 - 2*C) mod 7);
   end Day_Of;

   function Valid (Day, Month, Year : Integer)
                           return Boolean is
   begin
      if Year < 1901 or Year > 2099 or Day < 1 then
         return False;
```

```
      else
        case Month is
          when 1 | 3 | 5 | 7 | 8 | 10 | 12 =>
            return Day <= 31;
          when 4 | 6 | 9 | 11 =>
            return Day <= 30;
          when 2 =>
            if Year mod 4 = 0 then
              return Day <= 29;
            else
              return Day <= 28;
            end if;
          when others =>
            return False;
        end case;
      end if;
    end Valid;
  end Dates;
```

The package body can now be compiled and added to the library, and then we're finished. Note that we don't have to provide a **with** clause for Dates at the start of the package body; a package body is automatically granted access to its own specification. We can use this package in any of our programs in exactly the same way as any other package:

```
with Ada.Text_IO, Ada.Integer_Text_IO, Dates;
use  Ada.Text_IO, Ada.Integer_Text_IO;
procedure Weekday is
  Day, Month, Year : Integer;
begin
  Put ("Enter a date: ");
  Get (Day);
  Get (Month);
  Get (Year);

  if Dates.Valid(Day,Month,Year) then
    Put (Dates.Day_Of (Day, Month, Year));
  else
    Put_Line ("Invalid date!");
  end if;
end Weekday;
```

The program has to include the package in the **with** clause at the beginning; the declarations in the package specification are then accessible so that we can refer to the functions Dates.Day_Of and Dates.Valid. We could of course name Dates in a **use** clause so that Day_Of and Valid can be used without having to specify the package name as a prefix.

Note that only the package specification is accessed by a **with** clause; anything defined inside the package body is local to the package and hence invisible to programs which use the package. The package body might contain extra subprograms which are used to help implement the ones declared in the package specification; for example, there might be a function called Month_Length which returns the number of days in a given month:

```
package body Dates is

   -- Day_Of is accessible to users via the specification
   function Day_Of (Day, Month, Year : Integer)
                           return Integer is
     D : Integer := Day;
     M : Integer := Month;
     Y : Integer := Year;
     C : Integer;
   begin
     if M < 3 then
       Y := Y - 1;
       M := M + 10;
     else
       M := M - 2;
     end if;
     C := Y / 100;        -- first two digits of Year
     Y := Y mod 100;      -- last two digits of Year
     return (((26*M - 2)/10 + D + Y + Y/4 + C/4 - 2*C) mod 7);
   end Day_Of;

   -- This function is local to the package body and
   -- is not accessible via the package specification
   function Month_Length (Month : Integer) return Integer is
   begin
     case Month is
       when 2 =>
         return 28;
       when 4 | 6 | 9 | 11 =>
         return 30;
       when 1 | 3 | 5 | 7 | 8 | 10 | 12 =>
         return 31;
       when others =>
         return 0;
     end case;
   end Month_Length;
```

```
-- Valid is accessible to users via the specification
-- and is implemented using the local function Month_Length
function Valid (Day, Month, Year : Integer)
                      return Boolean is
begin
   if Year < 1901 or Year > 2099 or Day < 1 then
      return False;
   elsif Year mod 4 = 0 then
      return Day <= 29;
   else
      return Day <= Month_Length (Month);
   end if;
   end Valid;
end Dates;
```

Since Month_Length is not declared in the package specification, it cannot be accessed by programs which use the package; the only place it can be accessed is within the package body itself.

Note that any variables you might declare in the package specification will effectively be **global** variables rather than local variables; they will be created before executing the main program when the **with** clause for the package is elaborated, they will not be destroyed until after exiting from the main program, and they will be accessible wherever the package is accessible. Variables declared in the package body itself rather than inside a particular subprogram in the package body will also be created before the start of the program and destroyed after it finishes, although in this case they will not be accessible from outside the package body.

The package body shown above consists entirely of subprogram declarations. You are also allowed to put a series of statements in a package body in exactly the same way as you do in a subprogram (after any declarations, between **begin** and **end**):

```
with Ada.Text_IO;
package body Dates is
   ...        -- as above
begin
   Put_Line ("This program uses Dates by John English");
end Dates;
```

The statements after **begin** are executed when the package body is elaborated, typically at the point where the package is accessed by a **with** clause just before the main program is executed. They can be used to perform any initialisation that may be needed before the package is used for the first time. This is not a terribly common requirement, but one use for it might be to display a copyright notice of some sort at the start of the main program. In the example above, the message 'This program uses Dates by John English' will be displayed whenever any main program which uses the package starts up.

4.8 Child packages

To minimise namespace pollution even further, Ada allows us to define extensions to existing packages which are referred to as **child packages**. The **parent package** must have a unique name, but the children of this package have names which use the parent package's name as a prefix. Since the parent package's name is unique, this means that the child packages will also have unique names. The number of unique names needed is thus reduced to a handful of parent packages. This can also minimise the risk of bought-in package libraries from different suppliers having names that clash; each supplier can just provide a parent package with a unique name (their company name, for example). You've already come across child packages: Ada.Text_IO and Ada.Integer_Text_IO are typical examples. In fact, all the standard packages in Ada are children of one of three parent packages: Ada, Interfaces or System.

I'm going to do the same thing in this book. I'm going to define a parent package called JE (my initials) and make every other package in the book a child of that. Here it is:

```
package JE is
   -- an empty package!
end JE;
```

This package specification is only there to act as a parent for other packages. Since there's nothing in it, there's no need for a package body. In fact, you aren't allowed to provide a package body if it isn't needed (i.e. if there are no subprograms declared in the specification). All we need to do is compile the package specification and add it to the library. Now we can rewrite the previous package like this:

```
package JE.Dates is
   function Day_Of (Day, Month, Year : Integer) return Integer;
   function Valid  (Day, Month, Year : Integer) return Boolean;
end JE.Dates;
```

All I've done is to change the name of the package from Dates to JE.Dates. JE.Dates is effectively an extended version of the parent package JE; everything declared in JE is also part of JE.Dates (which doesn't give you anything extra in this case since JE is an empty package!). In other words, naming JE.Dates in a **with** clause automatically gives you access to the contents of the parent package JE.

Now the package body's name needs changing to match:

```
package body JE.Dates is
   function Day_Of (Day, Month, Year : Integer)
                              return Integer is
   begin
     -- as before
   end Day_Of;
```

```
     function Valid (Day, Month, Year : Integer)
                              return Boolean is
     begin
       -- as before
     end Valid;
   end JE.Dates;
```

and the main program needs changing to refer to JE.Dates instead of Dates:

```
   with Ada.Text_IO, Ada.Integer_Text_IO, JE.Dates;
   use  Ada.Text_IO, Ada.Integer_Text_IO;
   procedure Weekday is
     Day, Month, Year : Integer;
   begin
     Put ("Enter a date: ");
     Get (Day);
     Get (Month);
     Get (Year);
     if JE.Dates.Valid(Day,Month,Year) then
       Put (JE.Dates.Day_Of (Day, Month, Year));
     else
       Put_Line ("Invalid date!");
     end if;
   end Weekday;
```

The main effect of this change is that only the name JE needs to be unique in the library; something else called Dates will not clash with JE.Dates.

It is also possible to declare subprograms as children of packages; the function Day_Of could have been declared as a child of the package JE like this:

```
   function JE.Day_Of (Day, Month, Year : Integer)
                                 return Integer is
     D : Integer := Day;
     M : Integer := Month;
     Y : Integer := Year;
     C : Integer;
   begin
     if M < 3 then
       Y := Y - 1;
       M := M + 10;
     else
       M := M - 2;
     end if;
     C := Y / 100;      -- first two digits of Year
```

```
    Y := Y mod 100;    -- last two digits of Year
    return ((26*M - 2)/10 + D + Y + Y/4 + C/4 - 2*C) mod 7;
end JE.Day_Of;
```

All that's changed from the original version of the function is the name (JE.Day_Of instead of Day_Of). The main program will have to have a **with** clause referring to JE.Day_Of to use it:

```
with Ada.Text_IO, Ada.Integer_Text_IO, JE.Day_Of;
use  Ada.Text_IO, Ada.Integer_Text_IO;
procedure Weekday is
   Day, Month, Year, Century : Integer;
begin
   Put ("Enter a date: ");
   Get (Day);
   Get (Month);
   Get (Year);
   Put (JE.Day_Of (Day, Month, Year));
end Weekday;
```

Exercises

4.1 The procedure Ada.Integer_Text_IO.Get skips any leading spaces and then reads an integer, but Ada.Text_IO.Get reads a character without skipping leading spaces. Write a procedure called Get_Non_Space which skips leading spaces and reads the next non-space character into the variable supplied as its parameter and write a simple program which tests that it works properly.

4.2 Write a procedure which takes three integer parameters representing a date and a fourth integer parameter representing a number of days and adds the specified number of days to the date (so that, for example, adding 7 to December 26th 1995 will give January 2nd 1996). Add this procedure to the Dates package described in this chapter and write a simple program which tests that it works properly.

4.3 Write a function to calculate the greatest common divisor (GCD) of two integers. You can do this using 'Euclid's algorithm': the GCD of two values X and Y is X if Y is zero, otherwise the process should be repeated using the values Y and X mod Y instead of X and Y respectively (e.g. for X = 9, Y = 6, since Y isn't zero the process is repeated with X = 6, Y = 9 mod 6 = 3; since Y still isn't zero it's repeated again with X = 3, Y = 6 mod 3 = 0, and this time Y is zero so the result is 3). The absolute value (positive magnitude) of the result should be returned (you can get the absolute value of a number X using the expression 'abs X'). Write a simple program which tests that it works properly.

4.4 Many computers have an 'ANSI-compatible' display. Write a package to do simple screen handling for an ANSI-compatible display which contains procedures called Clear_Screen and Move_Cursor:

```
procedure Clear_Screen;
procedure Move_Cursor (Row, Column : in Integer);
```

You can perform these operations by using Put to display 'escape sequences' consisting of the 'escape' character (which can be referred to using the name ASCII.ESC) followed by a string representing a screen management command, e.g. "[2J" to clear the screen or "[5;6H" to move the cursor to row 5, column 6 on the screen.

CHAPTER 5

Defining new data types

So careful of the type she seems.
— Tennyson, *In Memoriam*

5.1 Standard data types

As I said earlier, when you write a program you are constructing a model of some aspect of the real world, and the more closely that model reflects reality the better your program will be. Ada programs represent different types of real-world objects using different **data types**. As you've already seen, Ada takes quite a strict approach to data types, which allows the compiler to spot many errors that might otherwise be overlooked.

A data type specifies what values are possible for the corresponding real-world objects as well as specifying what operations can be performed on those objects. Ada provides a number of built-in data types to get you started, but it also recognises that it is impossible to provide data types to cater for every imaginable situation. The language provides you with the ability to define your own data types so that your program can model reality as accurately as possible. This also has the advantage that the more precise you are about the data in the real world that you're modelling, the more the compiler can help you get your program right by checking it for errors.

The built-in data types are defined in a package called Standard which is always available automatically in every Ada program. Appendix B contains a listing of Standard. Unlike other packages, you do not have to use a **with** clause or a **use** clause to access the definitions provided in Standard. We have already met a few standard data types: the type Integer for dealing with whole numbers, the type String for dealing with sequences of characters, the type Character for dealing with individual characters, and the type Boolean for dealing with values which can be either True or False.

There are several other built-in types for dealing with numbers. Numbers in Ada are categorised as **integers** which are exact values with no fractional part (e.g. 123) or **real numbers** which have a fractional part (e.g. 1.23) but will not necessarily be represented with perfect accuracy; for example, the result of dividing 1.0 by 3.0 will be an infinitely long fraction 0.333333333333333... which can't be represented exactly since we don't have an infinite amount of memory. Also, since numbers are normally represented internally in binary, it will usually be impossible to represent 0.1 exactly, since this is a recurring fraction in binary.

5.2   Integers

The basic built-in integer type in Ada is called Integer. The exact range of numbers that type Integer can cope with is implementation defined; the only guarantee you have is that it will *at least* be able to hold values in the range ±32767. To allow you to find out the exact range of values available on a particular machine, all types in Ada have a set of **attributes** which can be used to discover various details about the type. Attributes are specified by putting an apostrophe (') and the attribute name after the type name. A complete list of attributes is given in Appendix C. In the case of integer types, the most important attributes are as follows:

```
First       -- the first (lowest) value of the type
Last        -- the last (highest) value of the type
Image(X)    -- convert the integer X to a string
Value(X)    -- convert the string X to an integer
Min(X,Y)    -- the smaller of the integers X and Y
Max(X,Y)    -- the larger of the integers X and Y
```

Thus Integer'Last will tell you what the largest value of type Integer is on your particular machine, and Integer'Image(X) will convert an Integer value X to a string. The following statement could be used to display the largest value of type Integer for a particular machine:

```
Ada.Text_IO.Put ( Integer'Image(Integer'Last) );
```

Integer types come with a full set of arithmetic operations, some of which you've already seen:

```
+       Addition              -       Subtraction
*       Multiplication        /       Division
rem     Remainder             mod     Modulus
**      Exponentiation        abs     Absolute value
```

The + and – operators can be used as **binary** operators which produce a result computed from two operands (e.g. 5 + 7 or 5 – 7) or as **unary** operators which produce a result computed from a single operand (e.g. +5 or –5). The **abs** operator is also unary; it discards the sign of its operand leaving only the (positive) magnitude, so that **abs** 7 and **abs** –7 both give a result of 7.

The division operator produces an integer result when dividing integers, so that 7/5 would give a result of 1 rather than 1.4. The operators **rem** and **mod** allow you to find out the remainder resulting from a division, so that 7 **rem** 5 would give you a result of 2. The same result could be obtained by using **mod**; 7 **mod** 5 would also be 2. The difference between **rem** and **mod** is the way they deal with negative numbers: **rem** gives a negative result if the dividend (the left hand operand) is negative, whereas **mod** gives a negative

Table 5.1

Operator precedence					
Highest priority (evaluated first):	**	abs	not		
	*	/	mod	rem	
	+	–		*(unary versions)*	
	+	–	&		
	=	/=	<	>	<= >=
Lowest priority (evaluated last):	and	or	xor		

result if the divisor (the right hand operand) is negative. Here are some examples which show the difference between them:

```
7/5   = 1        7 rem 5  = 2        7 mod 5  = 2
-7/5  = -1      -7 rem 5  = -2      -7 mod 5  = 3
7/-5  = -1       7 rem -5 = 2        7 mod -5 = -3
-7/-5 = 1       -7 rem -5 = -2      -7 mod -5 = -2
```

With **rem**, the result is the conventional remainder, i.e. the difference between A and (A/B)*B. For example, 7/5 is 1. Multiply this by 5 and you get 5. The remainder is the difference between 7 and 5, i.e. 2. With **mod**, a multiple of B is added to the remainder if necessary so that the result is always between 0 and B, excluding B itself. So in the case of –7/5, the remainder of –2 produced by **rem** has to have 5 added to it so that the result of 3 is between 0 and 5.

The exponentiation operator raises a value to a given power, so that A ** B means A to the power B. For example, 4 ** 3 is 4^3 (4 cubed), i.e. 64. The value of the right hand operand of ** cannot be negative since this will not give an integer result.

As was briefly mentioned in chapter 4, operators are evaluated in order of **precedence**; multiplications are done before additions, and so on. Table 5.1 above shows the precedence of all the operators in Ada (including some you haven't been introduced to yet). Evaluation of a sequence of operators with the same precedence is done from left to right, so that 12/2*3 means (12/2)*3 = 6*3 = 18, rather than 12/(2*3) = 12/6 = 2. If you are in any doubt, use extra parentheses to make it absolutely clear what you intend.

The standard type Integer may or may not provide a large enough range of values for what you need. For example, you might want to represent a time of day as a number of seconds since midnight, which requires a range of values between 0 and 86399. On some machines the type Integer might be able to represent values as high as 86399 but there's no guarantee that it will. However, it is easy enough to define your own integer types; all you have to do is to write a **type declaration** like this:

```
type Time_Of_Day is range 0..86399;
```

You now have a new data type called Time_Of_Day which is an integer type and which will have the same attributes and operators as the built-in type Integer. However, as far as

Ada is concerned, each type declaration creates a brand new type which is unrelated to all the other types (even if the range of values is identical), so you can't mix Integer values with Time_Of_Day values. In other words, if I is an Integer and T is a Time_Of_Day, the following statements are illegal:

```
T := I;          -- can't assign Integer to Time_of_Day
I := T;          -- can't assign Time_Of_Day to Integer
T := T + I;      -- can't add Integer to Time_Of_Day
T := I + I;      -- can't assign Integer to Time_of_Day
```

Operations such as + in the last statement above return a value of the same type as their operands (well, the **base type** of their operands actually, as described later; this is basically the same thing except that the range of values might be less restricted), so the addition I + I is legal and produces an Integer as its result. However, this can't be assigned to a Time_Of_Day variable because the types don't match. The problem doesn't arise with integer literals such as 1 or 99; these are **universal integers** which can be used with any integer type, so the following are all legal:

```
T := 99;
I := 99;
T := T + 99;
T := 99 + 99;
```

In the last example, adding two universal integers together gives a universal integer result.

Any numeric type can be converted to any other numeric type using a **type conversion** (which will involve rounding a real value to the nearest integer if you are converting a real type to an integer type). A type conversion consists of the name of the type you want to convert to, followed by the value to be converted enclosed in parentheses. The errors shown above can be avoided by using type conversions where necessary:

```
T := Time_Of_Day (I);
I := Integer (T);
T := T + Time_Of_Day (I);
T := Time_Of_Day (I + I);
```

Of course, the value might be out of the legal range of the target type; for example, I might be negative, in which case there is no corresponding Time_Of_Day value that it can be converted to. If this happens, a Constraint_Error exception will be raised.

If you want to display Time_Of_Day values on the screen or read them from the keyboard, you can't use Ada.Integer_Text_IO since this is for use with type Integer and type Time_Of_Day is quite distinct from this. You can always use Time_Of_Day'Image to convert a Time_Of_Day value to a String that you can display with Ada.Text_IO.Put:

```
Ada.Text_IO.Put ( Time_Of_Day'Image(T) );
```

but a better way is to create your own input/output package for Time_Of_Day that provides the same facilities as Ada.Integer_Text_IO. This is easy to do; here's the declaration of a package called Time_Of_Day_IO which will give you the same facilities for Time_Of_Day values that Ada.Integer_Text_IO does for Integers:

```
package Time_of_Day_IO is
        new Ada.Text_IO.Integer_IO (Time_Of_Day);
```

These lines can be put in the declaration section of a procedure after the declaration of Time_Of_Day itself. Ada.Text_IO must have been named in a **with** clause for this to work. What it does is to create a new package which is a copy of the **generic** package Ada.Text_IO.Integer_IO. This provides input/output facilities for integer types in general; all you have to do is to say which specific integer type you want to use it for. In the official terminology, we have **instantiated** (i.e. created a new **instance** of) the package Ada.Text_IO.Integer_IO for use with Time_Of_Day values. The standard package Ada.Integer_Text_IO is effectively predefined for use with Integers by the same process. The listing of Ada.Text_IO in Appendix B contains the definition of Integer_IO, so you can refer to that to find out what Ada.Integer_Text_IO provides.

5.3 Subtypes

The Ada notion of types is central to the issue of developing reliable software. If two integers represent quantities of chalk and cheese, we don't really *want* to be able to mix them indiscriminately. We want the compiler to be able to say 'sorry, you seem to be mixing chalk and cheese; what do you *really* mean?'. And of course if that's what you really want to do you can, but you have to tell the compiler that you're doing it deliberately rather than accidentally with an explicit type conversion. This seems to be an unnecessary complication to people who are used to other, less strict, programming languages, and you can usually spot code written by programmers who are new to Ada because they use Integer for absolutely everything. It takes time to get used to the idea of analysing what you're representing and going to the extra bother of writing a type declaration and doing type conversions where necessary. Once you do, the compiler can help you to spot all sorts of silly mistakes arising from muddled thinking. The extra effort is beneficial because it gives the compiler the means to check your programs for errors in a much more thorough way than it would otherwise be able to do; but since it's an extra effort it requires self-discipline on your part. However, self-discipline is essential if you're going to be a good programmer!

Sometimes, though, we may want to specify that a particular type of variable should hold a restricted range of the values covered by some other type without creating a brand new type which would need type conversion to be used in conjunction with the original type. We want to be able to mix different types freely when they're just different aspects of the same thing, but we still want the benefits which arise from telling the compiler what we're trying to do so that it can check if we're doing it right. For example, we want to specify that the right hand operand in an integer exponentiation is non-negative so that we don't end up with a real result. Ada allows us to define **subtypes** of existing types which behave just like the original type except that they have a restricted range of values:

```
subtype Natural  is Integer range 0..Integer'Last;
subtype Positive is Integer range 1..Integer'Last;
```

These declarations define two subtypes of type Integer: Natural is an Integer which cannot be less than zero, and Positive is an Integer which cannot be less than 1. In fact, both these subtypes are useful enough that they are already provided as built-in types declared in the package Standard, and the exponentiation operator is defined so that it requires a Natural value on its right hand side. Subtypes of a type can be used anywhere that the type itself or any of its subtypes can be used, so you can use a Natural variable anywhere an Integer is required and vice versa; however, if you use an Integer where a Natural is required the compiler will automatically insert checks into your program to ensure that the Integer isn't negative. If it *is* negative, a Constraint_Error exception will be raised. This lets you separate out the error handling into the exception handler section, which is more readable than having the error checking code jumbled together with the code for normal processing.

You don't have to restrict the range of values in a subtype declaration, as was done in the declarations of Natural and Positive:

```
subtype Whole_Number is Integer;
```

This means that Whole_Number has the same range of values as Integer, so it is effectively just another name for the same type.

To avoid raising exceptions you can test if a value is within the range of a particular subtype using the **in** and **not in** operators. For example, if I is an Integer variable and N is a Natural variable, you can test if I can be assigned to N like this:

```
if I in Natural then
    N := I;        -- OK, I is in Natural's range
else
    Put_Line ("I can't be assigned to N!");
end if;
```

All types in Ada are actually subtypes of anonymous types known as their **base types**, which I alluded to briefly above. Since the base types are anonymous you can't refer to them directly by name, but you can use the 'Base attribute to get at them; for example, Integer'Base is the base type of Integer. Base types may or may not have a wider range of values than their subtypes; the only significance of this is that intermediate values in expressions like A*B/C use the base type so that A*B might be able to exceed the limits of the type without raising an exception as long as the final result is within the required limits.

5.4 Derived types

Sometimes it's useful to define a new type in terms of an existing type, like this:

```
type Whole_Number is new Integer;
```

This defines a new type called Whole_Number which has exactly the same properties as Integer. Whole_Number is said to be **derived** from Integer; Integer is referred to as Whole_Number's **parent type**. The range of values and the operations available will be the same for Whole_Number as for Integer (Whole_Number is said to **inherit** all the operations of its parent type), but unlike the subtype declaration for Whole_Number shown earlier, Whole_Number will be a completely different type to Integer. However, it is always possible to use a type conversion to convert from a derived type to its parent type and vice versa. This means that if you want to mix Whole_Numbers and Integers in an expression, you will have to use a type conversion to convert one type to the other:

```
I : Integer;
W : Whole_Number := Whole_Number(I);
                    -- convert Integer to Whole_Number
```

The derived type declaration can also include a range constraint:

```
type Age is new Natural range 0..150;
```

Now Age is the name of a new integer type derived from Natural but restricted to values between 0 and 150.

Derivation creates a family of related types usually referred to as a **class**; for example, all integer types belong to the class of integer types. Also, you'll see later that the class of integer types is part of a larger class, the class of **discrete** types. The main reason for creating derived types is in situations where extra 'primitive operations' have been defined for a particular type. You could create a new type and then define an identical set of extra operations, but by using derivation you automatically inherit versions of all the primitive operations of the parent type so no rewriting is needed. Thus the class of discrete types provides the attribute 'First which all discrete types will inherit; the integer class adds arithmetic operations like '+' which integer types then inherit in addition to the properties they inherit by being discrete types. This is a subject that will be explored more fully in later chapters in connection with **tagged types**.

5.5 Modular integers

The integer types we have seen so far are properly known as **signed integer** types. These are defined by specifying the range of values allowed for that type. In the case of Time_Of_Day, this doesn't do quite what we want. Imagine that the time is one second before midnight, which would be stored in a Time_Of_Day variable as the value 86399. What happens if we try to add 1 to it? We will get the value 86400 which is outside the range of values allowed for a Time_Of_Day variable and a Constraint_Error will be reported as described above. What we really want here is for the value of the variable to wrap around from 86399 (one second to midnight) back to 0 (midnight).

One way to do this would be to do all arithmetic modulo 86400 using the **mod** operator described earlier:

```
T := (T + 1) mod 86400;
```

This is a bit risky, since evaluating T + 1 might give rise to a constraint error (although it's unlikely in this particular case; 86400 will almost certainly be within the range of the base type). A better way to do this would be to define Time_Of_Day as being a **modular integer** type:

```
type Time_of_Day is mod 86400;
```

Now all arithmetic on Time_Of_Day values is performed 'mod 86400' so that adding 1 to 86399 will wrap around back to 0, and subtracting 1 from 0 will wrap around to 86399. As a result arithmetic on modular integers will never raise a constraint error. However, the same is not true for type conversions. Attempting to convert a value outside the range 0 to 86399 to a Time_Of_Day value will still raise a Constraint_Error. Modular types provide an attribute called Modulus which gives the modulus of the type, so that Time_Of_Day'Modulus would give 86400. You can use this with the **mod** operator to ensure that values are in the correct range before assigning them to Time_Of_Day variables.

Text_IO provides a generic package for input and output of modular integers called Ada.Text_IO.Modular_IO. The following line can be used to instantiate Modular_IO for use with Time_Of_Day values, after which you'll have Get and Put procedures for Time_Of_Day values just like the ones for Integer values in Integer_Text_IO:

```
package Time_Of_Day_IO is
        new Ada.Text_IO.Modular_IO (Time_Of_Day);
```

5.6   Real types

Ada provides two ways of defining real types. **Floating point** types have a more or less unlimited range of values but are only accurate to a specified number of decimal places; **fixed point** types have a more limited range but are accurate to within a specified amount (the **delta** of the type). You can also have **decimal types**, but Ada compilers are not required to implement them so I'm not going to bother discussing them in detail. There is one standard floating point type called Float which is accurate to at least six significant figures and there is one standard fixed point type called Duration (used for representing times) which is accurate to at least the nearest 50 microseconds (a delta of 0.00005 seconds) up to a maximum of at least 86400.0 seconds (24 hours). There are no standard decimal types. You can define your own real types like this:

```
type My_Float is digits 10;          -- a floating point type
type My_Fixed is delta 0.01 range 0.0 .. 10.0;
                                     -- a fixed point type
type Decimal  is delta 0.01 digits 12;
                                     -- a decimal type (delta
                                     -- must be a power of 10)
```

Here My_Float is a floating point type which is accurate to at least ten significant figures, and My_Fixed is a fixed point type which is accurate to within 0.01 (i.e. to at least two decimal places) across the specified range. Decimal is a decimal type with 12 digits which is accurate to two decimal places (i.e. capable of representing decimal values up to 9999999999.99). You can find out the **digits** value of a floating point type by using the Digits attribute (e.g. Float'Digits) and the **delta** value of a fixed point type by using the Delta attribute (e.g. Duration'Delta). Many of the attributes already described for integers (First, Last, Image, Value and so on) also apply to real types; for a complete list of attributes which apply to real types, refer to Appendix C.

You can also have subtypes of real types; for example, there is a standard package called Ada.Calendar which defines a subtype of Duration called Day_Duration like this:

```
subtype Day_Duration is Duration range 0.0 .. 86400.0;
```

The same arithmetic operators are available for real numbers as for integers, except that dividing two real numbers gives a real result and so the **mod** and **rem** operators are not defined for real numbers. Also the exponentiation operator can be used to raise a real number to any integer power; raising a real number to a negative power will produce a real result, so the right hand operand is no longer restricted to belonging to the subtype Natural as it is for integer types.

There is a standard package called Ada.Float_Text_IO which provides Get and Put procedures for the standard type Float. You can also create your own for use with other real types; Ada.Text_IO provides two generic packages for input/output of floating point and fixed point values called Float_IO and Fixed_IO respectively. Ada.Float_Text_IO is effectively just an instantiation of Ada.Text_IO.Float_IO for type Float, so you can look at the listing of Ada.Text_IO in Appendix B to find out the details of Ada.Float_Text_IO. The specification of Put in this package is somewhat different to Put for integer types; in Ada.Float_Text_IO it looks like this:

```
procedure Put (Item : in Float;
               Fore : in Field := Default_Fore;
               Aft  : in Field := Default_Aft;
               Exp  : in Field := Default_Exp);
```

The optional parameters Fore, Aft and Exp can be used to control the layout of the values displayed on the screen. The default for floating point types is to display the number with a three-digit exponent, so that 1234.5678 would be displayed as 1.2345678E+003 (meaning 1.2345678×10^3); with fixed point values it would be displayed as 1234.5678, possibly with some extra spaces before and zeros afterwards. Fore specifies how many characters to display before the decimal point, Aft specifies how many digits to display after the decimal point (which will cause the value to be rounded to that many places if necessary) and Exp specifies how many digits there are in the exponent; a value of zero means that no exponent will be displayed. Here are some examples of how the version of Put for floating point values works:

```
Put (1234.5678);                    -- displays " 1.2345678E+003"
Put (1234.5678, Exp=>0);            -- displays "1234.5678"
Put (1234.5678, Fore=>5);           -- displays "    1.2345678E+003"
Put (1234.5678, Fore=>5, Aft=>2, Exp=>0);
                                    -- displays " 1234.57"
Put (1234.5678, Fore=>5, Aft=>2);
                                    -- displays "    1.23E+003"
```

Note that displaying an exponent means that the value is 'normalised' so that there is only one digit before the decimal point. Also, unlike the version of Put for integer types, real numbers can only be displayed in decimal; there is no equivalent of the Base parameter.

5.7   Numeric literals

To wind up the discussion of numeric types, let's look at how numbers are written in Ada. We've already seen integer values such as 86400 and real values such as 3.14159265; real values have a decimal point whereas integers don't. You can also use underline characters within numbers to improve readability (e.g. 86_400 or 3.14159_26536). What's more, you can use exponential notation: 86400 can be written as 864e2, meaning 864×10^2, and 3.14159_26536 can be written as 31415.926536e–4, meaning $31415.926536 \times 10^{-4}$. As usual, it doesn't matter whether you use upper or lower case; 864e2 and 864E2 mean exactly the same thing.

It's also possible to write numbers in binary or hexadecimal or any other base between 2 and 16. Here are three different ways of writing the decimal value 31:

```
2#11111#    -- the binary (base 2) value 11111
16#1F#      -- the hexadecimal (base 16) value 1F
6#51#       -- the base 6 value 51
```

The letters *A* to *F* (or *a* to *f*) are used for the digits 10 to 15 when using bases above 10. If you mix an exponent (*e*) part with a based number, the exponent is raised to the power of the base; thus 16#1F#e1 means hexadecimal 1F (= 31) $\times 16^1$, or 496 in decimal.

5.8 Constants

We can use the package Ada.Calendar mentioned earlier to improve on our good morning/good afternoon program. Instead of asking the user to tell us whether it's morning or afternoon, why not ask the computer? Ada.Calendar contains (among other things) a function called Clock whose result is the current date and time. This result is of type Time which is defined in Ada.Calendar. There is also a function called Seconds which takes a Time as its parameter and extracts the time of day, returning the number of seconds since midnight as a value of type Day_Duration which was mentioned earlier. Here are the specifications for Clock and Seconds:

```
function Clock return Time;
function Seconds (Date : Time) return Day_Duration;
```

This tells us that Clock is a function with no parameters which returns a result of type Time, and Seconds is a function with a parameter called Date of type Time which returns a Day_Duration result. All we have to do is to use Seconds to extract the time of day from the value produced by Clock and check if it is after noon (43200.0 seconds since midnight). Here is the new version of the program:

```
with Ada.Text_IO, Ada.Calendar;  use Ada.Text_IO;
procedure Greetings is
begin
  if Ada.Calendar.Seconds (Ada.Calendar.Clock) <= 43200.0 then
    Put_Line ("Good morning!");
  else
    Put_Line ("Good afternoon!");
  end if;
end Greetings;
```

The value 43200.0 in the new version of the program is remarkably uninformative. It would make the program much more readable if we used a name like Noon instead of this 'magic number'. This is generally true for practically all numbers except 0 and 1. Numbers almost always represent a quantity *of something*, and should therefore be given names which indicate what that something is. In many cases they are also subject to change as part of the maintenance process and should therefore be defined at a single place in the program so that any necessary change can be accomplished by altering just one line in the program. This can be done by defining **named numbers** like this:

```
Minute : constant := 60;
Hour   : constant := 60 * Minute;   -- i.e. 3600
```

These names can be used in exactly the same way as the numbers they stand for. They are universal integers just like the numbers 60 and 3600 so that they can be used whenever an integer of any type is needed. Universal real numbers can be used in exactly the same way. Although a named number declaration looks just like a variable declaration, the reserved word **constant** indicates that these values cannot be altered:

```
Hour := Hour + 1;          -- illegal!
```

Named numbers can be used anywhere that the corresponding numeric literal could be used, e.g. in a type declaration:

```
type Time_Of_Day is mod 24 * Hour;     -- same as "mod 86400"
```

One thing to remember is that in order for a named number to be usable anywhere that the corresponding 'magic number' could be used, the compiler must be able to work out its value at **compile time** (i.e. when the program is being compiled). This doesn't rule out using arithmetic expressions; for example, the declaration of Hour uses the expression 60*Minute as its value and Time_Of_Day uses 24*Hour as the modulus of the type. This is perfectly all right provided that the compiler can work out the value of the expression; in particular, it needs to know how much memory a Time_Of_Day object will require. An expression like this that can be evaluated at compile time is known as a **static** expression, meaning that its value is not dependent on extraneous factors such as input from the user or the time of day at which the program is being run. In this case the expression 24*Hour depends on knowing what Hour is at compile time, which in turn depends on knowing what Minute is. Since the compiler knows that Minute means 60, it can work out that Hour is 3600 and thus 24*Hour is 86400.

It is also possible to define constant values of a particular type by specifying the type name as part of the declaration:

```
Noon  : constant Day_Duration := Day_Duration (12 * Hour);
Start : constant Day_Duration := Seconds (Clock);
```

Named numbers must be static, but constants of a specific type like Start can have values which aren't known until **run time** (i.e. when the program is run); in the case of Start, its value will be the time at which it is declared. Variables and constants are collectively referred to as **objects** in Ada. Here is another version of the program, modified to show the use of some constants:

```
with Ada.Text_IO, Ada.Calendar;
use  Ada.Text_IO, Ada.Calendar;
procedure Greetings is
   Minute : constant := 60;
   Hour   : constant := 60 * Minute;
   Noon   : constant Day_Duration := Day_Duration (12 * Hour);
   Start  : constant Day_Duration := Seconds (Clock);
begin
```

```
   if Start <= Noon then
     Put_Line ("Good morning!");
   else
     Put_Line ("Good afternoon!");
   end if;
end Greetings;
```

Although this may seem quite long-winded, that's only because it's such a short example. If you compare the **if** statement above to the one in the previous example, I'm sure you'll agree that it's much easier to see exactly what this version is trying to achieve.

In many cases you can use attributes instead of constants to avoid using magic numbers. For example, you could use a constant to define type Time_Of_Day like this:

```
Maximum : constant := 86399;
type Time_Of_Day is range 0..Maximum;
```

and then you could use Maximum wherever you needed to refer to the largest possible Time_Of_Day value. But since Time_Of_Day'Last will give the same value as Maximum, why not just define Time_Of_Day like this:

```
type Time_Of_Day is range 0..86399;
```

and then use Time_Of_Day'Last wherever you would use Maximum or (perish the thought) 86399?

5.9 Enumerations

In many cases numbers are unsuitable for representing the types of data required by a program. Consider the days of the week as an example. We could use the numbers 0 to 6 or 1 to 7 to represent the days of the week, but they don't lend themselves to this naturally. The natural way to represent days of the week is by using their names (Monday, Tuesday, Wednesday and so on). We could of course define constants with the appropriate values, like this:

```
type Day_Of_Week is range 0..6;   -- or "mod 7" perhaps

Sun : constant Day_Of_Week := 0;
Mon : constant Day_Of_Week := 1;
Tue : constant Day_Of_Week := 2;
Wed : constant Day_Of_Week := 3;
Thu : constant Day_Of_Week := 4;
Fri : constant Day_Of_Week := 5;
Sat : constant Day_Of_Week := 6;
```

⇒   *Which would be better for type Day_Of_Week, 'range 0..6' or 'mod 7', and why?*

The disadvantage with this is that it would allow us to perform arithmetic on days of the week; for example, what do the expressions Wednesday + Tuesday or Monday * 2 mean?

Enumeration types allow us to define types as a list which **enumerates** the possible values of the type. We could define the type Day_Of_Week as an enumeration type like this:

```
type Day_Of_Week is (Sun, Mon, Tue, Wed, Thu, Fri, Sat);
```

This says that a Day_Of_Week object has seven possible values whose names are Sun, Mon, Tue and so on. You can compare values of an enumeration type (using =, /=, <, <=, > and >=) and assign them, but operations like addition and subtraction are not provided. For example, assuming D is a Day_of_Week variable, you can do the following:

```
D := Mon;
if D = Mon then
    Put_Line ("Oh no, it's Monday again...");
end if;
```

The ordering of the values is that defined by the list of values you provide, so that Sun is less than Mon and so on. There are a number of useful functions provided as attributes for enumeration types in addition to the ones mentioned earlier for integer types (First, Last, Image and Value):

```
Pos(X)      -- an integer representing the position of X in the
               list of possible values starting at 0
Val(X)      -- the X'th value in the list of possible values
Succ(X)     -- the next (successor) value after X
Pred(X)     -- the previous (predecessor) value to X
```

These can actually be used with integer types as well, but they aren't a lot of use since Pos and Val will convert an integer to itself and Succ and Pred can be replaced by addition and subtraction. They are only really useful for enumeration types. Pos and Val allow you to convert enumerations to integers and vice versa, while Succ and Pred effectively allow you to add or subtract 1 from an enumeration value. Here are a few examples:

```
Day_Of_Week'Pos(Sun)    = 0      Day_Of_Week'Pos(Wed)    = 3
Day_Of_Week'Val(0)      = Sun    Day_Of_Week'Val(3)      = Wed
Day_Of_Week'Succ(Mon)   = Tue    Day_Of_Week'Pred(Fri)   = Thu
```

Note that you will get a constraint error if you try to evaluate anything like Day_Of_Week'Val (7), Day_Of_Week'Succ (Sat) or Day_Of_Week'Pred (Sun) since in all these cases you are going outside the limits of the range of values available.

It is sometimes useful to use the same name for an enumeration value for two unrelated types. Here is a slightly artificial example:

```
type Weekday  is (Sun, Mon, Tue, Wed, Thu, Fri, Sat);
type Computer is (IBM, Apple, Sun, Cray);
```

Note that the name Sun is used as a value for Weekday as well as Computer. This shows that enumeration literals, like subprogram names, can be **overloaded**. The compiler will normally be able to distinguish between them from the type of value it expects to see at a particular point in the program. In the rare cases when it can't it will report an error, and you will then have to specify explicitly whether you mean Sun of type Weekday or of type Computer like this:

```
Weekday'(Sun)      -- the value Sun of type Weekday
Computer'(Sun)     -- the value Sun of type Computer
```

This looks similar to a type conversion but it isn't; the apostrophe between the type name and the parenthetical expression shows that this is a **qualified expression** which just tells the compiler what type you expect the parenthetical expression to have. No conversion is performed:

```
F1 : Float := Float(123);
                -- type conversion from Integer to Float
F2 : Float := Float'(123);
                -- qualified expression will be reported as an
                -- error since 123 isn't a valid Float value
```

The integer and enumeration types are collectively known as **discrete types** since they define a set of discrete values which can be listed in order. Real numbers can't be listed in this way since there are (in theory at least) an infinite number of them between any two real values you care to choose. Discrete types play a special role in various circumstances where discreteness is a useful property; I'll return to this point later. (A table showing the hierarchy of the types available in Ada and the relationships between them is given at the end of Appendix A.)

Like the packages for input and output of the numeric types, there is a generic package called Ada.Text_IO.Enumeration_IO that you can instantiate for input/output of enumeration types:

```
package Day_Of_Week_IO is
             new Ada.Text_IO.Enumeration_IO (Day_Of_Week);
```

This will provide Get and Put procedures for Day_Of_Week values. Put will by default display the enumeration value in upper case in the minimum possible width, but there are optional parameters Width and Set you can use to alter this. Here are some examples:

```
Put (Sun);                      -- displays "SUN"
Put (Sun, Width=>6);            -- displays "SUN   "
Put (Sun, Set=>Lower_Case);     -- displays "sun"
```

Unfortunately there is no 'Capitalised' value for the Set parameter which would display it as 'Sun'; the only possibilities are Upper_Case (giving 'SUN') and Lower_Case (giving 'sun').

We could use an enumerated type in a variant of the Greetings program from the previous chapter. Instead of asking the user to type M or A, we could define an enumeration type like this:

```
type Time_Of_Day is (AM, PM);
```

If we instantiate Enumeration_IO for use with type Time_Of_Day the user could then type in either AM or PM in either upper or lower case (or any mixture of the two) with or without leading spaces (which previous versions of the program didn't allow). Here's the reworked program:

```
with Ada.Text_IO;
use  Ada.Text_IO;
procedure Greetings is
   type Time_Of_Day is (AM, PM);
   package Time_IO is new Enumeration_IO (Time_Of_Day);
   use Time_IO;
   Answer : Time_Of_Day;
begin
   Put ("Is it morning (AM) or afternoon (PM)? ");
   Get (Answer);
   if Answer = AM then
     Put_Line ("Good morning!");
   else
     Put_Line ("Good afternoon!");
   end if;
end Greetings;
```

⇒   *An exception will be raised if anything other than AM or PM is typed in response to the prompt. Modify the program to deal with this.*

As with integers you can define subtypes of enumerated types:

```
subtype Working_Day is Day_Of_Week range Mon .. Fri;
```

Now you can use Working_Day wherever Day_Of_Week can be used but the values allowed are limited to those between Mon and Fri inclusive.

5.10 The type Boolean

The type Boolean is yet another one of Ada's standard data types, and is an enumeration type declared in the package Standard as follows:

```
type Boolean is (False, True);
```

Boolean plays a special role in Ada; it's used in the conditions of **if** and **exit when** statements as well as a few other places. Note that if you try putting a declaration for Boolean (or any other standard type) in your program you will be creating a brand new type; types in Ada which have different names are different even if their declarations are identical, and the full name for the standard Boolean type is Standard.Boolean. You will end up with two completely separate types called Boolean and Standard.Boolean, and since **if** statements and the like require conditions of type Standard.Boolean you won't be able to use your own Boolean type in this sort of context.

Comparison operators like '=' produce a Boolean result. The comparison operators available are as follows:

```
A = B      -- True if A is equal to B
A /= B     -- True if A is not equal to B
A < B      -- True if A is less than B
A <= B     -- True if A is less than or equal to B
A > B      -- True if A is greater than B
A >= B     -- True if A is greater than or equal to B
```

These can be used to compare values of any of the types described in this chapter. There are some other operators which combine Boolean values to produce Boolean results. We've already seen how **or** can be used; here is the full list:

```
A or B     -- True if either or both of A and B are True
A and B    -- True if both A and B are True
A xor B    -- True if either A or B is True (but not both)
not A      -- True if A is False
```

And, **or** and **xor** have the same precedence; if you want to mix them (e.g. using **and** and **or** together) in the same expression you must use parentheses to make the meaning unambiguous:

```
A and B or C      -- illegal due to ambiguity
(A and B) or C    -- one possible legal interpretation
A and (B or C)    -- the other possible legal interpretation
```

There are also variants of **and** and **or** to cater for a few tricky situations. Consider this situation as an example:

```
if B /= 0 and A/B > 0 then ...
```

The problem with this is that the expression on the right of the **and** operator is always evaluated, so that when B is zero the expression A/B will still be evaluated with the result that the division by zero will cause a constraint error to be raised. However, this is presumably what the check on B's value is supposed to avoid! The solution is to use the operator **and then** instead of **and**:

```
if B /= 0 and then A/B > 0 then ...
```

And then only evaluates its right hand side if it needs to; if B is zero, the overall result of the Boolean expression must be false so the right hand side won't be evaluated. This means that the division by zero won't happen, so a constraint error won't occur. The right hand side will only be evaluated if B is non-zero, in which case it's safe to divide A by B. The equivalent for **or** is **or else**, which only evaluates its right hand side if the expression on the left hand side is false:

```
if B = 0 or else A/B <= 0 then ...
```

You can of course define variables and constants of type Boolean:

```
Morning : constant Boolean := Start < Noon;
```

This refers to the constants Start and Noon defined earlier. Morning will be True if the program is run before noon and False otherwise. Boolean variables or constants can be used directly in **if** statements, **while** loops and any other context that expects a Boolean value:

```
if Morning then ...    -- same as "if Start < Noon then ..."
```

One common beginner's mistake is to write **if** statements involving Boolean values like this:

```
if Morning = True then ...
```

This is of course redundant; if you do this you are asking if True is equal to True, and if it is the result is True! Likewise, these are two different ways of saying the same thing:

```
if Morning = False then ...
if not Morning then ...
```

The second version is considered better style; it is certainly more easily understood than the first. A similar situation arises when assigning values to Boolean variables. Beginners sometimes write things like this:

```
if Start < Noon then
   Morning := True;
else
   Morning := False;
end if;
```

but you can achieve the same effect in a much less long-winded way, like this:

```
Morning := Start < Noon;
```

If Start is less than Noon, the expression 'Start < Noon' will evaluate to True, so Morning will be assigned the value True; if not, it will be assigned the value False.

5.11 The type Character

The other standard enumeration type is Character. This is an enumeration type whose values are the list of characters defined by the International Standardization Organization (ISO) in the standard ISO-8859. There are 256 possible characters in this character set which include letters, digits, punctuation marks, mathematical symbols and characters like å, ß and ç which are required in some European languages. The definition of type Character is given in the package Standard in Appendix B; this shows the characters it provides.

Some of the characters have no printable value; they are used as **control characters**. Examples include the 'carriage return' character which moves the cursor to the left of your screen when you display it and the 'form feed' character which is used to start a new page on a printer. To allow you to refer to them there is a package called ASCII (for American Standard Code for Information Interchange, the predecessor to ISO-8859) defined as part of the package Standard which provides names for these. Since ASCII is defined inside Standard you don't need to specify it in a **with** clause before you can use it. As a result, you can always refer to the carriage return character as ASCII.CR and the form feed character as ASCII.FF. However, this is a historical remnant from Ada 83; it only provides names for the first 128 characters of ISO-8859 and it might not be provided at all in future versions of the language. For these reasons it is better (if slightly less convenient) to use the package Ada.Characters.Latin_1 instead. This gives names for all the 256 available characters but it must be included using a **with** clause. Appendix B contains a listing of Ada.Characters.Latin_1.

The 256 characters are sufficient for European languages but doesn't cater for languages like Japanese or Russian. Ada provides another type Wide_Character which is similar to Character except that it provides 65536 different characters. There is also a type Wide_String corresponding to String; type String is a sequence of Characters, and Wide_String is a sequence of Wide_Characters.

As well as defining enumeration types using names like Sunday or Monday for the values you are allowed to use character literals like '+' or '*'. The declaration of Character in the package Standard makes use of this to define the set of printable characters. Here's the declaration of a data type which represents the operators used in the previous chapter's calculator program:

```
type Operator is ('+', '-', '*', '/');
```

Note that this is a completely different data type to Character, and there is no way to do a straight type conversion from Character to Operator or vice versa. Also, if you instantiate Enumeration_IO for Operator you might be in for a nasty shock; the values will be displayed complete with the enclosing quotes, and you must also type the quotes on input. This makes this facility somewhat less useful than it might otherwise be.

5.12   Renaming declarations

One of the things that contribute to maintainability is readability, and one of the things that contribute to readability is the use of meaningful names. However, most programmers find it a bit of a chore to write meaningful names, so that variables with short, almost meaningless names like I and J are quite common. You may have noticed that I do it myself from time to time; that's human nature. However, I tend to do it only where the name is going to be used in a small section of program where I'm not going to have to refer back across hundreds of lines to find out whether I stands for Interest_Rate or Idiocy_Ratio. Fully qualified names defined in external packages can be especially inconvenient to use; writing a name like Ada.Characters.Latin_1.ESC or even Ada.Characters.Latin_1.Registered_Trade_Mark_Sign (no, I'm not making this up!) is awkward if you need to use it more than once. This is why **use** clauses tend to get overused (pardon the pun). If you don't like having to write long names like Ada.Characters.Latin_1.ESC and you want to avoid **use** clauses you can always use a **renaming declaration** to give the package a more convenient name:

```
package Latin_1 renames Ada.Characters.Latin_1;
```

and then you can just write 'Latin_1.ESC' instead of 'Ada.Characters.Latin_1.ESC'. A renaming declaration like this just provides you with an extra name for an existing object.

If the individual names within the package are awkward to use you can rename them in the same way:

```
TM : Character renames
          Ada.Characters.Latin_1.Registered_Trade_Mark_Sign;
```

After this declaration you can just use the name TM whenever you want to refer to Ada.Characters.Latin_1.Registered_Trade_Mark_Sign in your program. TM acquires all the characteristics of the object it renames; in this case, since the object being renamed is a constant, TM is also a constant.

The moral is that you should try to use meaningful names (and, as mentioned in chapter 2, avoid **use** clauses), and then use renaming declarations where necessary to alleviate the burden if the resulting names get too long for comfort. This is quite a common use for **declare** blocks; long names can be abbreviated for use within a particular section of the program without making the abbreviation universally accessible.

You can also use renaming declarations to rename procedures and functions; you can also change the names and default values of the parameters if you want. The only requirement is that the number and the types of the parameters (and the type of result in the case of functions) are unchanged. So, if you always want floating point values to be displayed in the minimum possible width to two decimal places with no exponent, you can do this:

```
procedure Show (Value : in Float;
                Fore  : in Field := 1;
                Aft   : in Field := 2;
                Exp   : in Field := 0)
        renames Ada.Float_Text_IO.Put;
```

This gives you a procedure called Show instead of Put; its first parameter is called Value instead of Item and the default values for the other parameters are different to those for Put itself. Show can be used instead of Put like this:

```
Show (5.3);   -- displays "5.30"
              -- same as Put (5.3, Fore=>1, Aft=>2, Exp=>0);
```

The one situation where you're not allowed to use renaming declarations is with data types. This means that you can't say 'type Time renames Ada.Calendar.Day_Duration', for example. However, you can achieve the same effect by subtyping:

```
subtype Time is Ada.Calendar.Day_Duration;
```

Now Time is a subtype of Day_Duration so it can be used wherever Day_Duration can be used, but we haven't restricted its range of values. The result is a type called Time which has the same range of values as Day_Duration and which can be used interchangeably with Day_Duration; in other words they are identical, and Time is effectively just another name for Day_Duration.

Renaming a type like this may not be completely satisfactory; in the case of enumerated types you will also need to rename the enumeration literals. Enumeration literals behave as if they were parameterless functions, so if the type Day_Of_Week were defined in the package JE.Dates you could rename the type and its enumeration literals like this:

```
subtype  Weekday is JE.Dates.Day_Of_Week;
function Sun return JE.Dates.Day_Of_Week renames JE.Dates.Sun;
```

```
function Mon return JE.Dates.Day_Of_Week renames JE.Dates.Mon;
function Tue return JE.Dates.Day_Of_Week renames JE.Dates.Tue;
function Wed return JE.Dates.Day_Of_Week renames JE.Dates.Wed;
... and so on
```

This is quite awkward and long-winded, but fortunately it's rarely necessary in practice.

Exercises

5.1   Write a program to play a simple guessing game. Define an integer type with a range of values from 1 to 1000 and declare a secret value as a constant of this type, and then give the user ten chances to guess its value. A message should be displayed at the beginning to tell the user what to do. For each unsuccessful guess, the user should be told whether the guess was too low or too high. You will need to keep a count of the number of attempts. The program ends after the user has successfully guessed the secret value or after the tenth unsuccessful attempt. Display a message of congratulations or condolence at the end of the program. Modify the program so that the value to be guessed is chosen at random each time the program is run. You can generate random values of a discrete type X by instantiating the package Ada.Numerics.Discrete_Random for type X:

```
package Random_X is
              new Ada.Numerics.Discrete_Random (X);
  Gen : Random_X.Generator;    -- a random-value generator
```

You will of course need a **with** clause for Ada.Numerics.Discrete_Random. The random-value generator Gen can be initialised ready for use by calling the procedure Reset(Gen); you can then generate random values by calling the function Random(Gen), which will produce a new random value of type X from the generator Gen each time you call it.

5.2   Rewrite the date package from the previous chapter so that it includes a set of type declarations for days, months, years and days of the week. Use an enumeration type for the months and for the days of the week. Modify the functions in the package so that they use these types for their parameters and results instead of Integers and rewrite the main program Weekday so that it reads in a day, month and year as values of the appropriate types and displays the corresponding day of the week using input/output packages created from Ada.Text_IO.Integer_IO and Ada.Text_IO.Enumeration_IO as described earlier.

5.3   Write a function which takes a character as its parameter and returns it converted to lower case if it is an upper case letter, or returns it unchanged otherwise. Note that you can convert from upper case to lower case by adding the difference between an 'a' and an 'A', using Character'Pos and Character'Val to convert characters to and from integers.

5.4 Define data types to represent the suit and value of a playing card. Cards have four suits (Clubs, Diamonds, Hearts and Spades) and 13 cards in each suit (Ace, 2 to 10, Jack, Queen and King). Use Ada.Numerics.Discrete_Random as described in exercise 5.1 above to write a program to display three random cards, each of which is different.

CHAPTER 6

Composite data types

Yea, from the table of my memory I'll
wipe away all trivial fond records.
— William Shakespeare, *Hamlet*

6.1 Record types

In the last chapter you saw how Ada allows you to define data types which can be tailored fairly closely to the type of information that a particular program is concerned with modelling. Numeric types of various sorts can be defined to represent different types of numerical information; enumerated types can be used when a set of non-numerical values is needed; strings can be used when the information is textual in nature. Each of these data types that you define comes complete with a set of operations that you can perform on them, as for example the arithmetic operations provided for numeric types.

All the types described in the last chapter are used to represent individual values; they are known collectively as **scalar types** (see Appendix A for a complete list of the hierarchy of types in Ada). However, in most real-life situations the data you deal with can't be represented by simple numbers or enumerations of possible values. Most data is composite in nature, consisting of a collection of simpler data items. For example, a date consists of a day, a month and a year; a time consists of an hour and a minute. The data types we've used so far are adequate for representing each of these individual components; days, years, hours and minutes are all numerical and months are either enumerations or numbers. For example, here are some possible declarations for types to represent days, months and years:

```
subtype Day_Type   is Integer range 1..31;
type    Month_Type is (Jan, Feb, Mar, Apr, May, Jun,
                       Jul, Aug, Sep, Oct, Nov, Dec);
subtype Year_Type  is Integer range 1901..2099;
```

Although you could represent a date using three separate variables (day, month and year), this is not a very satisfactory solution. Every procedure or function that dealt with a date would require three parameters instead of one. Functions would not be able to return date results, since a function can only return a single result but a date consists of three separate values. Worse, it wouldn't necessarily be obvious that the three variables were parts of a common whole. You could end up supplying a procedure with the day from one date and the month from another by mistake as the result of a simple typing error. All this can lead to some pretty horrible debugging and maintenance problems.

The solution in Ada is to gather the components of the data type together into a single type known as a **record type**. Here is how we could define a record type to represent a date:

```
type Date_Type is
   record
      Day   : Day_Type;
      Month : Month_Type;
      Year  : Year_Type;
   end record;
```

Given this type declaration, variables of type Date_Type can be declared just like variables of any other data type:

```
Now, Later : Date_Type;
```

Notice that the individual components of the type defined between **record** and **end record** look just like variable declarations. You can if you like think of Date_Type as a type which acts as a container for three separate objects called Day, Month and Year, so that the variables Later and Now each contain three distinct subvariables, normally referred to as **components** (or sometimes **fields**). The components of a record type can be selected by using the same 'dot' notation you're already familiar with for selecting procedures from within a package, so that the Day component of Later can be referred to as Later.Day. In other words, you can treat Later.Day as a variable of type Day_Type, or Now.Month as a variable of type Month_Type. To copy one date into another you could do something like this:

```
Later.Day   := Now.Day;
Later.Month := Now.Month;
Later.Year  := Now.Year;
```

However, a variable of type Date_Type can also be treated as a single item, so that a Date_Type value can be passed as a parameter to a procedure or returned from a function. You can also assign one Date_Type variable to another in a single operation, so that the three assignment statements above can be written like this:

```
Later := Now;
```

Although the effect is exactly the same, it's much simpler and clearer than using three separate assignments as well as reducing the risk of error. The more statements you have to write to do something, the more chance there is of making a mistake. Also, if you have to change this when you maintain the program, you only have to change one statement instead of three; the more changes you have to make, the greater the risk of errors creeping in. The only other standard operations on record types are tests for equality and inequality:

```
if Later = Now then ...
if Later /= Now then ...
```

You can also use an **aggregate** to build a record from a set of components:

```
Later := (25,Dec,1995);
if Now = (25,Dec,1995) then ...
if Now /= (25,Dec,1995) then ...
```

An aggregate is simply a list of values of the appropriate types enclosed in parentheses. The assignment above is equivalent to the following longer-winded set of three assignment statements:

```
Later.Day   := 25;
Later.Month := Dec;
Later.Year  := 1995;
```

You can also use the names of the components in an aggregate:

```
Later := (Day=>25, Month=>Dec, Year=>1995);    -- same as above
```

If you do this you can write the values for the components in any order since the compiler can use the component names to arrange them into the correct order:

```
Later := (Month=>Dec, Year=>1995, Day=>25);    -- same as above
```

Aggregates are often used to provide an initial value for a variable as part of a declaration; they can also be used for declaring constants:

```
Birthday  : Date_Type := (25,Jan,1956);
Christmas : constant Date_Type := (25,Dec,1995);
```

Record types are types just like any other. You can use them in exactly the same way as any other type; they can be used for parameters to procedures, function results, even components of other records. If we declare a record type to represent a time of day like this:

```
subtype Hour_Type   is Integer range 0..23;
subtype Minute_Type is Integer range 0..59;
```

```
type Time_Type is
  record
     Hour   : Hour_Type;
     Minute : Minute_Type;
  end record;
```

we can define yet another record type which contains a date and a time, perhaps for recording the date and time of an appointment:

```
type Appointment_Type is
  record
     Date : Date_Type;
     Time : Time_Type;
  end record;
```

Given a variable A of type Appointment_Type, its components can be referred to like this:

```
A               -- the date and time as a whole (Appointment_Type)
A.Date          -- the date of the appointment (Date_Type)
A.Date.Day      -- the day of the appointment (Day_Type)
A.Date.Month    -- the month of the appointment (Month_Type)
A.Date.Year     -- the year of the appointment (Year_Type)
A.Time          -- the time of the appointment (Time_Type)
A.Time.Hour     -- the hour of the appointment (Hour_Type)
A.Time.Minute   -- the minute of the appointment (Minute_Type)
```

So, A is name of the date-and-time record as a whole. It's of type Appointment_Type, so we can select its Date component by saying A.Date; this is of type Date_Type, and so we can select the Day component of the date by saying A.Date.Day.

6.2 Strings

Of course, the one thing that's missing from the Appointment_Type above is a description of the appointment. We could represent this as a string using the standard type String. String is a predefined **array** type; an array is a collection of items of the same type. This is in contrast to record types, where the components can be different types. In the case of String, the individual components of the array are Characters. I'll describe how you can define your own array types in the next section, but for now I'll use String as an example of an array type to show you how arrays can be used.

To declare a string variable you have to specify how many characters it can hold:

```
Details : String (1..100);   -- a 100-character string
Name    : String (1..10);    -- a 10-character string
```

Another way of doing the same thing would be to declare subtypes to specify the length:

```
subtype Details_Type is String (1..100);
subtype Name_Type    is String (1..10);
Details : Details_Type;
Name    : Name_Type;
```

Both methods give you strings called Details and Name; Details can hold 100 characters numbered 1 to 100, while Name can hold ten characters numbered 1 to 10. You can select individual characters from Details using an **index** between 1 and 100:

```
Details(1)   := 'x';
Details(I+1) := 'x';
```

The range of possible index values is known as the **index subtype** of the array. If you try to access the array with an index which isn't within the range of the index subtype, you'll get a Constraint_Error. Both of the assignments above set a specified character in Details to **x**. In the first case it's the first character; in the second case the character selected depends on the value of the expression I + 1. If the value of I + 1 isn't within the range of the index subtype (i.e. 1 to 100) you'll get a Constraint_Error. Note that the individual elements of the string are of type Character.

As well as dealing with individual array elements, you can deal with **slices** of a string:

```
Details(1..5) := "Hello";
Details(2..6) := Details(1..5);
```

The first assignment copies the five-character string "Hello" into the first five characters of Details. The second assignment copies the first five characters into the five characters beginning at the second character of the string, so that after these two statements the first six characters of Details will be "HHello". As you can see, it doesn't matter if the slices overlap; a copy of the slice is taken and then the copy is stored in the destination slice. Note that slices are also arrays of characters, i.e. Strings.

The length of the string that you assign to a slice must be the same as the length of the slice; the same applies to Details as a whole:

```
Details := "a 100-character string                      ";
```

This will be all right provided that the length of the string being assigned to Details is in fact exactly 100 characters long. Extremely long strings like this might not fit on one line, in which case you can use the **concatenation** operator '&' to join two shorter strings end to end to create a longer one:

```
Details := "a 50-character string            " &
           "another 50-character string      ";
```

You could use slicing and the concatenation operator to interchange the two halves of Details (but I'm not sure why you would want to; this is only an example!). You would do it like this:

```
Details := Details(51..100) & Details(1..50);
```

The two slices are the last 50 characters and the first 50 characters of Details. These are then concatenated together to give a single 100-character string which can be assigned to Details.

If you want to fill an entire string with spaces, you can do it like this:

```
Name := "          "; -- exactly 10 spaces
```

The string literal above is actually an abbreviation for the following **array aggregate**:

```
Name := (' ', ' ', ' ', ' ', ' ', ' ', ' ', ' ', ' ', ' ');
                    -- an aggregate containing 10 spaces
```

This can be awkward with longer strings like Details. When all the characters are the same (and especially when there are a lot of them) you can simplify matters by writing the aggregate like this:

```
Details := (1..100 => ' ');
                    -- no need to write exactly 100 spaces!
```

This specifies that each character with an index in the range 1 to 100 is to be set to a space, and avoids having to write a string literal which contains exactly the right number of characters and to modify it if the string size needs to be changed. Better still, you can avoid mentioning the string bounds at all like this:

```
Details := (others => ' ');    -- fill string with spaces
```

You can use the same notations as in **case** statements:

```
Details := (1..10 => 'x',
            11..13 | 21..23 | 27 | 29 => 'y',
            others => ' ');
```

This sets each of the first ten characters of Details to *x*, characters 11 to 13, 21 to 23, 27 and 29 to *y* (a total of eight characters) and the remaining 82 characters to spaces.

The easiest way to read in a string is to use the procedure Get_Line defined in Ada.Text_IO:

```
Get_Line (Details, N);
```

This will read a line of up to 100 characters (the size of Details) into Details from the keyboard. N is an 'out Natural' parameter which is set by Get_Line to the actual number of characters read, so that you can then access the characters that you read in by using the slice Details (1..N).

Arrays can be compared using the comparison operators (=, /=, <, >, <=, >=). In the case of String, two strings are equal if they are the same length and contain the same characters. For comparing using '<' and so on, the characters of the strings are compared from left to right until either the strings are found to differ or the end of the shorter string is reached. This more or less gives alphabetical ordering (but not perfectly; 'a' comes after 'Z' in the definition of Character, and if you use accented characters as in French 'à' comes after 'z'). Here are some examples:

```
"abc" = "abc"          "abc" /= "ab"          "abc" /= ""
"abc" < "abd"          "abc" > "ab"           "abc" > ""
```

The comparison operations for other array types are defined in the same way. You can only compare arrays if the individual components can be compared, so that you couldn't use '<' to compare an array of records since you can't compare records using '<'. You could, however, compare two arrays of records for equality since you can compare individual records for equality. The logical operations **and**, **or**, **not** and **xor** are also defined for arrays provided that the individual components support these operations (e.g. an array of Booleans); the operation will be applied to corresponding components in the two arrays.

Now we can use String to finish off the appointment type defined earlier:

```
type Appointment_Type is
  record
    Date    : Date_Type;
    Time    : Time_Type;
    Details : String (1..50);
  end record;
```

Note that if A is an Appointment_Type value, A.Details is a 50-character string and A.Details(1) is the first character of the string.

6.3 Declaring array types

We can use Appointment_Type to represent appointments in an automated appointments diary program. However, an appointments diary program will need to manage more than one appointment so we'll need to be able to declare arrays of appointments. Here's how we could declare an array type to hold 100 appointments:

```
type Appt_Array is array (1..100) of Appointment_Type;
```

This defines Appt_Array as a type describing a collection of appointments which can be individually selected by an index between 1 and 100. Appt_Array variables can be declared in the normal way:

```
Appt_List : Appt_Array;       -- a list of 100 appointments
```

The individual appointments can then be accessed as Appt_List(1), Appt_List(2) and so on up to Appt_List(100), just like selecting an individual character from a string. You can slice any array in exactly the same way as you can slice a string; the first five appointments of Appt_List can be sliced out as Appt_List(1..5). As I mentioned earlier, anything you can do with a string (indexing it to select individual characters, slicing it to get a smaller string) can be done with any other array type; similarly all the new features of arrays I'll be describing below (array attributes and so on) apply to strings as well.

The first appointment in the array would be referred to as Appt_List(1). Since this is an individual array element of type Appointment_Type, we can refer to the details of the appointment as Appt_List(1).Details. Since this is a string you can then select its first character by referring to Appt_List(1).Details(1).

If you only want one array of a particular type, you can use the array type specification directly in the declaration of a variable:

```
Appt_List : array (1..100) of Appointment_Type;
```

The drawback with doing this is that it is equivalent to:

```
type ??? is array (1..100) of Appointment_Type;  -- not Ada!
                      -- "???" represents an anonymous type
Appt_List : ???;
```

You don't have a name for the type of Appt_List, so you can't declare any more arrays of the same type. This means you won't be able to assign one array to another in a single operation (or a slice of one array to another); you won't be able to use the name of the array type in a procedure parameter declaration so you won't be able to pass the array (or a slice of it) as a parameter to a procedure. However, you can still use individual array elements since each element has a known type, namely Appointment_Type.

One place where anonymous arrays are handy is in defining lookup tables; for example, the following declares an array containing the number of days in each month:

```
Month_Length : constant array (1..12) of Positive :=
              (31, 28, 31, 30, 31, 30, 31, 31, 30, 31, 30, 31);
```

Another way to declare the array is like this:

```
Month_Length : constant array (1..12) of Positive :=
              (4 | 6 | 9 | 11 => 30, 2 => 28, others => 31);
```

With this declaration, Month_Length(1) is 31, which tells us that January (month 1) has 31 days. The length of any month N is given by Month_Length (N), although it doesn't cater for February having 29 days in leap years.

The index subtype for an array type doesn't have to be a range of integers; it can be any discrete type (i.e. any integer or enumeration type) or a range of values of a discrete type:

```
Hours_Worked : array (Day_Of_Week range Mon..Fri) of Natural;
```

If you just give a range like 1..100 without specifying a particular type, the type Integer is assumed, so that the declaration of Appointment_Array given earlier is equivalent to this:

```
type Appt_Array is array (Integer range 1..100)
                          of Appointment_Type;
```

We could redefine Month_Length to use the enumeration type Month_Type declared earlier:

```
Month_Length : constant array (Month_Type) of Positive :=
               (31, 28, 31, 30, 31, 30, 31, 31, 30, 31, 30, 31);
```

Or equivalently:

```
Month_Length : constant array (Month_Type) of Positive :=
         (Apr | Jun | Sep | Nov => 30, Feb => 28, others => 31);
```

The individual elements of Month_Length would then be accessed as Month_Length(Jan), Month_Length(Feb) and so on. Here's another useful one using the type Day_Of_Week from chapter 5:

```
Tomorrow : constant array (Day_Of_Week) of Day_Of_Week :=
                     (Mon, Tue, Wed, Thu, Fri, Sat, Sun);
```

Tomorrow(Sun) is Mon, Tomorrow(Mon) is Tue, and so on up to Tomorrow(Sat) which is Sun. This can be used to get around the problem that Day_Of_Week'Succ can't be used to get the day after Saturday since Sat is the last value of the type.

6.4 Unconstrained types

It is usually better not to specify the exact size of an array in the type declaration; this ties you down so that all arrays of that type have to have exactly the same number of elements. It's much better to say that an array type is a collection of unspecified size to give yourself more room for manoeuvre. For example, the definition of String just says that a string is a collection of characters whose size must be specified when a String variable is declared. Here's what the declaration of String in the package Standard looks like:

```
type String is array (Positive range <>) of Character;
```

Here the index subtype for String is defined to be a subtype of Positive. The symbol '<>' is known as a **box**; it signifies that the exact range of values allowed is unspecified. This is referred to as an **unconstrained** array type; the actual range of values (the **constraint**) must be supplied whenever you declare a String variable so that the compiler knows how much memory to reserve to hold the string. One place where you are allowed to use an unconstrained type is as the type of a parameter in a procedure or function, which means that a procedure or function can be written to accept a string of any length as a parameter. This is acceptable because the compiler doesn't have to allocate any memory in this case; the actual parameter will refer to a constrained string whose memory space has already been allocated. If an array type declaration specifies the size you lose this level of flexibility.

Arrays have a number of useful attributes which can be used to find out details about the index subtype:

```
First    -- the lowest value of the index subtype
Last     -- the highest value of the index subtype
Range    -- the index subtype itself (First .. Last)
Length   -- the number of elements in the array
```

These can be applied to the types themselves (if they're constrained) or to individual array objects. The values of these attributes for the arrays Appt_List and Month_Length defined above would be as follows:

```
Appt_List'First  = 1       Month_Length'First  = Jan
Appt_List'Last   = 100     Month_Length'Last   = Dec
Appt_List'Range  = 1..100  Month_Length'Range  = Jan..Dec
Appt_List'Length = 100     Month_Length'Length = 12
```

The Range attribute can be used in situations where a range is expected, e.g. an array aggregate or a constraint in a declaration:

```
Another_Name : String (Name'Range);
And_Another  : String := (Name'Range => ' ');
```

We can declare Appt_Array as an unconstrained array in exactly the same way as String was declared:

```
type Appt_Array is array (Positive range <>)
                                of Appointment_Type;
```

To declare an Appt_Array, we have to provide the bounds of the range for the index subtype:

```
Appt_List : Appt_Array (1..100);          -- as before
```

The range constraint '1..100' is effectively used to fill in the box '<>' which is used in the declaration of Appt_Array, so the index subtype for Appt_List is 'Positive range 1..100'. Alternatively, an initial value in a declaration can be used to set the bounds of the index subtype:

```
String_1 : String := "Hello world";
                            -- bounds are set by initial value
```

In this case, the bounds are set to be 1..11 because the initial value has these bounds. String literals and array aggregates whose bounds aren't specified explicitly take their lower bounds from the lower bound of the index subtype; in the case of String the index is a subtype of Positive so the lower bound of a string literal is always Positive'First, i.e. 1. The initial value has to give the compiler enough information to figure out what the bounds are supposed to be, so an aggregate using **others** or the 'Range attribute won't be acceptable.

The bounds of an array don't have to be static; you're allowed to calculate them at run time:

```
Appts : Appt_Array (1..N);
               -- N might be calculated when the program is run
```

A **declare** block can be useful if you want to calculate the array size at run time; the array size can be read in and the **declare** block can then use the value read in to create the array accordingly:

```
Put ("How big do you want the array to be? ");
Get (N);
declare
   Appts : Appt_Array (1..N);
begin
   ...
end;
```

As you've seen with strings, you can supply the constraint as part of a subtype declaration and then use the subtype to declare variables:

```
subtype Hundred_Appts is Appt_Array (1..100);
Appt_List : Hundred_Appts;
               -- same as: Appt_List : Appt_Array (1..100);
```

6.5   For loops revisited

A normal requirement with arrays is to process each element of the array in turn. This can be done using a **for** loop, as mentioned briefly in chapter 3:

```
for P in Appt_List'First..Appt_List'Last loop
   Process ( Appt_List(P) );
end loop;
```

Here P takes on successive values in the range Appt_List'First to Appt_List'Last each time around the loop. The first time around, P will be 1 (Appt_List'First), the second time it will be 2, and so on up to 100 (Appt_List'Last). The range specification in a **for** loop is just like the range specification for an array index subtype: it can be any discrete type or a range of values of a discrete type; as with an array index, a range like 1..100 which doesn't mention a specific type will be assumed to be a range of type Integer.

There are a few significant points to note about **for** loops. The **control variable** P doesn't have to be declared in advance; P is declared automatically just by its appearance as the control variable for the loop. In fact, if you do declare a variable called P you won't be able to access it from inside the loop; using the name P inside the loop will refer to the control variable P rather than the variable called P declared outside the loop:

```
with Ada.Integer_Text_IO;   use Ada.Integer_Text_IO;
procedure Test is
   P : Integer := 0;
begin
   for P in 1..100 loop
      Put(P);     -- the control variable P
   end loop;
   Put(P);        -- the P declared at the beginning
end Test;          -- (which is still 0)
```

Also, the control variable can't be altered from inside the loop. This ensures that the number of times a **for** loop is executed is fixed in advance; you can still exit from the loop before it's finished using an **exit** statement, but you can't get stuck inside it forever. The control variable can't be accessed outside the loop (it only exists while the loop is being executed); if you do use an **exit** statement and you need to find out what the value of the control variable was when you exited the loop, you'll have to copy the control variable into an ordinary variable before executing the **exit** statement:

```
with Ada.Integer_Text_IO;   use Ada.Integer_Text_IO;
procedure Test is
   I : Integer;
   A : array (1..100) of Integer;
begin
```

```
for P in 1..100 loop
  I := P;                    -- copy the value of P
  exit when A(P) = 0;        -- maybe exit the loop early
end loop;
-- P is no longer accessible but I is
Put(I);                      -- the saved copy of P
end Test;
```

The Range attribute provides a simple way of specifying the range of values in a **for** loop to process an array:

```
for P in Appointment_List'Range loop
  Process ( Appointment_List(P) );
end loop;
```

The range of values in a **for** loop, like the range of an array index subtype, can be any discrete subtype. Here are some examples:

```
for P in 1..100 loop ...                  -- loop 100 times
for P in -100..100 loop ...               -- loop 201 times
for P in Positive range 1..100 loop ...   -- loop 100 times
for P in Day_Of_Week loop ...             -- loop 7 times
for P in Day_Of_Week range Monday..Friday loop ...
                                          -- loop 5 times
for P in 1..N loop ...                    -- loop N times
```

Note that the bounds of the range don't have to be constants; N in the last example might be a variable. The value of N at the time the loop is started will determine how many times the loop will be executed. Note that changing the value of N inside the loop won't change the number of times the loop is executed, which is determined by the value of N at the moment you enter the loop.

You can also go through a range of values in reverse order by specifying the word **reverse** before the index subtype:

```
for P in reverse 1..100 loop ...
```

P will take on the values 100, 99, 98 and so on all the way down to 1. Note that the following won't do what you might expect it to:

```
for P in 100..1 loop ...
```

Since there is no range of values starting from 100 and ending at 1, the loop will not be executed (or rather, it will be executed zero times, which is the number of values over 100 which are less than 1). This is quite sensible; the following loop will be executed N times:

```
for P in 1..N loop ...
```

If N is zero, the range of values will be 1..0, and so the loop will be executed zero times (i.e. it won't be executed at all). If it didn't behave this way and counted backwards from 1 to 0 you'd have to put in extra checks for the case where N is zero, which would make life much more complicated.

6.6   A simple sorting procedure

As a demonstration of using arrays, here's a procedure to sort an array of integers into ascending order. It shows how to use array attributes, slices and both forward and reverse **for** loops. It uses a method known as **shuffle sorting** (which is not particularly efficient for large arrays, but it *is* only an example!). Shuffle sorting works by looking through the array for items which are in the wrong order (i.e. a smaller integer follows a larger one). When such an item is found, a copy of it is made and the array is then scanned backwards until the correct place for the item is found. The array elements from this point to the point where the value was originally are then moved along one place to leave a gap to slot the value into. Here's the code for the procedure (which, since it uses a type called Array_Type, must be declared in the package or procedure where the declaration of Array_Type is given):

```
type Array_Type is array (Positive range <>) of Integer;

procedure Shuffle_Sort (X : in out Array_Type) is
   Position : Positive;
   Value    : Integer;
begin
   for I in X'First+1 .. X'Last loop
      if X(I) < X(I-1) then
         -- Misplaced item found: copy it
         Value := X(I);
         -- Scan backwards until correct position found
         for J in reverse X'First .. I-1 loop
            exit when X(J) < Value;
            Position := J;
         end loop;
         -- Move intervening values along
         X(Position+1 .. I) := X(Position .. I-1);
         -- Put saved copy of item in correct position
         X(Position) := Value;
      end if;
   end loop;
end Shuffle_Sort;
```

Notice how the procedure makes no assumptions about the values of the upper and lower bounds of the array; it uses the attributes First and Last to refer to them, which makes this procedure work with any array regardless of what its actual bounds are. You should always do this; never assume anything about the bounds of an array.

The innermost loop which searches backwards is an interesting one. It compares each item in turn with the saved item, starting with element I–1 and working back to the start of the array (X'First). The loop will always be executed at least once since I starts off as X'First+1; this means that I–1 cannot be less than X'First. Since we already know that element I–1 is greater than the saved item, the loop will always be executed in full at least once, so the value of Position will always be set. Position will end up holding the index of the last item which was greater than the saved item; if the loop terminates naturally rather than because of the **exit** statement, Position will be set to X'First and the saved item (which must be smaller than every other value before it if the **exit** statement was never triggered) will be slotted in at the very beginning of the array.

6.7 Multidimensional arrays

Ada allows arrays of any type of element. You can have arrays of integers or arrays of records; you can also have arrays of arrays. An array of strings is a good example of this:

```
Strings : array (1..5) of String(1..5) :=
    ("SATOR", "AREPO", "TENET", "OPERA", "ROTAS");
```

The value of Strings(4) will be the single String "OPERA"; as usual, this can be subscripted to extract a single character from the string so that the letter P in "OPERA" could be referred to as Strings(4)(2).

An alternative to declaring arrays of arrays like this is to declare **multidimensional** arrays. A multidimensional array like the one above can be declared like this:

```
Strings : array (1..5, 1..5) of Character :=
                      (('S', 'A', 'T', 'O', 'R'),
                       ('A', 'R', 'E', 'P', 'O'),
                       ('T', 'E', 'N', 'E', 'T'),
                       ('O', 'P', 'E', 'R', 'A'),
                       ('R', 'O', 'T', 'A', 'S'));
```

This declares Strings to be a 5×5 array of characters. The array aggregate is constructed as an array of array aggregates; hence the double parentheses. Individual elements are selected using a pair of subscripts, e.g. Strings(1,1) or Strings(1,5). The major difference between a two-dimensional array and an array of arrays is that you can only select individual elements of a two-dimensioanl array, but you can select an entire one-dimensional array from an array of arrays which you can then use in its entirety, or you can then slice it or subscript it like any other one-dimensional array.

You can have as many array dimensions as you like in a multidimensional array (subject to the overall limits on memory availability on your machine) and the index subtypes for each dimension can be different. For example, a chessboard consists of an 8×8 grid whose ranks (rows) are numbered 1 to 8 and whose files (columns) are lettered A to H, so that individual squares can be referred to as 'e5' or 'g6' or whatever. Here's a declaration of a chessboard in Ada:

```
type File is (A,B,C,D,E,F,G,H);
type Rank is range 1..8;
type Square is ... ;        -- some type declaration
Board : array (File, Rank) of Square;
```

You can now refer to Board(E,5) or Board(G,6) and so on. If you wanted to, you could create a three-dimensional array to hold the positions after each of the first 40 moves like this:

```
Game : array (File, Rank, 1..40) of Square;
```

You could then obtain the value of the e5 square on the 20th move by referring to Game(E,5,20).

When there is more than one dimension to the array, you have to specify which dimension you're referring to when you use the attributes 'Range, 'First, 'Last and 'Length. You do this by appending the dimension number to the attribute name, e.g. Board'First(1) or Board'Last(2). Here are the values of the attributes of the array Board above:

```
Board'Range(1)   = A..H      Board'Range(2)   = 1..8
Board'First(1)   = A         Board'First(2)   = 1
Board'Last(1)    = H         Board'Last(2)    = 8
Board'Length(1)  = 8         Board'Length(2)  = 8
```

6.8 Discriminants

Sometimes you may want to use an array as a component of a record but you don't necessarily want to tie yourself down to a specific array size. However, you can only use constrained arrays in a record type declaration so that the compiler knows how much space in memory to allocate when you declare a variable of that type. For example, consider a type to represent a variable-length string:

```
type Varying_String is
  record
    Length : Natural;
    Value  : String (1..100);
  end record;
```

The idea here is that Value holds the string itself, which is restricted to a maximum of 100 characters, and that Length is used to record how much of the string is actually in use at any one time. The problem is if we want a different maximum length we have to redefine Varying_String. It would be much more convenient to be able to declare an 'unconstrained' record. The way to get around the problem is to use a **discriminant** in the record declaration. A discriminant must be a value of either a discrete type or an access type (which will be discussed in chapter 11):

```
type Varying_String (Maximum : Positive) is
   record
     Length : Natural;
     Value  : String (1..Maximum);
   end record;
```

The discriminant effectively acts as a 'parameter' for the record. Varying_String is now an unconstrained type (like an unconstrained array, the compiler can't work out how much space to reserve in memory for a Varying_String unless the value of Maximum is known), so when you declare a Varying_String you will have to specify a value for the discriminant Maximum:

```
V1 : Varying_String (100);    -- a maximum of 100 characters
V2 : Varying_String (Maximum => 50);
                              -- a maximum of 50 characters
```

You can also provide the discriminant in a subtype declaration:

```
subtype Twenty is Varying_String (20);
V3 : Twenty;                  -- a maximum of 20 characters
```

The discriminant can be accessed just like any other component of the record:

```
V1.Length := V2.Maximum;      -- set V2's current length to 50
```

However, unlike other components, discriminants are constants; once they've been set in the declaration of the variable they can't be changed:

```
V2.Maximum := 100;            -- ILLEGAL!
```

Aggregates used to initialise record types must provide values for all the components. Since the discriminant is a component, you have to provide a value for the discriminant in the aggregate:

```
V4 : Varying_String := (Maximum=>20, Length=>5,
                        Value=>"Hello               ");
```

For convenience you can also provide a default value in the declaration of the original type:

```
type Varying_String (Maximum : Positive := 80) is
  record
    Length : Natural;
    Value  : String (1..Maximum);
  end record;

V1 : Varying_String;            -- default maximum of 80
V2 : Varying_String (100);      -- explicit maximum of 100
```

You can also provide default values for other record components:

```
type Varying_String (Maximum : Positive := 80) is
  record
    Length : Natural := 0;
    Value  : String (1..Maximum);
  end record;
```

Whenever a Varying_String is declared, the Value component will be 80 characters long by default and its Length component will be set to zero by default, so that newly created Varying_Strings will automatically be marked as containing zero characters but able to hold up to 80 characters. You can still set Length to a different value if you supply an initial value in the declaration:

```
V1 : Varying_String;       -- Maximum = 80, Length = 0 by default
V2 : Varying_String :=
            (Maximum=>15, Length=>5, Value=>"Hello           ");
  -- note that Value must be exactly Maximum characters long!
```

The defaults for record components don't have to be constants, they can be any expression. Whenever a variable is declared the expression will be evaluated. You could for example include a timestamp in every record to keep track of the time it was created:

```
type Time_Stamp is
  record
    Creation_Time : Ada.Calendar.Time := Ada.Calendar.Clock;
  end record;
```

In this case the function Clock from Ada.Calendar will be called when a Time_Stamp object is declared so that Creation_Time will be set by default to the time at which the object was created. Here's another example: a record type to represent a bank account which is automatically given a unique account number when it is created:

```
type Account_Number is range 1000_0000..9999_9999;
type Money_Type is delta 0.01 range 0.00 .. 1_000_000_000.00;
Last_Account : Account_Number := Account_Number_Type'First;

function Next_Account_Number return Account_Number is
   New_Account : Account_Number := Last_Account;
begin
   Last_Account := Last_Account + 1;
   return New_Account;
end Next_Account_Number;

type Bank_Account_Type is
   record
      Account : Account_Number := Next_Account_Number;
      Balance : Money_Type       := 0.00;
      -- and so on
   end record;
```

Now whenever an object of type Bank_Account_Type is created, the function Next_Account_Number will be called to initialise the Account component; this will use the value of Last_Account (so the first account created will be number 1000_0000) and it will also increment it (so the next account will be number 1000_0001, then 1000_0002, and so on). Note that Last_Account has to be declared outside Next_Account_Number so that it won't lose its value between one call of Next_Account_Number and another.

6.9 Limited types

In the case of bank accounts, you may want to prevent one bank account object being assigned to another. If you don't, assigning one account to another will result in two accounts with the same account number, and the original account number of the one being assigned to will have been lost. To prevent this, you can declare a record type to be **limited**:

```
type Bank_Account_Type is
   limited record
      Account : Account_Number := Next_Account_Number;
      Balance : Money_Type       := 0.00;
      -- and so on
   end record;
```

Now you can declare variables of type Bank_Account_Type in the normal way:

```
John, Fred : Bank_Account_Type;
```

The only operations available for ordinary record types are assignment (:=) and testing for equality or inequality (=, /=). Limited types don't have these operations, so you can't assign one bank account to another or test if they have the same value as each other. This also means that you can't assign an initial value to a bank account in its declaration. You can, however, alter the individual components within the record; the prohibition on assignment and comparison only applies to the record as a whole. There is a way around this, but I'll save it for later. Here are some examples involving the bank accounts John and Fred declared above:

```
John := Fred;                     -- illegal!
John.Balance := Fred.Balance;     -- legal (but is it sensible?)
```

Any array or record type involving limited components is automatically limited as well; you won't be able to assign or compare a record containing a limited component since this involves assigning or comparing each individual component.

6.10　Using packages with data types

In most cases, the declaration of a record type will rely on a number of closely related type declarations used for the record components. These type declarations will all need to be kept together; if you use the record type you will usually need to use the component types as well. The simplest way to do this is to put the type declarations in a package. That way you can get access to the complete set of related type declarations by specifying the package name in a **with** clause. For example, here's a package which contains the declarations of the types needed to represent dates:

```
package JE.Dates is
   subtype Day_Type   is Integer range 1..31;
   type    Month_Type is (Jan, Feb, Mar, Apr, May, Jun,
                          Jul, Aug, Sep, Oct, Nov, Dec);
   subtype Year_Type  is Integer range 1901..2099;

   type Date_Type is
     record
        Day   : Day_Type;
        Month : Month_Type;
        Year  : Year_Type;
     end record;
end JE.Dates;
```

Given this, any program which wants to use these declarations just has to specify JE.Dates in a **with** clause. Note that since the package does not contain any subprograms, there is no need for a package body since the specification does not include any incomplete declarations; in fact, you are forbidden to provide a package body unless the specification is incomplete in some way, e.g. if it declares any subprograms which then need to be defined in the package body.

If you want to define subprograms which have parameters of user-defined types, the type declarations must be available at the point where the subprogram is declared as well as at the point where it is called (so that the calling program can supply values of the correct type). The simplest way to do this is to put the type declarations and related subprograms together in a package so that the type declarations as well as the subprogram declarations are accessible to the calling program. Here is a modification of the date package from chapter 4 which uses Date_Type for the subprogram parameters instead of three individual integers, and which has Day_Of returning a result of the enumerated type Weekday_Type instead of an Integer:

```
package JE.Dates is
   subtype Day_Type     is Integer range 1..31;
   type    Month_Type   is (Jan, Feb, Mar, Apr, May, Jun,
                            Jul, Aug, Sep, Oct, Nov, Dec);
   subtype Year_Type    is Integer range 1901..2099;
   type    Weekday_Type is (Sun, Mon, Tue, Wed, Thu, Fri, Sat);

   type Date_Type is
     record
        Day   : Day_Type;
        Month : Month_Type;
        Year  : Year_Type;
     end record;
   function Day_Of (Date : Date_Type) return Weekday_Type;
   function Valid  (Date : Date_Type) return Boolean;
end JE.Dates;
```

The type declarations in the package specification are automatically visible in the package body so the package body will only need to contain the bodies of Day_Of and Valid. Any program which uses this package has access to the functions Day_Of and Valid as well as the type declarations it needs in order to use them.

Exercises

6.1   Write a program to count the number of occurrences of each letter of the alphabet typed as input at the keyboard. Using a subtype of Character as the index subtype of an array is a sensible way to do this.

6.2   Write a program which counts the number of occurrences of each word typed at the keyboard. Consider a word to be a sequence of up to 32 letters. You will need to use an array of records, where each record contains a word and the number of occurrences. Allow for a maximum of 100 different words, and ignore case differences. Functions to convert a character from upper case to lower case and to read the next word from the keyboard and return it as a string would be a good idea.

6.3   Produce a package defining data types to represent individual playing cards and also packs of cards (see exercise 5.4). Each card should be a record containing a suit and a value; the pack should contain an array of up to 52 cards (but try to avoid using the magic number 52 if you can!) together with the number of cards in the pack. Provide subprograms to initialise a pack (so that it contains a complete set of four suits of 13 cards each), to shuffle a pack (by interchanging each card with another randomly selected card from the same pack; see exercise 5.1), to deal a card (by removing the first card from the pack) and to replace a card (by adding it to the end of the pack). Write a simple test program to check that the package works correctly.

6.4   Write a program to encode a message using a simple substitution cipher, where each letter of the message is replaced by a different letter using a lookup table. The lookup table is generated using a keyword; the letters of the keyword are used for the first few positions in the table (ignoring any repeated letters) and the remaining letters of the alphabet are used to complete the table in alphabetical order. The output should be displayed in groups of five letters, all in upper case, with the last group padded out with Xs. For example, if the keyword is JABBERWOCKY, the lookup table will be as follows:

```
            A B C D E F G H I J K L M N O P Q R S T U V W X Y Z
encoded as: J A B E R W O C K Y D F G H I L M N P Q S T U V X Z
```

Note that B occurs twice in the keyword so the keyword actually appears as JABERWOCKY in the table, and the remaining letters of the alphabet (D, F, G, etc.) are then used to fill up the rest of the table. The message 'Cabbages and kings' would be encoded as BJAAJ ORPJH EDKHO PXXXX using this table.

CHAPTER 7

Exceptions

To err is human, to forgive, divine.
— Alexander Pope, *An Essay on Criticism*

7.1 The importance of exception handling

Exception handling was dealt with briefly at the end of chapter 3, but it's such an important topic that it's worth looking at in more detail. The Ada exception handling mechanism divides error handling into two separate concerns. One of them is detecting errors and the other is dealing with the errors in an appropriate way, and the two should be treated as two completely separate aspects of error handling. It also makes your programs easier to construct as well as more readable; a procedure is written as a section which deals with processing valid data and a separate section which deals with what to do when things go wrong. Thus, when you're writing the main part of the procedure you don't have to worry about how to deal with errors, and when you're reading it you don't have to get bogged down in the complexities of the error handling until after you've read and understood what happens with correct data. One way of writing a program is to do it incrementally: write the program without worrying too much about error handling initially, test it to make sure it works with correct data, and then concentrate on improving the exception handling once everything else is working. Debugging might also reveal exceptions that are raised in situations that you've overlooked, but it is much easier to add extra exception handlers than it is to disturb existing code and then have to go back and test it all again.

This separation of concerns is particularly important when designing packages which could be used by several different programs. It's always tempting to try and deal with errors as soon as you detect them, but one of the basic rules of package design is that you should never try to handle any errors within the package itself. The package may be able to detect errors but it will not usually know how to deal with them. Handling errors is something which is normally dependent on the overall program, and a package never knows anything about the program that is using it. What may be appropriate in one program may be totally inappropriate in another, and building in any assumptions about how an error should be handled will prevent you from reusing the package in more than one program. Displaying an error message on the screen and then halting may be appropriate in some situations, but in other situations there may not be a screen (e.g. your package is used by a program which controls a washing machine) or it may be a bad idea to halt (e.g. the package is used by a program in an aircraft's navigational system). Instead you should define your own exceptions and raise them if an error is detected; this will allow the main program to decide how best to deal with the error.

7.2   Declaring exceptions

Ada defines four standard exceptions. You've already met Constraint_Error; this is raised whenever a value goes outside the range allowed by its type. You're very much less likely to meet the others (Storage_Error, Tasking_Error and Program_Error). Storage_Error is raised when you run out of memory. This is only likely to happen when your program is trying to allocate memory dynamically, as explained in chapter 11. Tasking_Error can occur if a program is composed of multiple tasks executing in parallel, as explained in chapter 19, and a task can't be started for some reason or if you try to communicate with a task that has finished executing. Program_Error is raised in a variety of situations where the program is incorrect but the compiler can't detect this at compile time (e.g. run-time accessibility checks on access types as explained in chapter 11, or reaching the end of a function without executing a **return** statement).

Ada allows you to define your own exceptions in addition to the standard exceptions, like this:

```
Something_Wrong : exception;
```

This declares an exception called Something_Wrong. The standard exceptions are of course declared in the package Standard, just as the standard types like Integer are. Other exceptions are defined in other packages such as Ada.Text_IO; Data_Error is an example of this. You may have noticed that Data_Error is not in the list of standard exceptions above. It is actually declared in a package called Ada.IO_Exceptions, and redeclared by renaming inside Ada.Text_IO (and all the other input/output packages) like this:

```
Data_Error : exception
             renames Ada.IO_Exceptions.Data_Error;
```

Although an exception declaration *looks* like a variable declaration, it isn't; about the only thing you can do with an exception (apart from handling it when it is raised) is to raise it using a **raise** statement:

```
raise Something_Wrong;
```

When you raise an exception, the system looks for a handler for that exception in the current block. If there isn't one, it exits from the block (going to the line after **end** in the case of a **begin** ... **end** block, or returning to where it was called from in the case of a procedure or function body) and looks for a handler in the block it now finds itself in. In the worst case where there is no handler anywhere it will eventually exit from the main program, at which point the program will halt and an error will be reported.

Note that if an exception is raised inside an exception handler, you exit from the block immediately and then look for an exception handler in the block you've returned to. This prevents you getting stuck in an endless exception handling loop. The same thing happens if an exception is raised while elaborating declarations in a declaration section; this avoids the possibility of an exception handler referring to a variable that hasn't been created yet. Until you've got past the **begin** at the start of the block you're not counted as being inside it and hence not subject to the block's exception handlers; once an exception occurs and you've entered the exception handler section, you're counted as having left the block so once again you're not subject to that block's exception handlers. In other words, the exception handler only applies to the statements in the body of the block between **begin** and **exception**.

7.3   Re-raising exceptions

Sometimes you will want to do some tidying up before exiting a block even if you don't actually want to handle the exception at that point. For example, you may have created a temporary file on disk which needs to be deleted before you exit from the block. Here's how you can deal with this situation:

```
begin
  -- create a temporary file
  -- do something that might raise a Constraint_Error
  -- delete the temporary file
exception
  when Constraint_Error =>
    -- delete the temporary file
    raise Constraint_Error;
end;
```

The temporary file will be deleted whether an exception occurs or not, either in the course of normal processing or from within the exception handler. A **raise** statement is used inside the exception handler to raise the same exception again, so that you will immediately exit from the block and look for another handler to handle the exception properly.

Sometimes you don't know exactly which exception has occurred. If you have an **others** handler or a single handler for several different exceptions, you won't know which exception to raise after you've done your tidying up. The solution is to use a special form of the **raise** statement which is only allowed inside an exception handler:

```
begin
  -- create a temporary file
```

```
    -- do something that might raise an exception
    -- delete the temporary file
exception
  when others =>
    -- delete the temporary file
    raise;                    -- re-raise the same exception
end;
```

Raise on its own will re-raise the same exception, whatever it might be.

7.4   Getting information about exceptions

You may want to print out a message which says what the exception was as part of the handler. There is a standard package called Ada.Exceptions which contains some functions to give you this sort of information. Ada.Exceptions defines a data type called Exception_Occurrence and provides a function called Exception_Name which produces the name of the exception as a string from an Exception_Occurrence. You can get a value of type Exception_Occurrence by specifying a name for it as part of your exception handler:

```
begin
    ...
exception
  when Error : Constraint_Error | Data_Error =>
    Put ("The exception was ");
    Put_Line ( Exception_Name(Error) );
end;
```

The name of the Exception_Occurrence is prefixed to the list of exceptions in the handler (the name chosen was Error in this case). There are some other useful functions like Exception_Name; in particular, Exception_Message produces a string containing a short message giving some details about the exception, and Exception_Information produces a longer and more detailed message. Exception_Occurrence objects can also be useful for passing exception information to subprograms called from within an exception handler.

The standard exceptions will have a standard message associated with them. If you want to supply a message for an exception that you've defined yourself (or supply a different message for an existing exception) you can use the procedure Raise_Exception:

```
Raise_Exception (Constraint_Error'Identity,
                 "Value out of range");
```

This has the same effect as 'raise Constraint_Error' except that the message 'Value out of range' will be associated with the exception occurrence. Since an exception is not a data object, you can't use an exception as a parameter to a subprogram. You can get a data object representing an exception using the Identity attribute which produces a value of type Ada.Exceptions.Exception_Id, and it is this value which is passed as the first parameter to Raise_Exception..

7.5 File input/output

One of the major sources of exceptions is when dealing with input and output. Users will inevitably supply invalid input from time to time, due to typing errors if nothing else, and your program must be prepared to cope with this. A typical situation arises when a user types in the name of a file that the program is supposed to read some data from or write something to; the filename might be misspelt, the file might be in another directory or on another disk, the disk might be full, the directory might be write protected. In these cases it is often unfair just to terminate the program; the user should generally be given another chance to type a filename in again.

To illustrate this, I'll briefly describe how file input/output works in Ada. File input/output is fundamentally no different to dealing with the keyboard and screen. The Text_IO package provides all the necessary facilities. The main difference is that you need to **open** a file before you can use it, and you must **close** it when you've finished using it. To open a file you first of all have to declare an object of type File_Type (defined in Ada.Text_IO):

```
File : Ada.Text_IO.File_Type;
```

Now you can open the file using the procedure Open:

```
Open (File, Mode => Ada.Text_IO.In_File, Name => "diary");
```

This opens an input file whose name is *diary*. The Mode parameter is an enumeration with three possible values. In_File means the file is to be opened for input, as in this case. Out_File means the file is to be opened for output. Any existing contents of the file will be lost in this case; Out_File specifies that the existing contents of the file should be scrapped. If you don't want to do this you can use Append_File, which means that whatever output you write to the file will be appended to the end of the file's existing contents (if any). If the file doesn't already exist, Open will generate a Name_Error exception. If you want to create a brand new file for output, you can use the procedure Create:

```
Create (File, Name => "diary");
```

This will create a new output file with the given name if it doesn't already exist, or destroys the existing contents of the file if it does exist. You can optionally supply a Mode parameter as with Open; the default is Out_File, but you might want to use Append_File instead so that you will append your output to the file if it already exists. If the name isn't legal for some reason a Name_Error exception will be raised; for example, some systems can't handle filenames containing asterisks or question marks. The other exceptions that can occur when you try to open or create a file are Status_Error, which indicates that the file is already open, and Use_Error, which is raised if you can't open or create the file for any other reason (e.g. if there is no more disk space).

When you've finished using a file you should close it by calling the procedure Close:

```
Close (File);
```

While the file is open you can use Get to read it if it's an input file and Put or Put_Line to write to it if it's an output file. The only difference from using the keyboard and the screen is that you have to specify the file you want to read from or write to as the first parameter:

```
Get (File, C);           -- get a character from File into C
Put (File, "xyz");       -- write a string to File
Put_Line (File, "xyz");  -- same, and then start a new line
New_Line (File);         -- start a new line in File
Skip_Line (File);        -- skip to start of next line of File
```

If you try to read from a file when you've reached the end of it, an End_Error exception will be raised. To avoid this you can test if you're at the end of the file using the function End_Of_File, which is defined in Ada.Text_IO like this:

```
function End_Of_File (File : File_Type) return Boolean;
```

This returns the value True if you're at the end of the file.

To illustrate how exception handling is used with file I/O, here's an example program which counts the number of words in a file:

```
with Ada.Text_IO, Ada.Integer_Text_IO;
use  Ada.Text_IO, Ada.Integer_Text_IO;
procedure Word_Count is
   File    : File_Type;
   Name    : String(1..80);
   Size    : Natural;
   Count   : Natural := 0;
   In_Word : Boolean := False;
   Char    : Character;
begin
   -- Open input file
   loop
     begin
        Put ("Enter filename: ");
```

```
        Get_Line (Name, Size);
        Open (File, Mode => In_File, Name => Name(1..Size));
        exit;
      exception
        when Name_Error | Use_Error =>
          Put_Line ("Invalid filename -- please try again.");
      end;
    end loop;

    -- Process file
    while not End_Of_File (File) loop
      -- The end of a line is also the end of a word
      if End_Of_Line (File) then
        In_Word := False;
      end if;

      -- Process next character
      Get (File, Char);
      if In_Word and Char = ' ' then
        In_Word := False;
      elsif not In_Word and Char /= ' ' then
        In_Word := True;
        Count := Count + 1;
      end if;
    end loop;

    -- Close file and display result
    Close (File);
    Put (Count);
    Put_Line (" words.");
  end Word_Count;
```

The program is divided into the three traditional parts: initialisation (open the file), main processing (process the file) and finalisation (close the file and display the results). Opening the file involves getting the name of the input file from the user and then attempting to open it. This is done in a loop, and the loop is exited as soon as the input file is successfully opened. If attempting to open the file raises an exception, the exception handler for the block inside the loop displays the error message; the loop will then be executed again to give the user a chance to type in the filename correctly.

Once the file has been opened, the main processing loop begins. A variable called In_Word is used to keep track of whether we are in the middle of processing a word; initially it's set to False to indicate that we're not processing a word. A non-space character means that the start of a word has been seen, so In_Word is set True and the word count in Count is incremented. Once inside a word, characters are skipped until the end of the current line is reached or a space is read, using the function End_Of_Line to test if the current position is at the end of a line of input. Either of these conditions signals the end of a word, so In_Word gets set back to False. When the end of the file is reached, the loop terminates. The input file is then closed and the value of Count is displayed.

Exercises

7.1 Modify the guessing game program from exercise 5.1 to provide comprehensive exception handling to guard against input errors of any kind.

7.2 Write a program which asks the user for the name of an input file and an output file, reads up to 10000 integers from the input file, sorts them using the Shuffle_Sort procedure from the previous chapter, and then writes the sorted data to the output file. Check it to make sure it copes with errors arising from non-existent input files, write-protected destinations for output files, illegal filenames, and (one that often gets overlooked) using the same name for both files.

7.3 Modify the packages JE.Dates from the end of chapter 4 to define an exception called Date_Error, and get the Day_Of function to raise a Date_Error exception if it is called with an invalid date.

7.4 Modify the playing card package from exercise 6.3 to define an exception which will be raised if you try to deal a card from an empty pack or replace a card in a full pack. Use the package to implement a simple card game called 'Follow The Leader', in which a human player and the computer player are dealt ten cards each. The object of the game is to get rid of all the cards in your hand. The first player lays down a card, and each player in turn has to play a card which matches either the suit or the value of the previously played card (e.g. the Jack of Clubs could be followed by any Jack or any Club). If a player has no card that can be used to follow on, an extra card must be taken from the pack. If the pack becomes empty, the cards that were previously played (except the last one) must be returned to the pack. The first player to play out a hand and have no cards left is the winner.

CHAPTER 8

Program design and debugging

It is to be noted that when any part of this paper appears dull, there is a design in it.
— Sir Richard Steele, *The Tatler*

8.1 Stepwise refinement

So far I've said very little about how to design a program to solve a particular problem. The examples I've used until now have been small enough (tens of lines of code) that their design could effectively be ignored in favour of looking at language details and several of the exercises have involved making changes to the examples rather than writing new programs from scratch. You've now covered enough of the language that I can introduce a slightly larger problem here which demands a bit more effort. The solution is probably an order of magnitude larger than the previous examples. So, just what do you do when you're faced with a specification for a problem and a blank piece of paper to write the solution on?

A good way to start is to try to split your problem up into a number of smaller subproblems and then deal with each of them in turn. This is known as **stepwise refinement** or **top-down design**. It is a divide-and-conquer approach which lets you avoid having to deal with a large and complex design as a single monolithic unit. The problem can be broken down into a set of smaller steps, which can then be refined into more detail by applying the same process. The design of the calculator example at the end of chapter 3 used this approach.

Top-down design lets you avoid getting bogged down in details until the last possible moment. It's not entirely foolproof; to be able to do this effortlessly involves having an appreciation of where you're trying to get to and a vague idea of what kind of low-level details you'll end up having to deal with. In particular, it helps to know what packages are available that can provide pieces of the jigsaw puzzle you're trying to put together; if you can steer your breakdown of the solution in the general direction of being able to use some existing packages, you can save yourself some effort. This is part of the craft of programming which you have to learn through experience; if there was a formula you could apply to generate a 'correct' solution someone would have written a program to do it and programmers would find themselves out of a job. In fact, as you've already seen, there is no single 'correct' solution to a particular problem; different people will tend to find different solutions to the same problem.

Fortunately, there are some general principles that you can use as a guide to get you started. As I mentioned in chapter 3, a good start in most cases is to divide the problem up into an initialisation part, a main processing part and a finalisation part. The initialisation does any initial setting up that may be required (e.g. displaying a window on the screen or opening some files) and the finalisation does any final tidying up (destroying windows, closing files, etc.) before the program ends. The main processing in the middle is where all the hard work is done. This is usually a loop which repetitively processes 'events' such as user input, mouse movements, the passage of time or whatever. You may well end up designing the main processing section first and then identifying what initialisation and finalisation it requires.

Beyond this point you have to look at what sort of thing you're trying to do. Does it involve repeating some action over and over again? If so, you need a **loop** statement which encloses the required action. Alternatively, does it involve choosing between different actions? If so, you need an **if** or **case** statement. Now you've got one or more smaller actions inside your **loop**, **if** or **case** statement which you can now break down into smaller pieces using the same approach.

If you want to, you can just sweep some of the details under the carpet by inventing a procedure or function which will (eventually) deal with some aspect of the problem. Your initial implementation of the procedure or function might be a **stub** which does nothing or which cheats in some way (e.g. by getting the user to supply the value to be returned from a function); you can then test the general outline of the program before coming back to your stub and doing the job properly.

To illustrate all this I'm going to develop a larger example, an electronic diary which can be used to keep track of your appointments. It will need to provide as a minimum the ability to add new appointments, delete existing appointments, display the list of appointments and save the appointments to a file. Also, if there are any saved appointments the program should read them in when it starts up.

The initialisation part of this program will involve reading the diary file if it exists. The main processing will consist of displaying a menu of choices, getting the user's response and carrying out the specified operation. At the end, there isn't really anything more to do.

8.2 Initial design

As I said earlier, the initialisation part of this program will involve reading the diary file if it exists. The main processing will consist of displaying a menu of choices, getting the user's response and carrying out the specified operation. To make life easier, I will create a package called JE.Diaries to hold the procedures and related bits and pieces for this program; I'll worry about what will go into it as the design progresses. This gives us the following general structure:

```
with JE.Diaries; use JE.Diaries;
procedure Diary is
   -- declarations will go here
```

```
begin
  -- load diary from file (if any)
  -- process user commands (add, delete, list, save, etc.)
end Diary;
```

Loading the diary from a file can be delegated to a procedure which I'll call Load_Diary and define in JE.Diaries:

```
with JE.Diaries; use JE.Diaries;
procedure Diary is
  -- any declarations will go here
begin
  Load_Diary;
  -- process user commands (add, delete, list, save, etc.)
end Diary;
```

The main processing (dealing with commands from the user) is a repetitive task: repeatedly get a command and do it. This means that the main processing will be a loop of some sort:

```
with JE.Diaries; use JE.Diaries;
procedure Diary is
  -- any other declarations will go here
begin
  Load_Diary;
  loop
    -- process a single user command (add, delete, list, etc.)
  end loop;
end Diary;
```

Processing a command involves displaying a menu, getting a command in response to the menu, and then doing it. I'll use single characters for the command responses, so I'll need a Character variable to store it in which I'll call Command. The loop will be terminated when the user selects the Quit command. We can expand the design a bit further now:

```
with JE.Diaries; use JE.Diaries;
procedure Diary is
  Command : Character;
  -- any other declarations will go here
begin
  Load_Diary;
  loop
    -- display menu
    -- get a command
```

```
      -- perform selected command
   end loop;
end Diary;
```

Getting a command is trivial; it involves getting a single character using Get from Ada.Text_IO. This means that Ada.Text_IO must be added to the list of packages in the **with** clause:

```
with Ada.Text_IO, JE.Diaries;
use  Ada.Text_IO, JE.Diaries;
procedure Diary is
   Command : Character;
   -- any other declarations will go here
begin
   Load_Diary;
   loop
      -- display menu
      Get (Command);

      -- perform selected command
   end loop;
end Diary;
```

The menu just needs to list the command choices (A for add, D for delete, L for list, S for save, Q for quit; you can expand or alter the list of commands later if you need to). How you perform the selected command depends on which command it is; it's a choice of alternative actions, so an **if** or **case** statement is needed. A **case** statement is appropriate here since there are several possible choices which depend on the value of Command:

```
with Ada.Text_IO, JE.Diaries;
use  Ada.Text_IO, JE.Diaries;
procedure Diary is
   Command : Character;
   -- any other declarations will go here
begin
   Load_Diary;
   loop
      -- display menu
      New_Line (5);
      Put_Line ("Diary menu:");
      Put_Line ("    [A]dd appointment");
      Put_Line ("    [D]elete appointment");
      Put_Line ("    [L]ist appointments");
      Put_Line ("    [S]ave appointments");
```

```
        Put_Line ("    [Q]uit");
        New_Line;
        Put ("Enter your choice: ");

        -- get a command
        Get (Command);

        -- perform selected command
        case Command is
          when 'A' | 'a' =>
            -- add appointment
          when 'D' | 'd' =>
            -- delete appointment
          when 'L' | 'l' =>
            -- list appointments
          when 'S' | 's' =>
            -- save appointments
          when 'Q' | 'q' =>
            -- quit
          when others =>
            -- error: invalid menu choice
        end case;
      end loop;
    end Diary;
```

Displaying the menu and performing the selected command could easily be implemented as separate procedures, but I've left them in the main program so that it's easier to see the correspondence between the menu and the choices in the **case** statement, which ensures that if any changes are made to the menu it will be obvious whether the **case** statement has been changed to reflect this. However, others might prefer to use procedures to minimise code bulk in the main program. The difference in approach isn't major.

The Quit command is easy to deal with; this just involves exiting from the main loop. The **others** choice can simply display an error message, and the remaining commands can be handled by procedures in JE.Diaries:

```
case Command is
  when 'A' | 'a' =>
    Add_Appointment;
  when 'D' | 'd' =>
    Delete_Appointment;
  when 'L' | 'l' =>
    List_Appointments;
  when 'S' | 's' =>
    Save_Appointments;
```

```
      when 'Q' | 'q' =>
        exit;
      when others =>
        Put_Line ("Invalid choice -- " &
                  "please enter A, D, L, S or Q");
    end case;
```

So far so good. Now let's construct the specification of JE.Diaries from what we've got so far; all it needs is a list of the procedures referred to by the main program:

```
package JE.Diaries is
   procedure Load_Diary;
   procedure Add_Appointment;
   procedure Delete_Appointment;
   procedure List_Appointments;
   procedure Save_Appointments;
end JE.Diaries;
```

8.3   Diary package design

The procedures in the package all need to manipulate the diary, so we'll need to define the structure of the diary before we can go any further. Most of the necessary type declarations were developed in chapter 6, so I'll just take them from there:

```
subtype Day_Type    is Integer range 1..31;
type    Month_Type  is (Jan, Feb, Mar, Apr, May, Jun,
                        Jul, Aug, Sep, Oct, Nov, Dec);
subtype Year_Type   is Integer range 1901..2099;
subtype Hour_Type   is Integer range 0..23;
subtype Minute_Type is Integer range 0..59;

type Date_Type is
  record
     Day   : Day_Type;
     Month : Month_Type;
     Year  : Year_Type;
  end record;

type Time_Type is
  record
     Hour   : Hour_Type;
     Minute : Minute_Type;
  end record;
```

```
type Appointment_Type is
   record
      Date    : Date_Type;
      Time    : Time_Type;
      Details : String (1..50);      -- an arbitrarily chosen size
      Length  : Natural := 0;
   end record;
```

```
type Appointment_Array is array (Positive range <>)
                                 of Appointment_Type;
```

The only difference is that Appointment_Type now contains a Length component to record the actual length of the Details component; this will allow a maximum of 50 characters rather than exactly 50 characters. The maximum length is arbitrary; you can change it if you want longer appointment details.

Now we'll need an Appointment_Array together with a variable to keep track of how many appointments there actually are in the diary. This calls for another record type declaration:

```
type Diary_Type (Maximum : Positive) is
   record
      Appts : Appointment_Array (1..Maximum);
      Count : Natural := 0;
   end record;
```

Finally we can declare the diary itself:

```
Diary : Diary_Type (10);
```

I'm only allowing ten entries at the moment so that it'll be easy to test that the program behaves properly when the diary is full. The size of the diary and the length of the details string can both be changed by changing a single line of the declarations above, recompiling the package body and then relinking the main program. We'll need to be careful not to assume that those values will always be what they are now, and use the 'Last attribute for the length of the details string and the Maximum discriminant for the number of entries.

The procedures can be implemented as **stubs** for now. These are temporary versions of the procedures that we can use to complete the package body so that it can be compiled, and the bits that have been written so far can be tested. What I'll do is provide versions of the procedures that just display a message to say they've been called (which will also require a **with** clause for Ada.Text_IO at the top of the package body):

```
procedure Load_Diary is
begin
```

```
      Put_Line ("Load_Diary called");
   end Load_Diary;

   procedure Add_Appointment is
   begin
      Put_Line ("Add_Appointment called");
   end Add_Appointment;

   procedure Delete_Appointment is
   begin
      Put_Line ("Delete_Appointment called");
   end Delete_Appointment;

   procedure List_Appointments is
   begin
      Put_Line ("List_Appointments called");
   end List_Appointments;

   procedure Save_Appointments is
   begin
      Put_Line ("Save_Appointments called");
   end Save_Appointments;
```

The full version of the package body obtained by putting the above bits and pieces together looks like this:

```
with Ada.Text_IO;
use  Ada.Text_IO;
package body JE.Diaries is

   subtype Day_Type    is Integer range 1..31;
   type    Month_Type  is (Jan, Feb, Mar, Apr, May, Jun,
                           Jul, Aug, Sep, Oct, Nov, Dec);

   subtype Year_Type   is Integer range 1901..2099;
   subtype Hour_Type   is Integer range 0..23;
   subtype Minute_Type is Integer range 0..59;

   type Date_Type is
      record
         Day   : Day_Type;
         Month : Month_Type;
         Year  : Year_Type;
      end record;
```

```
type Time_Type is
   record
      Hour   : Hour_Type;
      Minute : Minute_Type;
   end record;

type Appointment_Type is
   record
      Date    : Date_Type;
      Time    : Time_Type;
      Details : String (1..50);     -- an arbitrary size
      Length  : Natural := 0;
   end record;

type Appointment_Array is array (Positive range <>)
                                 of Appointment_Type;

type Diary_Type (Maximum : Positive) is
   record
      Appts : Appointment_Array (1..Maximum);
      Count : Natural := 0;
   end record;

Diary : Diary_Type (10);

procedure Load_Diary is
begin
   Put_Line ("Load_Diary called");
end Load_Diary;

procedure Add_Appointment is
begin
   Put_Line ("Add_Appointment called");
end Add_Appointment;

procedure Delete_Appointment is
begin
   Put_Line ("Delete_Appointment called");
end Delete_Appointment;

procedure List_Appointments is
begin
   Put_Line ("List_Appointments called");
end List_Appointments;
```

```
procedure Save_Appointments is
begin
  Put_Line ("Save_Appointments called");
end Save_Appointments;
```

```
end JE.Diaries;
```

Once you've checked that the program works so far, you can replace the stubs with working versions of the code for each procedure. One of the advantages of top-down design is that it lets you postpone worrying about the finer details of your programs until the last possible moment; it also lets you do **incremental testing**, where you test each part of the program before you go any further.

8.4   Debugging the main program

At this point we want to be confident that the main program works. Once we know that it can cope with anything we throw at it we can get down to implementing the rest of the program. There isn't any point in proceeding until we know that everything so far works; apart from anything else, it's still only a small program which can be tested, fixed and then recompiled quite quickly.

The first thing to do is to test it with correct input. When the program starts up it should display the message 'Load_Diary called' followed by the menu. Try typing A, D, L and S to make sure that the correct procedure is called in each case. Now try a, d, l and s. Is everything all right? This has tested the three main menu commands; the remaining ones to try are Q and q. Type Q and the program should exit with the message 'Save_Diary called'. Now start it up again and try q instead.

So, the program so far works with correct input. Fortunately at this stage the possibilities can be tested exhaustively; in most cases you have to choose a representative set of test data since there are too many possibilities to test them all (unless you know somewhere where you can hire an infinite number of monkeys, that is!). Now what about incorrect input? First of all try typing X. You should get a message saying 'Invalid choice -- please enter A, D, L, S or Q'. So far so good. Now try typing *Add*. You should immediately spot that there's a problem.

You can probably see what the problem is straight away in this case, but to show you how to track down problems of this sort let's pretend we've been hit by an attack of stupidity. If you can't figure out what's happening, the first thing to do is to get more information about what's going wrong. You may have access to a **debugger** which will let you step through the program line by line, or set **breakpoints** so that the program halts whenever it gets to a particular line to let you inspect the values of selected variables as the program is running. Then again, you may not.

Using a debugger is the simplest thing to do as it doesn't involve making any changes to the program to find out what's going on. In the absence of a debugger, you have to modify the program to display a bit more information. In this case we know that the problem manifests itself in the **case** statement, so the simplest thing to do is to use Put to display the value of Command just before the **case** statement:

```
Put ("Command = ["); Put (Command); Put_Line ("]");    -- DEBUG
case Command is
   ...
end case;
```

Tinkering with the program like this means you have to be careful to fix all your changes and test everything again when you've finished debugging. The comment 'DEBUG' at the end of the line is to make it easy to find and remove lines added for debugging purposes once the bug has been fixed. It might also be a good idea to **comment out** the lines displaying the menu (i.e. make them into comments so that they have no effect but can be reinstated later) in case debugging information scrolls off the top of the screen:

```
-- DEBUG    New_Line (5);
-- DEBUG    Put_Line ("Diary menu:");
-- DEBUG    Put_Line ("    [A]dd appointment");
-- DEBUG    Put_Line ("    [D]elete appointment");
-- DEBUG    Put_Line ("    [L]ist appointments");
-- DEBUG    Put_Line ("    [S]ave appointments");
-- DEBUG    Put_Line ("    [Q]uit");
```

Again, the comment 'DEBUG' shows that the lines are commented out for debugging purposes so we can track down these lines and uncomment them after the bug has been fixed. Removing lines is far more risky; you might introduce extra bugs by doing so, or even remove the source of the bug you're trying to find! A better alternative would be to send debugging output somewhere else (e.g. into a file, or to a separate screen or window). Anyway, if you make the changes above, run the program and type in 'ADD', this is what you should see:

```
Load_Diary called

Enter your choice: ADD
Command = [A]
Add_Appointment called

Enter your choice: Command = [D]
Delete_Appointment called

Enter your choice: Command = [D]
Delete_Appointment called

Enter your choice:
```

It should now be fairly obvious what's going on. Each of the three characters on the line is being read in and treated as a command. A simple solution is to use Skip_Line to get rid of the rest of the line immediately after the call to Get:

```
-- get a command
Get (Command);
Skip_Line;
```

Now if you recompile and try again, this is what you should see:

```
Load_Diary called

Enter your choice: ADD
Command = [A]
Add_Appointment called

Enter your choice: XYZZY
Command = [X]
Invalid choice -- please enter A, D, L, S or Q

Enter your choice:
```

There's one more test to try. What happens if you type in the end-of-file character (which is usually control-Z or control-D)? You should find that the program halts with an End_Error exception. The solution to this one is obviously to add an exception handler for End_Error. However, after an end-of-file, the program might not be able to read any more input from the keyboard, so there probably isn't any point in going round the loop again. The simplest thing to do is to exit the program. The end-of-file test is always a good one to remember; it's surprising how many programs written by novices will just fall over gracelessly if you type the end-of-file character.

Here's a fixed version of the main program:

```
with Ada.Text_IO, JE.Diaries;
use  Ada.Text_IO, JE.Diaries;
procedure Diary is
   Command : Character;
begin
   Load_Diary;
   loop
      -- display menu
      ... as before

      -- get a command
      Get (Command);
```

```
      Skip_Line;            -- Bug fix added here
      -- perform selected command
      case Command is
         ... as before
      end case;
   end loop;

exception               -- Bug fix added here
   when End_Error =>
      null;               -- do nothing, just end the program
end Diary;
```

8.5 Displaying the appointments

The code to display the appointments is fairly simple. Since it will be needed to test the rest of the program, this is where I'll start. All that it'll need will be a loop to display each appointment in succession:

```
procedure List_Appointments is
begin
   for I in Diary.Appts'First .. Diary.Count loop
      Put ( Diary.Appts(I) );
   end loop;
end List_Appointments;
```

I'm assuming the existence of a Put procedure to display an appointment in an appropriate form on the screen; we'll need to provide this in the package body. The loop uses the value of the Count component of Diary to control the number of times the loop will be executed, and thus the number of appointments that will be displayed.

The trouble with this is that it's *too* simple; when Count is zero, the loop will be executed zero times, with the result that absolutely nothing will be displayed. It would be better to detect this as a special case and deal with it separately:

```
procedure List_Appointments is
begin
   if Diary.Count = 0 then
      Put_Line ("No appointments found.");
   else
      for I in Diary.Appts'First .. Diary.Count loop
         Put ( Diary.Appts(I) );
      end loop;
   end if;
end List_Appointments;
```

For the sake of simplicity, I'll assume that the appointments are stored in ascending order of date and time, so that listing them in sequence produces an ordered list rather than a random jumble of appointments. This will be something to bear in mind when we consider how to add new appointments. I've also ignored the situation where there are more appointments than will fit on the screen; if this happens the screen will scroll up so that you'll only be able to see the last screenful of appointments.

We need to implement Put before we can test this properly. Here's a possible implementation:

```
procedure Put (Item : in Appointment_Type) is
begin
   Put (Item.Date.Day,    Width => 2);  Put ("-");
   Put (Item.Date.Month);               Put ("-");
   Put (Item.Date.Year,   Width => 4);  Put (" ");
   Put (Item.Time.Hour,   Width => 2);  Put (":");
   Put (Item.Time.Minute, Width => 2);  Put (" ");
   Put_Line (Item.Details (1..Item.Length));
end Put;
```

This in turn requires versions of Put for the individual components of the appointment. These are all subtypes of Integer apart from Month_Type, so we can just instantiate Integer_IO for Integer and Enumeration_IO for Month_Type:

```
with Ada.Text_IO;
use  Ada.Text_IO;
package body JE.Diaries is
   subtype Day_Type    is Integer range 1..31;
   type    Month_Type  is (Jan, Feb, Mar, Apr, May, Jun,
                           Jul, Aug, Sep, Oct, Nov, Dec);
   subtype Year_Type   is Integer range 1901..2099;
   subtype Hour_Type   is Integer range 0..23;
   subtype Minute_Type is Integer range 0..59;

   package Int_IO   is new Integer_IO (Integer);
   package Month_IO is new Enumeration_IO (Month_Type);
   use Int_IO, Month_IO;

   ... etc.

end JE.Diaries;
```

You can test this before proceeding any further; you should just get a message saying 'No appointments found'. You'll need to implement Add_Appointment before you can test any further.

⇒ *If you enter a time like 10 o'clock you'll see that it gets displayed as 10: 0 (i.e. the minute part of the time is padded with a space rather than a leading zero). Fix this so that times are displayed properly, e.g. 10:00.*

8.6 Adding new appointments

The process of adding an appointment can be broken down into two smaller steps: read in the new appointment, and add it to the diary. You can start with a simple-minded version that doesn't keep the appointments in order; this will let you test that the Add_Appointment procedure works so far before going any further. All we need to do at this stage is to ask the user to enter the appointment details and then add the appointment to the end of the list. We'll need an Appointment_Type variable to hold the new appointment; we can write the code to get the appointment details like this:

```
procedure Add_Appointment is
   New_Appt : Appointment_Type;
begin
   Put_Line ("Enter appointment details...");
   Put ("Date: ");
   Get (New_Appt.Date);
   Put ("Time: ");
   Get (New_Appt.Time);
   Put ("Details: ");
   Skip_Line;
   Get_Line (New_Appt.Details, New_Appt.Length);

   -- Add the appointment to the list
end Add_Appointment;
```

⇒ *Why is the call to Skip_Line necessary? What happens if it is removed?*

This assumes that JE.Diaries will provide versions of Get to read in dates and times. Input is always an area where legitimate errors can occur due to typing mistakes, so you should always think about exception handling whenever input is done. You could just run the version of Add_Appointment above and find out which exceptions will occur by trial and error. You'll find that a constraint error or a data error will be raised if the input is incorrect, so an exception handler will be required to deal with these errors. Here's what it might look like:

```
exception
   when Data_Error | Constraint_Error =>
      Put_Line ("Invalid date or time");
      Skip_Line;
```

⇒ *Separate exception handlers for getting the date and for getting the time would improve things even more since you would be able to tell the user more precisely what's happened. Change the program so it does this.*

Simple versions of Get for dates and times can just use the versions of Get for Integers and Month_Types which are already available in Int_IO and Month_IO to read in the components of the record, like this:

```
procedure Get (Item : out Date_Type) is
begin
  Get (Item.Day);
  Get (Item.Month);
  Get (Item.Year);
end Get;

procedure Get (Item : out Time_Type) is
begin
  Get (Item.Hour);
  Get (Item.Minute);
end Get;
```

This does minimal checking; it might be a good idea to check that the date is valid in the version of Get for dates. You could use the function Valid from chapter 4 or a variant of it, or use Ada.Calendar.Time_Of as described in the previous chapter to do this. If the date is invalid, a sensible response would be to raise a Constraint_Error so that entering the 31st of February would be reported as the same sort of error you would get if you entered the 32nd of January.

⇒ *Think about what different formats you might want Get to be able to accept. See how close to the ideal you can make your version of Get.*

Now to add the appointment to the end of the diary. This involves incrementing the number of appointments (Diary.Count) so that it refers to the next free appointment and then storing the new appointment at that point in the array:

```
Diary.Count := Diary.Count + 1;
Diary.Appt (Diary.Count) := New_Appt;
```

If you try this out, you'll find that it will also raise a constraint error when the diary is full (i.e. when Diary.Count goes out of range). The code for reading the appointment details also needs to handle constraint errors, so it needs to go in a separate block with its own Constraint_Error handler to allow the code for adding the appointment to have a different Constraint_Error handler. The final version of Add_Appointment will look like this when you put all these bits together:

```
procedure Add_Appointment is
  New_Appt : Appointment_Type;
begin
  begin
    Put_Line ("Enter appointment details...");
    Put ("Date: ");
    Get (New_Appt.Date);
    Put ("Time: ");
    Get (New_Appt.Time);
    Put ("Details: ");
    Skip_Line;
    Get_Line (New_Appt.Details, New_Appt.Length);
  exception
    when Data_Error | Constraint_Error =>
      Put_Line ("Error in input -- appointment not added");
      Skip_Line;
  end;

  Diary.Count := Diary.Count + 1;
  Diary.Appts (Diary.Count) := New_Appt;

exception
  when Constraint_Error =>
    Put_Line ("Diary full -- appointment not added");
end Add_Appointment;
```

Now there are two separate Constraint_Error handlers: one in the inner block to cope with out-of-range input values and one in the outer block to cope with a full diary. When you test this you should discover that when there is an error in the input to Add_Appointment, an appointment is still added. This is because after the inner exception handler, execution continues with the statements after the inner block which will add a non-existent appointment to the diary. This can be fixed by adding a **return** statement to the inner exception handler:

```
exception
  when Data_Error | Constraint_Error =>
    Put_Line ("Invalid date or time");
    Skip_Line;
    return;
```

⇒   *Think of another way to fix this problem.*

At this point you can test List_Appointments more thoroughly. If you start with an empty diary you can add appointments one by one, listing the appointments before and after you do so, and see what happens. Your testing should reveal that there is still a bug in Add_Appointment.

⇒   *Well, have you spotted the bug? If not, try harder! Once you've found it you can discover the cause of it by printing out the values of some of the main variables used in Add_Appointment and List_Appointments. Fix it before you go any further.*

8.7   Deleting appointments

We need to have some way to describe a specific appointment when we come to deletions; the simplest way would be to number the appointments when they are listed and get the user to specify the appointment number when deleting an appointment. To do this, we'll need to modify List_Appointments to display an appointment number alongside each appointment:

```
procedure List_Appointments is
begin
   if Diary.Count = 0 then
      Put_Line ("No appointments found.");
   else
      for I in Diary.Appts'First .. Diary.Count loop
         Put (I, Width=>3); Put (") ");
         Put ( Diary.Appts(I) );
      end loop;
   end if;
end List_Appointments;
```

The steps involved in deleting an appointment will be to read in the appointment number, check that it's valid and then delete the corresponding appointment from the array. This means that we'll need to declare a variable to hold the appointment number that the user types in:

```
Appt_No : Positive;
```

Reading in the appointment number involves displaying a prompt and then reading a number into Appt_No:

```
Put ("Enter appointment number: ");
Get (Appt_No);
```

Of course, we'll need to check that the appointment number is valid. We'll need to provide an exception handler to check for input errors (constraint and data errors) as is nearly always the case when performing input:

```
exception
  when Constraint_Error | Data_Error =>
    Put_Line ("Invalid appointment number");
    Skip_Line;
```

Diary.Count gives the number of appointments that the diary currently holds, so Appt_No must not be greater than Diary.Count. An easy way to respond to this is to treat it as a constraint error:

```
if Appt_No not in Diary.Appts'First .. Diary.Count then
  raise Constraint_Error;
end if;
```

Deleting the appointment involves moving all the appointments after the one identified by Appt_No up one place in the array and decrementing Diary.Count. The appointments can be moved using a slice which selects all the entries from Appt_No+1 to Diary.Count:

```
Diary.Appt (Appt_No..Diary.Count-1) :=
                        Diary.Appt (Appt_No+1..Diary.Count);
Diary.Count := Diary.Count - 1;
```

Putting all this together gives us this procedure:

```
procedure Delete_Appointment is
  Appt_No : Positive;
begin
  Put ("Enter appointment number: ");
  Get (Appt_No);
  if Appt_No not in Diary.Appts'First .. Diary.Count then
    raise Constraint_Error;
  end if;
  Diary.Appts(Appt_No..Diary.Count-1) :=
                        Diary.Appts(Appt_No+1..Diary.Count);
  Diary.Count := Diary.Count - 1;
exception
  when Constraint_Error | Data_Error =>
    Put_Line ("Invalid appointment number");
    Skip_Line;
end Delete_Appointment;
```

Testing this will require typing in both valid and invalid appointment numbers and checking that the correct appointment disappears when a valid appointment number is given. Testing for **boundary cases** is always important, that is to say those values at the upper and lower limits of the range. If you've got appointments numbered 1 to 5, does the procedure work properly for 1 and 5 and does it correctly report an error for 0 and 6? Similarly, test the boundary cases for the number of appointments in the diary. Does it work correctly when the diary is full, or when it's empty, or when it just has a single appointment in it?

⇒ *There's a bug in the code above; try typing '1 X' when you're asked for the appointment number (assuming there is an appointment 1, of course). Track down the bug and fix it.*

8.8 Loading and saving

The final two procedures are Load_Diary and Save_Appointments. I'll consider these together since they both deal with the same file holding the diary. I'll assume that the diary will be stored in a file called 'Diary', but I'll define it as a string constant to make it easy to change later:

```
Diary_File_Name : constant String := "Diary";
```

Saving the appointments can be done just like List_Appointments except that the appointments don't need to be numbered and they're written to a file instead of being displayed on the screen. It would also be a good idea to write the number of appointments at the start of the file. A File_Type variable (Diary_File) will be needed to do the file accesses. Here's an outline:

```
procedure Save_Appointments is
   Diary_File : File_Type;
begin
   -- open the file
   -- write Diary.Count to the file
   for I in Diary.Appts'First .. Diary.Count loop
      -- write the I-th appointment to the file
   end loop;
   -- close the file
end Save_Appointments;
```

Opening the file can be done using Create as described in the previous chapter. Closing the file just involves using Close. Various exceptions can be raised by Create, so an exception handler will be needed. Use_Error indicates that the file couldn't be created; perhaps the disk is full or you don't have write access to it, so this should be reported to the user. Name_Error will be raised if the filename is invalid and Status_Error will be raised if the file is already open. Neither of these should occur unless a total disaster occurs (the constant string "Diary", which is presumably a valid filename, has been corrupted somehow, or you've opened the file and forgotten to close it elsewhere in the program), so they shouldn't be handled. That way if they ever do occur the exception will be reported as a genuine error which terminates the program:

```
procedure Save_Appointments is
   Diary_File : File_Type;
begin
   Create (Diary_File, Name => Diary_File_Name);
   -- write Diary.Count to the file
   for I in Diary.Appts'First .. Diary.Count loop
      -- write the I-th appointment to the file
   end loop;
   Close (Diary_File);
exception
   when Use_Error =>
      Put_Line ("Couldn't create diary file!");
end Save_Appointments;
```

Writing the appointments can be done using appropriate versions of Put for each of the appointment's components. A space should be output between each component to separate them in the file so that they can be read in by Load_Diary, and each appointment should go on a separate line in the file:

```
procedure Save_Appointments is
   Diary_File : File_Type;
begin
   Create (Diary_File, Name => Diary_File_Name);
   Put (Diary_File, Diary.Count);
   New_Line (Diary_File);

   for I in Diary.Appts'First .. Diary.Count loop
      declare
         Appt : Appointment_Type renames Diary.Appts(I);
      begin
         Put (Diary_File, Appt.Date.Day, Width=>1);
         Put (Diary_File, ' ');
         Put (Diary_File, Appt.Date.Month);
         Put (Diary_File, ' ');
         Put (Diary_File, Appt.Date.Year, Width=>1);
         Put (Diary_File, ' ');
         Put (Diary_File, Appt.Time.Hour, Width=>1);
         Put (Diary_File, ' ');
         Put (Diary_File, Appt.Time.Minute, Width=>1);
         Put (Diary_File, ' ');
         Put (Diary_File, Appt.Details (1..Appt.Length));
```

```
        New_Line (Diary_File);
      end;
    end loop;
    Close (Diary_File);
  exception
    when Use_Error =>
      Put_Line ("Couldn't create diary file!");
  end Save_Appointments;
```

Notice how I've used a local block inside the loop so that I can rename the current appointment to avoid having to use long-winded names like Diary.Appts(I).Date.Day.

One of the simplest mistakes to make is to write:

```
Put (' ');                    -- display space on screen
```

instead of:

```
Put (Diary_File, ' ');   -- write space to diary file
```

The effects of this sort of mistake can be easy to overlook if you're not being sufficiently careful. The program will compile and it will even appear to work. The spaces will be displayed invisibly on the screen instead of in the file, and if it weren't for the 'Width=>1' parameter in the calls to Put you might not notice it due to the number of spaces that will be output in front of each integer. The only way you'd notice it in this case is if you'd worked out exactly what the diary file should look like and discovered that the actual file didn't meet your expectations. This illustrates just how methodical you have to be if you don't want to end up with a buggy program.

Load_Diary will need to do the same as Save_Appointments but in reverse; it'll need to open the file for input, read the number of appointments, and then read in the appointment details one by one and then close the file:

```
procedure Load_Diary is
  Diary_File : File_Type;
begin
  -- open the file
  -- read Diary.Count
  for I in Diary.Appts'First .. Diary.Count loop
    -- read the I-th appointment from the file
  end loop;
  -- close the file
end Load_Diary;
```

The file can be opened using Open. The exception handling for Open will need to be slightly different to that for Create; Name_Error indicates that the file doesn't exist, and one way to handle this is to do nothing, so that the diary will just start off empty. Here's the next version, with a few more details filled in:

```
procedure Load_Diary is
  Diary_File : File_Type;
begin
  Open (Diary_File, Mode => In_File, Name => Diary_File_Name);
  -- read Diary.Count

  for I in Diary.Appts'First .. Diary.Count loop
    begin
      -- read the I-th appointment from the file
    exception
      when End_Error => exit;
    end;
  end loop;

  Close (Diary_File);

exception
  when Name_Error =>
    null;
  when Use_Error =>
    Put_Line ("Couldn't open diary file!");
end Load_Diary;
```

Reading the appointments from the file can be done using a series of calls to Get:

```
procedure Load_Diary is
  Diary_File : File_Type;
begin
  Open (Diary_File, Mode => In_File, Name => Diary_File_Name);
  Get (Diary_File, Diary.Count);
  Skip_Line (Diary_File);

  for I in Diary.Appts'First .. Diary.Count loop
    declare
      Appt : Appointment_Type renames Diary.Appts(I);
    begin
      Get (Diary_File, Appt.Date.Day);
      Get (Diary_File, Appt.Date.Month);
      Get (Diary_File, Appt.Date.Year);
      Get (Diary_File, Appt.Time.Hour);
      Get (Diary_File, Appt.Time.Minute);
```

```
        Get_Line (Diary_File, Appt.Details, Appt.Length);
      end;
    end loop;

    Close (Diary_File);

  exception
    when Name_Error =>
      null;
    when Use_Error =>
      Put_Line ("Couldn't open diary file!");
  end Load_Diary;
```

You can test this by starting the program up, adding some appointments, saving them and then quitting. You should then have a file called Diary which you can look at with a text editor to verify that it's correct. Make a copy of the file, and then start the program again. If you list the appointments you should see exactly what you had before. If you save the appointments again and quit the program, the Diary file and the copy of it that you saved earlier should be identical.

Unfortunately you'll find that they aren't identical; you should see two spaces between the time and the details in the latest version of the file but only one space in the saved copy. Of course, what's happened is that Load_Diary has read the separating space as the first character of Details, so it will need modifying to read and ignore the space:

```
procedure Load_Diary is
  Diary_File : File_Type;
begin
  Open (Diary_File, Mode => In_File, Name => Diary_File_Name);
  Get (Diary_File, Diary.Count);
  Skip_Line (Diary_File);

  for I in Diary.Appts'First .. Diary.Count loop
    declare
      Appt   : Appointment_Type renames Diary.Appts(I);
      Space : Character;                          -- bug fix
    begin
      Get (Diary_File, Appt.Date.Day);
      Get (Diary_File, Appt.Date.Month);
      Get (Diary_File, Appt.Date.Year);
      Get (Diary_File, Appt.Time.Hour);
      Get (Diary_File, Appt.Time.Minute);
      Get (Diary_File, Space);                    -- bug fix
      Get_Line (Diary_File, Appt.Details, Appt.Length);
    end;
```

```
   end loop;

   Close (Diary_File);

exception
   when Name_Error =>
      null;
   when Use_Error =>
      Put_Line ("Couldn't open diary file!");
end Load_Diary;
```

8.9 Assessing the program

So, at the end of all this you've got a working appointments diary. It's not quite finished yet; there are still some details to attend to. Add_Appointment needs quite a bit more work, even if you've managed to fix all the bugs in the current version; appointments aren't added in order yet, and as a result it's possible to make double bookings. Dates aren't validated either. Some more testing will be needed (e.g. what will happen if you've already got a file called Diary which doesn't hold appointments produced by this program the first time you run it?).

One of the advantages of top-down design is that it allows programs to be developed on a piecemeal basis, a bit at a time. That way you don't end up biting off more than you can chew. You can use stubs or incomplete versions to get yourself to a point where you can start testing; after your tests have been passed satisfactorily, you can incrementally implement a bit more, do a bit more testing, and so on until you're finished (phew!). Testing a program thoroughly is an essential part of development; you've got to try and think of everything that can go wrong and what to do about it. You can help track down bugs by adding extra code to display debugging information or commenting out code as necessary, or by using a debugger. If all else fails, I find that just explaining the problem to anyone who's prepared to listen usually helps. If they understand Ada, they might spot something you've overlooked; if they don't, you might find that you spot the problem as you're trying to explain what's happening (or at least come up with a theory as to what the problem is). Well, it works for me anyway!

Exhaustive testing is usually out of the question, so you have to come up with a representative set of test data and a plan of how you're going to carry out your testing. Plan your development steps in advance and do them in an order which will help you to test things. Make sure that valid data is handled correctly; look particularly closely at boundary conditions since these are usually where bugs can creep in. Make sure invalid data is detected and dealt with properly. Make sure you know what you expect the program to do, and check that it does *exactly* what you expect. Get used to looking at your code with a critical eye, and try to think of things that can go wrong as you're writing it (such as the user typing an end-of-file character unexpectedly). And when you think you've finished and there's no more to be done, spend a bit more time playing around with the program doing a mixture of sensible and silly things, because there might *still* be some combination of circumstances you've overlooked.

Exercises

8.1   It would be a good idea to ask the user whether or not to save any changes made to the diary before quitting. This is only necessary if any appointments have been added or deleted since the last time the diary was saved. Make the necessary modifications to the program.

8.2   Change the way that appointments are listed so that they are displayed a screenful at a time (or just under a screenful to allow room for prompts etc.) on the system that you're using. Provide the ability to go either forwards or backwards a screen or half a screen at a time.

8.3   Add a 'Find' command to display all appointments containing a specified string in the Details component. Ignore distinctions between upper and lower case when searching for the string.

8.4   Write a program which will read the diary file and display all appointments for the next three working days (where Saturday and Sunday do not count as working days), so that if you ran this program on a Thursday it would show you all appointments from that day until the following Monday inclusive, since the three working days involved are Thursday, Friday and Monday.

Part Two

Abstract data types

This part moves the focus from the mechanics of processing data in small examples to the representation of the data being processed. The previous part showed how Ada allows you to define new data types, but it often appears easier to use built-in types provided by the language. In larger-scale applications where maintenance is the dominant cost factor this turns out to be a false economy due to the increased testing and debugging costs incurred after every change. The data types are not faithful representations of the types of object being modelled in the real world, and so it is possible to perform unrealistic actions on them. The more a program is changed, the more likelihood there is of this happening.

Design approaches like stepwise refinement only attack the problem of processing data. Choosing a sensible organisation for the data to make it easier to process is also essential. Top-down design of programs can only work if you have a firm idea of the architecture of the bottom layer that you are trying to reach. It also takes no account of the seismic changes that will result if the nature of this bottom layer changes. This part introduces abstract data types as a way of providing a stable bottom layer towards which a program design can aim, and it shows how a design using abstract data types can be used to contain the impact that maintenance changes in one part of the design will have on other parts.

CHAPTER 9

Private types

What is essential is invisible to the eye.
— Antoine de Saint-Exupéry, *The Little Prince*

9.1 The need for abstraction

The program developed in the previous chapter works, but it's a very poor program all the same. It was designed oh-so-carefully using top-down design techniques; it was incrementally debugged, with each piece being tested and verified before going on to the next stage; it was carefully modularised using a set of procedures which were then encapsulated in a package. But even after all this, it's a terrible program.

So why do I say this? What's the matter with it? After applying all these design techniques, shouldn't we expect the result to be a shining example of program design? The unfortunate truth is that top-down design is a technique with some severe limitations. It doesn't necessarily take into account the need for reusability, portability or maintainability. It assists in producing maintainable programs in so far as you can replace low-level modules with improved versions, but not when the maintenance needs affect the outer levels of the design. It concentrates on the processing of the data and doesn't pay enough attention to the data itself.

Consider the following maintenance scenarios:

- You want to be able to look at several independent diaries at the same time. In order to schedule a meeting, you might want to be able to open the diaries of those involved and find a common free slot when you can hold your meeting and then book that slot in your own diary, if not in all of them. You might also want to be able to copy appointments from one diary into another.
- You want to move from a text-based environment to a graphical user interface. Commands to add or delete appointments might be accessed via a pull-down menu. Appointment details might be entered by filling in a form, and dates might be selected by pointing at a picture of a calendar using a mouse.
- You want to integrate your diary into another application: for example, an electronic mail system that will automatically send out reminders of important meetings to those involved or will add appointments to your diary which are embedded in incoming mail messages.

147

- You want to change the way dates are represented to make it easier to do arithmetic on dates. Rather than storing a date as a day, a month and a year you want to represent it by the number of days since January 1st 1901 (a **Julian date**).

In all of these cases you'll end up more or less rewriting the entire program. You need to do more than just fiddle about with low-level details in these situations. In the first case you suffer from the fact that there is a single diary buried in the package. You'll need to move the declaration into the package specification where it is visible to the rest of the program; you'll need to rejig the main program to provide extra commands for opening and closing and selecting different diaries; and you'll have to pass the selected diary as a parameter to each of the procedures in the package. There won't be any part of the program which escapes the effects of these changes. In the second case the input/output in the main program (displaying the menu and getting the user's response) will need changing, but so will the input/output in the package procedures (getting the details of a new appointment, selecting the appointment to be deleted, and so on). In the third case the package won't be reusable in the context of an electronic mail program since it does input and output to the screen and can't accept an appointment from another source. You'd have to add the ability to pass appointments around as parameters to the procedures in the package, which implies a complete rewrite. In the final case all the places where the components of dates are accessed will need rewriting since those components will no longer exist.

In other words, the program is inflexible in its present state. What top-down design as practised in the previous chapter gives you is a workable but brittle program. It will do exactly what you originally wanted, but what it won't necessarily do is adapt easily to changing requirements. None of these maintenance scenarios could have been anticipated at the time of the original development, but maintenance requirements are always going to be unpredictable unless you have an extremely high-class crystal ball in your desk drawer.

However, all is not lost. If you bear in mind the need for maintenance and reuse as you design, you can come up with designs that are a lot less naïve than the one in the previous chapter. The maintenance problems arise largely from the fact that the design concentrated on defining the processing required, and the design of the data structures involved was treated as a subsidiary problem of lesser importance. What is needed is a more data-centred approach. The representation of dates, appointments and so on used record types as containers for a collection of simpler types. Record types have a very limited repertoire of standard operations (assignment and equality testing only) unlike scalar types like Integer which have a rich set of predefined operations. The program just used standard operations to manipulate the record components rather than defining a set of procedures and functions to provide a range of operations for the record types themselves. What is really needed is a set of operations on appointments, dates and so on so that these types can be dealt with as entities in their own right rather than as containers for simpler types. We want to have a set of operations available for dates rather than having to deal with the day, month and year components of dates.

How will this help? Consider the final maintenance scenario described above. The program in its present form relies heavily on the internal representation of dates. If

Date_Type were defined in a package of its own which provided a function Day which returned the value of the day component, it would be a relatively simple matter to change the way dates are represented as long as the program using the package always used the function to access the day component rather than accessing it directly. Functions like Day would need rewriting to accommodate the new representation, but this would just be a change to the package body. Programs using the package would not need to be changed. And, as long the package provided a sufficiently rich set of operations on dates, it would be usable in any program which needed to operate on dates. What we would end up with is an **abstract data type** (ADT) whose operations would allow us to manipulate dates without worrying about the internal representation of the type. An abstract data type should be like a 'black box' whose internal workings are invisible to the user. If you think about it, this is what happens with types like Integer. We don't care how Integers are represented inside the computer; all we care about is that we can do addition and subtraction and so on. What we want to do is to elevate Dates to the point that they are indistinguishable from any of the 'built-in' data types like Integer. We should just be able to use them as if they too were 'built in' to the language.

9.2 Package design

Packages are the key to reuse in Ada; they allow you to take a **client–server** approach to program design. A package acts as a **server** which provides a set of services to its **clients** (programs or other packages). Packages are deliberately split into a specification part and a body part; this is in the interests of abstraction as described above. The specification tells you what services the package provides and the body provides the implementation of those services. Only the specification is accessible to clients of the package so that the implementation details are hidden from the clients. The specification can be viewed as a contract with the package clients; it tells the clients what services the package will provide, but not how it will provide them; it is the interface between the contents of the package and its clients. The more general the range of services provided, the more chance that the package will be able to be used and reused in a variety of different situations. This also implies that the package shouldn't assume anything about the properties of its clients, since this will reduce the range of possible clients to those that conform to the package's expectations.

Changes to the package body will not involve any changes to the clients, since the package body is not part of the package's contractual requirements (i.e. it isn't visible to the package's clients). Changes to the specification will involve changes to the clients as well, and since a package may be used by many different programs this can be expensive. Careful design is therefore required to reduce the risk that the package specification might need changing. Here are some important principles that should guide you when you design packages (which I deliberately ignored in the previous chapter!):

- *Avoid revealing implementation details.* The more information you can hide about implementation details, the more freedom you will have to make changes to them later. Anything visible in the package specification will be one of the contractual obligations for the package, so information should only be provided in the specification if you're willing to be tied down to the obligation that results. Programs will be written which rely on the things you reveal in the package specification, so any changes to the visible specification might make it necessary to rewrite a lot of client code with consequential costs in testing and debugging.

- *Avoid trying to handle errors in the package.* Undoubtedly there will be situations where error checks should be made, but don't confuse error detection and error handling. Although your package may be able to detect errors, this doesn't mean it should try to handle them. That's what exceptions are for; errors can be detected in one place and handled in another. In most cases, if you detect an error in a package you should just raise an exception and let the client decide how best to handle it. If you don't do this your package loses a lot of generality. Displaying an error message may seem like a good idea, but what happens if your package might be used in the control system for a washing machine with nowhere to display the message?

- *Avoid doing input/output in the package.* If your package does its own input and output it is tying itself down to a particular way of interacting with the user, and so it's making assumptions about the clients that it will be used with. It may work fine when it's being used in a program with a text-based user interface, but if the package displays prompts and reads input from the user this will prevent it from being used with a graphical interface where data is entered via dialog boxes which might involve choosing an option from a list rather than typing it in. Let the client program deal with user interface issues; the program should read the data in an appropriate fashion and pass it as parameters to procedures in the package. Likewise the program should be responsible for displaying any results in the appropriate form.

Hiding the data structure in the diary avoided revealing its implementation details, so this is apparently in accordance with the first of these three principles. However, it's a bad idea as you end up with a single data structure which is referenced from many different places and it becomes more and more difficult to untangle the program from the single instance of the data structure as the program grows. If at some point you want more than one instance of the data structure (as in the first maintenance scenario above) you're in real trouble. Here's one more design principle to round things off:

- *Avoid using global data structures.* By 'global' I mean something which is widely accessible, something which can be referred to directly from many places within a program. Direct access by subprograms produces an undesirable coupling between the subprograms and the data structure. The subprograms end up being dependent on the data structure so that even a simple change of name causes serious repercussions throughout the program. What you should almost always have is a data type rather than a single global instance of a type which can be accessed directly by subprograms. By declaring a data type, you can create as many instances of the type as you need. The data type (only its name, not its internal details!) should be widely visible, but individual instances of it should not. Instances should be passed as parameters to the subprograms that manipulate them This breaks the coupling between the subprogram and any particular object; the subprogram will be able to operate on *any* instance of the type that it is given.

Rather than saying to yourself 'I am writing a program to manage an electronic diary' you should say 'I am developing an electronic diary data type'; the program is then almost an afterthought, a particular client of the package that contains the data type and the operations it supports. Writing the program may help to identify the operations that a diary should support, but the diary should be the focus of attention rather than the program that uses it. That way there won't be any problems if the program then needs to be changed to handle multiple diaries.

In other words, a package should in most cases be a repository for one or more data types and a set of *client-neutral* operations on those data types. By 'client-neutral' I mean that the operations shouldn't assume anything about the clients which might use them, so they shouldn't try to handle errors or do input/output, both of which are very client-specific activities. Packages should just provide services to clients that need them without assuming any knowledge about who those clients might be. Occam's razor should be applied to package design: a package should provide those operations that are absolutely necessary but nothing more than is absolutely necessary.

9.3 Private types

Chapter 4 showed a small package called JE.Dates which was further revised in chapter 6. Here is the revised package specification from chapter 6, unchanged except for the function names:

```
package JE.Dates is
   subtype Day_Type     is Integer range 1..31;
   type     Month_Type  is (Jan, Feb, Mar, Apr, May, Jun,
                            Jul, Aug, Sep, Oct, Nov, Dec);
   subtype Year_Type    is Integer range 1901..2099;
   type    Weekday_Type is (Sun, Mon, Tue, Wed, Thu, Fri, Sat);
   type Date_Type is
     record
        Day   : Day_Type;
        Month : Month_Type;
        Year  : Year_Type;
     end record;
   function Weekday (Date : Date_Type) return Weekday_Type;
   function Valid   (Date : Date_Type) return Boolean;
end JE.Dates;
```

As discussed above, there is a fatal flaw in the package design as it stands. Clients which use the package just access the internal representation of Date_Type in order to extract the components of a date. Clients which directly access the components will need rewriting if the details of the data structure need to be changed at a later date. What is needed is a way of preventing direct access to the components of Date_Type. To solve this problem, Ada allows us to define **private types**.

A private type is one whose name is given in a package specification but whose internal workings are kept private. Only the package body is allowed to know about the internal representation, so that the body can use this information to implement the operations declared in the package specification. The only standard operations you can perform on values of a private type are assignment (':=') and testing for equality ('=' and '/='). Here's how you declare a private type in a package specification:

```
type Date_Type is private;
```

This lets you declare as many variables of type Date_Type as you like, but (except in the package body) the only things you can do with those variables is to assign them to each other using ':=', compare them for equality and inequality using '=' and '/=', and use the operations declared in the package specification to manipulate them.

At some point, of course, you *do* have to reveal the internal workings of the type. The package body has to know how the type is implemented and the compiler has to know how much space to allocate in memory when a variable of that type is declared. This is done by placing a section headed 'private' at the end of the package specification which divides it into two parts: a **visible part** which is visible to users of the package and a **private part** which is only accessible from within the package body.

```
package JE.Dates is
   -- Visible part of package
   subtype Day_Type    is Integer range 1..31;
   type    Month_Type  is (Jan, Feb, Mar, Apr, May, Jun,
                           Jul, Aug, Sep, Oct, Nov, Dec);
   subtype Year_Type   is Integer range 1901..2099;
   type    Weekday_Type is (Sun, Mon, Tue, Wed, Thu, Fri, Sat);
   type    Date_Type   is private;

   function Weekday (Date : Date_Type) return Weekday_Type;
   function Valid   (Date : Date_Type) return Boolean;

private                -- visible part ends here
   -- Private part of package
   type Date_Type is
     record
       Day   : Day_Type;
       Month : Month_Type;
```

```
        Year   : Year_Type;
    end record;
end JE.Dates;
```

It may seem strange to put the private information in the package specification rather than in the body, but the reason for this is that the compiler needs to know how much space to allocate when compiling programs that use the package (since the compiler only looks at the package specification in these situations). You may be able to look at the private information in the file containing the package specification but you aren't allowed to make any use of it in your programs. The compiler will refuse to let programs which use this package refer to anything defined in the package's private part. The only place where you can make use of the information in the private part of a package is in the package body, or in the bodies of any child packages (which are effectively treated as extensions to the parent package).

The great advantage of using private types is that it prevents anyone accessing the data structures directly in order to bypass the operations that your package provides. It also ensures that if you change the information in the private part during maintenance you can guarantee that only the package body (and the bodies of any of its child packages which use the private information) will need changing to match, since the package body is the only place where the private part is accessible. Package clients will need to be recompiled, but as long as there haven't been any changes to the visible part of the package specification (or the behaviour it implies) you can guarantee that no changes to the client code will be needed.

Of course, it is now impossible for clients of the package to do anything with dates except assign them to each other, test them for equality, test that they are valid and find out what day of the week they fall on. Since there's no access to the components of a date it's impossible to construct a date with a particular value or find out what day, month or year it is. What we need to do is to provide some extra functions to give clients these capabilities without revealing anything more about the internal structure of Date_Type. First we need a set of **accessor** functions to access the components of a date:

```
function Day   (Date : Date_Type) return Day_Type;
function Month (Date : Date_Type) return Month_Type;
function Year  (Date : Date_Type) return Year_Type;
```

We also need a **constructor** function to construct a date from its components:

```
function Date (Day   : Day_Type;
               Month : Month_Type;
               Year  : Year_Type) return Date_Type;
```

The constructor function is the only way to create dates, so we don't need to worry about possibilities like the month of a date being changed independently of the rest of it. This makes using dates much safer. In fact, since we can check dates for validity when they are first created by the constructor, the only place that a validity check is needed is inside the function Date itself, which means that Valid doesn't need to be made visible to clients. Date can just raise an exception if its parameters don't represent a valid date, so we need an exception declaration in the visible part of the package:

```
Date_Error : exception;    -- can be raised by Date
```

This is much more like a built-in type like Integer which doesn't rely on users calling a Valid function to check that Integer values are correct; instead, automatic error checking is done behind the scenes and an exception is raised whenever an error is detected. By adopting the same approach for Date_Type we start to make it look much more like a built-in type.

After these changes, the package specification so far looks like this:

```
package JE.Dates is

    -- Visible part of package
    subtype Day_Type    is Integer range 1..31;
    type    Month_Type  is (Jan, Feb, Mar, Apr, May, Jun,
                            Jul, Aug, Sep, Oct, Nov, Dec);
    subtype Year_Type   is Integer range 1901..2099;
    type    Weekday_Type is (Sun, Mon, Tue, Wed, Thu, Fri, Sat);

    type    Date_Type   is private;

    -- Accessor functions
    function Day     (Date : Date_Type) return Day_Type;
    function Month   (Date : Date_Type) return Month_Type;
    function Year    (Date : Date_Type) return Year_Type;
    function Weekday (Date : Date_Type) return Weekday_Type;

    -- Constructor function
    function Date    (Day   : Day_Type;
                      Month : Month_Type;
                      Year  : Year_Type) return Date_Type;

    -- Exception for error reporting
    Date_Error : exception;    -- can be raised by Date

private                  -- visible part ends here
    -- Private part of package
    type Date_Type is
      record
        Day    : Day_Type;
```

```
        Month : Month_Type;
        Year  : Year_Type;
      end record;
  end JE.Dates;
```

Notice that Weekday is in fact just another accessor function, although it has to do a bit more work than the other ones.

You can also define a child package or child subprogram to be **private**, in which case the entire package is private:

```
private package JE.Implementation_Details is
  ...
end JE.Implementation_Details;
```

The only place a private child can be accessed is from the body of its parent package or from the body of another child of the parent package. You can't access it from the specification of a non-private package at all. You can think of a private child as an extension of the private part of the parent package; it's completely inaccessible to external clients. Private children can be useful for providing operations which will be shared by the implementation of different children of a parent package.

9.4   Full and partial views

What a private type declaration does is to give you two separate **views** of the same type, according to where you are standing. The visible part of the package gives you a **partial view** of the type by saying it's private; this means that clients of the package see a type for which assignment and equality tests are allowed, but no more. The private part of the package provides the **full view** of the type; this provides more information than the partial view but can only be seen from the private part of the package specification or the package body. Child packages are treated as extensions of the parent package, so the full view of a type is also visible from the private part of a child package specification or from a child package body (or from anywhere within a private child).

The basic rule in Ada is that *the partial view should never provide more capabilities than the full view allows*. Limited types (see chapter 6) provide an excellent illustration of this. A type which is declared as **limited** in the private part of the package (the full view) must be declared **limited private** in the visible part (the partial view):

```
package Some_Package is
   type Some_Type is limited private;
   ...
private
   type Some_Type is limited record ... end record;
end Some_Package;
```

If you were allowed to declare Some_Type as **private** in the visible part of this package, this would mean that assignment would not be allowed if you had access to the full view but would be allowed if you only had access to the partial view, since non-limited private types allow assignment. However, you can declare a limited private type in the partial view which is non-limited in the full view, since the declaration in the visible part only restricts access in the partial view:

```
package Some_Package is
   type Some_Type is limited private;  -- assignment not allowed
   ...
private
   type Some_Type is record ... end record;
                                    -- assignment allowed
end Some_Package;
```

Package clients which only have access to the partial view cannot perform assignment or equality testing since they see Some_Type as a limited type, but anywhere which has access to the full view is allowed to do these things.

The idea of different parts of a program having different views of the same type is an important principle which makes the type restrictions associated with private types much easier to understand; you will meet it again in connection with generic type parameters and tagged types.

9.5 Deferred constants

Sometimes you might want to make a constant of a private type available to the user. For example, you might want to provide a constant representing an invalid date so that users of the date package can use this as an 'unknown date' value. The package doesn't provide any way to construct an invalid date; any attempt to do so will just raise a Date_Error exception. The only way it can be done is to use a knowledge of the internal structure of a date. If you want the value to be available to clients of the package (who can't see the internal structure of Date_Type) you have to define a constant in the visible part whose full definition is **deferred** to the private part where the full view of the type is available:

```
package JE.Dates is
   type Date_Type is private;
   Invalid_Date : constant Date_Type;        -- deferred constant
   ...
private
   type Date_Type is
      record
         Day   : Day_Type;
         Month : Month_Type;
```

```
      Year  : Year_Type;
   end record;

   Invalid_Date : constant Date_Type := (31,Feb,1901);
                                       -- full declaration
end JE.Dates;
```

The deferred declaration of Invalid_Date tells clients that there is a constant called Invalid_Date and that it's a Date_Type, but it does this without revealing anything about the internal structure of Date_Type. The full declaration of Invalid_Date is given in the private part of the package after the full declaration of Date_Type has been given. This is the only situation in Ada where you are allowed to omit the value of a constant in a constant declaration, and the omission can only be a temporary one; the full declaration must be given in the private part of the package.

9.6 The package body

Now let's look at the body for JE.Dates. Here's an outline generated directly from the specification:

```
package body JE.Dates is
   function Day      (Date : Date_Type) return Day_Type
                         is ... end Day;
   function Month    (Date : Date_Type) return Month_Type
                         is ... end Month;
   function Year     (Date : Date_Type) return Year_Type
                         is ... end Year;
   function Weekday  (Date : Date_Type) return Weekday_Type
                         is ... end Weekday;

   function Date     (Day   : Day_Type;
                      Month : Month_Type;
                      Year  : Year_Type) return Date_Type
                         is ... end Date;
end JE.Dates;
```

The function Valid will still be needed in the package body even if it isn't required in the specification since Date will need to use it to check if a date is valid. Valid can be made into a procedure which I'll call Validate; all it needs to do is to raise a Date_Error if its parameters don't form a valid date. It can be made much simpler than the Valid function from chapter 4 thanks to the fact that Day_Type, Month_Type and Year_Type ensure that the parameters to Date are at least in range, so the only thing it needs to check is that the value of Day isn't higher than the maximum allowed by Month and Year. It can also be amended to take a Date_Type parameter instead of three separate parameters. Here is the definition of Validate, which should be inserted at the start of the package body above:

```
procedure Validate (Date : in Date_Type) is
begin
  case Date.Month is
    when Apr | Jun | Sep | Nov =>
      if Date.Day > 30 then
        raise Date_Error;
      end if;

    when Feb =>
      if (Date.Year mod 4 = 0 and Date.Day > 29)
      or (Date.Year mod 4 /= 0 and Date.Day > 28) then
        raise Date_Error;
      end if;

    when others =>
      null;
  end case;
end Validate;
```

Date is now quite simple:

```
function Date (Day   : Day_Type;
               Month : Month_Type;
               Year  : Year_Type) return Date_Type is
  D : Date_Type := (Day, Month, Year);
begin
  Validate (D);
  return D;
end Date;
```

Most of the accessor functions are even simpler:

```
function Day (Date : Date_Type) return Day_Type is
begin
  return Date.Day;
end Day;

function Month (Date : Date_Type) return Month_Type is
begin
  return Date.Month;
end Month;
```

```
function Year (Date : Date_Type) return Year_Type is
begin
  return Date.Year;
end Year;
```

Weekday uses Zeller's Congruence as described in chapter 4:

```
function Weekday (Date : Date_Type) return Weekday_Type is
  D : Integer := Date.Day;
  M : Integer := Month_Type'Pos(Date.Month) + 1;
  Y : Integer := Date.Year;
  C : Integer;
begin
  if M < 3 then
    Y := Y - 1;
    M := M + 10;
  else
    M := M - 2;
  end if;

  C := Y / 100;     -- first two digits of Year
  Y := Y mod 100;   -- last two digits of Year

  return Weekday_Type'Val(((26*M - 2)/10 + D + Y + Y/4 +
                         C/4 - 2*C) mod 7);
end Weekday;
```

This just extracts the components of Date into a set of Integers, evaluates Zeller's Congruence and then uses Weekday_Type'Val to convert the result (0 to 6) into the corresponding Weekday_Type value. Thanks to the order in which the values of Weekday_Type were declared this will automatically give the correct result (0 = Sun, 1 = Mon and so on). The Month component is converted using Month_Type'Pos; this gives a value between 0 and 11 so the result is adjusted to the range 1 to 12 by adding 1 to it.

9.7 Overloaded operators

There are lots of other operations on dates we could add to round off this package. We could add a set of functions for doing date arithmetic: adding a number of days to a date to get a new date, subtracting a number of days from a date, subtracting two dates to find out the number of days between them, comparing dates to see which is the larger, and so on and so forth. Input/output operations (Get and Put) are another possibility, but these are worth avoiding for at least two reasons: firstly, they would only be of any use to a program with a text-mode interface, and secondly even in text-mode programs they would restrict the formats which could be used for entering dates and displaying them. Since the conventions used for representing dates vary widely from one country to another, this would make any program which actually used the Get and Put procedures provided by a date handling package unusable in any other country.

As mentioned earlier, Occam's razor should be used whenever you start to think of clever new things to put into a package. The operations mentioned above all require access to the private part of the package; they *could* be implemented outside the package using the accessor functions Day and Month and Year, but if the representation of Date_Type were ever changed to a Julian date it would be far easier to add a number of days to a Julian date directly instead of laboriously converting a Julian date into a day, month and year and then performing a much more complex process of addition. Similar arguments apply to comparison functions; Julian dates are easier to compare than dates composed of a day, a month and a year. This means that it is well worth providing these as part of the package itself. However, what about an operation to find when the next Monday (or any other day) after a given date will be? This isn't worth putting in a package like this: firstly, it's a very specialised operation that few programs will need, and secondly it can be implemented by adding 1 to a date up to a maximum of seven times (or by finding out what day of the week it is, calculating how many days it is from that day to the following Monday and then adding that number of days to the date). Putting this rarely used and relatively simple function into the package simply increases the bulk of the package to little effect. In general, operations like this are *not* worth building in as the costs outweigh the benefits. If they *do* turn out to be useful you can always define them in a child package to avoid bulking out the parent package.

Addition and subtraction could be done with functions declared like this:

```
function Add (Date : Date_Type; Days : Integer)
                                        return Date_Type;
function Sub (Date : Date_Type; Days : Integer)
                                        return Date_Type;
function Sub (First, Second : Date_Type) return Integer;
```

Thus to find out how many days there are from Now until Christmas you could use Sub (Christmas,Now) and to find out what the date is a week from Now you could use Add (Now,7).

⇒   *Write the bodies for these functions. Note that the first version of Sub can be defined in terms of Add since Sub(Now,N) is equivalent to Add(Now,–N).*

Note that the name Sub is **overloaded** in the two declarations above. You can use the same name for different subprograms provided that the compiler can work out which one you're referring to. Procedures and functions can always be distinguished since procedure calls are statements whereas function calls occur in expressions. You can also tell subprograms apart if they have different numbers of parameters or different parameter types (as with the two versions of Sub above). Functions can be distinguished by their return types, so you can have several functions with the same name and identical parameter types provided that they return different types of result.

Function calls are a very awkward notation compared to the arithmetic operations for standard types such as integers; if you were dealing with Integers instead of Date_Types you would write the above function calls as Now+7 and Christmas–Now respectively. Using function calls is far less readable than using the equivalent operators and adds to the number of things you have to remember about the data types you're dealing with. Overloading function names (as is done with Sub above) can reduce the burden a little, but it is still awkward and makes user-defined types visibly different from other types.

In fact, operators in Ada are just functions with special names. Writing 2 + 2 is actually equivalent to writing "+"(2,2). The name of the function corresponding to an operator is just the name of the operator enclosed in double quotes. Ada allows you to write functions which overload existing operators; all you have to do is to write a function whose name is the name of the operator enclosed in double quotes. The function must also have the correct number of parameters, which in the case of "<" is two; in the case of the "abs" or "not" operators you would only have one parameter, and in the case of "+" or "–" you can define functions with one parameter (the unary version of the operator) or two parameters (the binary version of the operator) or both. Also, you aren't allowed to provide default values for the parameters. **Operator overloading** means that instead of declaring functions called Add and Sub like the ones above, you can declare operators like this:

```
function "+" (Left : Date_Type; Right : Integer)
                                      return Date_Type;
function "-" (Left : Date_Type; Right : Integer)
                                      return Date_Type;
function "-" (Left, Right : Date_Type)    return Integer;
```

Overloading "+" and "–" like this means that it *is* now possible to write expressions like Now+7 or Christmas–Now.

All the operators in Ada can be overloaded except for **in**, **not in**, **and then** and **or else** which are not normal operators. There are also restrictions on overloading the inequality operator "/=" which I'll explain in a moment. The names of the operators that you can overload are therefore as follows:

+	–	*	/	**	rem	mod	abs
=	/=	<	>	<=	>=		
not	and	or	xor	&			

You cannot invent your own operators (e.g. you cannot invent a percentage operator called "%"); you are also unable to alter the precedence of operators, so that "*" will always be applied before "+". In the case of "=", if it produces a Boolean result then "/=" is automatically defined to produce the opposite result and you are not allowed to redefine "/=" yourself. You can only redefine "/=" if it produces a result of some other type than Boolean; for example, if you have a 'fuzzy logic' type like this:

```
type Fuzzy is (No, Maybe, Yes);
```

then you can define "=" to compare two values and return a Fuzzy result, but you won't automatically get a corresponding version of "/=". You'll have to define "/=" yourself in this case.

There is nothing special or magical about overloading operators; you can define a function named after an operator whenever you like. It doesn't have to be in a package specification, but this is normally where you want to do it, in connection with a type which is declared in the same package. The only time you can't use a name like "+" for a function is if you want to compile it as a free-standing library unit; overloaded operators must be enclosed within library units (packages or subprograms) which have normal alphanumeric names.

We can also overload "<", ">", "<=" and ">=" to compare pairs of dates:

```
function "<"  (Left, Right : Date_Type) return Boolean;
function ">"  (Left, Right : Date_Type) return Boolean;
function "<=" (Left, Right : Date_Type) return Boolean;
function ">=" (Left, Right : Date_Type) return Boolean;
```

Notice that it isn't necessary to overload "=" and "/="; private types already have these operators predefined and they will give the expected result. Given the definition of "<" above, we can now write things like this:

```
if Now < Date(25,Dec,1995) then ...
```

Here's how "<" for dates could be implemented:

```
function "<" (Left, Right : Date_Type) return Boolean is
begin
   if Left.Year /= Right.Year then
     return Left.Year < Right.Year;
   elsif Left.Month /= Right.Month then
     return Left.Month < Right.Month;
   else
     return Left.Day < Right.Day;
   end if;
end "<";
```

The version of "<" above is defined in terms of the versions of "<" predefined for Day_Type, Month_Type and Year_Type. There is no problem with this; the compiler always knows which version of "<" you are referring to by the types of the operands you use it with. This is exactly the same as having a number of procedures called Put with different types of parameters; the operands on either side of an operator are its parameters, and the compiler uses these to figure out what's happening in just the same way as it uses the type of parameter supplied for Put to figure out which version of Put you're talking about.

Here's how the other comparison operators can be implemented:

```
function ">"  (Left, Right : Date_Type) return Boolean is
begin
   return Right < Left;
end ">";

function "<=" (Left, Right : Date_Type) return Boolean is
begin
   return not (Left > Right);
end "<=";

function ">=" (Left, Right : Date_Type) return Boolean is
begin
   return not (Left < Right);
end ">=";
```

Since A>B means the same as B<A, we can define the ">" operator using the "<" operator defined above; similarly A<=B is True if A>B is False and A>=B is True if A<B is False. This makes the definitions nice and easy to write, and if the representation of Date_Type ever changes you'll only ever need to change the definition of "<" in order to change all of them.

9.8 'Use type' clauses

One of the problems with defining your own operators is that if you don't provide a **use** clause for the package that they're in, you can't use them in the normal way; operator names like "+" won't be accessible and you'll have to use fully qualified names like JE.Dates."+" instead. This means that in the absence of a **use** clause for JE.Dates you'd have to write this instead of 'Tomorrow := Weekday (Today + 1)':

```
Tomorrow := JE.Dates.Weekday (JE.Dates."+" (Today, 1));
```

This is seriously ugly, and in the absence of any other solution it would more or less force you to write **use** clauses for any packages declaring data types with overloaded operators. One solution would be to use renaming declarations for the operators you needed to use, like this:

```
function "+" (Left  : JE.Dates.Date_Type;
              Right : Integer) return JE.Dates.Date_Type
      renames JE.Dates."+";
```

In situations where there are lots of different operators, this is still extremely awkward. Fortunately there's a variant of the **use** clause designed to help in exactly this situation:

```
use type JE.Dates.Date_Type;
```

This gives you access to the operators of the specified type from the specified package (Date_Type from JE.Dates in this case) but not anything else, so with a **use type** clause you'd be able to write this:

```
Tomorrow := JE.Dates.Weekday (Today + 1);
```

Note that although operator names like "+" are directly accessible thanks to the **use type** clause, other names like Weekday are still not accessible and must still be fully qualified with the package name.

9.9 A word of caution

It is only ever a good idea to overload operators when the meaning will be absolutely obvious to anyone reading a program which uses them. There is nothing to prevent you from doing silly things like defining "+" to do subtraction or multiplication (or anything else for that matter); however, common sense should tell you never to use "+" as the name of a function which is not doing something addition-like. It is possible to be too cute for your own good; here is an example which shows how "−" can be redefined as a way of constructing dates:

```
subtype Day_Type   is Integer range 1..31;
type    Month_Type is (Jan, Feb, Mar, Apr,
                       May, Jun, Jul, Aug,
                       Sep, Oct, Nov, Dec);
subtype Year_Type  is Integer range 1901..2099;

type Date_Type is
  record
    Day   : Day_Type;
    Month : Month_Type;
    Year  : Year_Type;
  end record;

type Day_And_Month is
  record
    Day   : Day_Type;
    Month : Month_Type;
  end record;
```

```
function "-" (Left : Day_Type; Right : Month_Type)
                                  return Day_And_Month is
   Result : Day_And_Month := (Day => Left, Month => Right);
begin
   return Result;
end "-";


function "-" (Left : Day_And_Month; Right : Year_Type)
                                        return Date_Type is
   Result : Date_Type :=
        (Day => Left.Day, Month => Left.Month, Year => Right);
begin
   return Result;
end "-";
```

This means that you can write 25–Dec–1995 to mean Christmas Day, 1995: '25–Dec' gives a Day_And_Month value consisting of a Day component set to 25 and a Month component set to Dec; this is then combined with 1995 using the second version of "–" above to give a complete date. *I do not recommend doing this!* It may look nice but it is using "–" to do an operation which has no relationship at all to subtraction and this is a possible source of confusion; in another context where Dec is an Integer, the meaning of this expression will be completely different.

9.10   The package Ada.Calendar

Of course, there's not a lot of point in defining your own date handling package when the standard package Ada.Calendar already does practically everything you want. Here's the full specification of Ada.Calendar:

```
package Ada.Calendar is
   type Time is private;

   subtype Year_Number  is Integer range 1901 .. 2099;
   subtype Month_Number is Integer range 1 .. 12;
   subtype Day_Number   is Integer range 1 .. 31;
   subtype Day_Duration is Duration range 0.0 .. 86_400.0;

   function Clock return Time;

   function Year    (Date : Time) return Year_Number;
   function Month   (Date : Time) return Month_Number;
   function Day     (Date : Time) return Day_Number;
   function Seconds (Date : Time) return Day_Duration;
```

```
procedure Split  (Date    : in Time;
                  Year    : out Year_Number;
                  Month   : out Month_Number;
                  Day     : out Day_Number;
                  Seconds : out Day_Duration);


function Time_Of (Year    : Year_Number;
                  Month   : Month_Number;
                  Day     : Day_Number;
                  Seconds : Day_Duration := 0.0)
                          return Time;

function "+" (Left : Time;     Right : Duration)
                       return Time;
function "+" (Left : Duration; Right : Time)
                       return Time;
function "-" (Left : Time;     Right : Duration)
                       return Time;
function "-" (Left : Time;     Right : Time)
                       return Duration;

function "<" (Left, Right : Time) return Boolean;
function "<="(Left, Right : Time) return Boolean;
function ">" (Left, Right : Time) return Boolean;
function ">="(Left, Right : Time) return Boolean;

Time_Error : exception;

private
    ...    -- not specified by the language
end Ada.Calendar;
```

As you can see, this defines a private type Time which represents a date and time together
with a number of supporting scalar types. It defines a set of accessor functions (Year,
Month, Day, Seconds) and a constructor function (Time_Of). There is a 'deconstructor'
procedure called Split which splits a Time into its component parts. There are also
arithmetic operators and comparison operators and an exception Time_Error for reporting
any errors that are detected by the operations in the package. The only problem with the
package is that the time of day is expressed as a number of seconds rather than as an hour,
minute and seconds, and the month is represented by an integer instead of an enumerated
type. These could be provided in a separate package, but the disadvantage of this
approach is that users will end up having to use both Ada.Calendar and the new package
together. This means that the users would have to keep track of which operations belonged

to which packages, or provide **use** clauses for both. A simple solution is to write a 'wrapper' package which provides the extra operations as well as providing the existing operations by renaming. Although the result is not very pretty, it's a much easier solution from the user's point of view since all the operations and data types are then provided in a single package, and it's attractive (if ugly!) from an implementation point of view since it minimises the amount of new code that needs to be written. Here's the result:

```
with Ada.Calendar;
package JE.Times is
   subtype Time_Type     is Ada.Calendar.Time;

   subtype Year_Type     is Ada.Calendar.Year_Number;
   type    Month_Type    is (Jan, Feb, Mar, Apr, May, Jun,
                             Jul, Aug, Sep, Oct, Nov, Dec);
   subtype Day_Type      is Ada.Calendar.Day_Number;
   subtype Hour_Type     is Integer range 0..23;
   subtype Minute_Type   is Integer range 0..59;
   subtype Second_Type   is Integer range 0..59;

   subtype Day_Duration is Ada.Calendar.Day_Duration;

   function Clock return Ada.Calendar.Time
                      renames Ada.Calendar.Clock;

   function Interval (Days    : Natural := 0;
                      Hours   : Natural := 0;
                      Minutes : Natural := 0;
                      Seconds : Natural := 0) return Duration;
   function Year    (Date : Ada.Calendar.Time) return Year_Type
                      renames Ada.Calendar.Year;
   function Month   (Date : Time_Type) return Month_Type;
   function Day     (Date : Ada.Calendar.Time) return Day_Type
                      renames Ada.Calendar.Day;
   function Hour    (Date : Time_Type) return Hour_Type;
   function Minute  (Date : Time_Type) return Minute_Type;
   function Second  (Date : Time_Type) return Second_Type;

   function Time    (Year   : Year_Type;
                     Month  : Month_Type;
                     Day    : Day_Type;
                     Hour   : Hour_Type   := 0;
                     Minute : Minute_Type := 0;
                     Second : Second_Type := 0)
                                return Time_Type;
```

```
function "+" (Left  : Ada.Calendar.Time;
              Right : Duration)    return Ada.Calendar.Time
                         renames Ada.Calendar."+";
function "+" (Left  : Duration;
              Right : Ada.Calendar.Time)
                                    return Ada.Calendar.Time
                         renames Ada.Calendar."+";

function "-" (Left  : Ada.Calendar.Time;
              Right : Duration)    return Ada.Calendar.Time
                         renames Ada.Calendar."-";
function "-" (Left  : Ada.Calendar.Time;
              Right : Ada.Calendar.Time)    return Duration
                         renames Ada.Calendar."-";

function "<" (Left, Right : Ada.Calendar.Time)
                                            return Boolean
                         renames Ada.Calendar."<";
function "<="(Left, Right : Ada.Calendar.Time)
                                            return Boolean
                         renames Ada.Calendar."<=";
function ">" (Left, Right : Ada.Calendar.Time)
                                            return Boolean
                         renames Ada.Calendar.">";
function ">="(Left, Right : Ada.Calendar.Time)
                                            return Boolean
                         renames Ada.Calendar.">=";

Time_Error : exception  renames Ada.Calendar.Time_Error;

end JE.Times;
```

Interval is a new addition to the package which constructs a Duration from a number of days, hours, minutes and seconds. The parameters all have defaults of zero, so that you can define intervals like this:

```
Interval (Days => 7)                     -- a week
Interval (Hours => 48)                   -- 2 days
Interval (Minutes => 1, Seconds => 30)   -- a minute and a half
```

Apart from the functions Interval, Month, Hour, Minute, Second and Time, everything in this package is just a renaming of the corresponding parts of Ada.Calendar (with subtyping being used for type renaming). However, the renamed subprograms have to use the original type names since the types of the parameters in a renaming declaration must be identical to those in the original subprogram. The extra functions are easy enough to implement:

```ada
package body JE.Times is
   Seconds_Per_Minute : constant := 60;
   Minutes_Per_Hour   : constant := 60;
   Hours_Per_Day      : constant := 24;
   Seconds_Per_Hour   : constant :=
                        Minutes_Per_Hour * Seconds_Per_Minute;
   Seconds_Per_Day    : constant :=
                        Hours_Per_Day * Seconds_Per_Hour;

   type Integer_Time is range 0 .. Seconds_Per_Day - 1;

   function Convert_Time (Time : Day_Duration)
                                       return Integer_Time is
      type Extended_Integer_Time is
           range Integer_Time'First .. Integer_Time'Last + 1;
      T : Extended_Integer_Time := Extended_Integer_Time(Time);
   begin
      return Integer_Time (T mod Integer_Time'Last);
   end Convert_Time;

   function Interval (Days    : Natural := 0;
                      Hours   : Natural := 0;
                      Minutes : Natural := 0;
                      Seconds : Natural := 0)
                                       return Duration is
   begin
      return Duration( Days * Seconds_Per_Day +
                       Hours * Seconds_Per_Hour +
                       Minutes * Seconds_Per_Minute +
                       Seconds );
   end Interval;

   function Month  (Date : Ada.Calendar.Time)
                                 return Month_Type is
   begin
      return Month_Type'Val (Ada.Calendar.Month(Date) - 1);
   end Month;

   function Hour (Date : Time_Type) return Hour_Type is
      S : Ada.Calendar.Day_Duration :=
                          Ada.Calendar.Seconds (Date);
```

```
begin
   return Hour_Type( Convert_Time(S) / Seconds_Per_Hour );
end Hour;

function Minute (Date : Time_Type) return Minute_Type is
   S : Ada.Calendar.Day_Duration :=
                        Ada.Calendar.Seconds (Date);
begin
   return Minute_Type( (Convert_Time(S) / Seconds_Per_Minute)
                        mod Minutes_Per_Hour );
end Minute;

function Second (Date : Time_Type) return Second_Type is
   S : Ada.Calendar.Day_Duration :=
                        Ada.Calendar.Seconds (Date);
begin
   return Second_Type( Convert_Time(S)
                        mod Seconds_Per_Minute );
end Second;

function Time (Year    : Year_Type;
               Month   : Month_Type;
               Day     : Day_Type;
               Hour    : Hour_Type    := 0;
               Minute  : Minute_Type  := 0;
               Second  : Second_Type  := 0)
                        return Time_Type is
   Seconds : Day_Duration :=
           Day_Duration( Hour * Seconds_Per_Hour +
                         Minute * Seconds_Per_Minute +
                         Second );
begin
   return Ada.Calendar.Time_Of (Year,
                        Month_Type'Pos(Month) + 1,
                        Day, Seconds);
end Time;

end JE.Times;
```

So by reusing what's already available instead of reinventing the wheel, we end up with a fully functional package in a fraction of the time it would have otherwise taken. There's a moral in this somewhere, I'm sure!

There's one nasty little trap in the package body which I've carefully avoided. Since real values are converted to integers by rounding, Day_Duration is rounded to an integer in the range 0 to 86400. We actually want a value in the range 0 to 86399, so the result of the rounding needs to be taken modulo 86400. If I'd forgotten to do this the program would crash in the last half-second before midnight, but would work perfectly the rest of the time. Bugs like this can be quite hard to detect, since very few people do their debugging at exactly half a second before midnight!

I've defined the function Convert_Time to do the conversion from Day_Duration to Integer_Time. I've had to define an internal type called Extended_Integer_Time with a range of 0..86400 rather than 0..86399 to avoid constraint errors when rounding from Day_Duration. The **mod** operator is then used to produce a result in the range 0..86399 which is then converted to an Integer_Time result. Using a modular type for Integer_Time wouldn't help since values aren't forced into range when converting to a modular type; you'd still get a constraint error in the last half-second before midnight. If Duration were a floating point type, you could get around this problem by using the 'Truncation attribute (see Appendix C) to do the conversion by truncation instead of rounding. Unfortunately there is no 'Truncation attribute for fixed point types, which appears to be an oversight on the part of the language standards committee; there is no easy way to do fixed point truncation without using an integer type with a wider range than you actually require.

Exercises

9.1 Write a package which defines an abstract data type to represent fractions like 1/2 or 2/3. A fraction consists of a numerator (an Integer) which is divided by a denominator (a Positive). Fractions should always be stored in their lowest possible form, so that 2/4 is always reduced to 1/2; you can do this by always dividing the numerator and denominator by their greatest common divisor, using Euclid's algorithm (see exercise 4.3) to find the greatest common divisor. Provide a complete set of arithmetic operations between pairs of Fractions (e.g. 1/2 + 1/3) as well as between Fractions and Integers (e.g. 1/2 + 2) and between Integers and Fractions (e.g. 2 + 1/2) as well as a function to convert a rational number to a Float. Note that the "/" operator can be overloaded for use as a constructor, dividing an Integer by an Integer to return a Fraction as its result.

9.2 Modify the playing card package from exercise 7.4 to use private types for cards and packs of cards. A card should have a Boolean component called Valid with a default value of False to indicate whether a card variable contains a valid card or not, and a pack should have a Boolean component called Initialised with a default value of False to show whether it has been initialised. All operations on a pack of cards should check the Initialised member and initialise the pack if necessary so that it contains a full set of 52 cards. Note that cards and packs should be limited private types so that it isn't possible to duplicate them by assignment. Provide a Move operation which moves a valid card into an invalid variable, leaving the destination valid and the original card invalid, so that it is impossible to create duplicate cards. It should be an error to move a card into another card which is marked as valid, since this would allow existing cards to be destroyed. You will also need functions to access the suit and value of a card.

9.3 One of the remaining shortcomings in the Ada type system is that if a numeric type is declared to represent physical values such as lengths in metres, the inherited multiplication operator will multiply two lengths to produce another length. In reality, multiplying metres by metres gives square metres. Produce a package to represent dimensioned physical quantities by recording the dimensions of mass (in kilograms), length (in metres) and time (in seconds) involved together with the magnitude of the quantity. For example, acceleration is measured in metres per second squared (m s^{-2}), so the dimensions are 0 for mass, 1 for length and -2 for time. Provide a set of arithmetic operators for dimensioned quantities. They can only be added or subtracted if the dimensions match (so you can't add density and acceleration); they can be multiplied or divided by multiplying or dividing the magnitudes and adding or subtracting the corresponding dimensions.

9.4 Modify the diary program from chapter 8 so that it uses the package JE.Times defined in this chapter, and modify the Load procedure so that appointments with dates prior to today's date (without taking the time into account) are ignored.

CHAPTER 10

Designing with abstract data types

We explain the behaviour of a component at any given level in terms of interactions between subcomponents whose own internal organization, for the moment, is taken for granted.
— Richard Dawkins, *The Blind Watchmaker*

10.1 The design process revisited

Having looked at how private types can be used to implement abstract data types (ADTs) in Ada, let's return to the electronic diary program of chapter 8 and try to redesign it using abstract data types to avoid the sorts of maintenance problems highlighted at the beginning of chapter 9. Rather than starting by trying to break down the program into smaller subproblems as in the top-down approach, the starting point with a design based around abstract data types is to decide what types of **objects** in the real world the program is going to need to represent. This is the basis of an object-oriented approach to the design. In the case of an electronic appointments diary the answer is fairly obvious; the program needs to model a diary, so we'll need an ADT called Diary_Type. The diary contains a collection of appointments, so we'll need another ADT which I'll call Appointment_Type. A good rule of thumb is to look at the program specification; the nouns it uses (*diary*, *appointment*, and so on) describe the objects it deals with and are therefore possible candidates for ADTs, although some (e.g. *user*) will be red herrings. By examining the nouns used in the specification you can draw up a list of potential ADTs and then eliminate synonyms and red herrings. At this point the types can just be described as 'private' so that their internal workings don't have to be considered until later. Each ADT should go in a separate package unless there's a very good reason to the contrary (e.g. they need to be able to see each other's full declaration for some reason).

The next step is to identify the operations that each ADT supports. Again, a useful rule of thumb is to look at the verbs in the specification which are used in connection with the corresponding nouns: *add* an appointment to the diary, *list* the appointments in the diary, and so on. These describe the actions to be performed by the objects. From this you can build up a list of the operations that each ADT must provide and write subprogram specifications to match. By now you should have an outline of the visible part of the package specification for each of the ADTs and you can concentrate on writing the program in terms of these ADTs and the operations they provide.

This is no longer a top-down approach; the top-down approach only works if you know where the 'bottom' is that your design is heading towards. By sketching out the design of the ADTs in advance you are providing yourself with a known 'bottom' layer to aim for, and you can then steer your top-down design towards it. In other words, you combine a top-down approach with a 'bottom-up' approach with the aim of getting the two to meet in the middle. The nitty-gritty implementation details of each ADT operation can then be the subject of another iteration of the same design process, so that each ADT is implemented in terms of further ADTs. The result will be an **object-oriented design**; each type of object (i.e. each ADT) provides a set of services that other objects can use without revealing how those services are implemented, and in turn uses the services provided by other ADTs without needing to know how they are implemented. At the bottom level the ADTs are those provided for in the language specification: Integer, Float, Boolean, String, Ada.Exceptions.Exception_Id, Ada.Calendar.Time and so on. As long as the set of services that an ADT provides is sufficient for the needs of its clients and independent of any particular implementation you should be able to reimplement any of the ADTs without affecting the overall design of the system. Defining the interaction of the ADTs is the most important part of the design process; implementing them is a secondary concern.

10.2   Separating out the user interface

One of the most important aspects in a successful design is separating the modelling of the aspects of the real world that the program is concerned with (e.g. the functions of a diary) from the **user interface** which allows a user to interact with it. The user interface should always be the outermost layer of a program; it's the part of the program that's most likely to change and nothing else in the program should depend on it. At the moment the diary has a simple textual interface, but this might need to be a graphical interface in another program or another version of the same program. The program uses a **model** (an abstract data type of some sort) to represent something in the real world. It also provides a user interface, a **view** of the data represented in the model which gives the users a way of interacting with (viewing and controlling) that model. Different views of the same model might be required; you might want to be able to view a table of numbers as a pie chart or some sort of graph. The way that you interact with the program is likely to depend on how you're viewing the data; if it's a graph, you might want to alter it by dragging points on the graph around the screen rather than by typing in numbers. You might also want multiple different views of the same data at the same time. In the case of a diary you might want to be able to look at the appointments or you might want a 'day-planner' view which shows the times you are free and the times you are busy, or you might want both views at once.

   With this approach, the program is responsible for tying together the model and the view. The model itself should be completely independent of the program; this can be achieved by defining the model as an abstract data type in a package. The view will of course be heavily dependent on the model and will be tailored to the needs of the particular program, but the program shouldn't have any special knowledge of the internal details of the view's implementation so that these can be changed if necessary. One way to manage this would be to define a set of user interface procedures which could be compiled separately from the main program, but a better way is to define the view in yet another package. This will give us the freedom to hide additional implementation details in the package body (data types, procedures, etc.) which are specific to the view and which the main program should not need to see.

Since views are program specific, the package defining the view might actually be defined inside the main program. Here's the sort of thing you might do in the diary program:

```
with JE.Diaries;
procedure Diary is
   package Diary_View is
      type Command_Type is (Add, List, Delete, Save, Quit);
      function  Next_Command return Command_Type;
      procedure Load_Diary
               (Diary : in out JE.Diaries.Diary_Type);
      procedure Save_Diary
               (Diary : in JE.Diaries.Diary_Type);
      procedure Add_Appointment
               (Diary : in out JE.Diaries.Diary_Type);
      procedure List_Appointment
               (Diary : in JE.Diaries.Diary_Type);
      procedure Delete_Appointment
               (Diary : in out JE.Diaries.Diary_Type);
   end Diary_View;

   package body Diary_View is separate;

   ...      -- etc.

begin
   ...      -- body of program
end Diary;
```

The subprograms declared in Diary_View will all be concerned with the user interface, interacting with the user to get the details of an appointment and then using the facilities of JE.Diaries to add the appointment to the diary.

Notice that a package can be defined inside a procedure rather than being made into a separate library unit. Both the specification and the body must be declared at the same level, so for library packages they are both library units. Inside a procedure they must be declared in the same declaration section.

The package specification tells us absolutely nothing about the appearance of the user interface; it just provides a list of possible commands, a function for getting the next command, and a set of procedures to interact with the user in order to implement those commands. The commands themselves are completely abstract; they may be characters typed at a keyboard or items selected from a pull-down menu. All the program ever sees is values of type Command_Type.

The package body is defined as **separate**, so somewhere else we need to define it like this:

```
separate (Diary)
package body Diary_View is
   . . .
end Diary_View;
```

The great advantage of this approach is that the package body can provide any internal data structures or subprograms that it needs as well as its own initialisation code (e.g. creating a window on the screen) without the main program having to know anything about it at all. I described in chapter 4 how a package initialisation section could be used to display copyright notices when a program starts up; the same facility can be used to perform any other package-specific initialisation (although you have to be careful to handle every exception that might occur, since any unhandled exceptions will abort the program before the main procedure gets started!). The separate package body can also have its own **with** clauses to allow it to reference any external packages it needs. If the user interface changes, only the procedures in the package body need to be changed; if multiple views of the diary are needed, List_Appointments can display whatever views the user selects and Next_Command can respond to the user's interactions with any of those views without the program having to be involved in view management. All the program ends up doing is providing the model and using the package Diary_View to get and respond to commands from the user:

```
with JE.Diaries;
procedure Diary is

   package Diary_View is
      type Command_Type is (Add, List, Delete, Save, Quit);
      function  Next_Command return Command_Type;

      procedure Load_Diary
                     (Diary : in out JE.Diaries.Diary_Type);
      procedure Save_Diary
                     (Diary : in JE.Diaries.Diary_Type);
      procedure Add_Appointment
                     (Diary : in out JE.Diaries.Diary_Type);
      procedure List_Appointments
                     (Diary : in JE.Diaries.Diary_Type);
      procedure Delete_Appointment
                     (Diary : in out JE.Diaries.Diary_Type);
   end Diary_View;
```

```
      package body Diary_View is separate;

      Diary_Model : JE.Diaries.Diary_Type;
   begin
      begin
         Diary_View.Load_Diary (Diary_Model);
      exception
         when JE.Diaries.Diary_Error =>
            null;     -- ignore errors when trying to load the diary
      end;

      loop
         case Diary_View.Next_Command is
            when Diary_View.Add =>
               Diary_View.Add_Appointment (Diary_Model);
            when Diary_View.List =>
               Diary_View.List_Appointments (Diary_Model);
            when Diary_View.Delete =>
               Diary_View.Delete_Appointment (Diary_Model);
            when Diary_View.Save =>
               Diary_View.Save_Diary (Diary_Model);
            when Diary_View.Quit =>
               exit;
         end case;
      end loop;
   end Diary;
```

The program tries to load the diary, and then processes commands one after another. I've assumed an exception called Diary_Error will be reported if anything goes wrong during loading so that errors encountered when loading the diary can be ignored by the exception handler. Each command is directed to the appropriate operation in Diary_View except for Quit, which just breaks out of the main loop to end the program.

10.3   Designing the model

Now it's time to consider the design of the types used to represent the diary and its appointments. We know we need to represent a diary, so we'll need a type which I've called Diary_Type. Diary_Type will need to be declared in a package which I've called JE.Diaries. Should Diary_Type be visible? No, because we might want to change the implementation at a later date. It needs to be a private type or a limited private type. In general only scalar types like Day_Type and Month_Type should be made visible; they are usually needed as their values are the building blocks used to construct composite values like dates. Do we want to be able to assign one diary to another? Probably not, since this would allow an existing diary to be overwritten (but merging the appointments from one diary with the appointments in another might be a sensible operation to provide). If we don't want to allow assignment, the diary should be declared **limited private**. The diary will be a collection of appointments, so we'll need to define another type Appointment_Type for the individual appointments. This can go in another package called JE.Appointments. We don't want users to be able to see how we've implemented these, so the type should be private, but we probably do want to be able to copy appointments so it won't need to be a limited type.

Next we need to identify the operations that a diary should provide. We can do this by looking at the specification for the original problem:

> *It will need to provide as a minimum the ability to add new appointments, delete existing appointments, display the list of appointments and save the appointments to a file. Also, if there are any saved appointments we should read them in when the program starts up.*

(Most specifications that you'll be given will hopefully be more detailed than this!) The operations are similar to those from chapter 8; we need to be able to add appointments, delete specified appointments, extract individual appointments in order to list them, save the diary to a file and load it from a file.

Here's a package specification based on these initial thoughts:

```
with JE.Appointments;
use  JE.Appointments;
package JE.Diaries is

   type Diary_Type is limited private;

   procedure Load    (Diary : in out Diary_Type;
                       From  : in String);
   procedure Save    (Diary : in Diary_Type;
                       To    : in String);
   procedure Add     (Diary : in out Diary_Type;
                       Appt  : in Appointment_Type);
   procedure Delete  (Diary : in out Diary_Type;
                       Appt  : in Positive);
   function  Choose  (Diary : Diary_Type;
                       Appt  : Positive) return Appointment_Type;

   Diary_Error : exception;

private
   ...    -- it's a secret!
end JE.Diaries;
```

Load and Save both take a diary and a string as their parameters; the diary will be loaded from or saved to the filenamed by the Name parameter. Add takes a diary and an appointment as its parameters and adds the appointment to the diary. Delete takes a diary and an appointment number as its parameters and deletes the specified appointment; Choose also takes a diary and an appointment number as its parameters and returns a copy of the selected appointment. Earlier I assumed the existence of an exception called Diary_Error which would be reported if anything went wrong when loading the diary, which is declared here. It can also be used for reporting errors arising from other operations. In the case of Add, the diary might be full, and in the case of Delete and Choose the appointment number might be out of range, so Diary_Error can be used to report these errors. An extra function to return the number of appointments in the diary would also be useful, since this will allow clients to test if an appointment number is valid before calling Delete or Choose:

```
function Size (Diary : Diary_Type) return Natural;
```

The chances are that you'll overlook a few minor details like this in the early stages of any design and then discover the need for them as you get more involved in the implementation. This is normal; don't worry about it. As you get more and more experienced you'll start spotting these things earlier, but in the meantime there's nothing wrong with having to go back and make a few minor changes occasionally.

Appointment_Type needs to be dealt with next. An appointment consists of a date (day, month, year, hour and minute) and a description; we will need to be able to extract these via accessor functions and construct an appointment from its components with a constructor function so that values can be transferred to and from the user interface. The package JE.Times from the previous chapter provides Time_Type which can be used for the date, and the description will just be a String.

Here's an outline for JE.Appointments which shows the specifications for the accessor and constructor functions that Appointment_Type requires:

```
with JE.Times;
use  JE.Times;
package JE.Appointments is

   type Appointment_Type is private;

   -- Accessor functions
   function Date    (Appt : Appointment_Type) return Time_Type;
   function Details (Appt : Appointment_Type) return String;

   -- Constructor
   function Appointment (Date    : Time_Type;
                         Details : String)
                                    return Appointment_Type;
```

```
private
   ...   -- it's a secret!
end JE.Appointments;
```

10.4   Defining the view package

Given the design described above for JE.Diaries and JE.Appointments, we can turn to
considering the body of the internal package Diary_View. This version will be a textual
interface based on Ada.Text_IO. In outline it will look like this:

```
with Ada.Text_IO, Ada.Integer_Text_IO;
use  Ada.Text_IO, Ada.Integer_Text_IO;
separate (Diary)
package body Diary_View is
   function Next_Command return Command_Type is
      ...
   end Next_Command;

   procedure Load_Diary
            (Diary : in out JE.Diaries.Diary_Type) is
      ...
   end Load_Diary;

   procedure Save_Diary
            (Diary : in JE.Diaries.Diary_Type) is
      ...
   end Save_Diary;

   procedure Add_Appointment
            (Diary : in out JE.Diaries.Diary_Type) is
      ...
   end Add_Appointment;

   procedure List_Appointments
            (Diary : in JE.Diaries.Diary_Type) is
      ...
   end List_Appointment;

   procedure Delete_Appointment
            (Diary : in out JE.Diaries.Diary_Type) is
      ...
   end Delete_Appointment;
end Diary_View;
```

Let's consider each of these in turn. Next_Command will be responsible for displaying a menu and getting the user's response. Most of this code can be taken from the program in chapter 8:

```
function Next_Command return Command_Type is
   Command : Character;
begin
   loop
      -- display menu
      New_Line (5);
      Put_Line ("Diary menu:");
      Put_Line ("    [A]dd appointment");
      Put_Line ("    [D]elete appointment");
      Put_Line ("    [L]ist appointments");
      Put_Line ("    [S]ave appointments");
      Put_Line ("    [Q]uit");
      New_Line;
      Put ("Enter your choice: ");

      -- get a key
      Get (Command);
      Skip_Line;

      -- return selected command
      case Command is
         when 'A' | 'a' =>
            return Add;
         when 'D' | 'd' =>
            return Delete;
         when 'L' | 'l' =>
            return List;
         when 'S' | 's' =>
            return Save;
         when 'Q' | 'q' =>
            return Quit;
         when others =>
            Put_Line ("Invalid choice -- " &
                      "please enter A, D, L, S or Q");
      end case;
   end loop;
exception
   when End_Error =>    -- quit if end-of-file character entered
      return Quit;
end Next_Command;
```

The function displays the menu, gets the user's choice and then returns the appropriate Command_Type value for the choice. If the user enters an incorrect character an error message is displayed before looping back to display the menu again. End-of-file errors are handled by treating them as Quit commands.

Listing the appointments is also done in much the same way as before, except that the procedure Choose must be used to get the appointment; since Diary_Type is private, we can't just access it as an array:

```
procedure List_Appointments
          (Diary : in JE.Diaries.Diary_Type) is
  Appt : JE.Appointments.Appointment;
begin
  if JE.Diaries.Size(Diary) = 0 then
    Put_Line ("No appointments found.");
  else
    for I in 1 .. JE.Diaries.Size(Diary) loop
      Put (I, Width=>3); Put (") ");
      Put (JE.Diaries.Choose(Diary,I));
      New_Line;
    end loop;
  end if;
end List_Appointments;
```

A version of Put for Appointment_Type values will be needed within Diary_View. This will be a private operation hidden inside the package body; the implementation of it could be based on the version which was given in chapter 8.

Add_Appointment just needs to get the date, time and details of an appointment from the user and then use the Add procedure from JE.Diaries to add the new appointment to the diary:

```
procedure Add_Appointment
          (Diary : in out JE.Diaries.Diary_Type) is
  package Month_IO is
          new Ada.Text_IO.Enumeration_IO (JE.Times.Month_Type);
  use Month_IO;

  Day       : JE.Times.Day_Type;
  Month     : JE.Times.Month_Type;
  Year      : JE.Times.Year_Type;
  Hour      : JE.Times.Hour_Type;
  Minute    : JE.Times.Minute_Type;
  Details   : String (1..50);
  Length    : Natural;
  Separator : Character;
```

```
begin
   Put ("Enter date:   ");
   Get (Day);
   Get (Separator);
   Get (Month);
   Get (Separator);
   Get (Year);
   Skip_Line;
   Put ("Enter time:   ");
   Get (Hour);
   Get (Separator);
   Get (Minute);
   Skip_Line;
   Put ("Description: ");
   Get_Line (Details, Length);

   JE.Diaries.Add
      ( Diary,
        JE.Appointments.Appointment
           ( JE.Times.Time (Day, Month, Year, Hour, Minute),
             Details(1..Length) )
      );
exception
   when Data_Error | Constraint_Error | JE.Times.Time_Error =>
      Put_Line ("Invalid input.");
end Add_Appointment;
```

A single separator character is read between each component of the date and time; this allows the user to enter any separator rather than requiring the components to be separated by spaces (e.g. 25-Dec-1995 for a date or 10.15 for a time).

⟹   *Try using a colon as the separator (e.g. 10:15; try 2:30 as well). This won't work since the colon is a synonym for # (see sections 2.4.2 and J.2 of the Language Reference Manual), and Get will think it's dealing with a based number like 10#15# as described in chapter 5. Try and think of a way of solving this problem.*

The appointment details will be read into a string which is defined arbitrarily as being 50 characters long; this is done without reference to the diary package which just uses String as the type for the appointment details without revealing what the maximum length it allows is. The length of the string that the user is allowed to type in is then a property of the user interface rather than the diary and the maximum length that an appointment can hold is a property of the diary package; the two are kept independent of each other.

   Deleting an appointment involves asking the user to enter an appointment number, checking that it's valid and then calling JE.Diaries.Delete to handle the actual deletion:

```
procedure Delete_Appointment
         (Diary : in out JE.Diaries.Diary_Type) is
   Appt_No : Positive;
begin
   Put ("Enter appointment number: ");
   Get (Appt_No);
   if Appt_No not in 1 .. JE.Diaries.Size(Diary) then
      raise Constraint_Error;
   end if;
   JE.Diaries.Delete (Diary, Appt_No);

exception
   when Constraint_Error | Data_Error =>
      Put_Line ("Invalid appointment number");
      Skip_Line;
end Delete_Appointment;
```

Finally, here are Load_Diary and Save_Diary. These just call JE.Diaries.Load to load the diary and JE.Diaries.Save to save the diary:

```
procedure Load_Diary (Diary : in out JE.Diaries.Diary_Type) is
begin
   JE.Diaries.Load (Diary, Diary_Name);
end Load_Diary;

procedure Save_Diary (Diary : in JE.Diaries.Diary_Type) is
begin
   JE.Diaries.Save (Diary, Diary_Name);
end Save_Diary;
```

The diary name can be defined as a constant inside the package body:

```
Diary_Name : constant String := "Diary";
```

An alternative implementation might search a predefined list of places to find the file or might ask the user for the filename; it might also allow multiple files to be loaded and merged.

10.5   Implementing the ADT packages

So far we haven't needed to consider how the diary and appointment packages are actually implemented. One of the interesting things about an object-oriented approach to design is that, once the behaviour of the objects has been defined, writing the code to provide that behaviour can be treated as mere detail. It still needs to be done, though! First we'll need to define the actual representations of the private types:

```
with JE.Times;   use JE.Times;
package JE.Appointments is
   type Appointment_Type is private;
   ...      -- etc.
private
   type Appointment_Type is
     record
        Time    : Time_Type;
        Details : String (1..50);          -- an arbitrary size
        Length  : Natural := 0;
     end record;
end JE.Diaries;

with JE.Appointments;   use JE.Appointments;
package JE.Diaries is
   type Diary_Type is limited private;
   ...      -- etc.
private
   type Appointment_Array is
     array (Positive range <>) of Appointment_Type;

   type Diary_Type is
     limited record
        Appts : Appointment_Array (1..10);  -- an arbitrary size
        Count : Natural := 0;
     end record;
end JE.Diaries;
```

These declarations are the same as the ones given in chapter 8, except that the date and time are represented using JE.Times.Time_Type and that Diary_Type doesn't use a discriminant for the number of appointments any more. The package body for JE.Appointments will look like this in outline:

```
package body JE.Appointments is
   function Date (Appt : Appointment_Type) return Time_Type is
      ...
   end Date;

   function Details (Appt : Appointment_Type) return String is
      ...
   end Details;
```

```
         function Appointment (Date    : Time_Type;
                               Details : String)
                                            return Appointment_Type is
            . . .
         end Appointment;
      end JE.Appointments;
```

The package body for JE.Diaries needs to provide bodies for the subprograms declared in the package specification, so in outline it will look like this:

```
      package body JE.Diaries is
         function Size (Diary : Diary_Type) return Natural is
            . . .
         end Size;

         procedure Load (Diary : in out Diary_Type;
                         From  : in String) is
            . . .
         end Load;

         procedure Save (Diary : in Diary_Type;
                         To    : in String) is
            . . .
         end Save;

         procedure Add (Diary : in out Diary_Type;
                        Appt  : in Appointment_Type) is
            . . .
         end Add;

         procedure Delete (Diary : in out Diary_Type;
                           Appt  : in Positive) is
            . . .
         end Delete;

         function Choose (Diary : Diary_Type;
                          Appt  : Positive)
                                     return Appointment_Type is
            . . .
         end Choose;
      end JE.Diaries;
```

These outlines are taken directly from the package specifications. All that remains is to implement the bodies of the subprograms in each package. I'll deal with the appointment package first. The appointment accessors are very straightforward; they can be implemented like this:

```
function Date (Appt : Appointment_Type) return Time_Type is
begin
   return Appt.Time;
end Date;

function Details (Appt : Appointment_Type) return String is
begin
   return Appt.Details (1..Appt.Length);
end Details;
```

The constructor for appointments is marginally more complex since it needs to take into account the fact that the Details parameter might be longer than the appointment can hold, in which case only the first part of the string should be copied into the appointment:

```
function Appointment (Date    : Time_Type;
                      Details : String)
                                return Appointment_Type is
   A : Appointment_Type;
begin
   A.Time := Date;
   if Details'Length > A.Details'Length then
     A.Details := Details(Details'First ..
                          Details'First+A.Details'Length-1);
     A.Length := A.Details'Length;
   else
     A.Details (1 .. Details'Length) := Details;
     A.Length := Details'Length;
   end if;
   return A;
end Appointment;
```

10.6 Diary operations

Now for the operations on Diary_Type objects. Size is the simplest of these; it's just an accessor function for the Count component of a diary:

```
function Size (Diary : Diary_Type) return Natural is
begin
   return Diary.Count;
end Size;
```

Choose is likewise an accessor for a specific appointment within the array of appointments in a diary. It needs to check that the appointment number is valid and raise a Diary_Error exception if it isn't:

```
function Choose (Diary : Diary_Type;
                    Appt  : Positive) return Appointment_Type is
begin
   if Appt not in 1 .. Diary.Count then
      raise Diary_Error;
   else
      return Diary.Appts(Appt);
   end if;
end Choose;
```

Deleting an appointment involves checking that the appointment number is valid and then moving appointments up the array to overwrite the appointment being deleted:

```
procedure Delete (Diary : in out Diary_Type;
                    Appt  : in Positive) is
begin
   if Appt not in 1 .. Diary.Count then
      raise Diary_Error;
   else
      Diary.Appts(Appt..Diary.Count-1) :=
                        Diary.Appts(Appt+1..Diary.Count);
      Diary.Count := Diary.Count - 1;
   end if;
end Delete;
```

Adding an appointment involves locating the correct place in the array for the new appointment, moving appointments down the array to make room for it and then inserting the new appointment into the vacated array element. Diary_Error will need to be raised if the diary is full:

```
procedure Add (Diary : in out Diary_Type;
                 Appt  : in Appointment_Type) is

   use type JE.Times.Time_Type; -- to allow use of ">"
   Pos : Positive;              -- position for insertion

begin
   if Diary.Count = Diary.Appts'Length then
      raise Diary_Error;
   else
```

```
      Pos := 1;
      for I in 1 .. Diary.Count loop
        exit when Date(Diary.Appts(I)) > Date(Appt);
        Pos := Pos + 1;
      end loop;

      Diary.Appts(Pos+1 .. Diary.Count+1) :=
                      Diary.Appts(Pos .. Diary.Count);
      Diary.Appts(Pos) := Appt;
      Diary.Count := Diary.Count + 1;
    end if;
  end Add;
```

A **use type** clause is needed to allow the operator ">" to be accessed directly. The package body will of course need a **with** clause for JE.Times.

Rather than saving the diary as a text file (which would involve unpicking each appointment into its component parts) the appointments can be saved in their internal form using the package Ada.Sequential_IO. This is a generic package that needs to be instantiated for the type of data to be stored in the file; the full specification is given in Appendix B. It provides essentially the same facilities as Ada.Text_IO except that the input and output procedures are called Read and Write instead of Get and Put. The package body will need a **with** clause for Ada.Sequential_IO and an instantiation for Appointment_Type:

```
with Ada.Sequential_IO, JE.Times;
package body JE.Diaries is
  package Appt_IO is new Ada.Sequential_IO (Appointment_Type);
  ...
end JE.Diaries;
```

Save needs to try to create the output file and then to write each appointment in turn into the file. Diary.Count can't be written to the file any more since only Appointment_Type values can be written:

```
procedure Save (Diary : in Diary_Type;
                To    : in String) is
  File : Appt_IO.File_Type;
begin
  Appt_IO.Create (File, Name => To);
  for I in 1..Diary.Count loop
    Appt_IO.Write (File, Diary.Appts(I));
  end loop;
  Appt_IO.Close (File);
end Save;
```

Load essentially reverses the process; there is no appointment count in the file now, so it needs to check for End_Of_File to discover when it's finished reading the file. Here's how Load can be implemented:

```
procedure Load (Diary : in out Diary_Type;
                From  : in String) is
   File : Appt_IO.File_Type;
begin
   Diary.Count := 0;
   Appt_IO.Open (File, Name => From,
                       Mode => Appt_IO.In_File);
   while not Appt_IO.End_Of_File(File) loop
      Diary.Count := Diary.Count + 1;
      Appt_IO.Read (File, Diary.Appts(Diary.Count));
   end loop;
   Appt_IO.Close (File);
exception
   when Appt_IO.Name_Error =>
      raise Diary_Error;
end Load;
```

The diary size (Diary.Count) is set to zero at the very beginning of the procedure so that it's guaranteed to be valid if an exception occurs. The exception handler will handle Name_Errors by raising a Diary_Error exception so that the main program can decide how to deal with it, in accordance with the principle that package operations shouldn't do their own error handling.

⇒   *What will happen if a file called Diary exists that wasn't created by this program? Add the necessary exception handling code to Load to deal with this possibility. Don't forget to close the file if it's been opened!*

10.7   Maintenance issues

So, how much better is this design than the one in chapter 8? We can assess this by considering the maintenance scenarios described at the beginning of chapter 9: having multiple diaries, using a graphical user interface, and integrating the diary into an electronic mail system. The last of these will now be easy to do; JE.Diaries is completely independent of the program in this chapter so it could be used unchanged in any other application that needed it. Multiple diaries could be handled by declaring an array of Diary_Types in the program and providing extra commands to open and close diaries as well as selecting a particular diary as the 'current diary' to be used when adding or deleting appointments. The appropriate array element could then be passed as the parameter to Add_Appointment, Delete_Appointment and so on.

The way that the model has been separated from the view will make it fairly easy to revise for use with a graphical user interface. In a graphical environment the commands might be selected from pull-down menus; Next_Command will just need to return command codes whenever one of the diary handling commands is selected. Extra commands might be needed to manage aspects of the user interface, e.g. commands to control the placement and size of windows. These commands wouldn't affect the model, so they could be handled internally within the Diary_View package. The List command might be redundant since in a graphical environment the appointments would probably be visible in a window at all times. This is no problem; if this were the case, the interface's menu wouldn't provide a List command and Next_Command would never return List as its result. Add_Appointment would be quite easy to rewrite since it does all the necessary interaction with the user to get the appointment details; you'd just need to replace the procedure with a version which used a graphical dialog to get the details instead. When deleting appointments, the appointment to be deleted might be selected by pointing at one of the appointments displayed on the screen. It would still be possible for the user interface code to work out what the corresponding appointment number was by keeping track of which appointments were visible, so the fact that the Diary_Type abstraction identifies appointments by number shouldn't be a problem. Also, the user might be able to select multiple appointments for deletion; Delete_Appointment would then need to incorporate a loop to get the numbers corresponding to the selected appointments and delete them one by one.

The program now exhibits the object-oriented structure that I described at the beginning of the chapter. The program defines the user interface and uses the services provided by the other ADTs in the design (the diary and the appointments). Appointments rely on an ADT which provides date and time services (JE.Times), and so on. Individual ADTs can be changed independently as long as the set of services needed by their clients is still available. However, we haven't eliminated maintenance problems completely. Maintenance requirements like the ones described will still involve a fair amount of work, but the way that the different aspects of the program have been compartmentalised will make maintenance much easier than it was before. Also, as we'll see in later chapters, there are other maintenance issues which the current design will *still* have difficulties coping with.

Exercises

10.1   Modify the diary program in this chapter to allow the user to specify the name of the diary file to be used.

10.2   Modify the diary program to allow the user to open multiple diaries at the same time and switch from using one diary to another.

10.3   Once the ability to open multiple diaries has been provided, add the ability to copy or move appointments from one diary to another.

10.4 Once the ability to open multiple diaries has been provided, add a command which allows the user to display a merged list of all the appointments in all the diaries that are currently open. The appointments should still be listed in order of date and time.

CHAPTER 11

Dynamic memory allocation

The memory strengthens as you lay burdens on it.
— Thomas De Quincey, *Confessions of an English Opium-Eater*

11.1 Access types

There's still room for improvement in the current appointments diary design. Using an array of appointments limits us to a fixed number of appointments; the size of an array must be specified when the array is declared. If the size chosen is too big, memory will be wasted on unused array elements (and the program may or may not run on different machines with different amounts of memory); if it's too small, the array will get filled up and the user will not be able to add any more appointments.

To solve this problem we need some way of allocating extra memory as and when it is needed. Since this depends on the dynamic behaviour of the program as it is run, this sort of memory allocation scheme is known as **dynamic allocation**. Ada allows memory to be allocated dynamically like this:

```
X := new Appointment_Type;
                -- create a new Appointment_Type record
```

New takes a free block of memory from a **storage pool** of available memory (often referred to as a **heap**) and reserves it for use as an Appointment_Type variable. A reference to its location is then assigned to the variable X so that we then have some way of accessing it. An initial value can be specified for the new appointment like this, assuming that the full declaration of Appointment_Type from the previous chapter is visible:

```
X := new Appointment_Type'(Time => Time(25,Dec,1999,10,00),
                           Details => "Open presents       ",
                           Length => 13);
```

As this example shows, an initial value is specified in parentheses and appended to the type name by an apostrophe ('); this is actually a **qualified expression** as described in chapter 5.

So how do we declare X in this case? First of all, we need to define an **access type** (which I'll call Appointment_Access) and then declare X to be an Appointment_Access variable:

```
type Appointment_Access is access Appointment_Type;
                                        -- the access type
X, Y : Appointment_Access;              -- access variables
```

Variables of type Appointment_Access can only be assigned references to Appointment_Type variables generated by **new**. In many programming languages variables like this are referred to as **pointers** since they 'point to' a dynamically allocated block of memory, and although this is not official Ada terminology it's in such widespread use that I'm going to risk offending some language purists by using the terms 'access value' and 'pointer' interchangeably.

Having set X to point to a dynamically allocated Appointment_Type variable, you can then use 'X.all' to access the appointment itself. You can then select components of the appointment in the usual way:

```
X.all.Time := Time(25,Dec,1995,21,00);
if Month(X.all.Time) = Jan then ...
```

As a convenience, when you access components of a dynamically allocated record you can just say 'X.Time' and so on instead of 'X.all.Time':

```
X.Time := Time(25,Dec,1995,21,00);    -- as above
if Month(X.Time) = Jan then ...       -- as above
```

Be careful not to confuse 'X' and 'X.all'; 'X' on its own is the name of the access variable, but 'X.all' is the value that X points to:

```
X.all := Y.all;    -- copy one appointment into another
X := Y;            -- set X to point to the same thing as Y
```

Assuming that X and Y point to different appointments, the first assignment will copy the contents of one appointment into the other so that you end up with two identical appointments. In the second case X and Y will both end up pointing to the same appointment, and the appointment that X pointed to before is now inaccessible unless there's another access variable which points to it. After the first assignment, you can alter X.Date and it won't affect Y.Date since X and Y point to different appointments, but after the second assignment X.Date and Y.Date both refer to the same thing, so any change to X.Date will also be a change to Y.Date.

Apart from assigning a value generated by **new** to X, you can assign the special value **null** to X to indicate that it doesn't point to anything (a 'null pointer'). Access variables are automatically set to **null** when they are declared unless **new** is used to initialise them:

```
X : Appointment_Access;              -- a null pointer
Y : Appointment_Access := null;      -- another null pointer
Z : Appointment_Access := new Appointment_Type;
                                     -- an initialised pointer
```

Attempting to access the value that a null pointer points to will generate a constraint error. It's a good idea to check for null first:

```
if X = null then ...    -- do something sensible if X is null
```

11.2 Linked lists

On the face of it, this doesn't get us much further since for every dynamically allocated appointment there must still be an access variable which points to it. If all we end up with is an array of access variables instead of an array of appointments we won't have actually achieved very much!

The solution is to build a **linked list** of appointments. We need to extend Appointment_Type to include an Appointment_Access value which will be used to point to the next appointment. Then all we need is a single variable to point to the first appointment; the first appointment then points us to the second appointment, which then points us to the third appointment, and so on. It might also be convenient to have a variable which points to the last appointment in the list, but I'll ignore that possibility for the moment. Here are declarations for types Appt_Type and Appt_Access to handle this:

```
type Appt_Type;                        -- 1

type Appt_Access is access Appt_Type;  -- 2

type Appt_Type is
   record
      Time    : JE.Times.Time_Type;
      Details : String (1..50);
      Length  : Natural := 0;
      Next    : Appt_Access;           -- 3
   end record;
```

The reason for line 1 in the code above is to resolve the circularity in the declarations of Appt_Type and Appt_Access. The declaration of Appt_Access (line 2) refers to Appt_Type and the declaration of Appt_Type refers to Appt_Access (line 3). Line 1 is an **incomplete declaration** which simply tells the compiler that Appt_Type is the name of a type of some sort so that the name can be used on line 2 where Appt_Access is declared. If Appt_Type had any discriminants, we'd have to use the following incomplete declaration:

```
type Appt_Type (<>);
          -- (<>) means that the type has discriminants
```

We don't need to know anything about Appt_Type other than its name in order to declare an access type for it; typically, all access values will occupy the same amount of memory no matter what type of data they point to so that no major burdens are imposed on the compiler. Then, once Appt_Access is declared, we can give the full declaration of Appt_Type which includes an Appt_Access component.

Diary_Type will now contain a pointer to the first appointment in the diary instead of an array of appointments:

```
type Diary_Type is
  record
    First : Appt_Access;
    Count : Natural := 0;
  end record;
```

Since access values reflect the precise memory location where an appointment has been created it's no use saving them in a file and expecting them to make any sense when the program is run again, since the actual locations of the appointments will probably be quite different each time the program is run. For this reason it's unwise to use Ada.Sequential_IO to store Appt_Type values directly; a better way would be to embed the original Appointment_Type from chapter 10 (containing Time, Details and Length) as a component in a larger record which includes the pointer to the next appointment:

```
type Appointment_Record;

type Appointment_Access is access Appointment_Record;

type Appointment_Record is
  record
    Appt : Appointment_Type;        -- see chapter 10
    Next : Appointment_Access;
  end record;
```

The Appt component can then be saved to a file and restored from it, rather than saving and restoring the whole record.

The following diagram illustrates what a list like this will look like:

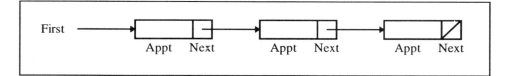

The variable First points to the first appointment in the list, which consists of an appointment component Appt and a pointer Next. Next points in turn to the second appointment, and the second appointment's Next field points to the last appointment. The last appointment in the list does not have an appointment after it, so its Next pointer is set to **null** to indicate this (symbolised by a diagonal bar in the diagram). We can work through a list of this sort processing each appointment in some way like this:

```
Current := Diary.First;
while Current /= null loop
   Process (Current.Appt);
   Current := Current.Next;
end loop;
```

This assumes that Current is an Appointment_Access variable used to keep track of the current position in the list. Remember, Current.Next and Current.Appt are abbreviations for Current.all.Next and Current.all.Appt.

Inserting a new item into the list is quite easy. Given that Current points to an appointment somewhere in the list, here's how you can insert a new item immediately after that appointment:

```
New_Item := new Appointment_Record;          -- 1
New_Item.Next := Current.Next;                -- 2
Current.Next := New_Item;                     -- 3
```

The diagrams below illustrates the steps involved:

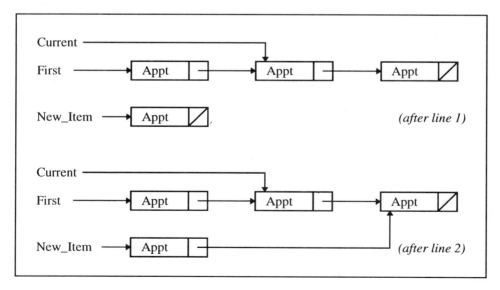

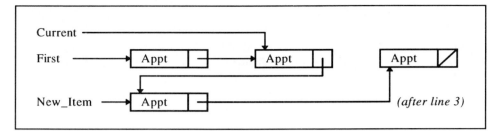

(after line 3)

Line 1 creates a new appointment and stores a pointer to it in New_Item, which I'll assume was declared to be a variable of type Appointment_Access. Line 2 sets its Next field so that the appointment after it is the same appointment that follows Current. Current's Next pointer is then changed so that the new item is the one after the current item.

Deleting an item is just as easy; the drawback is that to delete a particular item you have to have a pointer to the item before it (since the Next pointer of the item before needs to be altered so that it no longer points to the item being deleted). Assuming that Current points to the item *before* the one you want to delete, here's what you have to do:

```
Current.Next := Current.Next.Next;
```

In other words, make the item which follows Current be the one after the one that follows it now. The one that follows it now is thus left with nothing pointing to it, and so the memory allocated for it can now be recycled for use elsewhere. I'll explain how this is done in a moment.

There are a couple of problems here that I've glossed over: one of them is inserting an item at the beginning of the list (or into an empty list) rather than after an existing item, and another is deleting the first item in the list. One way to get around these problems is to provide extra procedures to deal with these specific situations, so that you would need two insertion procedures and two deletion procedures. This is not particularly elegant. Another solution would be to use a value of **null** for the current position to indicate that an item should be inserted before the first item or that the first item should be deleted. Here's how insertion into a diary called Diary would be done:

```
New_Item := new Appointment_Record;
if Current /= null then      -- insert after another appointment
  New_Item.Next := Current.Next;
  Current.Next := New_Item;
else                         -- insert at start of list
  New_Item.Next := Diary.First;
  Diary.First := New_Item;
end if;
```

Here's how deletion would be done:

```
if Current /= null then     -- delete appointment after Current
   Current.Next := Current.Next.Next;
else                        -- delete first appointment
   Diary.First := Diary.First.Next;
end if;
```

11.3 Doubly linked lists

The list structure described above is known as a **singly linked** list, since each item has a single pointer linking it to the next item in the list. This makes it possible to go forwards through the list but not to go backwards. The solution is simple: add another pointer to each item which points to the previous appointment.

```
type Appointment_Record is
   record
      Appt : Appointment_Type;
      Next : Appointment_Access;
                            -- pointer to next appointment
      Prev : Appointment_Access;
                            -- pointer to previous appointment
   end record;
```

What you now have is a **doubly linked list**. There will need to be a pointer to both the first and last items in the list so that you can start at either end and traverse the list in either direction. This arrangement makes it much easier to delete appointments. In the case of a singly linked list you have to have a pointer to the item *before* the one you want to delete; in a doubly linked list the item you want to delete points to its neighbours on each side, so this is what you have to do to delete the item that Current points to:

```
Current.Prev.Next := Current.Next;      -- 1
Current.Next.Prev := Current.Prev;      -- 2
```

In other words, the item before Current is changed to point to the one after Current, and the item after Current is changed to point to the one before Current. The items on either side of Current will therefore bypass it completely. leaving it isolated from the list.

Here's a diagram showing the initial state of the list:

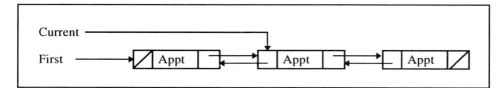

The next diagram illustrates what the state of the list is after the two steps above:

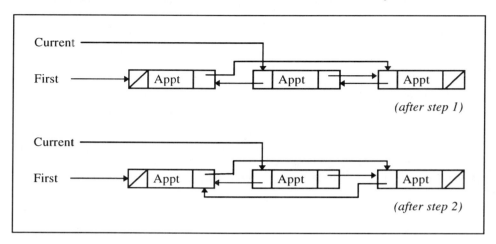

(after step 1)

(after step 2)

Inserting an appointment into the list involves setting the Prev pointers as well as the Next pointers. This is how you would insert a new appointment in front of the one that Current points to:

```
New_Item := new Appointment_Record;    -- 1
New_Item.Prev := Current.Prev;         -- 2
New_Item.Next := Current;              -- 3
Current.Prev.Next := New_Item;         -- 4
Current.Prev := New_Item;              -- 5
```

This sequence of steps creates a new record (line 1) and links it to the current item and the previous one so that it will appear between the current item and the previous one (lines 2 and 3). The Next pointer of the previous item is then set to point to the new item (line 4), as is the Prev pointer of the current item (line 5).

Here's a diagram which illustrates what the situation is after the new item has been created by line 1:

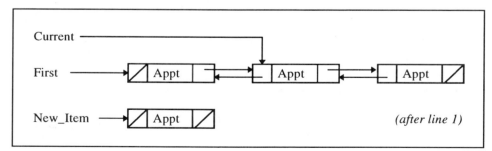

(after line 1)

Lines 2 and 3 link the new item to the existing list, and lines 4 and 5 then modify the existing list to include the new item. Here's a diagram which shows you how it happens:

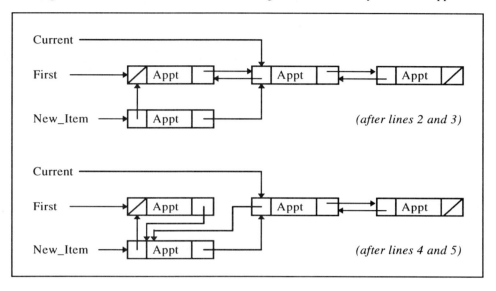

As with singly linked lists, you can detect the end of the list by the fact that Next contains a null pointer; you can also detect the beginning of the list by the fact that Prev contains a null pointer.

There are several other variations on this theme; for example, it's sometimes useful to have **circular lists** where the ends of the list are joined together (i.e. the last item points to the first item and vice versa).

11.4 Iterators

The variable Current that I've been using so far could be made into another component of Diary_Type so that each diary would keep track of its own current position for insertion, deletion, etc. A better solution is to define a separate type to represent positions within the list (often called an **iterator**) which points to the list itself as well as the current position. The advantage of this approach is that you can have more than one 'current' position in a single list, and you can save a copy of the iterator for the current position so you can go back to it later. The only problem is when one iterator is used to delete an item that another one is pointing to. Using the second iterator can be catastrophic since the item it points to might not exist any more. There is no easy solution to this; one approach is to keep a count of the number of iterators that are referring to each item, but this is quite complicated to administer and is still not foolproof. The simplest way out is to ignore the problem and just try to avoid getting into such a situation. This is the solution I'm going to adopt here.

⇒ *I've ducked the problem; see if you can devise a scheme (e.g. using an iterator count in each list item) which will be safe when items are deleted.*

Here are the type declarations we need for this approach:

```
type Appointment_Record;
type Appointment_Access is access Appointment_Record;

type Appointment_Record is
  record
    Appt : Appointment_Type;
    Next : Appointment_Access;
    Prev : Appointment_Access;
  end record;

type List_Header is
  record
    First : Appointment_Access;
    Last  : Appointment_Access;
    Count : Natural := 0;
  end record;

type List_Access is access List_Header;

type Diary_Type is
  record
    List : List_Access := new List_Header;
  end record;

type Diary_Iterator is
  record
    List    : List_Access;
    Current : Appointment_Access;
  end record;
```

The declarations above involve a delicate balancing act. A List_Header contains pointers to the first and last items in the list as well as a count of the number of items in the list. Since access variables can only point to objects created using **new**, the List pointer in Diary_Iterator can't point to a List_Header unless the List_Header is created using **new**. A diary is then just a pointer to a List_Header; this is what the declarations of List_Access and Diary_Type do. When a Diary_Type object is declared, its List component is automatically initialised to point to a newly created List_Header, and an iterator can then point to the same List_Header object. The iterator references the list it's associated with as well as the current position in the list; I'll adopt the convention that if the current position is **null** it means that the iterator is past the end of the list, so that inserting an item when the current position is **null** will add the item being inserted to the end of the list. When an iterator is declared, its List component will be **null** which indicates that it isn't associated with a list; this will need to be checked by the subprograms which operate on iterators.

Now we'll need some operations to get iterators from a diary and to manipulate them. We can define functions which return iterators pointing to the start of the list and the end of the list (the position after the last item):

```
function First (Diary : Diary_Type) return Diary_Iterator is
begin
   return (List => Diary.List, Current => Diary.List.First);
end First;

function Last (Diary : Diary_Type) return Diary_Iterator is
begin
   return (List => Diary.List, Current => null);
end Last;
```

The names have been chosen to echo the names of the attributes of a discrete type to make them easy to remember. We'll also need functions to move an iterator forwards or backwards through the list; we can call them Succ and Pred to match the attribute names. These need to check that the iterator is valid (i.e. it points to a list) and that we aren't trying to go past the end of the list in either direction. We'll need an Iterator_Error exception which can be raised if anything is wrong:

```
Iterator_Error : exception;

function Succ (Iterator : Diary_Iterator)
                                   return Diary_Iterator is
begin
   if Iterator.List = null or else Iterator.Current = null then
     raise Iterator_Error;
   else
     return (List => Iterator.List,
             Current => Iterator.Current.Next);
   end if;
end Succ;

function Pred (Iterator : Diary_Iterator)
                                   return Diary_Iterator is
begin
   if Iterator.List = null or else
           Iterator.Current = Iterator.List.First then
```

```
      raise Iterator_Error;
  elsif Iterator.Current = null then
    return (List => Iterator.List,
            Current => Iterator.List.Last);
  else
    return (List => Iterator.List,
            Current => Iterator.Current.Prev);
  end if;
end Pred;
```

Both these functions check that Iterator.List isn't null; Succ also checks that the current position isn't null (i.e. that we're not already at the end of the list) and Pred checks that we're not at the start of the list. Pred also needs to check if the current position is null (i.e. just past the last appointment in the list) and if so set the current position to point to the last appointment.

We'll also need a function to get the appointment that an iterator points to:

```
function Value (Iterator : Diary_Iterator)
                        return Appointment_Type is
begin
  if Iterator.List = null or else Iterator.Current = null then
    raise Iterator_Error;
  else
    return Iterator.Current.Appt;
  end if;
end Value;
```

These functions can be used to process each appointment in a diary called Diary like this:

```
declare
  I : Diary_Iterator;
begin
  I := First(Diary);
  while I /= Last(Diary) loop
    Process ( Value(I) );
    I := Succ(I);
  end loop;
end;
```

11.5 Deallocating memory

There is one remaining detail to be considered, and that is how to deallocate memory allocated using **new** when you don't need it any more. If you don't deallocate it, it will still be there even if you don't have any way of accessing it any more and you will gradually run out of memory. The memory is only guaranteed to be reclaimed when the access type goes out of scope. If the access type is declared in a library package this won't happen until after the main program has terminated, which is probably too late to be of any use.

One way to deal with this problem is to keep a **free list**; that is, a list of items which have been deleted and are free to be used again. All you need to do when you want to delete an item from a list is to detach it from the list and then attach it to the free list instead. When you want to allocate a new item, you just take one from the free list. If the free list is empty, you just use **new** in the normal way.

The problem with this approach is that your memory usage will only ever increase. If you ever need to allocate an object of a different type using **new**, there may not be enough free memory available even though you have plenty of 'free' memory on your free list. What is needed is a way of telling the system to deallocate the memory so that it can be reused by anything that needs it. The way to do this is to use the standard procedure Ada.Unchecked_Deallocation. As the name implies, there is no check made that the memory is actually free and that you don't still have an access variable pointing to it; it's entirely your responsibility to ensure that once you've used Unchecked_Deallocation to get rid of something, you never try to refer to it again. If you do the result will be unpredictable and might well crash your program.

Ada.Unchecked_Deallocation is a **generic** procedure, in just the same way as Ada.Text_IO.Integer_IO is a generic package. Like Ada.Text_IO.Integer_IO, you have to **instantiate** it before you can use it by specifying what sort of object you're going to delete with it. Here's how you do it:

```
procedure Delete_Appt is new Ada.Unchecked_Deallocation
                    (Appointment_Type, Appointment_Access);
```

You need to mention Ada.Unchecked_Deallocation in a **with** clause before you can do this. What you get out of this is a procedure called Delete_Appt which will deallocate Appointment_Type objects which are pointed to by Appointment_Access values. Delete_Appt takes an Appointment_Access parameter which points to the object you want to delete:

```
X : Appointment_Access :=
        new Appointment_Type;      -- create an appointment
...                                -- use the appointment
Delete_Appt (X);                   -- then delete it
```

We can use this in a procedure to delete an appointment that an iterator is pointing to:

```
procedure Delete (Iterator : in Diary_Iterator) is
begin
   if Iterator.List = null or else Iterator.Current = null then
```

```
         raise Iterator_Error;
      else
         if Iterator.Current.Next = null then
            Iterator.List.Last := Iterator.Current.Prev;
         else
            Iterator.Current.Next.Prev := Iterator.Current.Prev;
         end if;

         if Iterator.Current.Prev = null then
            Iterator.List.First := Iterator.Current.Next;
         else
            Iterator.Current.Prev.Next := Iterator.Current.Next;
         end if;

         Delete_Appt (Iterator.Current);
         Iterator.List.Count := Iterator.List.Count - 1;
      end if;
   end Delete;
```

This procedure needs to check if the appointment being deleted is the first or last one in the list; if not, the pointers in the adjoining appointment records are adjusted, but if it is, the list's First or Last component must be adjusted instead.

To round off the set of operations, we need an Insert procedure to insert a new item in front of the position that an iterator points to:

```
   procedure Insert (Iterator : in Diary_Iterator;
                      Appt     : in Appointment_Type) is
      New_Appt : Appointment_Access;
   begin
      if Iterator.List = null then
         raise Iterator_Error;
      else
         New_Appt.Next := Iterator.Current;
         New_Appt.Appt := Appt;
         if Iterator.Current = null then
            New_Appt.Prev := Iterator.List.Last;
            Iterator.List.Last := New_Appt;
         else
            New_Appt.Prev := Iterator.Current.Prev;
            Iterator.Current.Prev := New_Appt;
         end if;
         if Iterator.Current = Iterator.List.First then
            Iterator.List.First := New_Appt;
         else
```

```
      New_Appt.Prev.Next := New_Appt;
    end if;
    Iterator.List.Count := Iterator.List.Count + 1;
  end if;
end Insert;
```

This creates a new appointment record which points to the current position as the next appointment after it. There are two special cases to consider. The first is when inserting at the end of the list (i.e. when the current position is **null**); in this case the appointment needs to be linked to what was the last item in the list and the list's Last pointer needs adjusting to point to the new appointment. The other is when inserting at the start of the list, in which case the list's First pointer needs updating.

11.6   Designing a linked list diary

At this point we can start redesigning JE.Diaries to use a linked list of appointments. Here's a package specification containing a set of type declarations based on the types I defined above:

```
with JE.Appointments;
use  JE.Appointments;
package JE.Diaries is
   type Diary_Type is limited private;
   ...     -- etc.
private
   type Appointment_Record;
   type Appointment_Access is access Appointment_Record;

   type Appointment_Record is
     record
       Appt : Appointment_Type;
       Next : Appointment_Access;
       Prev : Appointment_Access;
     end record;

   type List_Header is
     record
       First : Appointment_Access;
       Last  : Appointment_Access;
       Count : Natural := 0;
     end record;

   type List_Access is access List_Header;
```

```
type Diary_Type is
   limited record
      List : List_Access := new List_Header;
   end record;

type Diary_Iterator is
   record
      List    : List_Access;
      Current : Appointment_Access;
   end record;
end JE.Diaries;
```

The package body will need to provide an instantiation of Ada.Unchecked_Deallocation, so we'll need a **with** clause for Ada.Unchecked_Deallocation; the operations on iterators will also need to go into the package body:

```
with Ada.Sequential_IO, Ada.Unchecked_Deallocation, JE.Times;
package body JE.Diaries is
   use JE.Appointments;
   package Appt_IO is new Ada.Sequential_IO (Appointment_Type);
   procedure Delete_Appt is new Ada.Unchecked_Deallocation
                     (Appointment_Type, Appointment_Access);

   function First (Diary : Diary_Type) return Diary_Iterator
            is ... ;
   function Last (Diary : Diary_Type) return Diary_Iterator
            is ... ;
   function Succ (Iterator : Diary_Iterator)
            return Diary_Iterator is ... ;
   function Pred (Iterator : Diary_Iterator)
            return Diary_Iterator is ... ;
   function Value (Iterator : Diary_Iterator)
            return Appointment_Type is ... ;
   procedure Insert (Iterator : in Diary_Iterator;
                     Appt     : in Appointment_Type) is ... ;
   procedure Delete (Iterator : in Diary_Iterator) is ... ;

   -- Diary operations declared in package spec go here
end JE.Diaries;
```

These operations were all defined earlier. It would also be a good idea to put declarations of these operations in the private section of the package specification rather than in the package body; this will prevent client packages from using them but it will allow child packages to use them to navigate through the diary if necessary.

```
package JE.Diaries is
   ...    -- as before

private
   ...    -- as before

   function  First  (Diary    : Diary_Type)
                            return Diary_Iterator;
   function  Last   (Diary    : Diary_
                            return Diary_Iterator;
   function  Succ   (Iterator : Diary_Iter
                            return Diary_Iterator;
   function  Pred   (Iterator : Diary_Iter
                            return Diary_Iterator;
   function  Value  (Iterator : Diary_Iter
                            return Appointment_Type;
   procedure Insert (Iterator : in Diary_Iterator;
                     Appt     : in Appointment_Type);
   procedure Delete (Iterator : in Diary_Iterator);

end JE.Diaries;
```

11.7 Implementing a linked list diary

Now for the operations on Diary_Type objects. These are very similar to the way they were in the previous chapter. Size is the same as it was before except that it needs to refer to Diary.List.Count instead of Diary.Count:

```
function Size (Diary : Diary_Type) return Natural is
begin
   return Diary.List.Count;
end Size;
```

Choose is a bit more difficult. It needs to step through the list from the beginning to the requested position:

```
function Choose (Diary : Diary_Type;
                 Appt  : Positive) return Appointment_Type is
   Iterator : Diary_Iterator;
begin
   if Appt not in 1 .. Diary.List.Count then
      raise Diary_Error;
   else
```

```
      Iterator := First(Diary);
      for I in 2 .. Appt loop
        Iterator := Succ(Iterator);
      end loop;
      return Value(Iterator);
   end if;
end Choose;
```

Deleting an appointment also involves stepping through the list to the correct position:

```
procedure Delete (Diary : in out Diary_Type;
                  Appt  : in Positive) is
   Iterator : Diary_Iterator;
begin
   if Appt not in 1 .. Diary.Count then
      raise Diary_Error;
   else
      Iterator := First(Diary);
      for I in 2 .. Appt loop
        Iterator := Succ(Iterator);
      end loop;
      Delete (Iterator);
   end if;
end Delete;
```

Adding an appointment involves locating the correct position for the appointment just like it did with the array implementation. If we're out of memory a Storage_Error exception will be raised, so this will need to be reported as a Diary_Error:

```
procedure Add (Diary : in out Diary_Type;
               Appt  : in Appointment_Type) is
   use type JE.Times.Time_Type;    -- to allow use of ">"
   Iterator : Diary_Iterator;
begin
   Iterator := First(Diary);
   while Iterator /= Last(Diary) loop
      exit when Date(Value(Iterator)) > Date(Appt);
      Iterator := Succ(Iterator);
   end loop;
   Insert (Iterator, Appt);
exception
   when Storage_Error =>
      raise Diary_Error;
end Add;
```

Load is very similar to the way it was before, except that it has to make sure the diary is empty by deleting all the appointments in the list rather than just by setting the Count component to zero:

```
procedure Load (Diary : in out Diary_Type;
                From  : in String) is
  File : Appt_IO.File_Type;
  Appt : Appointment_Type;
begin
  while Diary.List.Count > 0 loop
    Delete (First(Diary));
  end loop;
  Appt_IO.Open (File, In_File, From);
  while not Appt_IO.End_Of_File(File) loop
    Appt_IO.Read (File, Appt);
    Insert (Last(Diary), Appt);
  end loop;
  Appt_IO.Close (File);

exception
  when Name_Error =>
    raise Diary_Error;
end Load;
```

The diary can be assumed to be saved in date order, so each appointment can be added to the end of the list by using Last(Diary) as the insertion position. Save is also very similar to the previous version, except that the number of appointments isn't stored in the file:

```
procedure Save (Diary : in Diary_Type;
                To    : in String) is
  File : Appt_IO.File_Type;
  I : Diary_Iterator := First(Diary);
begin
  Appt_IO.Create (File, To);
  while I /= Last(Diary) loop
    Appt_IO.Write (File, Value(I));
    I := Succ(I);
  end loop;
  Appt_IO.Close (File);
end Save;
```

The diary program from the previous chapter will not need changing; the visible interface in the package hasn't been touched, so all the facilities that the program used are still usable in exactly the same way. Only the internal implementation has been affected.

11.8   General access types

Sometimes it is useful to be able to create pointers to ordinary variables rather than just to objects created using **new**. Ada refers to such objects as **aliased objects** since any such object already has a name by which it can be accessed; a pointer to the object acts as an 'alias' for it, in other words another name which can be used to access it. To enable the compiler to keep track of which objects are aliased and which ones aren't, you have to use the reserved word **aliased** in the object declaration:

```
I : aliased Integer;
```

You can also declare aliased array elements and record components:

```
type Array_Type is array (Positive range <>)
                                  of aliased Integer;
type Record_Type is
  record
    I : aliased Integer;
  end record;
```

Access variables which can be used with aliased objects as well as those allocated using **new** are declared like this:

```
type Integer_Access is access all Integer;
```

The use of **access all** in the declaration of Integer_Access means that a variable of type Integer_Access is allowed to point to aliased integers like I as well as integers created using **new**. Integer_Access is known as a **general access type** as opposed to the **pool-specific** access types that you've seen so far.

You can get a pointer to an aliased variable by using the 'Access attribute:

```
IA : Integer_Access := I'Access;       -- pointer to I (above)
A  : Array_Type(1..10);                -- see above
AA : Integer_Access := A(5)'Access;    -- pointer to A(5)
B  : Record_Type;                      -- see above
BA : Integer_Access := B.I'Access;     -- pointer to B.I
```

There are some limitations placed on this for the sake of safety. The scope of any aliased Integer which IA is going to point to must be at least as large as that of the scope of the type declaration for Integer_Access. This means that the following is illegal in Ada:

```
procedure Illegal is         -- outer scope for declarations
   type Integer_Access is access all Integer;
   IA : Integer_Access;
```

```
begin
   ...
   declare                         -- inner scope for declarations
      I : aliased Integer;
   begin
      IA := I'Access;              -- illegal!
   end;                            -- end of I's scope
   IA.all := IA.all + 1;           -- eek! I doesn't exist any more!
end Illegal;                       -- end of Integer_Access's scope
```

The reason for this is that IA is assigned a pointer to I inside the inner block. At the end of the block, I ceases to exists so that at the point where the assignment statement is executed, IA points to a non-existent variable. This is what is known as a **dangling pointer**. The restriction may seem a bit severe but it guarantees that any objects that an Integer_Access variable can point to must exist for at least as long as any Integer_Access variable. In particular, if Integer_Access is declared in a library package, the scope of Integer_Access is the entire program so that only variables declared at **library level** (i.e. declared inside a package which is compiled as a library unit) can be used with Integer_Access. You can get around this to some extent by using generic packages as described in the next chapter, but if the restriction is still too severe you can subvert it by using the attribute 'Unchecked_Access instead of 'Access. As the name implies, no checks on accessibility are performed and it's up to you to make sure that you don't do anything stupid:

```
procedure Legal_But_Stupid is
   type Integer_Access is access all Integer;
   IA : Integer_Access;
begin
   ...
   declare
      I : aliased Integer;
   begin
      IA := I'Unchecked_Access;    -- dangerous!
   end;
   IA.all := IA.all + 1;           -- it's your own fault when
end Legal_But_Stupid;              -- this crashes!
```

Using 'Unchecked_Access is not recommended unless you are *completely* sure you know what you're doing!

General access variables must be set to point to variables since they can be used to assign a new value to the object they point to; if you want to point to constants as well as variables you must use **access constant** instead of **access all** in the type declaration:

```
type Constant_Integer_Access is access constant Integer;
```

A Constant_Integer_Access variable can't be used to alter the object it points to, whether that object is a constant or a variable. One use for this is to create arrays of strings of different lengths. If you want an array of strings to hold the names of the days of the week the individual strings must all be the same size:

```
Day_Names : constant array (Day_Of_Week) of String (1..9) :=
   ("Sunday   ", "Monday   ", "Tuesday  ", "Wednesday",
    "Thursday ", "Friday   ", "Saturday ");
                              -- all exactly 9 characters long
```

However, you can have an array of pointers to strings instead, which allows the individual strings to have different lengths:

```
Sun_Name : aliased constant String := "Sunday";
Mon_Name : aliased constant String := "Monday";
Tue_Name : aliased constant String := "Tuesday";
Wed_Name : aliased constant String := "Wednesday";
Thu_Name : aliased constant String := "Thursday";
Fri_Name : aliased constant String := "Friday";
Sat_Name : aliased constant String := "Saturday";

type Name_Type is access constant String;

Day_Names : array (Day_Of_Week) of Name_Type :=
   (Sun_Name'Access, Mon_Name'Access, Tue_Name'Access,
    Wed_Name'Access, Thu_Name'Access, Fri_Name'Access,
    Sat_Name'Access);
```

You are also allowed to use the 'Access attribute to create pointers to subprograms:

```
type Menu_Operation is access procedure;

procedure Add;
procedure List;
procedure Delete;

Menu : constant array (1..3) of Menu_Operation :=
                  (Add'Access, List'Access, Delete'Access);

type Math_Function  is access function (I : Float)
                                        return Float;
function Sin (F : Float) return Float;
function Cos (F : Float) return Float;
function Tan (F : Float) return Float;
```

```
Ops : constant array (1..3) of Math_Function :=
                  (Sin'Access, Cos'Access, Tan'Access);
```

The number and types of the parameters and the result type of functions must match those given in the access type declaration (but the parameter names don't need to). Thus a Menu_Operation can point to any parameterless procedure and a Math_Function can point to any function with a single Float parameter and a Float result. You can call these subprograms like this:

```
Menu(I).all;        -- call I'th procedure from array Menu
F := Ops(I)(F);     -- call I'th function from array Ops
                    -- with parameter F
```

Note that you have to use '.all' to call a parameterless subprogram, but you don't if there are any parameters; 'Ops(I)(F)' is an abbreviation for 'Ops(I).all(F)'.

The same scope rules apply for pointers to subprograms as for pointers to aliased objects, so that an **access procedure** type declared in a library package can only point to library-level procedures (i.e. procedures compiled as library units in their own right or procedures inside packages compiled as library units). You can't use the 'Unchecked_Access attribute with subprograms; to get around this, you have to use generic packages as I mentioned earlier. The way this is done is described in the next chapter.

11.9   Access parameters and discriminants

There are two final features of access types which I'll describe briefly here but which I'll come back to in later chapters. An **access parameter** is a special form of **in** parameter for a function or procedure:

```
function  F (A : access Integer) return Integer;
procedure G (A : access Integer);
```

The keyword **access** is used in place of **in**, **out** or **in out**. The actual parameter you supply when you call a subprogram with an access parameter is any access value which points to the correct type of object:

```
type Integer_Access is access Integer;
IA : Integer_Access := new Integer'(1);
AI : aliased Integer;

X : Integer := F(IA);
Y : Integer := F(AI'Access);
Z : Integer := F(new Integer);
```

The parameters to F in the example above are all pointers to an Integer of one sort or another. Within the subprogram the access parameter may be used to inspect or alter the object it points to. The parameter can't be a null pointer; if it is you'll get a Constraint_Error when you attempt to call the subprogram. Inside the subprogram the parameter acts like an access value which is a constant (i.e. you can't alter the pointer itself, although you *can* alter what it points to) and which belongs to an anonymous access type. Since you haven't got a name for the access type you can't declare any more objects of the same type, and any attempts to convert the value to a named access type will be checked to make sure you aren't breaking the scope rules described earlier for general access types, and a Program_Error exception will be raised if you are.

In a similar way you can use **access discriminants** in type declarations:

```
type T (P : access Integer) is
   limited record
      . . .
   end record;
```

Any type with an access discriminant must be a limited type, so you can't use assignment as a way of breaking the scope rules. When you declare an object of type T you must supply an appropriate access value of some sort for the discriminant:

```
type Integer_Access is access Integer;
Int_Access   : Integer_Access := new Integer'(1);
Aliased_Int : aliased Integer;

X : T (Int_Access);
Y : T (Aliased_Int'Access);
Z : T (new Integer);
```

Again, the discriminant value can't be **null** and its type is anonymous so you can't declare any other objects of the same type.

Exercises

11.1   Produce a package which implements strings with no maximum size limit. This can be done by allocating space in linked blocks of (say) 100 characters at a time, and linking extra blocks to the end of the existing allocation when more space is needed. Define operations to convert to and from normal strings as well as the standard operations of copying, slicing, concatenating and indexing individual characters.

11.2   Write a program which asks the user to pick an animal and then tries to identify it by asking a series of yes/no questions (see exercise 3.3). Use a record containing a string and two pointers. If the pointers are null, the string is the name of an animal; if not, the string is a question to ask and the pointers point to further records of the same type, one for a 'yes' answer and one for a 'no'. The program should ask questions and follow the appropriate pointers until an animal's name (e.g. 'aardvark') is reached, at which point the question 'Is it an aardvark?' should be asked. If the user responds 'no', the program should ask for the name of the animal and a question to distinguish it from an aardvark (or whatever). The question can be used to replace the animal's name in the last node visited and two extra nodes can be created containing the original animal's name and the new name entered by the user.

11.3 Write a procedure to sort a linked list of integers into ascending order. There are lots of ways this could be done!

11.4 Write a program which counts the number of occurrences of each word typed at the keyboard, as in exercise 6.3, but use a linked list to avoid imposing any limit on the maximum number of words which can be handled. As in exercise 6.3, consider a word to be a sequence of up to 32 letters, and ignore case differences.

CHAPTER 12

Generics

I am made all things to all men.
— Corinthians I, *9:22*

12.1   Generic packages

Linked lists as presented in the previous chapter are the sort of data structure that are useful in a wide variety of situations. We could take the linked list operations from the diary package to create a separate linked list package like this:

```
package JE.Lists is
   type Appointment_Type is private;
   type List_Type        is limited private;
   type List_Iterator    is private;

   function  First (List     : List_Type)
                                 return List_Iterator;
   function  Last  (List     : List_Type)
                                 return List_Iterator;
   function  Succ  (Iterator : List_Iterator)
                                 return List_Iterator;
   function  Pred  (Iterator : List_Iterator)
                                 return List_Iterator;
   function  Value (Iterator : List_Iterator)
                                 return Appointment_Type;
   procedure Insert (Iterator : in List_Iterator;
                     Appt     : in Appointment_Type);
   procedure Delete (Iterator : in List_Iterator);
private
   ...    -- as in chapter 11
end JE.Lists;
```

Unfortunately it wouldn't be terribly useful since the lists it would define would be lists of diary appointments. We wouldn't need lists of appointments that often, but lists of strings

219

or integers or personnel details or playing cards could conceivably be useful. The actual list handling would be the same no matter what type of data the list actually held, so why not define a **generic** list management package which could be used to manage linked lists of any data type we happen to require?

At present, the linked list package uses Appointment_Type throughout as the type of the items to be stored in the lists. One way to generalise the package would be to include the following subtype declaration:

```
subtype Item_Type is Appointment_Type;
```

This means that Item_Type is effectively a renaming of Appointment_Type. If the package is amended so that it uses Item_Type as the type of the items to store in the list, it's easy to change the package to deal with items of a different type; all you have to do is make a copy of the package (and give it a new name), then change the declaration of Item_Type and recompile. However, Ada provides a mechanism for defining **generic packages** that can give you the same effect without any copying, editing or recompiling.

You've already met some generic packages; the package Ada.Text_IO contains several generic packages like Integer_IO which can be instantiated for use with any integer type and Enumeration_IO which can be instantiated for use with any enumerated type. If you look at the declaration of Ada.Text_IO in Appendix B, you'll see that Integer_IO is declared inside it like this:

```
generic
   type Num is range <>;
package Integer_IO is
   -- subprograms with parameters of type Num
end Integer_IO;
```

Before you can use this package, you have to **instantiate** it by supplying the name of the actual type you want to use as a parameter. The result of this is a brand new package:

```
package My_Integer_IO is
        new Ada.Text_IO.Integer_IO (My_Integer_Type);
```

What effectively happens is that the compiler creates a new package called My_Integer_IO which is identical to Ada.Text_IO.Integer_IO except that all occurrences of the type Num have been replaced by My_Integer_Type. So where Ada.Text_IO.Integer_IO provides a procedure Put which takes a parameter of type Num, My_Integer_IO provides a procedure Put which takes a parameter of type My_Integer_Type instead. You can use a named parameter association when instantiating a generic package, just as you can for the parameters in a procedure call:

```
package My_Integer_IO is
        new Ada.Text_IO.Integer_IO (Num => My_Integer_Type);
```

This shows explicitly that the type Num in Integer_IO is to be replaced by My_Integer_Type when the package is instantiated.

The specification of the parameter Num as 'range <>' shows that Num can be any integer type, since the reserved word **range** in a type declaration indicates that the type being declared is an integer type. All the normal integer operations can be used with type Num inside the package; the compiler will ensure that when the package is instantiated the actual type supplied as a parameter really is an integer type so that those operations are guaranteed to be legitimate. However, the actual range of values for Num is unspecified (as shown by the box symbol '<>') so the package should be careful to avoid unwarranted assumptions. For example, putting anything like this in the package body would be a bad idea:

```
X : Num := 0;           -- Argh! Can't assume 0 will always be
                        -- a legal value of Num!
```

If an integer type that doesn't include 0 in its range (e.g. Positive) is used to instantiate the package, the declaration above will raise a constraint error. Attributes like Num'First and Num'Last should always be used instead of specific values for safety.

Generics are not restricted to use with packages; generic procedures and functions can also be defined. For example, Ada.Unchecked_Deallocation (which was described in the previous chapter) is a generic procedure. In the case of a generic package, the generic parameter list goes before the package specification but not in front of the package body; the compiler knows about the generic parameters when it's compiling the body because it's already dealt with the specification. A similar thing is done with generic procedures and functions; a specification of the procedure or function *must* be given which gives the generic parameter list, and the procedure or function is then defined without repeating the generic parameter list.

12.2 Generic parameters

In the case of a linked list package, we want a linked list of any type. Linked lists of arrays, records, integers or any other type should be equally possible. The way to do this is to specify the item type in the package declaration as **private**, like this:

```
generic
   type Item_Type is private;
package JE.Lists is
   ...
end JE.Lists;
```

The only operations that will be allowed in the package body are those appropriate to private types, namely assignment (:=) and testing for equality and inequality (= and /=). When the package is instantiated, any type that meets these requirements can be supplied as the actual parameter. This includes records, arrays, integers and so on; the only types excluded are limited types. Also, you must give a constrained type (so String would not be allowed, but a subtype of String which is constrained to a particular length would be); if you wanted to allow unconstrained types as well as constrained types to be used to instantiate the package, you would need to declare the generic parameter like this:

```
generic
   type Item_Type(<>) is private;
package JE.Lists is
   ...
end JE.Lists;
```

The '(<>)' after the type name means that unconstrained types are allowed as well as constrained types. One effect of this is that you would only be able to use Item_Type in ways which are allowed for unconstrained types; using Item_Type as a procedure parameter would be allowed but declaring an uninitialised Item_Type variable wouldn't.

As you can see, the way you declare your generic type parameters puts restrictions on what operations you can perform on the type inside the package as well as what types you can supply as parameters. Specifying the parameter as 'range <>' allows the package to use all the standard operations on integer types but restricts you to supplying an integer type when you instantiate the package. Specifying the parameter as 'private' gives you greater freedom when you instantiate the package but reduces the range of operations that you can use inside the package itself. There are numerous ways of specifying generic parameters; table 12.1 gives the complete list, the last half-a-dozen of which are related to **tagged types** (which will be described in chapter 14). For example, you can use 'mod <>' as a generic parameter, in which case you can use any modular type in your instantiation; inside the package you can use any of the standard operations on modular types (e.g. the 'Modulus attribute).

Something that table 12.1 doesn't show is that the generic parameter can also be specified as having discriminants, in which case the actual type you supply for the parameter must have matching discriminants:

```
type X (Count : Integer) is private;
         -- any non-limited type with an Integer discriminant
```

Also, as I mentioned above, you can specify for any generic parameter that its actual type may or may not have discriminants by putting '(<>)' after the type name:

```
type X (<>) is private;
         -- any non-limited type with or without discriminants
```

Note that in the cases of access types and derived types you must specify X in terms of another specific type (called Y in the examples in table 12.1). This is so that the compiler knows what to do with the object that an X points to in the case of an access type, and so

Table 12.1

Generic type specifications

```
limited private            -- any type at all
private                    -- any non-limited type
(<>)                       -- any discrete (integer or
                              enumeration) type
range <>                   -- any signed integer type
mod <>                     -- any modular integer type
digits <>                  -- any floating point type
delta <>                   -- any fixed point type
delta <> digits <>         -- any decimal type
access Y                   -- any access-to-Y type
access all Y               -- any "access all Y" type
access constant Y          -- any "access constant Y" type
array (Y range <>) of Z    -- any unconstrained array-of-Z
                              type with a subtype of Y as
                              its index subtype
array (Y) of Z             -- any constrained array-of-Z
                              type with a subtype of Y as
                              its index subtype
new Y                      -- any type derived from Y
new Y with private         -- any non-abstract tagged type
                              derived from Y
abstract new Y with private
                           -- any tagged type (abstract or
                              not) derived from Y
tagged private             -- any non-abstract non-limited
                              tagged type
tagged limited private     -- any non-abstract tagged type
abstract tagged private    -- any non-limited tagged type
abstract tagged limited private
                           -- any tagged type at all
```

that it knows what the parent type is (and hence what operations are available) in the case of a derived type. Similarly, in array types you must specify the type of the individual items as well as the index subtype so that the compiler knows what operations are allowed on the index type and the individual array elements; also you cannot use a constrained array type for an unconstrained generic array parameter or an unconstrained array type for a constrained generic array parameter. Typically the specific types used in access, array and derived type parameters will be other generic parameters; for example, the standard procedure Ada.Unchecked_Deallocation (which was described in the previous chapter) is declared like this:

```
generic
   type Object(<>) is limited private;
   type Name       is access Object;
package Ada.Unchecked_Deallocation (X : in out Name);
```

Here Name is an access type defined in terms of Object, which is also a generic parameter. Thus when you instantiate Unchecked_Deallocation you have to specify the access type that you want to deallocate as well as the type of object it points to. The declaration of Object allows this to be any type at all, either constrained or unconstrained.

Generic packages, like any other packages, can have child packages. Child packages of generic packages must also be generic:

```
generic
   type Other_Type is private;
package JE.Lists.Child is
   ...
end JE.Lists.Child;
```

To instantiate JE.Lists.Child you have to instantiate the parent package first. The child package is then effectively a generic child of the instantiated parent package so that it can be instantiated like this:

```
package Int_Lists      is new JE.Lists (Item_Type => Integer);
package Int_List_Child is new Int_Lists.Child
                                       (Other_Type => Boolean);
```

If you don't need any extra generic parameters for the child package you can just leave them out, although the child package must still be specified as being generic:

```
generic
   -- it's generic but there are no generic parameters
package JE.Lists.Child is
   ...
end JE.Lists.Child;
```

In this case, you would first need to instantiate JE.Lists as before, and then instantiate JE.Lists.Child without supplying any generic parameters:

```
package Int_Lists      is new JE.Lists (Item_Type  => Integer);
package Int_List_Child is new Int_Lists.Child;
```

Here's what the linked list package from the beginning of the chapter (including the full version of the private part, which is taken from the previous chapter) looks like once it's been modified to be a generic package:

```
generic
   type Item_Type is private;
package JE.Lists is
   type List_Type      is limited private;
   type List_Iterator is private;

   function  First   (List     : List_Type)
                                   return List_Iterator;
   function  Last    (List     : List_Type)
                                   return List_Iterator;
   function  Succ    (Iterator : List_Iterator)
                                   return List_Iterator;
   function  Pred    (Iterator : List_Iterator)
                                   return List_Iterator;
   function  Value   (Iterator : List_Iterator)
                                   return Item_Type;
   procedure Insert (Iterator : in List_Iterator;
                     Item     : in Item_Type);
   procedure Delete (Iterator : in List_Iterator);

private
   type Item_Record;
   type Item_Access is access Item_Record;

   type Item_Record is
      record
         Item : Item_Type;
         Next : Item_Access;
         Pred : Item_Access;
      end record;

   type List_Header is
      record
         First : Item_Access;
         Last  : Item_Access;
         Count : Natural := 0;
      end record;
   type List_Access is access all List_Header;

   type List_Type is
      record
         List : List_Access := new List_Header;
      end record;
```

```
type List_Iterator is
  record
    List     : List_Access;
    Current : Item_Access;
  end record;

end JE.Lists;
```

The package body is exactly the same as it was before with the type names changed appropriately to match the new names used in the specification (Item_Type instead of Appointment_Type, List_Type instead of Diary_Type, List_Iterator instead of Diary_Iterator, Item_Access instead of Appointment_Access and so on).

Once the generic package has been compiled, using it is simply a matter of instantiating it with the item type you want to use:

```
package Appointment_Lists is
    new JE.Lists (Item_Type => Appointment_Type);

package Integer_Lists is
    new JE.Lists (Item_Type => Integer);
```

The generic package doesn't need changing or recompiling at all when you do this, but all the type safety checks are still enforced.

12.3   Revising the diary package

Now that we've got a generic linked list package, we can use it to reimplement the diary package from the previous chapter. The definition of Diary_Type in the private part of the specification will need changing to use the generic package:

```
with JE.Appointments, JE.Times, JE.Lists;
use  JE.Appointments;
package JE.Diaries is
  type Diary_Type is limited private;
  ...     -- etc.

private
  type Appointment_Type is
    record
      Time    : JE.Times.Time_Type;
      Details : String (1..50);
      Length  : Natural := 0;
    end record;
```

```
   package Lists is
          new JE.Lists (Item_Type => Appointment_Type);

   type Diary_Type is
      limited record
        List : Lists.List_Type;
      end record;
end JE.Diaries;
```

The subprograms in the package body will need minor changes to use operations from the list package rather than doing things 'by hand'. For example, the definition of Size will need changing to use the Size operation from Lists:

```
function Size (Diary : Diary_Type) return Natural is
begin
   return Size(Diary.List);
end Size;
```

The implementation of Choose involves the same sort of minor changes. Compare this version with the previous version:

```
function Choose (Diary : Diary_Type;
                 Appt  : Positive) return Appointment_Type is
   Iterator : List_Iterator;
begin
   if Appt not in 1 .. Size(Diary.List) then
     raise Diary_Error;
   else
     Iterator := First(Diary.List);
     for I in 2 .. Appt loop
       Iterator := Succ(Iterator);
     end loop;
     return Value(Iterator);
   end if;
end Choose;
```

Here are amended versions of the other subprograms:

```
procedure Delete (Diary : in out Diary_Type;
                  Appt  : in Positive) is
   Iterator : List_Iterator;
begin
   if Appt not in 1 .. Size(Diary.List) then
     raise Diary_Error;
```

```
      else
         Iterator := First(Diary.List);
         for I in 2 .. Appt loop
            Iterator := Succ(Iterator);
         end loop;
         Lists.Delete (Iterator);
      end if;
   end Delete;

   procedure Add (Diary : in out Diary_Type;
                  Appt  : in Appointment_Type) is
      use type JE.Times.Time_Type;   -- to allow use of ">"
      Iterator : List_Iterator;
   begin
      Iterator := First(Diary.List);
      while Iterator /= Last(Diary.List) loop
         exit when Value(Iterator).Time > Appt.Time;
         Iterator := Succ(Iterator);
      end loop;
      Insert (Iterator, Appt);
   exception
      when Storage_Error =>
         raise Diary_Error;
   end Add;

   procedure Load (Diary : out Diary_Type;
                   From  : in String) is
      File : Appt_IO.File_Type;
      Appt : Appointment_Type;
   begin
      while Size(Diary.List) > 0 loop
         Delete (First(Diary.List));
      end loop;

      Appt_IO.Open (File, In_File, From);
      while not Appt_IO.End_Of_File(File) loop
         Appt_IO.Read (File, Appt);
         Insert (Last(Diary.List), Appt);
      end loop;
      Appt_IO.Close (File);
   exception
      when Name_Error =>
         raise Diary_Error;
   end Load;
```

```
procedure Save (Diary : in Diary_Type;
                To     : in String) is
  File : Appt_IO.File_Type;
  I : Iterator := First(Diary.List);
begin
  Appt_IO.Create (File, In_File, To);
  while I /= Last(Diary.List) loop
    Appt_IO.Write (File, Lists.Value(I));
    I := Succ(I);
  end loop;
  Appt_IO.Close (File);
end Save;
```

Appointment_Type wasn't affected by any of the changes to Diary_Type, so none of the operations on Appointment_Type need any modifications.

12.4   A generic sorting procedure

The sorting procedure defined in chapter 6 is another obvious candidate for making generic. It doesn't matter if we're sorting integers or appointments, as long as we can compare them to determine their relative ordering. Here's a possible declaration for a procedure Generic_Sort that can sort arrays of any discrete type:

```
generic
  type Item_Type  is (<>);
  type Index_Type is (<>)
  type Array_Type is array (Index_Type range <>) of Item_Type;
procedure Generic_Sort (X : in out Array_Type);
```

Here's a possible instantiation of Generic_Sort:

```
type Character_Count is array (Character) of Integer;

procedure Sort is
            new Generic_Sort (Item_Type  => Integer,
                              Index_Type => Character,
                              Array_Type => Character_Count);
```

Since Generic_Sort defines Item_Type to be a discrete type, we can use the comparison operator "<" to compare the relative ordering of items in the array. Unfortunately this rules out using this procedure to sort an array of appointments since Appointment_Type is a record type, not a discrete type, and there is no "<" operator defined for record types. The only way to define Item_Type which would allow it to be used with record types is as a private type, but this prevents us from using "<" for our comparisons since "<" is not a standard operation on private types (only assignment and tests for equality and inequality are allowed). However, you can also specify procedures, functions or packages as generic parameters. What you need to do is to supply a comparison function as a generic parameter:

```
generic
   type Item_Type  is private;
   type Index_Type is (<>)
   type Array_Type is array (Index_Type range <>) of Item_Type;
   with function Compare (Left, Right : Item_Type)
                         return Boolean;
procedure Generic_Sort (X : in out Array_Type);
```

Note that procedure, function and package parameters are preceded by 'with'; if you left out 'with' in the example above the compiler would think that you were declaring a generic function called Compare.

Now when you instantiate it you just have to supply the name of a suitable function which has the right number and types of parameters and the right result type:

```
type Character_Count is
   record
     Char  : Character;
     Count : Integer := 0;
   end record;

type Count_Array is array (Character) of Character_Count;

function Less (X, Y : Character_Count) return Boolean is
begin
   return X.Count < Y.Count;
end Less;


-- Instantiation of Generic_Sort to sort Count_Arrays:
procedure Sort is
            new Generic_Sort (Item_Type  => Character_Count,
                              Index_Type => Character,
                              Array_Type => Count_Array,
                              Compare    => Less);
```

Here Sort will sort an array of records using the function Less to decide on the order of the array items. Supplying the comparison function as a generic parameter also has the advantage that you can supply any comparison function you like; for example, here are two instantiations which sort an array of integers into ascending and descending order:

```
type Character_Count is array (Character) of Integer;

procedure Ascending_Sort is
            new Generic_Sort (Item_Type  => Integer,
                              Index_Type => Character,
                              Array_Type => Character_Count,
                              Compare    => "<");
procedure Descending_Sort is
            new Generic_Sort (Item_Type  => Integer,
                              Index_Type => Character,
                              Array_Type => Character_Count,
                              Compare    => ">");
```

The first one uses "<" to compare the items so that they'll be sorted into ascending order, the second uses ">" instead so that the ordering will be reversed.

In many cases, "<" will be the function we will want to use to do the comparisons. To avoid having to specify it as a parameter in every instantiation, it's possible to provide a default value. Here's how it's done:

```
generic
   type Item_Type  is private;
   type Index_Type is (<>)
   type Array_Type is array (Index_Type range <>) of Item_Type;
   with function "<" (Left, Right : Item_Type)
                                        return Boolean is <>;
procedure Generic_Sort (X : in out Array_Type);
```

The 'is <>' at the end of the function declaration means that you don't need to provide a function for the parameter if a suitable function already exists with the same name as the parameter (in this case "<"). This means that we can now define Ascending_Sort like this:

```
procedure Ascending_Sort is
            new Generic_Sort (Item_Type  => Integer,
                              Index_Type => Character,
                              Array_Type => Character_Count);
            -- Integer < Integer will be used to do
            -- comparisons in Ascending_Sort
```

So here, finally, is the sort procedure from chapter 6 generalised into a generic procedure. Remember that a separate specification is required for the procedure which is prefixed by the generic parameter list; the procedure definition is given separately without repeating the generic parameter list. A common mistake is to try and put the generic parameter list in front of the procedure definition and not bother with a specification, but the compiler won't like it if you do this.

```
-- Generic procedure specification
generic
   type Item_Type  is private;
   type Index_Type is (<>);
   type Array_Type is array (Index_Type range <>)
                           of Item_Type;
   with function "<" (Left, Right : Item_Type)
                           return Boolean is <>;
procedure Generic_Sort (X : in out Array_Type);

-- Procedure definition
procedure Generic_Sort (X : in out Array_Type) is
   Position : Index_Type;
   Value    : Item_Type;
begin
   for I in Index_Type'Succ(X'First)..X'Last loop
     if X(I) < X(Index_Type'Pred(I)) then
        Value := X(I);
        for J in reverse X'First .. Index_Type'Pred(I) loop
          exit when X(J) < Value;
          Position := J;
        end loop;
        X(Index_Type'Succ(Position)..I) :=
                         X(Position..Index_Type'Pred(I));
        X(Position) := Value;
     end if;
   end loop;
end Generic_Sort;
```

$\Rightarrow$ *See what your compiler says if you leave out the specification and try to put the*
  generic parameter list in front of the procedure definition.

Notice how the attributes 'Succ, 'Pred, 'First and 'Last have been used throughout the
procedure body to avoid making any assumptions about the index subtype of Array_Type.
You have to be *very* careful about this sort of thing when writing generic code. Don't take
anything for granted, and test everything with unusual types (e.g. arrays whose bounds are
100 .. 200).

Note that as well as using types and subprograms as generic parameters, you can also
use packages, constants or variables; the complete list of possibilities is shown in table
12.2. In the first two cases, you can also supply a default value like this:

```
generic
    Size : Integer := 100;
procedure Something_Or_Other;
```

Table 12.2

```
┌─────────────────────────────────────────────────────────────────────┐
│                    Other generic parameters                          │
│                                                                       │
│  X : T;                      -- any object of type T                  │
│  X : in T;                   -- the same (any object of type T)       │
│  X : in out T;               -- any variable of type T                │
│  with procedure X;           -- any procedure matching the            │
│                                 specification of X                    │
│  with function X return T;   -- any function returning a result       │
│                                 of type T which matches the           │
│                                 specification of X                    │
│  with package X is new Y(<>); -- any package which is an              │
│                                 instantiation of Y                    │
└─────────────────────────────────────────────────────────────────────┘
```

When you instantiate this, you can omit specifying a value for Size:

```
procedure X is new Something_Or_Other (Size => 100);
procedure X is new Something_Or_Other;       -- same as above
```

12.5   Generics and general access types

As I mentioned in the previous chapter, you can also use generic packages to finesse your way out of the accessibility restrictions on general access types. If you declare a general access type as a package and then access it via a **with** clause, the scope of the type is the scope of the entire program and so you can only use it to point to objects whose scope is also the scope of the entire program; that is, only to objects declared in library packages (or to library subprograms). This is restrictive, but fortunately (by design!) the scope of a type declared in a generic package is the scope at the point it is instantiated. This means that you can 'smuggle' a package containing a general access type into an inner block by instantiating it in that inner block.

You can use this to design a general purpose menu package. The idea is to create a linked list containing a menu item, a character used to select it, and a pointer to a procedure to be executed when the menu item is selected. This reduces the amount of work involved in displaying menus, getting responses and validating them, and selecting the action to be performed. Here's an outline of a possible specification for the package:

```
with JE.Lists;
generic
package JE.Menus is
   type Action_Type is access procedure;
   type Menu_Type   is limited private;
   ...        -- operations on Menu_Type go here
```

```
private
   type Menu_Item_Type is
      record
         Title  : String (1..40);
         Length : Natural;
         Choice : Character;
         Action : Action_Type;
      end record;
   package Menu_Lists is new JE.Lists (Menu_Item_Type);
   type Menu_Type is
      limited record
         Menu_List : Menu_Lists.List_Type;
      end record;
end JE.Menus;
```

This uses the private part of the package to define the types needed to support Menu_Type. Menu_Type is a limited record because it contains a list of menu items, and lists are limited types. Menu_Item_Type declares the structure of an individual menu item: a title to be displayed together with its length, a character used to select it and an action procedure to be called. The package as a whole is generic even though there are no generic parameters needed; this is so that we can 'smuggle' it into inner scopes as described above by instantiating it at the same scope as the action procedures we want to use:

```
package Menus is new JE.Menus;
```

We'll need operations to add new menu items to the menu and to allow the user to select menu choices:

```
procedure Add     (Menu   : in out Menu_Type;
                   Title  : in String;
                   Key    : in Character;
                   Action : in Action_Type);

function  Execute (Menu   : Menu_Type) return Boolean;
```

The idea is that the Execute function will display the menu, get and validate the user's choice and then call the selected procedure. It will provide a Q (Quit) option automatically and will return True if the user doesn't select the Quit option, so that it can be used in a loop like this:

```
while Execute(Menu) loop
   ...    -- do anything that needs doing between menu actions
end loop;
```

Here's what the body of Add will look like:

```
procedure Add (Menu   : in out Menu_Type;
               Title  : in String;
               Key    : in Character;
               Action : in Action_Type) is
   Item : Menu_Item_Type;
   use Menu_Lists;

begin
   if Title'Length > Item.Title'Length then
     Item.Title := Title (Title'First ..
                          Item.Title'Length-Title'First+1);
     Item.Length := Item.Title'Length;
   else
     Item.Title (Item.Title'First ..
                 Title'Length-Item.Title'First+1)
                 := Title;
     Item.Length := Title'Length;
   end if;

   Item.Choice := Ada.Characters.Handling.To_Upper(Key);
   Item.Action := Action;
   Insert( Last(Menu.Menu_List), Item );
end Add;
```

Notice how this procedure carefully avoids assuming anything about the length or index range of the Title parameter and the Title component of Item. It constructs the menu item from the parameters and then uses the linked list operation Insert to add the new item to the end of the list. Since case differences should be ignored, it uses a function called To_Upper from the package Ada.Characters.Handling (see Appendix B) which converts its parameter to upper case if it's a lower case letter. The body of JE.Menus will need a **with** clause for Ada.Characters.Handling so that it can be referenced from Add.

Now for the body of Execute:

```
function Execute (Menu : Menu_Type) return Boolean is
   Item   : Menu_Item_Type;
   Choice : Character;
   use Menu_Lists;
   I : List_Iterator;

begin
   loop
     New_Line (3);
```

```
   -- Display the menu
   I := First(Menu.Menu_List);
   while I /= Last(Menu.Menu_List) loop
      Item := Value(I);
      Put ("    [");
      Put (Item.Choice);
      Put ("] ");
      Put_Line (Item.Title(1..Item.Length));
      I := Succ(I);
   end loop;

   -- Display the Quit option and prompt
   Put_Line ("    [Q] Quit");
   Put ("Enter your choice: ");

   -- Get user's choice in upper case
   Get (Choice);
   Choice := Ada.Characters.Handling.To_Upper(Choice);

   if Choice = 'Q' then
      -- Quit chosen, so return
      return False;
   else
      -- Search menu for choice
      I := First(Menu.Menu_List);
      while I /= Last(Menu.Menu_List) loop
         if Choice = Value(I).Choice then
            -- Choice found, so call procedure and return
            Value(I).Action.all;
            return True;
         end if;
         I := Succ(I);
      end loop;
   end if;

   -- Choice wasn't found, so display error message and loop
   Put_Line ("Invalid choice -- please try again.");
   end loop;
end Execute;
```

This uses procedures from Ada.Text_IO, so the package body for JE.Menus will need **with** and **use** clauses for Ada.Text_IO.

Here's how the menu package could be used to display the menu for the electronic diary program:

```
with JE.Menus, JE.Diaries;
procedure Diary is
   package Diary_View is
      ...      -- user interface procedures
   end Diary_View;

   ...        -- declarations of the diary etc.

   procedure Add    is separate;
   procedure Delete is separate;
   procedure List   is separate;

   package Menus is new JE.Menus;
   Menu : Menus.Menu_Type;
begin
   Menus.Add (Menu, "Add appointment",    'A', Add'Access);
   Menus.Add (Menu, "Delete appointment", 'D', Delete'Access);
   Menus.Add (Menu, "List appointments",  'L', List'Access);

   while Menus.Execute(Menu) loop
      null;
   end loop;
end Diary;
```

Add, Delete and List would just be procedures to call the corresponding user interface procedures in the internal Diary_View package with the appropriate parameters.

Exercises

12.1   Convert the diary package and main program from the previous chapter to use JE.Menus and JE.Lists.

12.2   Produce a generic version of the calculator program from chapter 3 as a procedure which can be instantiated to work with any integer type and test it with some different integer types.

12.3   Write a generic procedure which will apply a function given as a generic parameter to each element of an array, so that for example it could be used to square every value in an array of integers or convert all lower case letters in a string to upper case.

12.4   Modify the dimensioned units package from exercise 9.3 so that the dimensions are specified by a discrete type supplied as a generic parameter. The dimensions can be represented as an array of integers whose index subtype is the supplied discrete type. For example, the original package used dimensions of mass, length and time; this could be handled by instantiating the new package with an enumeration type consisting of the three values (Mass, Length, Time).

CHAPTER 13

Building a calculator

No reckoning made, but sent to my account
With all my imperfections on my head.
— Shakespeare, *Hamlet*

13.1   Handling operator precedence

It's time to return to the calculator program that was developed in chapter 3, which was capable of evaluating arithmetic expressions like 2+3*4. Expressions were dealt with on a strict left-to-right basis, so that 2+3*4 would evaluate to 20. However, the normal rules of arithmetic tell us that the value of this expression should be 14, since the conventional interpretation involves performing multiplication before addition.

Modifying the calculator to deal with this will require delaying the addition operation until the multiplication has been performed. This is a well-known problem; algorithms to deal with this were first developed in the 1950s and refined in the 1960s. One approach is to use a data structure known as a **stack**. A stack is a collection with specific restrictions on how it can be accessed; the traditional comparison is with a pile of plates. New items can be added to the top of the stack (i.e. you can put more plates on top of the pile) and items can be removed from the top of the stack (i.e. you can remove plates from the top of the pile). The conventional names for these operations are **pushing** an item onto the stack and **popping** an item off the top. You can generally tell if someone is a programmer by asking what the opposite of 'push' is; programmers say 'pop', everyone else says 'pull'! There may be a few extra operations; for example, you may be able to find out how many items the stack contains or inspect the top item without removing it. What you can't do is add or remove items anywhere except at the top of the stack; if you were to try with a stack of plates the result might be a 'stack crash'! A stack is said to have a **last-in first-out (LIFO)** organisation: the last item pushed onto the stack is the first one to be popped off.

Stacks are one of the most generally useful data structures around. They crop up in all sorts of situations; for example, the compiler relies on using a stack to keep track of procedure calls. When you call a procedure, your return address (the point in the calling procedure that you want to return to) is pushed onto a stack; returning from a procedure is simply a matter of popping the return address off the top of the stack and going back to the place it specifies. Stacks can also be used for evaluating arithmetic expressions according to the conventional rules of arithmetic.

239

The method for doing this requires two stacks, one for operands and one for operators. Whenever you see an operand, you put it on the operand stack; when you see an operator, you compare it with the operator on top of the operator stack. Each operation is given a priority (or precedence); multiplication has a higher priority than addition. If the operator you've just read has a higher priority than the one on top of the stack, you just push it onto the stack. This defers dealing with high-priority operators until you've had a chance to see what comes next. Otherwise, you remove the operator from the top of the stack, remove the top two values from the operand stack, apply the operator to the two operands and push the result onto the operand stack. You then repeat the process until the operator you're considering does have a higher priority than the one on top of the operator stack. In other words, when you see a low-priority operator you first of all deal with any deferred operators on the stack which have the same priority or higher. Finally, you push the operator you're considering onto the operator stack until you see what comes next.

To make this work, you need to prime the operator stack with an operator which has a lower priority than any other. At the end of the expression, operators must be removed one by one from the operator stack together with the top two operands from the operand stack; each operator is applied to its two operands and the result is pushed onto the operand stack. When you reach the low-priority operator on the bottom of the stack, the operand stack will contain a single value which is the result of the expression. Here's what happens if you evaluate 2+3*4+5 using this algorithm:

	Input	Symbol	Operands	Operators	Action
1)	2+3*4+5.			#	(start state)
2)	+3*4+5.	2	2	#	Push 2
3)	3*4+5.	+	2	# +	+ > #; push +
4)	*4+5.	3	2 3	# +	Push 3
5)	4+5.	*	2 3	# + *	* > +; push *
6)	+5.	4	2 3 4	# + *	Push 4
7)	5.	+	2 12	# +	+ < *; apply *
8)	5.	+	14	#	+ = +; apply +
9)	5.	+	14	# +	+ > #; push +
10)	.	5	14 5	# +	Push 5
11)	.		19	#	. < +; apply +

The result is 19. I've used '#' to represent the low-priority operator used to prime the operator stack. Operands and operators are pushed onto their respective stacks until step 7 is reached. Here we've got '+' and the operator stack has '*' on top. So the multiplication operator is removed from the operator stack, the top two items are removed from the operand stack (3 and 4), the multiplication operator is applied to the two operands, and the result (12) is pushed back onto the operand stack. Now we have a '+' on top of the operator stack, so step 8 repeats the process; 2+12 gives 14 which is pushed onto the operand stack. Now the top of the operator stack is '#', which has a lower priority than '+', so the '+' finally gets pushed onto the operator stack in step 9. At step 11 we've reached the full stop which signifies the end of the expression, so the '+' on top of the operator stack is removed, the two operands 14 and 5 are removed from the operand stack, and the result (19) is pushed onto the operand stack. The top operator on the stack is now '#', so the value on top of the operand stack (19) is the final result.

13.2 A stack package

At this point it's worth considering the design of a package to implement a stack type. The stack type itself should be private to prevent users fiddling about with implementation details; it should also be limited to prevent attempts to copy one entire stack to another or comparing two stacks for equality. The package needs to be generic so that a stack of any type of item can be created; the generic parameter should be **private** for maximum flexibility, so that any type which supports assignment can be used. The package only needs to use assignment to store and retrieve the items, so this is no problem.

The two basic operations to be provided are Push and Pop. These will need the stack to be operated on as a parameter; it will need to be an **in out** parameter since it needs to be copied into the procedure and then modified. For convenience and completeness we can provide a few extra operations: a function Top which returns a copy of the top item on the stack, a function Size which returns the number of items on the stack, and a function Empty which returns a Boolean result to indicate whether or not the stack is empty.

There are two things that can go wrong: the stack can overflow as the result of attempting to push too many items onto the stack, or the stack can 'underflow' as the result of attempting to access the top item of an empty stack. This means that we need two exceptions, Stack_Overflow and Stack_Underflow. Here's the resulting package specification, with the private part omitted for the moment:

```
generic
   type Item_Type is private;
package JE.Stacks is
   type Stack_Type is limited private;

   procedure Push  (Stack : in out Stack_Type;
                    Item  : in Item_Type);
   procedure Pop   (Stack : in out Stack_Type;
                    Item  : out Item_Type);
   function  Top   (Stack : Stack_Type) return Item_Type;
   function  Size  (Stack : Stack_Type) return Natural;
   function  Empty (Stack : Stack_Type) return Boolean;

   Stack_Overflow, Stack_Underflow : exception;

private
   -- to be dealt with later
end JE.Stacks;
```

Here's a modified version of chapter 3's calculator program which uses this stack package. I've tried to keep the structural changes to a minimum so that you can compare this with the original version more easily:

```ada
with Ada.Text_IO, Ada.Integer_Text_IO, JE.Stacks;
use  Ada.Text_IO, Ada.Integer_Text_IO;
procedure Calculator is
   package Operand_Stacks  is new JE.Stacks (Integer);
   package Operator_Stacks is new JE.Stacks (Character);
   use Operand_Stacks, Operator_Stacks;

   Operand_Stack  : Operand_Stacks.Stack_Type;
   Operator_Stack : Operator_Stacks.Stack_Type;

   Operator : Character;
   Operand  : Integer;

   procedure Apply is
      Left, Right : Integer;
      Operator    : Character;
   begin
      Pop (Operand_Stack, Right);
      Pop (Operand_Stack, Left);
      Pop (Operator_Stack, Operator);
      case Operator is
         when '+'    => Push (Operand_Stack, Left + Right);
         when '-'    => Push (Operand_Stack, Left - Right);
         when '*'    => Push (Operand_Stack, Left * Right);
         when '/'    => Push (Operand_Stack, Left / Right);
         when others => raise Program_Error;
                                   -- should never happen (!)
      end case;
   end Apply;

   function Prio (Operator : Character) return Natural is
   begin
      case Operator is
         when '+' | '-' => return 1;
         when '*' | '/' => return 2;
         when '#'       => return 0;
         when others    => raise Program_Error;
                                   -- should never happen (!)
      end case;
   end Prio;
```

```
begin        -- main program
  Push (Operator_Stack, '#');
  Put ("Enter an expression: ");
  Get (Operand);
  Push (Operand_Stack, Operand);

  loop
    loop
      Get (Operator);
      exit when Operator /= ' ';
    end loop;
    if Operator = '.' then
      while Top(Operator_Stack) /= '#' loop
        Apply;
      end loop;
      Put (Top(Operand_Stack), Width => 1);
      exit;
    end if;
    case Operator is
      when '+' | '-' | '*' | '/' =>
        while Prio(Operator) <= Prio(Top(Operator_Stack)) loop
          Apply;
        end loop;
        Push (Operator_Stack, Operator);
      when others =>
        Put ("Invalid operator '");
        Put (Operator);
        Put ("'");
        exit;
    end case;
    Get (Operand);
    Push (Operand_Stack, Operand);
  end loop;

  New_Line;
end Calculator;
```

This program uses an internal procedure called Apply which pops two operands and an operator and then pushes the result of applying the operator to the two operands; there is also an internal function called Prio which returns the priority of a selected operator. These procedures should never be called with anything except a valid operator, but I've written them defensively; Murphy's Law states that 'what can go wrong, will' so rather than taking anything for granted I've made sure that Program_Error will be raised by Apply and Prio if they come across an illegal operator character.

13.3   An improved calculator

The program as it stands expects its input to be a sequence of integers separated by operators and ending with a full stop. However, we might want to be able to deal with expressions like '2*(3+4)' which do not follow this pattern. In order to deal with parentheses, we need to read the input a character at a time rather than blindly assuming that the first thing on the line is an integer or that an integer follows every operator. Fortunately, Text_IO provides a procedure called Look_Ahead to enable us to look at the next input character without actually reading it. Look_Ahead takes two output parameters: a Character variable which will be set to the value of the next character and a Boolean variable which will be set True if we're at the end of the line (in which case the character parameter won't be affected). Here's how we could use Look_Ahead to get either an operator or an integer, assuming the existence of a Character variable Ch, a Boolean variable EOL and an Integer variable I:

```
loop
   Look_Ahead (Ch, EOL);
   if EOL then
      Skip_Line;          -- end of line, so go to next line
   elsif Ch = ' ' then
      Get (Ch);           -- space, so read it and ignore it
   else
      exit;               -- non-space, so exit loop
   end if;
end loop;

-- At this point, Ch is a copy of the next character, but the
-- next character hasn't actually been read yet.  We can read
-- an Integer or a Character, as appropriate...

if Ch in '0'..'9' then
   Get (I);               -- digit, so get an integer in I
else
   Get (Ch);              -- non-digit, so read it into Ch
end if;
```

Parentheses need to be dealt with in a special way. An opening parenthesis '(' is given a priority of 0, just like the '#' which is used to prime the stack. Any operators which follow this will have a higher priority and so will be stacked up above it. When we get to the closing parenthesis we clear operators by applying them to their operands until the opening parenthesis is the top item on the stack. It is then discarded, as is the closing parenthesis. We'll also need to check that there are no opening parentheses that haven't been left unmatched at the end of the expression. This is what happens when '2*(3+4)' is evaluated:

	Input	Symbol	Operands	Operators	Action
1)	2*(3+4).			#	(start state)
2)	*(3+4).	2	2	#	Push 2
3)	(3+4).	*	2	# *	* > #; push *
4)	3+4).	(	2	# * (	Push (
5)	+4).	3	2 3	# * (	Push 3
6)	4).	+	2 3	# * (+	+ > (; push +
7)	).	4	2 3 4	# * (+	Push 4
8)	.	)	2 7	# * (	Apply +
9)	.	)	2 7	# *	Remove (
10)	.		14	#	. < *; apply *

Here's a modified version of the program which allows for parentheses. Since Look_Ahead tells us when we've reached the end of the input line, we can use this as the expression terminator instead of requiring a full stop. Also, an exception Syntax_Error is used to respond to syntax errors in the input:

```
with Ada.Text_IO, Ada.Integer_Text_IO, JE.Stacks;
use  Ada.Text_IO, Ada.Integer_Text_IO;
procedure Calculator is
    package Operand_Stacks  is new JE.Stacks (Integer);
    package Operator_Stacks is new JE.Stacks (Character);
    use Operand_Stacks, Operator_Stacks;

    Operand_Stack  : Operand_Stacks.Stack_Type;
    Operator_Stack : Operator_Stacks.Stack_Type;

    Operator     : Character;
    Operand      : Integer;
    Line_End     : Boolean;
    Got_Operand  : Boolean := False;

    procedure Apply is
        Left, Right : Integer;
        Operator    : Character;
    begin
        Pop (Operand_Stack, Right);
        Pop (Operand_Stack, Left);
        Pop (Operator_Stack, Operator);

        case Operator is
            when '+'   => Push (Operand_Stack, Left + Right);
            when '-'   => Push (Operand_Stack, Left - Right);
            when '*'   => Push (Operand_Stack, Left * Right);
```

```
         when '/'    => Push (Operand_Stack, Left / Right);
         when others => raise Program_Error;
      end case;
   end Apply;


   function Prio (Operator : Character) return Natural is
   begin
      case Operator is
         when '+' | '-' => return 1;
         when '*' | '/' => return 2;
         when '#' | '(' => return 0;
         when others    => raise Program_Error;
      end case;
   end Prio;


   Syntax_Error : exception;

begin                                   -- main program
   Push (Operator_Stack, '#');
   Put ("Enter an expression: ");
   loop
      -- Get next non-space character
      loop
         Look_Ahead (Operator, Line_End);
         exit when Line_End or Operator /= ' ';
         Get (Operator);                -- got a space, so skip it
      end loop;

      -- Exit main loop at end of line
      exit when Line_End;

      -- Process operator or operand
      if Operator in '0'..'9' then    -- it's an operand
         if Got_Operand then          -- can't have an operand
            Put ("Missing operator"); -- immediately after
            exit;                     -- another
         end if;
         Get (Operand);               -- read the operand
         Push (Operand_Stack, Operand);
         Got_Operand := True;         -- record we've got an
                                      -- operand
      else                            -- it's not an operand
         Got_Operand := False;        -- so record the fact
         exit when Operator = '.';    -- exit at end of expr.
```

```
   Get (Operator);                    -- else read the operator
   case Operator is                   -- and apply it
     when '+' | '-' | '*' | '/' =>
        while Prio(Operator) <=
                      Prio(Top(Operator_Stack)) loop
           Apply;
        end loop;
        Push (Operator_Stack, Operator);

     when '(' =>                       -- stack left parenthesis
        Push (Operator_Stack, Operator);

     when ')' =>                       -- unwind stack back to '('
        while Prio(Top(Operator_Stack)) > Prio('(') loop
           Apply;
        end loop;
        Pop (Operator_Stack, Operator);
        if Operator /= '(' then
           Put ("Missing left parenthesis");
           raise Syntax_Error;
        end if;

     when others =>
        Put ("Invalid operator '");
        Put (Operator);
        Put ("'");
        raise Syntax_Error;
   end case;
  end if;
end loop;

-- Apply remaining operators from stack
while Prio(Top(Operator_Stack)) > Prio('#') loop
  Apply;                        -- unwind stack, apply operations
end loop;

-- Display result or report error
if Top(Operator_Stack) = '#' then
  Put (Top(Operand_Stack), Width => 1);
  New_Line;
else
  Put ("Missing right parenthesis");
  raise Syntax_Error;
end if;
```

```
exception
  when Syntax_Error =>
    Put_Line (" -- program terminated.");
end Calculator;
```

The main loop is executed until Look_Ahead reports the end of the line has been reached. If the character in Operator is a digit, an integer is read into Operand and pushed onto the stack and a Boolean variable called Got_Operand will be set to indicate that an operand has just been read. This is used to guard against two operands being entered one after the other; if this happens an error message is displayed and a Syntax_Error is raised. The processing of the operators is as it was earlier except that two extra cases are provided to deal with the left and right parentheses. A left parenthesis is just pushed onto the stack; a right parenthesis applies operators from the operator stack until an operator with a priority of zero is reached. If this isn't a left parenthesis it means that there are too many right parentheses in the expression, so an error message is displayed and a Syntax_Error is raised.

The main loop ends when Look_Ahead reports that the end of the line has been reached. Operators are then applied to their operands until an operator with a priority of zero is reached; if this isn't the '#' used to prime the stack it must be an unmatched left parenthesis, which means that there is a right parenthesis missing somewhere.

⇒   *One problem is that the program won't report operators with missing operands, so that '*2' will be accepted and will produce a Stack_Underflow. See if you can figure out how to fix this.*

13.4   Implementing the stack package

We've seen how to use the stack package to improve on the calculator design from chapter 3; now it's time to return to the stack package itself and look at ways of implementing its body. Since a stack is a collection, we could use an array or a linked list to implement it. Let's consider an array implementation first. We'll need an array of items for the stack itself together with a count to tell us how many items there are on the stack. The private section of the package specification might look like this:

```
package JE.Stacks is
  -- as before

private
  Max_Items : constant := 100;
                    -- an arbitrary maximum size for stacks

  type    Stack_Array   is array (1..Max_Items) of Item_Type;
  subtype Stack_Pointer is Natural range 0..Max_Items;
```

```
   type Stack_Type is
      record
         Value : Stack_Array;
         Top   : Stack_Pointer := 0;
      end record;
end JE.Stacks;
```

The package has a built-in arbitrary limit of 100 items per stack. The stack pointer (Top) is set to zero by default so that all stacks will automatically start off empty. Pushing an item involves incrementing Top and storing the item at the array position it indicates; popping an item off the stack is the reverse process, i.e. the item at position Top is retrieved and then Top is decremented. The other functions are equally straightforward. Here's the package body:

```
package body JE.Stacks is
   procedure Push (Stack : in out Stack_Type;
                   Item  : in Item_Type) is
   begin
      Stack.Top := Stack.Top + 1;
      Stack.Value(Stack.Top) := Item;
   exception
      when Constraint_Error =>
         raise Stack_Overflow;
   end Push;

   procedure Pop (Stack : in out Stack_Type;
                  Item  : out Item_Type) is
   begin
      Item := Top(Stack);
      Stack.Top := Stack.Top - 1;
   end Pop;

   function Top (Stack : Stack_Type) return Item_Type is
   begin
      return Stack.Value(Stack.Top);
   exception
      when Constraint_Error =>
         raise Stack_Underflow;
   end Top;

   function Size (Stack : Stack_Type) return Natural is
   begin
      return Stack.Top;
   end Size;
```

```
function Empty (Stack : Stack_Type) return Boolean is
begin
   return Size(Stack) = 0;
end Empty;
end JE.Stacks;
```

Note how Pop uses Top to get the value of the topmost stack item, including the necessary checks for stack underflow, so as to avoid code duplication.

A linked list approach is just as simple. Here's what the private part of the specification looks like if we decide to take this approach:

```
with JE.Lists;
package JE.Stacks is
   -- as before
private
   package Item_Lists is new JE.Lists (Item_Type);
   type Stack_Type is new Item_Lists.List_Type;
end JE.Stacks;
```

Notice that Stack_Type is effectively just a renaming of Item_Lists.List_Type. However, since Stack_Type was declared as a private type, you can't declare it as a subtype in the private part of the specification in order to effect a renaming; it must be declared as a type, so I've declared it as a derived type. The only problem with this is that Stack_Type values will need to be explicitly converted to Item_Lists.List_Type values before operations on List_Type values can be applied:

```
function Size (Stack : Stack_Type) return Natural is
begin
   return Item_Lists.Size (Item_Lists.List_Type(Stack));
end Size;
```

This is awkward; another approach which leads to more readable code is to declare Stack_Type as a record containing a List_Type component:

```
with JE.Lists;
package JE.Stacks is
   -- as before
private
   package Item_Lists is new JE.Lists (Item_Type);
   type Stack_Type is
      record
         L : Item_Lists.List_Type;
      end record;
end JE.Stacks;
```

The Size function above can now be written like this:

```
function Size (Stack : Stack_Type) return Natural is
begin
   return Item_Lists.Size (Stack.L);
end Size;
```

This is much less complicated; using a record type like this is a trick worth remembering for future reference. Now we can use the operations on lists defined in Lists to implement the package body:

```
with JE.Lists;
package body JE.Stacks is

   package ILP renames Item_Lists;

   procedure Push (Stack : in out Stack_Type;
                   Item  : in Item_Type) is
   begin
      ILP.Insert (ILP.First(Stack.L), Item);
   exception
      when Storage_Error =>
         raise Stack_Overflow;
   end Push;

   procedure Pop (Stack : in out Stack_Type;
                  Item  : out Item_Type) is
   begin
      Item := Top(Stack);
      ILP.Delete (ILP.First(Stack.L));
   end Pop;

   function Top (Stack : Stack_Type) return Item_Type is
   begin
      return ILP.Value(ILP.First(Stack.L));
   exception
      when ILP.List_Error =>
         raise Stack_Underflow;
   end Top;

   function Size (Stack : Stack_Type) return Natural is
   begin
      return ILP.Size(Stack.L);
   end Size;
```

```
   function Empty (Stack : Stack_Type) return Boolean is
   begin
      return Size(Stack) = 0;
   end Empty;
end JE.Stacks;
```

13.5 Opaque types

The problem with the approaches above is that if we decide to change the implementation from an array to a linked list or vice versa, the package specification needs changing. This will mean recompiling any existing code that uses the stack package, which may be very inconvenient if it's used in library units totalling hundreds of thousands of lines. A better approach is to try to hide all the implementation details inside the package body, so that any changes affect only the body and not the specification. That way we have to recompile the body, but since the specification won't have changed the client units won't need to be recompiled. The only thing that will need doing to client code is relinking it with the new body which will be much quicker than recompiling it.

How can we achieve this state of ultimate privacy? The answer is to use one of the features of access types that was mentioned when I first started talking about them; if you tell the compiler the name of a type in an **incomplete declaration** you can define an access type for it without the compiler needing to know anything more about the type. All access values are the same size, no matter what type of thing they point to, so the compiler can allocate memory for access variables without needing to know any details about what they point to. What we end up with is an **opaque type** whose name is mentioned but whose definition can be hidden inside the package body:

```
package JE.Stacks is
   -- as before
private
   type Stack_Item;        -- defined in package body
   type Stack_Type is access Stack_Item;
end JE.Stacks;
```

The package body gets a little bit more complicated since a Stack_Type variable will start off set to **null**, so we'll need to create a Stack_Item variable with **new** the first time an item is pushed onto it. We'll also need to check for **null** in all the package's procedures and functions. Here's how it's done using an array:

```
package body JE.Stacks is
   Max_Items : constant := 100; -- arbitrary maximum stack size

   type    Stack_Array  is array (1..Max_Items) of Item_Type;
   subtype Stack_Pointer is Natural range 0..Max_Items;
```

```
-- Completion of type declaration

type Stack_Item is
   record
      Value : Stack_Array;
      Top   : Stack_Pointer := 0;
   end record;

procedure Push (Stack : in out Stack_Type;
                Item  : in Item_Type) is
begin
   if Stack = null then
      Stack := new Stack_Item;
   end if;
   Stack.Top := Stack.Top + 1;
   Stack.Value(Stack.Top) := Item;
exception
   when Storage_Error | Constraint_Error =>
      raise Stack_Overflow;
end Push;

procedure Pop (Stack : in out Stack_Type;
               Item  : out Item_Type) is
begin
   Item := Top(Stack);
   Stack.Top := Stack.Top - 1;
end Pop;

function Top (Stack : Stack_Type) return Item_Type is
begin
   return Stack.Value(Stack.Top);
exception
   when Constraint_Error =>
      raise Stack_Underflow;
end Top;

function Size (Stack : Stack_Type) return Natural is
begin
   if Stack = null then
      return 0;
   else
      return Stack.Top;
   end if;
end Size;
```

```
function Empty (Stack : Stack_Type) return Boolean is
begin
   return Size(Stack) = 0;
end Empty;

end JE.Stacks;
```

Push will allocate a new stack if it's null; if we run out of memory to allocate the stack, a Storage_Error exception will be raised. Like Constraint_Error, this is simply reported back to the caller as a stack overflow. Pop and Top don't need changing; any attempt to access the top of a stack which hasn't been allocated (i.e. which is still null) will raise Constraint_Error, which will then be turned into a Stack_Underflow exception by Top. Size and Empty are modified so that if you use either of them with a stack that hasn't been allocated they'll behave as if the stack exists but is empty.

Changing the package to use a linked list is fairly straightforward:

```
with JE.Lists;
package body JE.Stacks is

   package Lists is new JE.Lists (Item_Type);

   type Stack_Item is
      record
         L : Lists.List_Type;
      end record;

   procedure Push (Stack : in out Stack_Type;
                   Item  : in Item_Type) is
   begin
      if Stack = null then
         Stack := new Stack_Item;
      end if;
      Lists.Insert (Lists.First(Stack.L), Item);
   exception
      when Storage_Error =>
         raise Stack_Overflow;
   end Push;

   procedure Pop (Stack : in out Stack_Type;
                  Item  : out Item_Type) is
   begin
      Item := Top(Stack);
      Lists.Delete (Lists.First(Stack.L));
   end Pop;
```

```
function Top (Stack : Stack_Type) return Item_Type is
begin
   return Lists.Value(Lists.First(Stack.L));
exception
   when Lists.List_Error =>
      raise Stack_Underflow;
end Top;

function Size (Stack : Stack_Type) return Natural is
begin
   if Stack = null then
      return 0;
   else
      return Lists.Size (Stack.L);
   end if;
end Size;

function Empty (Stack : Stack_Type) return Boolean is
begin
   return Size(Stack) = 0;
end Empty;

end JE.Stacks;
```

This reveals another advantage of burying the list in a record rather than using a derived type; if a derived type were used, you would need to write things like this in order to use Lists operations on a Stack_Type value:

```
return Lists.Value(Lists.First(Lists.List_Type(Stack.all)));
   -- instead of "return Lists.Value(Lists.First(Stack.L));"
```

Since Stack_Type is an access type, the value that a Stack_Type object called Stack points to would have to be be accessed using Stack.all; this would then need to be converted to List_Type before any List_Type operations could be performed on it.

13.6   Formalising the syntax of expressions

Trying to detect and deal with all the possible errors that can occur in an arithmetic expression is really quite difficult. An alternative way of dealing with expressions known as **recursive descent parsing** can make life quite a bit easier. This is based on having a formal definition of the syntax of an expression. We can define an expression as a sequence of **terms** separated by adding operators. A term can then be defined as a sequence of **primaries** separated by multiplying operators, and a primary as either a number or an expression enclosed in parentheses. This is usually written using a formal notation similar to this:

```
Expression    = Term { AddOp Term }
Term          = Primary { MulOp Primary }
Primary       = Number | ( Expression )
AddOp         = + | -
MulOp         = * | /
```

Here the curly brackets '{ ... }' indicate that what they enclose can be repeated any number of times (including zero times) and the vertical bar 'I' means 'or'. The first rule is equivalent to an infinitely long rule that looks like this:

```
Expression    = Term
              | Term AddOp Term
              | Term AddOp Term AddOp Term
              | Term AddOp Term AddOp Term AddOp Term
              ... and so on
```

Primary is defined as being a number or an expression enclosed in parentheses. This seems slightly odd when you think about it; Expression is defined in terms of Term which is defined in terms of Primary which is defined in terms of Expression which is defined in terms of ... It seems completely circular, but actually it makes perfect sense. Look at how 2*(3+4) is analysed using these rules:

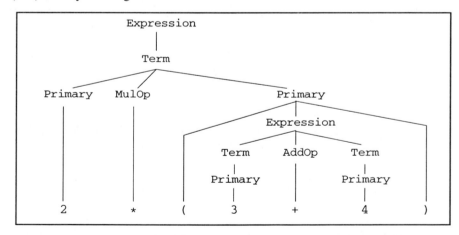

An apparently circular definition like this is known as a **recursive** definition. It may seem like a bit of a curiosity, but recursion turns up in all sorts of problems. Want to sort an array? Split it in two and sort each half, and then merge the sorted halves. This may sound silly, but it's the basis of a well-known technique called **merge sorting** which outperforms all of the 'obvious' ways of sorting that generally spring to people's minds (e.g. the shuffle sort described in chapter 6). Want to generate all possible permutations of a sequence? Take each item in turn as the start of a permutation and append all possible permutations of the items that are left, so that the possible permutations of [1,2,3] are generated by 1 followed by all permutations of [2,3], 2 followed by all permutations of [1,3], and 3 followed by all permutations of [1,2]; this gives you [1,2,3], [1,3,2], [2,1,3], [2,3,1], [3,1,2] and [3,2,1].

All recursion has to stop somewhere; the merge sort stops recursing when the array to be sorted contains a single item and the permutation algorithm stops when you have to generate all possible permutations of a single item. In the case of parsing an expression recursion only occurs when you see a left parenthesis, so it's impossible to get stuck in an infinite loop. In programming terms, recursion is where a function or procedure calls itself either directly or indirectly. Here's an example of a recursive function to calculate factorials: factorial N is the product of $1 * 2 * 3 * ... * N$ (and as a special case, factorial 0 is 1), which means that factorial N is $N * $ factorial $(N - 1)$ for all $N > 0$, and 1 when N = 0:

```
function Factorial (N : Natural) return Positive is
begin
   if N = 0 then
      return 1;
   else
      return N * Factorial(N-1);
   end if;
end Factorial;
```

The recursion always stops because N gets smaller every time and eventually gets down to 0 which is where the recursion ends.

13.7   A recursive descent parser

Writing a recursive descent parser involves converting the syntax rules given earlier into Ada procedures. The first thing we need is a function Next_Character which uses Look_Ahead to find out what the next non-space character is without reading it:

```
function Next_Character return Character is
   Ch  : Character;
   EOL : Boolean;
begin
   loop
      Look_Ahead (Ch, EOL);
      if EOL then
         return '.';
```

```
      elsif Ch /= ' '
        return Ch;
      else
        Get (Ch);
      end if;
    end loop;
  end Next_Character;
```

This produces a full stop as its result when it reaches the end of the current line. The next step is to implement a function called Expression:

```
function Expression return Integer is
   Value    : Integer;
   Operator : Character;
begin
   Value := Term;
   loop
     Operator := Next_Character;
     exit when Operator /= '+' and Operator /= '-';
     Get (Operator);
     if Operator = '+' then
       Value := Value + Term;
     else
       Value := Value - Term;
     end if;
   end loop;
   return Value;
end Expression;
```

This gets a Term (using another function we'll have to implement in a moment) and then sits in a loop accumulating more Terms as long as it sees an adding operator. Term is very similar to Expression:

```
function Term return Integer is
   Value    : Integer;
   Operator : Character;
begin
   Value := Primary;
   loop
     Operator := Next_Character;
     exit when Operator /= '*' and Operator /= '/';
     Get (Operator);
     if Operator = '*' then
       Value := Value * Primary;
```

```
      else
         Value := Value / Primary;
      end if;
   end loop;
   return Value;
end Term;
```

This is defined in terms of Primary, which looks like this:

```
function Primary return Integer is
   Value : Integer;
   Ch    : Character;
begin
   Ch := Next_Character;
   case Ch is
      when '0'..'9' =>
         Get (Value);
      when '(' =>
         Get (Ch);
         Value := Expression;
         if Next_Character /= ')' then
            raise Syntax_Error;
         else
            Get (Ch);
         end if;
      when others =>
         raise Syntax_Error;
   end case;
   return Value;
end Primary;
```

A primary must be either a number or a parenthesised expression, so the **case** statement in this function checks for a digit or a left parenthesis as the valid characters which can start an operand. If the character is anything other than a digit or left parenthesis, a Syntax_Error exception gets raised. This deals with errors arising from missing operands, as in '* 2' or '1 + * 2' where Primary will see an operator rather than a digit or left parenthesis.

If the character is a digit, an integer is read from the input and returned as the value of the function; if it's a left parenthesis, an expression is read and its value used as the function's return value. It is, however, necessary to check that a parenthesised expression ends with a right parenthesis, so Next_Character is used after reading the expression to check for this. If the next character is a right parenthesis, it is simply read in and ignored; if not, a Syntax_Error exception is raised. This deals with errors arising from missing right parentheses.

A main program using these functions simply needs to call Expression and then check that the next character is a full stop. If it isn't, there's a syntax error arising from a missing left parenthesis, a missing operator or an illegal character. If the character is a right parenthesis, this indicates a missing left parenthesis, e.g. '1 + 2)'; if it's a digit there's a missing operator, e.g. '1 2', and if it's anything else it's an illegal character, e.g. '1 & 2'. The functions above can be embedded in a program together with the exception Syntax_Error; here's what the main program might look like:

```
with Ada.Text_IO, Ada.Integer_Text_IO, JE.Parser;
use   Ada.Text_IO, Ada.Integer_Text_IO;
procedure Evaluate is
   Syntax_Error : exception;

   function Next_Character return Character is separate;
   function Expression     return Integer   is separate;
   function Term           return Integer   is separate;
   function Primary        return Integer   is separate;

   Value : Integer;

begin
   Put ("Enter an expression: ");
   Value := Expression;
   if Next_Character /= '.' then
      raise Syntax_Error;
   end if;
   Put (Value);
   New_Line;

exception
   when Syntax_Error =>
      Put_Line ("Syntax error!");
end Evaluate;
```

The functions themselves will need modifying to include **separate** clauses at the beginning, like this:

```
separate (Evaluate)
function Expression return Integer is
   ...
end Expression;
```

⇒ *Compile this program and test that it works, especially the error handling. How could you improve the error reporting?*

Exercises

13.1 Using a doubly linked list for a stack is overkill since items are only ever added to or removed from the front of the list. Modify the stack package to use a simple singly linked list which is manipulated directly by the operations in the package body, and test it using the calculator program.

13.2 Write a program to generate all possible anagrams of a word using the recursive method described in this chapter. If you want to get a list in alphabetical order, sort the characters making up the word into ascending order before generating the anagrams. To avoid generating duplicates, don't use the same letter twice. For example, to generate all unique anagrams of 'apple' in alphabetical order, sort the letters to give *aelpp*, then display *a* followed by all anagrams of *elpp*, *e* followed by all anagrams of *alpp*, *l* followed by all anagrams of *aepp*, *p* followed by all anagrams of *aelp*, but don't do it again for the second *p*.

13.3 The double-ended queue (or *deque*) is yet another data structure that is useful in many situations. A deque is a sequence of items which allows you to add new items to either end or remove items from either end. Produce a deque package which uses an opaque type to represent a deque and write a test program to allow you to exercise the package. Model your package on the stack package shown in this chapter.

13.4 The data structure described in exercise 11.2 is known as a *binary tree*. It is a fundamentally recursive structure; the node at the root of the tree points to two other nodes which can be considered to be the roots of two smaller subtrees with the same structure. Modify your solution to exercise 11.2 using a recursive algorithm for searching the tree.

Part Three

Designing extensible software

This part deals with problems arising from the need to extend the existing capabilities of a program as part of the maintenance process. The object-oriented design approach using abstract data types which was described in the previous part simplifies many maintenance problems where the services provided by individual objects comprising a program need to be reimplemented to meet changing requirements such as a change in the user interface. However, it assumes that the set of services provided by each type of object will remain unchanged. What it doesn't address are issues arising from maintenance problems which require an extension to the services provided by a particular type of object.

The ability to extend the capabilities of existing data types by inheritance is an essential feature of object-oriented programming languages, and the main changes between Ada 83 and Ada 95 were in the area of support for object-oriented programming. This part shows how the object-oriented facilities that Ada 95 provides can be used to improve the designs of the examples from the previous part to make them easier to extend. The appointments diary is extended so that it can handle a variety of different appointment types, including any we may care to add in the unknown future, and the calculator is redesigned so that new types of operators or operands can be added or the syntax of expressions can be changed. The new improved calculator is then extended for use as a building block for a spreadsheet, and finally the spreadsheet itself is extended to accommodate multitasking capabilities.

CHAPTER 14

Tagged types

Profit comes from what is there,
usefulness from what is not there.
— Lao Tsu, *Tao Te Ching*

14.1 Extending existing software

The design techniques based on abstract data types which were discussed in the previous part allowed us to produce a fairly robust appointments diary and calculator which could be changed fairly easily to cope with changing requirements during the maintenance process. You may feel that all is now well with the world. To see how wrong you can be, consider another maintenance scenario. You have a working appointments diary and you need to adapt it to produce a new version to deal with meeting schedules. This means that in addition to the existing information that is kept about each appointment you need to maintain extra information for each appointment, such as a room number, an attendance list, an agenda and so on. How much new code does this involve writing? Can it be integrated into the existing diary system or will you end up with two separate systems, one for day-to-day use which doesn't record these details explicitly (although you could put them into the description of appointments) and another for meetings which will insist on you providing a room number and all the other extra bits and pieces? Putting room numbers into the descriptions of the day-to-day appointments may not be adequate if you want to find out what a particular room has been booked for or when it is booked; on the other hand for certain appointments (lunch dates etc.) the level of formality involved in a meetings diary might be excessive. Where are you having lunch, who with, what's the agenda?

This is quite a different sort of problem to the ones addressed in the preceding part; it's about **extensibility**. Can you extend an existing system to cope with new requirements and still maintain compatibility with what's already there or do you have to rewrite everything? Can you produce a new version of the diary to cope with different types of appointments so that existing appointments are left unchanged (so that you don't have to specify spurious agendas for parties or lunch dates) while allowing new types of appointments to be integrated smoothly into what's already there?

To do this you would seem to need some sort of foresight which will allow you to predict the things you might need to change at some point in the future when you first design a system. This is where object-oriented programming languages like Ada 95 come into their own. They provide mechanisms for writing programs which will still work when confronted with undreamt-of variations on what they already do. It is yet another shift from a processor-centric view of the world as exemplified in the first part of this book towards a more data-centric view as described in the preceding part. Object-oriented programming languages take the data-centric view a step further: not only is the data concealed so that its structure can be altered if necessary, but the data directs its own processing. In the object-oriented view of the world, you do not perform operations on data items; instead, you ask the data items to perform operations on themselves, and different data items might perform these operations in quite distinct ways. If you want to extend the diary program to add a type of appointment, you arrange for the program to ask each appointment to perform its own operations so that any new appointment type's operations get used automatically by the existing program.

This might not sound terribly revolutionary; after all, you saw in chapter 13 how you can build different versions of a stack. You can always push an item of data onto a stack, but in one case the stack in question might be implemented as an array and in another case it might be a linked list. You neither know nor care; all you know is that when you say 'Push!' it pushes and when you say 'Pop!' it pops. Different stacks might be performing the same operation in different ways; who knows, who cares, as long as it works? However, abstract data types as described thus far only really help with changes in the implementation of existing types; they don't cater for extending a program to cope with new data types, whereas the object-oriented techniques described in this part do.

Let's begin by considering what to do in order to extend the appointment type as it currently exists. Here's a package specification which is nearly identical to the appointment package in chapter 10:

```
with JE.Times;   use JE.Times;
package JE.Appointments is
   type Appointment_Type is private;

   function Date     (Appt : Appointment_Type) return Time_Type;
   function Details (Appt : Appointment_Type) return String;

   procedure Appointment (Date    : in Time_Type;
                          Details : in String;
                          Result  : out Appointment_Type);
   procedure Put (Appt : in Appointment_Type);
private
   type Appointment_Type is
      record
        Time    : Time_Type;
        Details : String (1..50);
        Length  : Natural := 0;
      end record;
end JE.Appointments;
```

The only change is that the constructor function Appointment is now a procedure instead of a function, for reasons which I'll explain later, and I've added a Put procedure to display an appointment on the screen. Now let's consider what's needed in order to produce a new appointment type for meetings which includes a room number. Other details apart from room numbers can be added in the same way, so I'll stick to just adding a room number in order to simplify matters. One way to add a room number would be to define a type called Meeting_Type which contains an appointment and a room number:

```
subtype Room_Type is Integer range 100 .. 999;

type Meeting_Type is
   record
      Appt : Appointment_Type;
      Room : Room_Type;
   end record;
```

We can now declare a set of operations for Meeting_Type objects similar to those defined for Appointment_Type objects:

```
function  Date    (Meeting : Meeting_Type) return Time_Type;
function  Details (Meeting : Meeting_Type) return String;
function  Room    (Meeting : Meeting_Type) return Room_Type;
procedure Meeting (Date    : in Time_Type;
                   Details : in String;
                   Room    : in Room_Type;
                   Result  : out Meeting_Type);
procedure Put     (Meeting : in Meeting_Type);
```

These are the same as the operations for Appointment_Type except that Meeting (which constructs a Meeting_Type object from its components) has an extra parameter for the room number, and there is an extra function Room to extract the Room component of a meeting. Most of these operations are very similar to the equivalent operations for Appointment_Type; in fact, Date and Details will be identical. As an example, here's how Meeting and Date could be implemented:

```
procedure Meeting (Date    : in Time_Type;
                   Details : in String;
                   Room    : in Room_Type;
                   Result  : out Meeting_Type) is
   A : Appointment_Type;
begin
   Appointment (Date, Details, A);
   Result := (Appt => A, Room => Room);
end Meeting;
```

```
function Date (Meeting : Meeting_Type) return Time_Type is
begin
   return Date (Meeting.Appt);
end Date;
```

Most of the work in these subprograms involves calling Appointment_Type operations to do the standard appointment-related work; any extra work involving the room number is then done as an afterthought.

14.2   Variant records

Another approach is to use a record discriminant to merge the two record types into a single **variant record**, like this:

```
type Appointment_Kind is (Appointment, Meeting);

type Appointment_Type (Kind : Appointment_Kind) is
   record
      Time    : Time_Type;
      Details : String (1..50);
      Length  : Natural := 0;

      case Kind is
         when Appointment =>
            null;
         when Meeting =>
            Room : Room_Type;
      end case;

   end record;
```

The record declaration consists of a **fixed part** which applies to all Appointment_Type objects, so that all Appointment_Type objects will have Date, Time, Details and Length components, followed by a **variant part** which looks very much like a **case** statement. What the variant part says is that when the Kind discriminant is set to Appointment, there will be no more components (as signified by **null**) but when Kind is set to Meeting you will also have a Room component. You can then declare objects of either variety like this:

```
A : Appointment_Type(Appointment);   -- A has no Room component
M : Appointment_Type(Meeting);       -- M has a Room component
```

You can then process generalised Appointment_Types by using a **case** statement which inspects the discriminant and decides what to do in each case:

```
procedure Put (Appt : in Appointment_Type) is
begin
  Put (Appt.Time);
  Put (Appt.Details(1..Appt.Length));

  case Appt.Kind is
    when Appointment =>
      null;                -- do nothing for plain appointments
    when Meeting =>
      Put (Appt.Room);  -- display Room component for meetings
  end case;

  New_Line;
end Put;
```

In this case the parameter to Put is unconstrained, which means that either variant of Appointment_Type can be passed as a parameter to Put. Inside Put, a **case** statement is used to select alternative courses of action depending on the value of the discriminant, which is what determines whether there is a Room component or not.

14.3 Tagged types

Although either of the approaches above will work, they are both fairly awkward ways of doing things. Putting an Appointment_Type inside a Meeting_Type involves defining a whole bunch of operations which are effectively just **forwarding** operations; each call is simply forwarded to the equivalent Appointment_Type operation where the real work gets done. All these new operations must still be tested, so there is a cost penalty for testing as well as development. Also, Meeting_Type and Appointment_Type are completely unrelated from the point of view of clients who can't see the full declaration of Meeting_Type; there's no easy way to convert an ordinary appointment to a meeting by tagging on a room number and you can't treat a meeting as an appointment by ignoring the room number. You would laboriously have to extract the date, time and details components and then put them back together again in order to perform a type conversion.

Using a variant record is simpler in some respects; you only have one copy of each subprogram. The disadvantage is that you have to know in advance what type variants you are going to support. Adding a new one involves modifying the original type declarations, and at every point where you discriminate between the variants you will have to add extra code to deal with the new variant. This will involve modifying, recompiling and retesting everything you've already written.

Fortunately, there is a much simpler way of defining extensible data types. A record type can be declared to be a **tagged record** which allows it to be extended later. Here's what the declaration of Appointment_Type would look like if we'd defined it as a tagged record:

```
type Appointment_Type is
  tagged record
    Time    : Time_Type;
    Details : String (1..50);
    Length  : Natural := 0;
  end record;
```

The only difference is that the declaration says **tagged record** instead of just plain **record**. However, we can now define Meeting_Type by extending Appointment_Type like this:

```
type Meeting_Type is new Appointment_Type with
  record
    Room : Room_Type;
  end record;
```

This is another variation on derived types as described in chapter 5. Meeting_Type is **derived from** Appointment_Type; we say that Appointment_Type is Meeting_Type's **parent type**. What the declaration of Meeting_Type says is that Meeting_Type is just like Appointment_Type except that it has an extra component called Room. A Meeting_Type object called M will therefore have five components called M.Date, M.Time, M.Details, M.Length and M.Room.

Bearing in mind that you can perform type conversions between derived types, you can convert M from a Meeting_Type to an Appointment_Type like this:

```
A : Appointment_Type := Appointment_Type (M);
```

All this does is to discard the extra components of M that were added to Appointment_Type when Meeting_Type was defined (which is just Room in this case). To convert the other way you have to use an **extension aggregate** to supply the missing components (namely, the value of Room):

```
M := (A with Room=>101);
```

This takes the value of A and adds a value of 101 for the room number to produce a Meeting_Type value.

14.4   Inheriting primitive operations

More important is that, since Meeting_Type is derived from Appointment_Type, it inherits all the **primitive operations** of Appointment_Type (or **primitive subprograms**; the terms 'operation' and 'subprogram' are essentially synonymous in this context) just as a type derived from Integer would inherit all the primitive operations defined for Integer like "+", "–" and so on. So what are the primitive operations of Appointment_Type? They are simply those operations on Appointment_Type values which were declared in the same package specification as Appointment_Type; in other words, any procedures or functions with an Appointment_Type parameter (a **controlling parameter**) as well as any functions which return an Appointment_Type result (a **controlling result**). Access parameters (as described in chapter 11) are also treated as controlling parameters, so you can also arrange for subprograms which need an access-to-Appointment_Type parameter to be primitive operations of type Appointment_Type.

Note that Appointment_Type *must* be declared in a package specification if it is to have any primitive operations; declaring a tagged type in a procedure and then declaring some operations on it doesn't mean that those operations are primitive operations of the type. Also, once a type like Meeting_Type is derived from Appointment_Type, you can't declare any more primitive operations for Appointment_Type (since otherwise this would mean allowing Meeting_Type to inherit operations which haven't been declared yet):

```
package JE.Appointments is
   type Appointment_Type is
          tagged record ... end record;

   procedure X (Appt : in Appointment_Type);
          -- primitive, since it's in the same package
          -- specification as Appointment_Type

   type Meeting_Type is new Appointment_Type with ... ;

   procedure Y (Appt : in Appointment_Type);        -- ILLEGAL!
          -- would be primitive, but not allowed since it
          -- follows the declaration of Meeting_Type
end JE.Appointments;
```

The declaration of Appointment_Type is said to be **frozen** by the declaration of Meeting_Type; it would also be frozen if any Appointment_Type objects were declared. Once a type is frozen, you cannot declare any more primitive operations for it. The best way to avoid falling foul of the type-freezing rules is to declare all the primitive operations of a type immediately after the type declaration so that it's obvious what the primitive operations of each type are.

The way inheritance works for primitive operations like X in the example above is that operations are implicitly declared immediately after the derived type declaration which are identical to the parent type's primitive operations except that all uses of the parent type's name in their specifications are effectively replaced by the name of the derived type. In the example above, Meeting_Type inherits a primitive operation called X; it is as if X were declared immediately after the declaration of Meeting_Type like this:

```
procedure X (Appt : in Meeting_Type);
```

14.5   A package for representing meetings

Here's a revised version of JE.Appointments which declares Appointment_Type as a tagged type:

```
with JE.Times;
use  JE.Times;
package JE.Appointments is
   type Appointment_Type is tagged private;

   function Date    (Appt : Appointment_Type) return Time_Type;
   function Details (Appt : Appointment_Type) return String;

   procedure Appointment (Date    : in Time_Type;
                          Details : in String;
                          Result  : out Appointment_Type);

   procedure Put (Appt : in Appointment_Type);

private
   type Appointment_Type is
      tagged record
         Time    : Time_Type;
         Details : String (1..50);
         Length  : Natural := 0;
      end record;
end JE.Appointments;
```

Note that Appointment_Type is declared as **tagged private** in the visible part of the specification. Using **tagged private** reveals to clients of the package that Appointment_Type is a tagged type. Of course, the full declaration in the private part must be a tagged type as advertised so that the full view of the type has at least the same capabilities as the partial view given in the visible part; alternatively you can just declare the type as **private** in the visible part of the package if you don't want to let clients know whether the actual type is tagged or not.

We can now define Meeting_Type in a child package; this avoids having to modify the existing diary package and so avoids having to recompile all the diary package's clients. Remember that a child package is treated as an extension of its parent package and that the private part of the child (as well as the child package body) can use the information in the private part of its parent. Here's a specification for the child package:

```
package JE.Appointments.Meetings is
   subtype Room_Type is Integer range 100 .. 999;
   type Meeting_Type is new Appointment_Type with private;
```

```
      procedure Meeting (Date    : in Time_Type;
                         Details : in String;
                         Room    : in Room_Type;
                         Result  : out Meeting_Type);
      function  Room    (Appt    : Meeting_Type) return Room_Type;

   private
      type Meeting_Type is new Appointment_Type with
         record
            Room : Room_Type;
         end record;
   end JE.Appointments.Meetings;
```

If Appointment_Type had simply been declared **private** rather than **tagged private**, the declaration of Meeting_Type in the visible part would be illegal. The visible part of the child package only has access to the visible part of its parent to ensure that the child can't reveal any private information from its parent in its visible part. As a result, Appointment_Type has to be declared to be a tagged type in the visible part of JE.Appointments so that, in the visible part of the package above, Meeting_Type can be declared to be derived from Appointment_Type. If Appointment_Type wasn't visibly declared to be tagged, the visible declaration of Meeting_Type couldn't extend it.

Notice that Meeting_Type extends Appointment_Type using **with private** in the visible part of the package. This lets clients of the package know that Meeting_Type is derived from Appointment_Type without providing any information about the extra components it provides. Because of this the compiler will allow clients of the package to use operations inherited from Appointment_Type on Meeting_Type objects. On the other hand, Meeting_Type could simply have been declared to be **private**:

```
   type Meeting_Type is private;
```

The disadvantage of doing this would be that clients of the package wouldn't be able to see that Meeting_Type is related to Appointment_Type so that operations inherited from Appointment_Type wouldn't be accessible to its clients (although they *would* be accessible in the package body, where the full declaration of Meeting_Type is visible).

The functions Date, Details, etc., are inherited from Appointment_Type and can be used unchanged on Meeting_Type objects; there are also two new primitive operations for Meeting_Type called Meeting and Room which allow a meeting to be constructed from its components and the room number to be extracted from a Meeting_Type object. If a further type were to be derived from Meeting_Type, it would inherit all the primitive operations of Meeting_Type; this would mean that it would inherit the primitive operations that Meeting_Type inherited from Appointment_Type (Date, Details, etc.) as well as the new primitive operations Meeting and Room. Room is just an accessor function for the Room component, and Meeting just needs to create an appointment and convert it to a Meeting_Type result with an extension aggregate:

```
procedure Meeting (Date    : in Time_Type;
                   Details : in String;
                   Room    : in Room_Type;
                   Result  : out Meeting_Type) is
   A : Appointment;
begin
   Appointment (Date, Details, A);
   Result := (A with Room => Room);
end Meeting;
```

Meeting_Type also inherits the procedure Put from Appointment_Type. What Put will do is to output a Meeting_Type in exactly the same way as an Appointment_Type; in other words, the extra room number component will be ignored. This is not what we want in this particular case, so we need to **override** the inherited version of Put with one which can deal with the room numbers as well. This is done by declaring a procedure with *exactly* the same specification as the inherited procedure (and it must be exact!):

```
procedure Put (Appt : in Meeting_Type);
```

The new version of the package now looks like this:

```
package JE.Appointments.Meetings is
   subtype Room_Type is Integer range 100 .. 999;
   type Meeting_Type is new Appointment_Type with private;

   procedure Meeting (Date    : in JE.Times.Time_Type;
                      Details : in String;
                      Room    : in Room_Type;
                      Result  : out Meeting_Type);
   function  Room    (Appt    : Meeting_Type) return Room_Type;
   procedure Put     (Appt    : in  Meeting_Type);

   -- Date and Details inherited unchanged
   -- from Appointment_Type

private
   type Meeting_Type is new Appointment_Type with
      record
         Room : Room_Type;
      end record;
end JE.Appointments.Meetings;
```

Note that the rules for child packages mean that if you access JE.Appointments.Meetings in a **with** clause, you also get access to the parent package JE.Appointments automatically (as well as the ultimate parent package JE, although since this is empty it doesn't give you any extra benefits). This means that given a **with** clause for the package JE.Appointments.Meetings, you don't need a separate **with** clause for the package JE.Appointments. However, a **use** clause for JE.Appointments.Meetings allows you to refer to Meeting_Type directly but it does not let you refer to Appointment_Type directly; you'd need a separate **use** clause for JE.Appointments if you wanted to do this:

```
with JE.Appointments.Meetings;
use  JE.Appointments.Meetings, JE.Appointments;
procedure X is
  A : Appointment_Type;
              -- i.e. JE.Appointments.Appointment_Type
  M : Meeting_Type;
              -- i.e. JE.Appointments.Meetings.Meeting_Type
begin
  ...
end X;
```

Alternatively, you could just have a **use** clause for JE.Appointments and then refer to Meetings.Meeting_Type since the **use** clause for JE.Appointments lets you refer to JE.Appointments.Meetings simply as Meetings.

14.6   The dangers of inheritance

The way I've declared Meeting_Type above is much simpler than the first version at the beginning of the chapter. The version at the beginning contained an Appointment_Type component, which meant that the two types were completely unrelated to each other and that a full set of operations for Meeting_Type had to be defined explicitly, using forwarding to perform the appointment-related work. The new version involving tagged types involves less coding and hence less testing; only the operations that are different and additional operations need to be written and tested, which can reduce the costs of development considerably. What's more, you can convert between the two types, which means that you can use any procedures you've already written to deal with Appointment_Type objects to deal with Meeting_Type objects; all you have to do is to use a type conversion to convert your Meeting_Type object to an Appointment_Type when you call the procedure.

There is, however, a downside to all this. The derived type does not explicitly list the operations it inherits, so without looking at the parent package (and the grandparent package, and so on) it's difficult to know what the complete set of operations for the derived type actually is. You may be very lucky and have access to automated tools which can generate this information automatically from the relevant package specifications (using a **class browser**), but in general the only reliable solution to this is to provide information about the inherited operations in the documentation, including the use of comments inside the package specification. This requires self-discipline; the compiler won't check what you've written so it's up to you to get it right. If you don't provide this sort of information (or if you get it wrong or miss something out) the users of the package will find it much harder to figure out what's going on.

As an example of this, I didn't mention the procedure Appointment which was inherited from Appointment_Type. Without reading the original package specification you wouldn't realise that there was any such procedure available. However, the reason I didn't mention it was that it illustrates yet another danger arising from inheritance in Ada. In many other object-oriented languages certain operations are not inheritable (particularly constructors), but in Ada, *all* primitive operations are inherited. The specification of the procedure that Meeting_Type inherits will look like this:

```
procedure Appointment (Date    : in Time_Type;
                        Details : in String;
                        Result  : out Meeting_Type);
```

The result of calling this procedure will be that the Meeting_Type result will be created in exactly the same way as it was when the result was an Appointment_Type; the room number won't have been set up. The procedure Meeting doesn't override this because the name is different, and even if Meeting was renamed Appointment it wouldn't override it since the parameter lists are different (Meeting has an extra parameter for the room number) so that there would just be two procedures called Appointment. This is a serious problem because it provides a way to construct Meeting_Type objects incorrectly. One solution is to override Appointment so that it provides a default value for the room number; another possibility is to raise an exception if Appointment is called to create a meeting:

```
procedure Appointment (Date    : in Time_Type;
                        Details : in String;
                        Result  : out Meeting_Type) is
begin
   -- This procedure should never be called
   raise Program_Error;
end Appointment;
```

This is unsatisfactory because it involves declaring an unnecessary procedure which should never be called; it is also unsatisfactory because if Appointment is accidentally called to initialise a meeting, detection of the error will happen at run time instead of at compile time.

In the original package Appointment was declared as a function:

```
function Appointment (Date    : Time_Type;
                      Details : String)
            return Appointment_Type;
```

If a function is a primitive operation of a tagged type and it returns a result of that type, any derived types inherit what is called an **abstract operation**, in other words a function for which no implementation exists. Since Meeting_Type is an extension of Appointment_Type, it's no good just returning an Appointment_Type result and pretending it's a Meeting_Type since the room number won't have been set up. The compiler will insist that you explicitly override any inherited abstract operations:

```
function Appointment (Date    : Time_Type;
                      Details : String)
        return Meeting_Type;
```

You might be able to set the room number to some sort of default value, but the most sensible definition you could provide for this function would be one that raises an exception as described above since you'll probably need a similar function for meetings anyway:

```
function Meeting (Date    : Time_Type;
                  Details : String;
                  Room    : Room_Type)
        return Meeting_Type;
```

At least if you use a function the compiler will tell you that you've got a problem; when you have a problem like this involving a procedure it's up to you to realise that you've got a problem and to do something about it. For this reason you should be very careful whenever you've got a type with a primitive procedure which has an **out** or **in out** parameter of the type in question.

Another solution is to declare Appointment in a separate package so that it isn't a primitive operation of Appointment_Type and so it won't be inherited by Meeting_Type. One way to do this is to use another package inside Appointments:

```
package JE.Appointments is
   type Appointment_Type is tagged private;
   ...     -- as before

   -- Internal package containing constructor function:
   package Create is
      function Appointment (Date    : Time_Type;
                            Details : String)
              return Appointment_Type;
   end Create;

private
   ...     -- as before
end JE.Appointments;
```

Now since Appointment is declared in a different package it won't be a primitive operation of Appointment_Type. The inner package body will need to be defined within the body of the outer package, like this:

```
package body JE.Appointments is
   ...      -- bodies of primitive subprograms go here

   package body Create is
      function Appointment (Date    : Time_Type;
                            Details : String)
              return Appointment_Type is

       ...
      end Appointment;
   end Create;
end JE.Appointments;
```

The constructor can now be called using the name JE.Appointments.Create.Appointment, or if you've chosen to provide a **use** clause for JE.Appointments you can refer to it more simply as Create.Appointment.

Of course, there are other cases where you want to override an existing primitive operation but you make a silly mistake:

```
procedure Appointment (Details : in String;
                       Date    : in Time_Type;
                       Result  : out Meeting_Type);
```

The parameters are now in a different order, so the procedure's signature is different. The compiler will interpret this as *overloading* the procedure name with a separate meaning rather than *overriding* the existing procedure with a new meaning, and you'll end up with two procedures called Appointment. To be safe, you should copy the parent specification and then edit it (carefully!) so that you don't make mistakes like this when you're defining your derived type.

The final verdict? **Beware!** Inheritance is powerful but potentially dangerous. There are lots of subtle traps that the compiler can't detect. You have to be *very* careful what you do. All the same, you have to risk it; the alternative is to end up trapped in a non-extensible cul-de-sac when it's maintenance time.

14.7   Inheritance or containment?

I started off this chapter by using *containment* to simulate inheritance, where the 'derived' type contained an object of the 'parent' type. This is always a possibility, but inheritance can sometimes make things easier. So how can you tell when to use inheritance rather than containment (or vice versa) to establish relationships between things?

Inheritance is often characterised as an 'is-a' or an 'is-kind-of' relationship between two types. By deriving type Derived from type Parent, what you're saying is that a Derived is a kind of Parent. For example, it would make sense to derive a type Car from another type Vehicle, since a car is a kind of vehicle. However, it would not make sense to derive type Engine from type Car since an engine is not a type of car; it is instead a component of a car. The relevant declarations might look something like this in Ada:

```
type Vehicle is
   tagged record
      ...                         -- properties common to all Vehicles
   end record;

type Car is new Vehicle with    -- Car is inherited from Vehicle
   record
      E : Engine;                -- Engine is a component of Car
      ...
   end record;
```

The relationship between an engine and a car is a 'has-a' or an 'is-part-of' relationship (a car has an engine; an engine is part of a car) rather than an 'is-kind-of' relationship, or in other words a **containment** relationship (since a car 'contains' an engine). Identifying the correct relationship is very important; you've already seen how complicated things can get if containment is used instead of inheritance at the beginning of this chapter. Similarly, inappropriate use of inheritance can cause problems. Imagine that Car had a Headlight component and an operation called Flash_Headlights, and that we derived Engine from Car by mistake. Engine would inherit Headlight and Flash_Headlights from Car. I don't know about you, but I've never come across an engine with headlights, still less one that could flash them! What's more, you could convert an engine into a car whenever you wanted to; this would not go down well with the licensing authorities.

What about a Driver? It's obviously not a kind of Car, so there isn't an inheritance relationship between Car and Driver; neither is a driver a component of a car, since a car can exist without a driver or can have different drivers at different times; similarly a driver might drive different cars at different times. This shows that there's another possible relationship between types: an association which can be characterised as an 'is-used-by' or an 'is-associated-with' relationship.

In the case of vehicles, cars, engines and drivers the relationships are fairly obvious, but there are other cases that are much less straightforward. For example, consider a point in a two-dimensional plane which is represented by its X and Y coordinates. If you want to generalise this to a three-dimensional point represented by three coordinates (X, Y and Z) you could use either containment (a 3D point contains a 2D point together with a Z coordinate) or inheritance (a 3D point is a kind of 2D point with an extra Z coordinate). The main difference is that if inheritance is used it becomes possible to convert a 3D point to a 2D point by discarding the Z coordinate. Depending on the sort of primitive operations defined for 2D points, you might inherit inappropriate operations if a 3D point were derived from a 2D point. For this reason I would probably prefer to use containment since it is likely that you would want to choose which two-dimensional plane you project a three-dimensional point on to; there might also be considerations such as the need for perspective transformations.

Another interesting case is the relationship between squares and rectangles. A square is a kind of rectangle, or is it the other way round? A square has a width (which is also its length), but a rectangle might be considered to be an extension of this which has an extra length component independently of its width:

```
type Square is
   tagged record
      Width : Float;
   end record;

type Rectangle is new Square with
   record
      Length : Float;
   end record;
```

However, most people would prefer to say that a square is a special case of a rectangle rather than saying that a rectangle is a generalisation of a square. Inheritance doesn't let us remove existing features, so this is something we can't represent using inheritance. A good way to choose between containment and inheritance is to ask yourself if you would want to be able to convert a rectangle to a square (or vice versa). In difficult cases like this where the two types are obviously related in some way (e.g. for use in a drawing program which can draw squares, rectangles and other shapes), but where the relationship isn't at all obvious, you can usually break the Gordian knot by deriving them both from some other parent type Shape:

```
type Shape is
   tagged record
      ...           -- properties common to all shapes
   end record;

type Square is new Shape with
   record
      Width : Float;
   end record;

type Rectangle is new Shape with
   record
      Width  : Float;
      Length : Float;
   end record;
```

This illustrates a useful design principle: difficult decisions about the relationship between two types can quite often be resolved by introducing a third type which is used to encapsulate the common features of the other two types.

Exercises

14.1 Modify the linked list package JE.Lists to define List_Iterator as a tagged type. Derive a new Sorted_List_Iterator with an overridden Insert operation which always inserts items into the list in the correct position so that the items in the list are always in ascending order. You will need to supply a suitable comparison operation as a generic parameter. Test that it works by modifying the diary program to use it for inserting appointments into the diary.

14.2 Use a variant record to define a shape which can be a circle (with a radius) or a square (with a width) or a rectangle (with a width and length). Define a function Area to return the area of a given shape. Write a test program to create some shapes and display their areas.

14.3 Define a tagged type to represent a bank account with operations to deposit and withdraw money and to query the balance of the account. Derive another bank account type which allows the account to be overdrawn up to a defined limit and another one which charges a fixed fee for every withdrawal. Write a test program to test the different account types.

14.4 Define a new appointment type which records the duration of an appointment in minutes, and modify the diary program so that it asks for the duration of new appointments and so that it displays the start and end times of each appointment (e.g. '10:00 – 10:30' for a 30 minute appointment at 10:00).

CHAPTER 15

Polymorphism and dispatching

Every kind of thinking, without exception, is
stamped with the brand of a class.
— Mao Tse-tung, *On Practice*

15.1 Class-wide types

The last chapter showed how new types of appointment for an appointments diary can be
created by inheritance from the original appointment type. However, it assumed that the
diary would only need to deal with a single type of appointment. It would be more
realistic to produce a diary capable of holding different types of appointments at the same
time: some meetings, some social appointments, and so on. The diary can be listed by
displaying each appointment in turn using Put.   Here are the declarations of some
appointment types and the associated versions of Put:

```
type Appointment_Type is
   tagged record
      . . .                -- properties common to all appointments
   end record;
procedure Put (Appt : in  Appointment_Type);
                  -- primitive operation


type Meeting_Type is new Appointment_Type with
   record
      . . .               -- extra properties of meetings
   end record;
procedure Put (Appt : in  Meeting_Type);
                  -- override inherited Put


type Deadline_Type is new Appointment_Type with
   record
      . . .               -- extra properties of deadlines
   end record;
procedure Put (Appt : in  Deadline_Type);
                  -- override inherited Put
```

Notice that you can guarantee that you'll be able to use Put to display any appointment, since any type derived directly or indirectly from Appointment_Type either inherits a version of Put from its parent type or overrides the inherited version. In either case there will be a procedure called Put with a single parameter which can be used to display the appointment.

We could create a linked list of Appointment_Types or a linked list of Meeting_Types using the linked list package from chapter 12, but what we want is a list that can contain a mixture of appointments. It wouldn't be any good creating a list of Appointment_Types since this would mean converting meetings and deadlines to normal appointments before they could be stored in the list, and this would mean stripping off the extra components that they have in addition to any components that Appointment_Type provides.

Tagged types provide an attribute called 'Class which gives a type describing an entire family of types (a **class-wide** type) which can be used to solve this problem. For example, Appointment_Type'Class consists of Appointment_Type itself, together with any types derived from Appointment_Type (in this case Meeting_Type and Deadline_Type). Any other types that we derive from Appointment_Type or Meeting_Type or Deadline_Type will also be members of Appointment_Type'Class. This means that a linked list of Appointment_Type'Class objects could be used to hold appointments, meetings, deadlines, or any other type of appointment that we decide to add later.

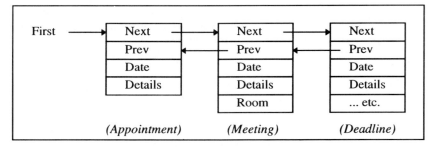

Notice that you can guarantee that you'll be able to use Put to display any appointment, since any type derived directly or indirectly from Appointment_Type either inherits a version of Put from its parent type or overrides the inherited version. In either case there

However, Appointment_Type'Class is an unconstrained type. Different appointments will occupy different amounts of memory, so you can't declare an Appointment_Type'Class variable since the compiler won't know how much memory to allocate for it (unless you specify an initial value for it, in which case it is permanently constrained to be the same type of appointment as the initial value). What you *can* do is to create an access type for Appointment_Type'Class:

```
type Appointment_Access is access Appointment_Type'Class;
```

Since Shape_Access is a pointer to the class-wide type Shape'Class, a Shape_Access variable can be used to point to any shape at all:

```
M : Appointment_Access := new Meeting_Type;
D : Appointment_Access := new Deadline_Type;
```

This means that we can have a linked list of Appointment_Access objects and have each list element point to any kind of appointment we feel like:

```
package Appointment_Lists is
                    new JE.Lists (Appointment_Access);
```

M and D above can point to any type of appointment at all. This means that if you get at the appointments that M and D point to using 'M.all' and 'D.all', the only thing the compiler knows is that they're some sort of appointment. It doesn't know whether they're going to be meetings or deadlines (and they could be different at different times), so you can't apply any meeting-specific or deadline-specific operations. The only things you can do with M.all and D.all are operations common to all appointments, namely the primitive operations of Appointment_Type. If you want to do something to M.all which is unique to Meeting_Type, you have to use a type conversion to convert M.all to a Meeting_Type:

```
Meeting_Specific_Operation( Meeting_Type(M.all) );
```

If you do this, it's your responsibility to make sure that M does actually point to a meeting. If it doesn't you'll get a Constraint_Error when you try to do the type conversion. How you check what M really points to is discussed below.

A consequence of class-wide types is that you aren't allowed to declare derived types at a deeper level than the parent type. Library units are at **library level**, and each time you enter a subprogram (or go into a **declare** block) you are going one level deeper, so that inside the main program you are one level deeper than the library level. Basically, entering any block which can have a declaration section increases the depth, and exiting from the block decreases it again. Packages do not affect the level. The reason for the restriction is similar to the reason for the accessibility limitations on general access types described in chapter 11; for example, if you declared a derived type in a procedure called from the main program and the main program had a pointer to a class-wide type, the procedure would be able to set the pointer to point to an object of the derived type. On exit from the procedure, the pointer would be pointing to an object of a type that no longer exists, and any attempt to use this pointer in the main program would probably be disastrous.

15.2 Dispatching

Since Appointment_Type'Class is an unconstrained type, one of the few things you can use it for is as the type for a procedure parameter:

```
procedure Display (A : in Appointment_Type'Class) is
begin
   ...            -- display an appointment using Put
end Display;
```

This lets you pass a meeting or a deadline or any other type of appointment to Display as its parameter. You could use this procedure to process individual appointments from a list of appointments like this:

```
procedure List_Diary (A : in Appointment_Lists.List_Type) is
   I : Appointment_Lists.List_Iterator :=
                              Appointment_Lists.First(A);
begin
   while I /= Appointment_Lists.Last(A) loop
     Display( Appointment_Lists.Value(I).all );
   end loop;
end List_Diary;
```

This uses an iterator I to go through each item in the list. Appointment_Lists.Value(I) extracts the current Appointment_Access value from the list, and then '.all' is used to get the Appointment_Type'Class value it points to for use by Display.

Display will need to deal with each appointment in an appropriate way. The parameter might be a meeting or a deadline or any other type of appointment, so we need to ensure that the correct version of Put is called according to the actual type of the parameter. Tagged types contain a **tag** (hence the name 'tagged type') which identifies their actual type, so that we can inspect the parameter's tag to find out if it's actually a meeting or a deadline or whatever. One way to do this is to use the **in** operator to check for membership of a particular class:

```
procedure Display (A : in Appointment_Type'Class) is
begin
   if A in Meeting_Type'Class then
     Put( Meeting_Type(A) );
   elsif A in Deadline_Type'Class then
     Put( Deadline_Type(A) );
   else
     Put( Appointment_Type(A) );
   end if;
end Display;
```

The test 'A in Meeting_Type'Class' tests if the actual type of A belongs to Meeting_Type'Class, i.e. Meeting_Type itself or any types derived from Meeting_Type. If so, A is converted to a Meeting_Type so that the version of Put which takes a Meeting_Type parameter will be called to display the meeting. The same is done for deadlines, and if all else fails the version of Put for the parent type Appointment_Type will be called.

This is not particularly satisfactory since the version of Put for meetings will be called for any type derived from Meeting_Type. If you want to add a derived type called Urgent_Meeting_Type, the version of Put for Meeting_Type will be called instead of the version for Urgent_Meeting_Type. One way to solve this is to get at the parameter's tag directly using the 'Tag attribute:

```
if A'Tag = Meeting_Type'Tag then ...
```

This will check whether A is actually a Meeting_Type rather than a member of Meeting_Type's family of derived types. The tag belongs to the private type Ada.Tags.Tag; you can also get a printable form of the tag using the attribute 'External_Tag (e.g. A'External_Tag) whose value is a String.

Using the tag to identify the type is still not a particularly satisfactory solution. Regardless of whether you decide to identify an object using 'A in Meeting_Type'Class' or 'A'Tag = Meeting_Type'Tag', you'll still run into problems whenever a new type of appointment is added to the program. Any class-wide operations like Display will need modifying whenever a new appointment is derived from Appointment_Type, with resultant costs in recompiling and testing.

Fortunately you don't actually need to go to all this trouble. When you have a class-wide type like Appointment_Type'Class and you call a primitive operation like Put, the tag is used to identify the correct version of the primitive operation automatically. This automatic selection of primitive operations is known in Ada as **dispatching**. It only applies to class-wide values where the actual type isn't known until run time; if the compiler can identify the actual type at compile time it knows which version of the operation to use so no dispatching is necessary. It also only applies to primitive operations, since these are the only ones that are guaranteed to be available for all types derived from the parent type. So for Appointment_Type'Class, a call to any primitive operation of Appointment_Type will be a dispatching operation. This means that Display can be written like this:

```
procedure Display (A : in Appointment_Type'Class) is
begin
   Put( A );   -- A is class-wide and Put is primitive, so
               -- dispatching happens; the version of Put that
               -- gets called depends on the actual type of A
end Display;
```

If A is actually a meeting, the version of Put for Meeting_Type will be called; if it's a deadline, the version of Put for Deadline_Type will be called. In fact, you can eliminate Display altogether:

```
procedure List_Diary (A : in Appointment_Lists.List_Type) is
   I : Appointment_Lists.List_Iterator :=
                    Appointment_Lists.First(A);

begin
   while I /= Appointment_Lists.Last(A) loop
```

```
    Put( Appointment_Lists.Value(I).all );
        -- Appointment_Lists.Value(I).all is class-wide and Put
        -- is primitive, so dispatching happens; the version
        -- of Put that gets called depends on the actual type
        -- of Appointment_Lists.Value(I).all
    end loop;
 end List_Diary;
```

In effect, you can think of calls to primitive operations of a class-wide object as asking the object to perform the primitive operation on itself. How each object satisfies this request will depend on what type of object it really is. You're asking each appointment to display itself, and how this is done depends on the actual type of appointment involved. Primitive operations of tagged types are **polymorphic** (literally 'many shaped'); what the 'shape' of the operation will be depends on the type of object being operated on.

One possible complication arises if two tagged types are declared within the same package specification. What will happen if you declare a subprogram which takes two parameters, one of each type? The subprogram would end up being a primitive operation of both types, and the compiler would need some way of deciding which parameter to use for dispatching. For example, consider the following (illegal) example:

```
type Appointment_Type is
   tagged record
     . . .
   end record;

type Output_Device is
   tagged record
     . . .
   end record;

procedure Put (A : in Appointment_Type; D : in Output_Device);
       -- write A to output device D (ILLEGAL!)
```

The idea is to be able to have various types of output device and to have a procedure to output a given appointment to a given device (e.g. a display, or a speech synthesiser, or whatever). Each appointment can override Put to output itself appropriately; also each Output_Device can override Put to use the operations appropriate to a particular output device. If Put is called the compiler won't know whether to call the overridden version for the derived Appointment_Type or the overridden version for the derived Output_Device.

Ada adopts a brutally simple approach to resolving this problem. Subprograms which are primitive operations of two tagged types (like Put above) are not allowed. Either you could move the operation itself out of the package specification so that it is no longer a primitive operation of either type or you could move one of the type declarations out of the package so that the operation is a primitive operation of only one of the two types.

Alternatively, you could change the procedure specification so that it only uses one of the two types. Here's how you could modify Put to eliminate the Output_Device parameter:

```
procedure Put (A : in Appointment_Type;
               D : in Output_Device'Class);
```

The parameter D isn't an Output_Device any more so the procedure is no longer a primitive operation of Output_Device. However, inside Put an Output_Device'Class value will cause dispatching to occur if there is a call to a primitive operation of Output_Device. This technique is known as **double dispatching** or **redispatching**. For example, imagine that Output_Device has a primitive operation called Write_Output that looks like this:

```
procedure Write_Output (D : in Output_Device; S : in String);
```

Meeting_Type might override Put to output a meeting like this:

```
procedure Put (A : in Appointment_Type;
               D : in Output_Device'Class) is
begin
  Put (Appointment_Type(A), D);   -- parent's version of Put
  Write_Output (D, "Room: ");     -- display the meeting's room
  Write_Output (D, Room_Type'Image(A.Room));
end Put;
```

A call to Put involving class-wide parameters corresponding to a meeting and a particular type of output device will result in the call being dispatched to the version of Put above. This will output the meeting's details using calls to Write_Output, each of which will be dispatched to the correct version of Write_Output for the particular type of device.

You are still allowed to have two parameters of the same tagged type. For example, imagine a primitive operation to determine the time between two appointments. The declaration might look like this:

```
function Interval (A,B : Appointment_Type) return Time_Type;
```

This means that the inherited operations for Meeting_Type and Deadline_Type will look like this:

```
function Interval (A,B : Meeting_Type)  return Time_Type;
function Interval (A,B : Deadline_Type) return Time_Type;
```

The reason that declarations like this are allowed is that the parameters in situations like this will always be the same type as each other so there will never be a choice of types to dispatch the operation to. This means that if you call Interval with two class-wide parameters, the actual types of the class-wide parameters must match. The compiler will insert a run-time check in your program to make sure that the types do in fact match, and a Constraint_Error will be raised if you ever try to call Interval with parameters whose actual types don't match.

15.3 Abstract types

In many cases it can be difficult to define the contents of a parent type or the implementation of its primitive operations. Consider the Shape type mentioned at the end of the previous chapter. The components of Shape will be those that are common to all shapes we could ever imagine: not just squares and rectangles, but triangles, circles, ellipses, parallelograms and so on as well. Quite often in these situations there are no components at all that will be common to everything, so Shape needs to be a **null record**:

```
type Shape is
   tagged record
      null;        -- no components!
   end record;
```

This happens often enough that there is a special abbreviated form of this declaration:

```
type Shape is tagged null record;
```

You can also use null records as type extensions if you don't want to add any extra components when you derive from a tagged type:

```
type Deadline_Type is new Appointment_Type with null record;
```

For example, the only difference between Deadline_Type and Appointment_Type might be in the way they're displayed; you might want a Deadline_Type to be displayed in a way that makes it stand out on the screen (e.g. in bright red or boldface characters).

We might want all shapes to have a primitive operation called Draw to guarantee that there'll always be a way of drawing any derived shape. Now, how can we implement Draw when Shape is a null record? The answer is that we can't; each shape will have its own requirements, but there's no way to draw a generalised Shape without knowing what sort of shape it is. One solution is to define Draw so that it does nothing:

```
procedure Draw (S : in Shape) is
begin
   null;    -- do nothing
end Draw;
```

An alternative would be to raise a Program_Error exception, since there's surely something wrong if we ever get into the situation of drawing an amorphous shape.

However, there's an easy way to overcome this problem: Ada allows us to declare Shape as an **abstract type** (which is not the same thing as an abstract data type!) by adding the word **abstract** to the declaration:

```
type Shape is abstract tagged null record;
```

You can't create objects of an abstract type; the only reason for its existence is to act as a parent type for a family of related types. Its main purpose is to provide a set of primitive operations such as Draw which will be inherited by all types derived from it. Since you can't declare a Shape once it's made abstract, you don't run the risk of calling Draw for an indeterminate Shape. You have to derive **concrete** (non-abstract) types such as Square and Rectangle so that objects of these types can be created. These can override Draw in an appropriate way, and the version of Draw that will be called from a class-wide (Shape'Class) reference will then be the overridden versions defined for Square or Rectangle.

There is still one risk to be guarded against, and that is that when you derive a new type from Shape you might forget to override Draw. As it is, you will simply end up with an invisible shape (or an exception, depending on how the Shape version of Draw was implemented), but it would be far better to identify this sort of problem at compile time rather than leaving it until run time. The way to do this is to declare Draw as an **abstract operation**:

```
procedure Draw (S : in Shape) is abstract;
```

This is used as the specification of Draw in the package specification, and it indicates to the compiler that this version of Draw will not actually be implemented (i.e. there will be no definition of Draw in the package body). Only abstract types can have abstract operations. When you derive a concrete type from an abstract type, the compiler requires you to override all the abstract primitive operations, so that it's impossible to forget to provide them. If you want to you can derive another abstract type from a parent abstract type, in which case the derived type will just inherit the abstract operations from its parent:

```
type Coloured_Shape is abstract new Shape
                    with record ... end record;
```

Coloured_Shape inherits Draw as an abstract primitive procedure, just as if you'd written this:

```
procedure Draw (S : in Coloured_Shape) is abstract;
```

Since you're not allowed to create objects belonging to an abstract type, functions which return a result of an abstract type must be declared to be abstract, since you can't provide an implementation; there's no way to create an object to return as the function's result.

15.4 An object-oriented diary

Let's reconsider the appointment diary design using the tagged types for appointments and meetings from the previous chapter. If we want a diary which holds a mixture of appointments and meetings and any other derivations we may care to add at some future date, we'll need to have a list of pointers to Appointment_Type'Class objects rather than a list of Appointment_Types. The main difficulty is in preserving the separation of model and view. Different types of appointment will need to be displayed in different ways, so we'll need to provide a primitive operation of Appointment_Type (which we can call Put, as usual) to do this:

```
procedure Put (Appt : in Appointment_Type);
```

Since the appointment list contains class-wide pointers, the availability of Put as a primitive operation will mean that Put can just be called for each appointment in the list and dispatching will ensure that the correct version for the actual appointment type will be used. However, this will mean that the model (Appointment_Type) is once again entangled with a particular view.

Derivation provides a simple solution to this difficulty. If the user interface needs to be redesigned you can just derive a new type from Appointment_Type which overrides Put. In fact, by making Appointment_Type an abstract type and Put an abstract operation, you can preserve the independence of the model from the view; each program which uses the Appointment_Type abstraction will need to derive a concrete type from it to be able to use it and will be forced to provide an appropriate implementation of Put. Since functions returning abstract types have to be abstract, the constructor has to be made into a procedure so that an implementation can be given for it; it also has to be inherited by derived classes (with all the potentially nasty consequences described in the previous chapter) since derived classes will need to use it to set up the Date and Details components that they inherit from Appointment_Type. The appointment package from the previous chapter will need some minor modifications as a result:

```
with JE.Times;
use  JE.Times;
package JE.Appointments is
   type Appointment_Type is abstract tagged private;

   function Date    (Appt : Appointment_Type) return Time_Type;
   function Details (Appt : Appointment_Type) return String;

   procedure Appointment (Date    : in Time_Type;
                          Details : in String;
                          Result  : out Appointment_Type);

   procedure Put (Appt : in Appointment_Type) is abstract;
```

```
private
   type Appointment_Type is
      abstract tagged record
         Time    : Time_Type;
         Details : String (1..50);
         Length  : Natural := 0;
      end record;
end JE.Appointments;
```

The diary will need changing to be a linked list of class-wide pointers. Add will need to take a class-wide pointer as its parameter and Choose will need to return a class-wide result.

```
with JE.Appointments, JE.Lists;
use  JE.Appointments;
package JE.Diaries is
   type Diary_Type is limited private;

   procedure Add     (Diary : in out Diary_Type;
                      Appt  : in Appointment_Type'Class);
   function  Choose (Diary : Diary_Type;
                     Appt  : Positive)
                         return Appointment_Type'Class;

   ...    -- other declarations as before

private
   type Appointment_Access is access Appointment_Type'Class;
   package Lists is
            new JE.Lists (Item_Type => Appointment_Access);

   type Diary_Type is
      limited record
         List : Lists.List_Type;
      end record;
end JE.Diaries;
```

Meetings can be derived from Appointment_Type as in the previous chapter, but Meeting_Type will need to be an abstract type which inherits an abstract Put procedure:

```
package JE.Appointments.Meetings is
   subtype Room_Type is Integer range 100 .. 999;
   type Meeting_Type is abstract new Appointment_Type
                        with private;
```

```
procedure Meeting (Date    : in Time_Type;
                   Details : in String;
                   Room    : in Room_Type;
                   Result  : out Meeting_Type);
function  Room (Appt : Meeting_Type) return Room_Type;

-- Date, Details and Put inherited unchanged from
-- Appointment_Type; so is Appointment, but don't use it!

private
   type Meeting_Type is
     abstract new Appointment_Type with
     record
        Room : Room_Type;
     end record;

end JE.Appointments.Meetings;
```

Meeting_Type inherits the constructor procedure Appointment from Appointment_Type and also provides its own constructor called Meeting. Meeting can be implemented using the inherited version of Appointment:

```
procedure Meeting (Date    : in Time_Type;
                   Details : in String;
                   Room    : in Room_Type;
                   Result  : out Meeting_Type) is
begin
   Appointment (Date, Details, Result);
                              -- set up Result's date & details
   Result.Room := Room;       -- and its room component
end Meeting;
```

The main program will need to derive concrete appointment types from the abstract types Appointment_Type and Meeting_Type as part of the view package. Because of the restrictions about where derived types can be declared (as described at the beginning of this chapter), it's no longer possible to declare the view package inside the main program; it'll have to be declared at library level. To do this, I'll create another empty parent package called JE.Views:

```
package JE.Views is
   -- another empty package!
end JE.Views;
```

and then I'll make a child package of JE.Views called JE.Views.Diary:

```
with JE.Diaries, JE.Appointments.Meetings;
package JE.Views.Diary is
   type Appointment_Type is
          new JE.Appointments.Appointment_Type
          with null record;
   procedure Put (Appt : in Appointment_Type);

   type Meeting_Type is
               new JE.Appointments.Meetings.Meeting_Type
               with null record;
   procedure Put (Appt : in Meeting_Type);

   type Command_Type is (Add, List, Delete, Save, Quit);
   function  Next_Command return Command_Type;

   procedure Load_Diary
          (Diary : in out JE.Diaries.Diary_Type);
   procedure Save_Diary
          (Diary : in JE.Diaries.Diary_Type);
   procedure Add_Appointment
          (Diary : in out JE.Diaries.Diary_Type);
   procedure List_Appointments
          (Diary : in JE.Diaries.Diary_Type);
   procedure Delete_Appointment
          (Diary : in out JE.Diaries.Diary_Type);

end JE.Views.Diary;
```

15.5   Stream input/output

One problem that arises from using a linked list of class-wide pointers is that Load and
Save will need modifying because they won't be able to use Ada.Sequential_IO. After all,
it's a bit difficult to read a value into a variable when you don't know the exact type of
value that you're about to read until you've already read it! However, all tagged types like
Appointment_Type have attributes called Input and Output which are subprograms for
reading and writing values; these use **streams** rather than files, but there is a package
called Ada.Streams.Stream_IO (see Appendix B) which lets you associate a stream with a
file. Input and Output are also defined for class-wide types; if you use the procedure
Appointment_Type'Class'Output, the tag of the appointment will be written to the stream
followed by the actual appointment, whatever type within Appointment_Type'Class it
might be. Appointment_Type'Class'Input reads the tag, and then it reads the appropriate
type of object from the stream. The specifications for these two subprograms look like this
(see Appendix C):

```
procedure Appointment'Class'Output
   (Stream : access Ada.Streams.Root_Stream_Type'Class;
    Item   : in Appointment_Type'Class);

function  Appointment'Class'Input
   (Stream : access Ada.Streams.Root_Stream_Type'Class)
            return Appointment_Type'Class;
```

The package Ada.Streams.Stream_IO provides similar facilities to Text_IO and Sequential_IO. It also contains a function Stream which takes a file as a parameter and returns a value suitable for use as the Stream parameter of the Input and Output subprograms above:

```
type Stream_Access is
            access all Ada.Streams.Root_Stream_Type'Class;
function Stream (File : in Ada.Streams.Stream_IO.File_Type)
            return Stream_Access;
```

The **with** clause at the start of the package body will need changing to refer to Ada.Streams.Stream_IO instead of Ada.Sequential_IO. Here's what Save will look like:

```
procedure Save (Diary : in Diary_Type;
                To    : in String) is
   File   : Ada.Streams.Stream_IO.File_Type;
   Stream : Ada.Streams.Stream_IO.Stream_Access;
   I : List_Iterator := First(Diary.List);
begin
   Ada.Streams.Stream_IO.Create (File, Name => To);
   Stream := Ada.Streams.Stream_IO.Stream(File);

   while I /= Last(Diary.List) loop
     Appointment_Type'Class'Output (Stream, Value(I).all);
     I := Succ(I);
   end loop;

   Ada.Streams.Stream_IO.Close (File);
end Save;
```

Load just has to use Appointment_Type'Class'Input to read successive appointments of whatever type from the file:

```
procedure Load (Diary : in out JE.Diaries.Diary_Type;
                From  : in String) is
   File   : Ada.Streams.Stream_IO.File_Type;
```

```
   Stream : Ada.Streams.Stream_IO.Stream_Access;
begin
   while Size(Diary) > 0 loop
      Delete (First(Diary.List));
   end loop;

   Ada.Streams.Stream_IO.Open
            (File, Name => From,
             Mode => Ada.Streams.Stream_IO.In_File);
   Stream := Ada.Streams.Stream_IO.Stream(File);

   while not Ada.Streams.Stream_IO.End_Of_File(File) loop
      Add (Diary, Appointment_Type'Class'Input (Stream));
   end loop;

   Ada.Streams.Stream_IO.Close (File);

exception
   when Ada.Streams.Stream_IO.Name_Error =>
      raise Diary_Error;
end Load;
```

First of all the diary is emptied by repeatedly deleting the first appointment until there are none left. Then the file is opened and the main loop reads appointments one by one, adding them to the diary using Add.

15.6   Other diary operations

Apart from these changes, the other changes to the diary are fairly minor. References to 'Value(I)' need to be changed to 'Value(I).all', as for example in Choose:

```
function Choose (Diary : Diary_Type;
                 Appt  : Positive)
                          return Appointment_Type'Class is
   Iterator : List_Iterator;

begin
   if Appt not in 1 .. Size(Diary) then
      raise Diary_Error;
   else
      Iterator := First(Diary.List);
      for I in 2 .. Appt loop
         Iterator := Succ(Iterator);
```

```
        end loop;
        return Value(Iterator).all;
      end if;
  end Choose;
```

Delete needs to deallocate the appointments when the pointers to them are removed from the list:

```
    procedure Delete (Diary : in out Diary_Type;
                      Appt  : in Positive) is
      Iterator : Lists.Iterator;
      procedure Delete_Appt is new Ada.Unchecked_Deallocation
                      (Appointment_Type'Class, Appointment_Access);
    begin
      if Appt not in 1 .. Size(Diary) then
        raise Diary_Error;
      else
        Iterator := First(Diary.List);
        for I in 2 .. Appt loop
          Iterator := Succ(Iterator);
        end loop;
        Delete_Appt (Value(Iterator));
        Delete (Iterator);
      end if;
    end Delete;
```

The only changes to Add are the change to the type of its parameter and the use of **new** to create a class-wide object initialised to hold a copy of the parameter:

```
    procedure Add (Diary : in out Diary_Type;
                   Appt  : in Appointment_Type'Class) is
      use type JE.Times.Time_Type;    -- to allow use of ">"
      Iterator : Iterator;
    begin
      Iterator := First(Diary.List);
      while Iterator /= Last(Diary.List) loop
        exit when Value(Iterator).Time > Appt.Time;
        Iterator := Succ(Iterator);
      end loop;
      Insert (Iterator, new Appointment_Type'Class'(Appt));
    exception
      when Storage_Error =>
        raise Diary_Error;
    end Add;
```

Adding a new appointment will involve asking the user if it's an ordinary appointment or a meeting. The date, time and details are then read in. Finally, the appointment is created and added to the diary depending on the appointment type; if it's a meeting, the extra meeting-specific information (the room number) is read in first:

```
procedure Add_Appointment (Diary : in out Diary_Type) is
   Day       : JE.Times.Day_Type;
   Month     : JE.Times.Month_Type;
   Year      : JE.Times.Year_Type;
   Hour      : JE.Times.Hour_Type;
   Minute    : JE.Times.Minute_Type;
   Details   : String (1..50);
   Length    : Natural;
   Separator : Character;
   Appt_Kind : Character;

begin
   -- Get appointment type
   Put ("Appointment (A) or meeting (M)? ");
   Get (Appt_Kind);
   if Appt_Kind /= 'A' and Appt_Kind /= 'a' and
            Appt_Kind /= 'M' and Appt_Kind /= 'm' then
      raise Data_Error;
   end if;

   -- Get date
   Put ("Enter date:  ");
   Get (Day);
   Get (Separator);
   Get (Month);
   Get (Separator);
   Get (Year);
   Skip_Line;

   -- Get time
   Put ("Enter time:  ");
   Get (Hour);
   Get (Separator);
   Get (Minute);
   Skip_Line;

   -- Get description
   Put ("Description: ");
   Get_Line (Details, Length);
```

```
    if Appt_Kind = 'M' or Appt_Kind = 'm' then
      -- Get meeting-specific details and construct a meeting
      declare
        Room : JE.Diaries.Meetings.Room_Type;

        Appt : Meeting_Type;
      begin
        Put ("Room number: ");
        Get (Room);
        Skip_Line;
        Meeting (JE.Times.Time(Year,Month,Day,Hour,Minute),
                 Details(1..Length), Room, Appt);
        JE.Diaries.Add (Diary, Appt);
      end;
    else
      -- Construct a normal appointment
      declare
        Appt : Appointment_Type;
      begin
        Appointment (JE.Times.Time(Year,Month,Day,Hour,Minute),
                     Details(1..Length), Appt);
        JE.Diaries.Add (Diary, Appt);
      end;
    end if;
  exception
    when Data_Error | Constraint_Error
                    | JE.Diaries.Diary_Error =>
      Put_Line ("Invalid input.");
  end Add_Appointment;
```

15.7   Extending the diary

If at some point in the future you decide to add another appointment type (e.g.
Deadline_Type) all you'll need to do is to create a new child package which derives
Deadline_Type from Appointment_Type and provides any overridden operations as well
as any extra operations (of which there are none in this case):

```
package JE.Appointments.Deadlines is
  type Deadline_Type is
          abstract new Appointment_Type with null record;
  -- Date, Details, Put and Appointment inherited unchanged
  -- from Appointment_Type
end JE.Appointments.Deadlines;
```

The view package will need modifying to provide a new concrete type with a suitable implementation of Put:

```
type Deadline_Type is
        new JE.Appointments.Deadlines.Deadline_Type
        with null record;
procedure Put (Appt : in Deadline_Type);
```

Put will also need to be defined in the package body. It might simply display the message 'URGENT' at the end; the rest of the appointment can be displayed by converting the urgent appointment to an ordinary appointment so that the Appointment_Type version of Put can be called, although it's a bit fiddly since it involves converting to the abstract parent type Appointment_Type and then using an aggregate extension to convert this to the derived concrete Appointment_Type:

```
procedure Put (Appt : in Deadline_Type) is
begin
   Put(Appointment_Type'(JE.Appointments.Appointment_Type(Appt)
                        with null record));
   Ada.Text_IO.Put (" (URGENT)");
end Put;
```

Note that even when a derived type adds no extra data components to its parent type, an extension aggregate must still be used to convert from the parent type to the derived type, but the extension to the parent type is specified as 'with null record'. We need to use a qualified expression to tell the compiler which type we expect the extension aggregate to be, since there might be any number of derived types like Deadline_Type which have a null extension and an inherited version of Put, and it would otherwise be ambiguous.

Add_Appointment will need modifying to ask if the appointment is a deadline or not and to create and initialise deadlines when necessary:

```
procedure Add_Appointment
                    (Diary : in out JE.Diaries.Diary_Type) is
   ...      -- as before
begin
   Put ("Appointment (A), meeting (M) or deadline (D)? ");

   if Appt_Kind /= 'A' and Appt_Kind /= 'a' and
          Appt_Kind /= 'M' and Appt_Kind /= 'm' and
          Appt_Kind /= 'D' and Appt_Kind /= 'd' then
      raise Data_Error;
   end if;

   ...      -- as before
```

```
   if Appt_Kind = 'M' or Appt_Kind = 'm' then
      ...    -- as before
   elsif Appt_Kind = 'D' or Appt_Kind = 'd' then
     declare
        Appt : Deadline_Type;
     begin
        Appointment (JE.Times.Time(Year,Month,Day,Hour,Minute),
                     Details(1..Length), Appt);
        JE.Diaries.Add (Diary, Appt);
     end;
   else
      ...    -- as before
   end if;

 exception
    when Data_Error | Constraint_Error
                    | JE.Diaries.Diary_Error =>
      Put_Line ("Invalid input.");
 end Add_Appointment;
```

The diary package will not need changing; a Deadline_Type will be a member of Appointment_Type'Class so it will be able to be stored in the diary along with the other appointments. Calls to Put will be dispatched to the overridden version of Put defined for Deadline_Type, so no modifications will be needed to the operations in the diary package itself. The only changes will be the introduction of the new child package JE.Appointments.Deadlines and the modifications to the view package described above. None of the existing code in the other packages will need changing; these packages won't even need to be recompiled. You'll need to compile the new child package and the modified view package, recompile the main program (because JE.Views.Diary's specification has been changed) and then test the changes that you've made. This is an enormous maintenance saving compared with any non-object-oriented solution.

Exercises

15.1 Write a program which allows you to create any of the bank accounts from exercise 14.3 and then lets you deposit and withdraw money and inspect the balance, regardless of which account type you created.

15.2 Modify the diary program to incorporate an appointment type which records the duration of an appointment in minutes, as in exercise 14.4.

15.3 Define a tagged type to represent the details of a publication (title, author and year of publication) which could be used to display an entry in a bibliography. Derive specialised publication types to represent journal articles (with journal name and volume and issue numbers), books (with publisher's name) and articles in collections (with the details of the book containing the article: title, editor, publisher and so on). Write a program similar to the appointments diary example in this chapter which uses this to implement a bibliographic database. You should be able to add the details of a publication to the database, display the contents of the database in alphabetical order of author, delete publications, and save the database to a file.

15.4 A chessboard consists of an 8×8 grid of squares, each of which can be empty or can hold a piece. Each piece is coloured white or black. Different pieces can move in different ways: for example, a rook can move along either the row or the column it is on, whereas a bishop can move along either of the two diagonals through the square it is on. Rooks and bishops cannot move through other pieces; they must stop on the square before a piece of the same colour or on the same square as a piece of the opposite colour (in which case the opposing piece is captured and removed from the board). Define a tagged type to represent a chess piece with a primitive operation which takes a chessboard and a position on the board as its parameters and returns a linked list of board positions that the piece can move to, then derive types from this to represent rooks and bishops. Write a program which will read the positions of a set of rooks and bishops on a chessboard and generate a list of all legal moves for each piece.

CHAPTER 16

Controlled types

*A retentive memory is a good thing, but the
ability to forget is the true token of greatness.*
— Elbert Hubbard, *Epigrams*

16.1 Memory leaks

It's time to take another look at the linked list package, since there's still one problem with it that I've been carefully ignoring. When you declare a linked list, memory is allocated using **new**. At the end of the block where the list is declared, the list object is destroyed. Since the list object contains a pointer to an object allocated by **new**, this pointer is lost and there is no longer any way of accessing the object it pointed to. This is known as a **memory leak** and if it happens often enough you will eventually run out of memory. Memory leaks can be a major headache. You may not notice there is a problem until the program is at full stretch, which usually happens after it's been debugged and released for use in a production environment. Also, it's usually very difficult to track down the leak since it's caused by the *absence* of something in your code.

Some systems (but not all) use a **garbage collector** as a way of solving this problem. At some point (e.g. when you try to allocate some memory) the garbage collector scans the heap looking for blocks of memory that are no longer accessible and reclaims them for recycling. Unfortunately, since not all systems use garbage collection, you can't rely on it being there to tidy up after you. The only time that Ada guarantees to reclaim inaccessible objects is at the point where the declaration of the access type itself goes out of scope, since by then there won't be any access variables left which might point to the objects. In the case of a generic package the access type is effectively declared at the point where you instantiate the package so this isn't as bad as it might sound. The only other alternative is to use Unchecked_Deallocation as described in chapter 11. As the name implies, this is done at your own risk; if you deallocate something and you still have an access variable which points to it (a **dangling pointer**) you run the risk of crashing your system. Using a dangling pointer to access something that isn't there any more can make a real mess of things. However, in the case of a linked list you can usually make sure that this doesn't happen.

So to guarantee that your linked lists don't cause memory leaks you will need to provide a procedure which will use Unchecked_Deallocation to clean up the linked list (possibly called Close by analogy with closing a file):

```
declare
   X : List_Type;
begin
   Process (X);      -- use the list X
   Close (X);        -- free memory allocated to X
end;
```

The disadvantage of doing this is that it puts an extra burden on the users of your linked list package; they will have to remember to call Close at the end of every block where a list is declared, and if they forget they will end up with memory leaks.

16.2   User-defined finalisation

Ada provides a way of automating the clearing up process. The package Ada.Finalization defines two tagged types called Controlled and Limited_Controlled (collectively referred to as **controlled types**). As the names imply, Controlled is a non-limited type and Limited_Controlled is a limited type. Both types are abstract so that you can't directly declare Controlled or Limited_Controlled objects.

You can derive new controlled types by deriving them from Controlled or Limited_Controlled. Controlled types inherit a primitive operation called Finalize from their parent type:

```
procedure Finalize (Object : in out Controlled);
procedure Finalize (Object : in out Limited_Controlled);
```

Finalize is unusual in that it is automatically called when a controlled object goes out of scope (i.e. at the end of the block where it is declared). Finalize is therefore like the Close procedure described above except that you don't need to call it explicitly; the compiler will automatically provide a call to Finalize at the end of the block. Finalize can be used for any last-minute cleaning up (**finalisation**) that needs to be done; this often involves deallocating memory, but you could use it to save the object automatically to disk, add an entry to a log file, clear the screen, play a tune, or do anything else you might think is appropriate. The versions of Finalize that you inherit from Controlled and Limited_Controlled do nothing, so that you don't have to override Finalize for your derived type if you don't need to do any finalisation operations.

British readers should be careful not to use the normal British spelling ('Finalise' instead of 'Finalize') when attempting to override operations of controlled types. If you declared a procedure called Finalise, you'd end up with a brand new primitive operation called Finalise in addition to the inherited version of Finalize, and Finalise would *not* be called automatically. A good compiler should warn you about this!

In the case of a linked list you can define Finalize to deallocate all the items in a list automatically at the end of its scope. Here's how the linked list package from chapter 12 can be modified to allow this:

```
with Ada.Finalization;    use Ada.Finalization;
generic
   type Item_Type is private;
package JE.Lists is
   type List_Type is limited private;
   ...                   -- as before
private
   ...                   -- as before
   type List_Type is new Limited_Controlled with
     record
       Header : List_Access := new List_Header;
     end record;

   procedure Finalize (Object : in out List_Type);
   ...                   -- as before
end JE.Lists;
```

List_Type is automatically a limited type because it is derived from the limited type Limited_Controlled. Finalize is declared in the private part of the package; this makes it a primitive operation of List_Type (so that it overrides the 'do-nothing' version inherited from Limited_Controlled) but it's invisible to package clients. Child packages can still access it; this means that if a further type derived from List_Type wants to override Finalize, it can call List_Type's version of Finalize as part of its own finalisation code. Note that if the visible part of the package revealed that List_Type were derived from Limited_Controlled, package clients could call Finalize directly since Finalize is visibly known to be a primitive operation of Limited_Controlled types and so would be known to be inherited by List_Type.

The definition of Finalize for a linked list might look like this:

```
procedure Finalize (Object : in out List_Type) is
   procedure Delete_Header is
      new Ada.Unchecked_Deallocation
                        (List_Header, List_Access);
begin
   while First(Object) /= Last(Object) loop
     Delete (First(Object));
   end loop;
   Delete_Header (Object.List);
end Finalize;
```

This loops until the list is empty, removing and deleting the first element of the list each time around the loop, and then deletes the list header.

As well as Finalize, controlled types have another primitive operation called Initialize. Initialize is declared in exactly the same way as Finalize is:

```
procedure Initialize (Object : in out Controlled);
procedure Initialize (Object : in out Limited_Controlled);
```

Like Finalize, the default behaviour is to do nothing. If you override Initialize for a derived controlled type, it is called automatically whenever an object of that type is created that has no initial value specified. If an initial value *is* specified in the object declaration, Initialize doesn't get called.

16.3 Smart pointers

One remaining problem is what to do in the case of a list of pointers. Finalising the list will deallocate the elements of the list, but this will cause a memory leak since the pointers that they contain will disappear. One solution to this is to define a **smart pointer** type which finalises itself automatically and to use this as the type of list element to be used instead of a plain access type:

```
type Pointer_Type is new Controlled with
  record
    Value : Some_Access_Type;
  end record;

procedure Finalize (Object : in out Pointer_Type);
```

The Finalize operation for Pointer_Type can be used to delete the pointer it contains. We'll also need an accessor function to let us get at the pointer inside the Pointer_Type object:

```
function Value (Pointer : Pointer_Type)
                 return Some_Access_Type is
begin
  return Pointer.Value;
end Value;
```

This is best done in a generic package so that we can instantiate it for use with any access type:

```
generic
  type Item_Type(<>) is limited private;
  type Access_Type   is access Item_Type;

package JE.Pointers is
  ...
end JE.Pointers;
```

Note that Item_Type is defined to be an unconstrained limited private type; this means that it can be instantiated using absolutely any type at all. Access_Type can be any (pool-specific) access type which accesses Item_Type.

Inside the package, the declaration of Pointer_Type doesn't need to specify publicly that Pointer_Type is a tagged type since this would give clients the freedom to derive from Pointer_Type and override the Finalize operation if they wanted to, so the package can look something like this:

```
with Ada.Finalization;
generic
   type Item_Type(<>) is limited private;
   type Access_Type    is access Item_Type;
package JE.Pointers is
   type Pointer_Type is private;
   function Value (Pointer : Pointer_Type) return Access_Type;
private
   type Pointer_Type is new Ada.Finalization.Controlled with
      record
         Value : Access_Type;
      end record;
   procedure Finalize (Object : in out Pointer_Type);
end JE.Pointers;
```

Here's how the package might be used:

```
with JE.Pointers;
package JE.Coords is
   type Coord_Type is
      record
         X, Y : Float;
      end record;
   type Coord_Access is access Coord_Type;

   package Coord_Pointers is
      new JE.Pointers (Item_Type    => Coord_Type,
                       Access_Type => Coord_Access);

   A : Coord_Access;
   B : Coord_Pointers.Pointer_Type;
end JE.Coords;
```

This instantiates JE.Pointers in a library-level package; this is necessary because of the rule that derived types must be declared at the same level as the parent type. Since Ada.Finalization.Controlled is a library-level type, all controlled types must be derived by instantiation at library level; remember that generic packages are treated as being declared at the point of instantiation. This means that JE.Pointers can only be instantiated at library level, usually within another library package as shown above.

There are two objects declared in this package: A is a normal access variable while B is a smart pointer. Where you would refer to the components of the object that A points to as A.X, A.Y or A.all, you refer to Value(B).X, Value(B).Y and Value(B).all to get at the components of the object that B points to. B starts off as a null pointer, so you'll need a constructor function that generates a Pointer_Type object from an Access_Type value:

```
function Pointer (Value : Access_Type) return Pointer_Type is
   Object : Pointer_Type;
begin
   Object.Value := Value;
   return Object;
end Pointer;
```

This just takes a copy of the parameter and encapsulates it in a smart pointer. This means that you should avoid using the parameter elsewhere; don't deallocate it using Ada.Unchecked_Deallocation or use it to initialise another smart pointer, since it will then end up being deallocated twice. This will usually be fatal for the memory management system and your program will probably crash shortly afterwards in a mystifying way. Here is how you should use Pointer:

```
B : Coord_Pointers.Pointer_Type :=
        Coord_Pointers.Pointer( new Coord_Type'(1.0,1.0) );
```

The parameter to Pointer is a value created using **new** which won't be used elsewhere. As you can see, you can use Pointer to generate an initial value for use in a declaration; if a declaration doesn't provide an initial value, the variable will start off with a null pointer as usual.

16.4   User-defined assignment

One problem with this is that it's still possible to cause a disaster by assigning one Pointer_Type object to another. If you do this you will end up with two Pointer_Type objects pointing to the same thing so that when they are finalised the same object will be deleted twice, generally with disastrous results as mentioned above. The ideal solution would be to overload the assignment operator ':=', but you can't do this because in fact ':=' isn't counted as being an operator in Ada. Fortunately the Finalization package provides a solution to this problem too. The type Controlled has a primitive operation called Adjust which is used during assignment operations, so that types derived from Controlled can override this to modify the behaviour of assignments. Adjust looks just like Initialize and Finalize:

```
procedure Adjust (Object : in out Controlled);
```

There is of course no version of Adjust for Limited_Controlled since Limited_Controlled (as well as any type derived from it) is a limited type and so assignment isn't possible anyway.

When a value is assigned to a controlled object, Adjust is automatically called after copying the new value into the object. If A and B are objects of the same controlled type, the assignment A := B involves taking a copy of B, finalising the current value of A before it gets destroyed by being overwritten, copying the copy of B into A, adjusting A, and then finalising the copy of B before it's destroyed:

```
A := B;   -- compiled as:   Temp := B;
                            Finalize(A);
                            A := Temp;
                            Adjust(A);
                            Finalize(Temp);
```

This looks like a laborious business but the compiler can generally optimise it so that it ends up like this:

```
A := B;   -- compiled as:   Finalize(A);
                            A := B;
                            Adjust(A);
```

The extra copy of B is usually unnecessary, but it caters for the case where an object is assigned to itself:

```
B := B;   -- compiled as:   Temp := B;
                            Finalize(B);
                            B := Temp;
                            Adjust(B);
                            Finalize(Temp);
```

A copy of B's value is made before B is finalised, and it's this copy that's assigned back into B and then adjusted.

Adjust can take care of any post-assignment adjustments that may be needed. In the case of Pointer_Type we can make assignment work properly by using Adjust and Finalize to maintain a **reference count** showing how many references there are to the same object, and only deleting an object when the reference count reaches zero. This means that Pointer_Type will need to point to an object which holds the reference count as well as the actual pointer to the data; keeping the reference count in the Pointer_Type object wouldn't work since other Pointer_Type objects would have no idea it was there. Having multiple Pointer_Type objects point to a common item means that the item itself can keep track of the reference count. This means that we'll need Pointer_Type objects to point to **reference counted objects** which contain a reference count and a pointer to the actual data being managed. This will involve a number of changes to the existing package:

```ada
with Ada.Finalization;
generic
   type Item_Type(<>) is limited private;
   type Access_Type   is access Item_Type;

package JE.Pointers is
   type Pointer_Type is private;
   function Pointer (Value   : Access_Type)
                                       return Pointer_Type;
   function Value   (Pointer : Pointer_Type)
                                       return Access_Type;

private
   type Reference_Counted_Object is
     record
       Value : Access_Type;
       Count : Natural;
     end record;

   type Reference_Counted_Pointer is
                       access Reference_Counted_Object;

   type Pointer_Type is new Ada.Finalization.Controlled with
     record
       Pointer : Reference_Counted_Pointer;
     end record;

   procedure Finalize (Object : in out Pointer_Type);
   procedure Adjust   (Object : in out Pointer_Type);
end JE.Pointers;
```

Pointer_Type now points to a Reference_Counted_Pointer which contains the actual pointer value together with a reference count. You still have to be a bit careful since circular lists of reference counted objects will never be deallocated because each object will always be pointed to by the preceding object in the list so the reference count will never become zero. A Pointer_Type object will start off as a null pointer, so it'll be necessary to check for **null** within each of the operations provided by the package. The definitions of Pointer and Value both need changing to reflect this:

```ada
procedure Delete_Item is
     new Ada.Unchecked_Deallocation (Item_Type, Access_Type);
```

```
function Pointer (Value : Access_Type)
                             return Pointer_Type is
   Object : Pointer_Type;
begin
   Object.Pointer :=
           new Reference_Counted_Object'(Value => Value,
                                         Count => 1);
   return Object;
end Pointer;

function Value (Pointer : Pointer_Type) return Access_Type is
begin
   if Pointer.Pointer = null then
     return null;
   else
     return Pointer.Pointer.Value;
   end if;
end Value;
```

Pointer has to create an object which points to a new Reference_Counted_Object with a reference count of 1 while Value has to check whether its parameter contains a null pointer and then return either **null** or the access value in the Reference_Counted_Object it points to.

If a Pointer_Type object being finalised doesn't contain a null pointer, Finalize will need to decrement the reference count and then delete the object if the count has reached zero:

```
procedure Delete_Pointer is
   new Ada.Unchecked_Deallocation (Reference_Counted_Object,
                                   Reference_Counted_Pointer);

procedure Finalize (Object : in out Pointer_Type) is
begin
   if Object.Pointer /= null then
     Object.Pointer.Count := Object.Pointer.Count - 1;
     if Object.Pointer.Count = 0 then
       Delete_Item (Object.Pointer.Value);
       Delete_Pointer (Object.Pointer);
     end if;
   end if;
end Finalize;
```

Adjust will need to increment the reference count when a non-null value is assigned to a Pointer_Type object:

```
procedure Adjust (Object : in out Pointer_Type) is
begin
  if Object.Pointer /= null then
    Object.Pointer.Count := Object.Pointer.Count + 1;
  end if;
end Adjust;
```

Assigning another Pointer_Type value to Object means that Object will just point to the same reference counted object as the other one does. The old value of Object will be finalised, so that the reference counted object it points to will have its reference count decremented and will be deleted if necessary. The new value will then be copied into Object. Finally, Adjust will increment the reference count if it isn't a null pointer to mark the fact that there is now one extra Pointer_Type object pointing to the same Reference_Counted_Object.

Note that Adjust will also be called if an initial value is specified as part of the declaration of a Pointer_Type object:

```
A : Point_Access.Pointer_Type;    -- as defined earlier
B : Point_Access.Pointer_Type := A;
```

The value of A will be copied into B so that A and B will end up pointing to the same reference counted object, and then Adjust will be called to increment the object's reference count.

16.5   Testing controlled types

One of the problems with testing controlled types lies in the fact that the procedures Initialize, Finalize and Adjust are called automatically without there being any sign in your program that they are being called. A good way to test that controlled types work as expected is to make Initialize, Finalize and Adjust display a message to show when they are being called:

```
procedure Initialize (Object : in out Pointer_Type) is
begin
  ...    -- do initialisation
  Put_Line ("Initialize called for Pointer_Type");
end Initialize;

procedure Finalize (Object : in out Pointer_Type) is
begin
  ...    -- do finalisation
  Put_Line ("Finalize called for Pointer_Type");
end Finalize;
```

```
procedure Adjust (Object : in out Pointer_Type) is
begin
   ...      -- do post-assignment adjustment
   Put_Line ("Adjust called for Pointer_Type");
end Adjust;
```

A little ingenuity with global variables in the package body where these functions are declared will let you associate unique identifiers with each Pointer_Type object that's created (as in the Bank_Account example mentioned in chapter 6) to display even better messages to keep track of what's going on. In the case of Pointer_Type, you might want to include a numeric ID in each Reference_Counted_Object and display the object ID and reference count every time the object is updated:

```
type Reference_Counted_Object is
   record
      Value : Access_Type;
      Count : Natural;
      Ident : Positive;    -- a unique object number
   end record;
```

The function Pointer will need to allocate numbers for the Ident component of Reference_Counted_Objects as they are created:

```
-- In the package body:
RCO_Number : Positive := 1;

function Pointer (Value : Access_Type) return Pointer_Type is
   Object : Pointer_Type;
begin
   Object.Pointer :=
       new Reference_Counted_Object'(Value => Value,
                                     Count => 1,
                                     Ident => RCO_Number);
   RCO_Number := RCO_Number + 1;
   return Object;
end Pointer;
```

Finalize and Adjust can display the Ident component and the corresponding reference count as changes are made:

```
procedure Finalize (Object : in out Pointer_Type) is
begin
   if Object.Pointer /= null then
     Put ("Finalising ");
```

```
      Put (Object.Pointer.Ident, Width => 1);
      Object.Pointer.Count := Object.Pointer.Count - 1;
      Put (", reference count is now ");
      Put (Object.Pointer.Count, Width => 1);
      if Object.Pointer.Count = 0 then
        Put (" so deleting it");
        Delete_Item (Object.Pointer.Value);
        Delete_Pointer (Object.Pointer);
      end if;
      New_Line;
    end if;
end Finalize;

procedure Adjust (Object : in out Pointer_Type) is
begin
   if Object.Pointer /= null then
     Put ("Adjusting ");
     Put (Object.Pointer.Ident, Width => 1);
     Object.Pointer.Count := Object.Pointer.Count + 1;
     Put (", reference count is now ");
     Put (Object.Pointer.Count, Width => 1);
     New_Line;
   end if;
end Adjust;
```

This will make it much easier to track down the exact order of events when you're dealing
with controlled objects. You can't use your text editor to track down the places where
Initialize, Finalize and Adjust are called since the compiler inserts invisible calls to these
procedures, so you need to design controlled types so that they will provide the debugging
information automatically. At this point it's worth pointing out a possible use for the
parent package JE:

```
package JE is
   procedure Debug (On : in Boolean);     -- set a hidden flag
   function  Debugging return Boolean;    -- test the hidden flag
end JE;
```

This lets you turn a flag on or off and then test it in the child units to determine whether to
display debugging information. You could even use an enumeration or an integer value
instead of a Boolean to choose between different levels of detail. That way if anything
goes wrong, your debugging tools are ready and waiting to be turned on if you need them.
They make your application larger when you don't need them, but discarding your
debugging tools to save space has been compared to leaving your parachute at home once
you get your pilot's licence. Need I say more?

Exercises

16.1   Modify the playing card package from exercise 9.2 to make a pack of cards a controlled type. Declaring a pack of cards should create a shuffled set of all 52 cards automatically.

16.2   Create a generic package which defines a controlled type containing a random number generator from Ada.Numerics.Discrete_Random (see exercise 5.1). The controlled type's Initialize operation should call Reset to guarantee that the random number generator is initially randomised.

16.3   Modify the diary program so that diaries are loaded and saved automatically at initialisation and finalisation. For the sake of simplicity, use filenames suffixed by a number (Diary1, Diary2 and so on) for each diary object you declare; to do this, use a global diary number which is incremented every time a diary object is declared and use the diary number to generate the filename.

16.4   Modify the linked list package to make it possible to do 'deep copying' of lists. This means that when one list is assigned to another, copies of all the items in the list are made so that a completely separate duplicate copy is produced. You can do this by making List_Type a controlled type and overriding Adjust.

CHAPTER 17

An object-oriented calculator

> *We shall have to evolve problem-solvers galore —*
> *since each problem they solve creates ten problems more.*
> — Piet Hein, *More Grooks*

17.1 Expression handling objects

In this chapter I'm going to try and show you another side to object-oriented programming by taking another look at the calculator program from chapter 13. I'm going to leave it operating on Integer values although it would be possible to modify it to deal with Floats or make it generic to be able to be instantiated with different numeric types. What I want to concentrate on here is redesigning it so that it will be possible to extend it easily to handle new types of operand and operator, which at the moment would involve some fairly fundamental changes to the program. What I want to produce is something that will evaluate an expression which is stored in a string. Using a string as the source of the expression is a useful generalisation; you could read the string from the keyboard or a file, or you could generate it within your program.

Apart from the string containing the expression to be recognised, the other main component of the evaluation process is a specification of the expression's syntax. In previous versions of the program, the syntax was implicit in the subprograms which did the analysis. This means that it couldn't be altered without modifying the existing subprograms. By using a tagged type Expression_Type, the subprograms can be made primitive operations of the type and overridden in derived classes as necessary. This will allow new types of operators and operands to be added without affecting existing code, as well as allowing changes to be made to the syntax of expressions. A tagged type can therefore be seen as a *collection of subprograms* rather than just as an extensible collection of data components. This view is central to the object-oriented way of looking at the world. Here's the declaration of Expression_Type:

```
type Expression_Type is tagged limited private;
```

Expression_Type doesn't need to contain any data, since it's just a collection of primitive operations. The full declaration in the private part of the package will just look like this:

```
type Expression_Type is tagged limited null record;
```

Expression_Type is a limited type because there is no need to allow assignment and comparison of Expression_Type values. All Expression_Type objects will effectively be identical since they'll all embody the same syntax rules. The main primitive operation will be a function called Evaluate to evaluate a string representing an expression and produce an integer result:

```
function Evaluate (Syntax : Expression_Type;
                   Expr   : String) return Integer;
```

The parameter Syntax will in effect embody the syntax rules for an expression, and Evaluate will use these rules to process the expression given in the Expr parameter to produce an integer result. Evaluate will be a primitive operation of Expression_Type so that it can be overridden by descendants of Expression_Type if the format of an expression needs to be changed. We'll also need an exception that Evaluate can use to report syntax errors:

```
Syntax_Error : exception;
```

These declarations are the only ones that clients of the package need to be able to see. Everything else can be put into the private part of the package so that it's hidden from clients but is still accessible to allow child packages to define types derived from Expression_Type.

17.2 Tokens

An expression consists of a series of **tokens** arranged according to the syntax rules embodied in Evaluate. The types of token that the calculator in chapter 13 handled included numbers, various operators, left and right parentheses, and an 'end-of-expression' marker (the end of the line or a full stop or something similar). To allow the set of legal tokens to be extended we need yet another tagged type:

```
type Token_Type is abstract tagged null record;
```

This is an abstract type since we won't want to allow clients to create amorphous Token_Type objects; you should only be able to deal with specific tokens like numbers, the addition operator and so on. There isn't any data that all tokens will have in common, so I've declared it to be a null record. Token_Type is there so that all tokens will have a common parent and the class-wide type Token_Type'Class will be able to be used for any token at all. We can derive some concrete classes directly from Token_Type:

```
type Left_Parenthesis  is new Token_Type with null record;
type Right_Parenthesis is new Token_Type with null record;
type End_Of_Expression is new Token_Type with null record;
```

We can also derive further abstract types to represent specific classes of token which add some necessary primitive operations:

```
type      Priority_Type  is range 0..9;
subtype   Operator_Priority_Type is
                Priority_Type range 1..Priority_Type'Last;

type      Operator_Type is
                abstract new Token_Type with null record;
function Priority (Operator : Operator_Type)
                return Operator_Priority_Type is abstract;

type      Operand_Type is
                abstract new Token_Type with null record;
function Value (Operand : Operand_Type)
                return Integer is abstract;
```

We know that there are a number of different operators; these obviously all have something in common, so I've introduced a type called Operator_Type to capture the features which are common to all operators. Operators have a priority (i.e. a precedence), so there is a primitive function of Operator_Type called Priority which returns the operator's priority as a value of type Operator_Priority_Type. This allows for nine different levels of priority; I'll use 1 for the highest priority and 9 for the lowest. The reason for making Operator_Priority_Type a subtype of Priority_Type is to allow 0 to be used for operands; I'll explain this in more detail later. Priority is an abstract function so concrete derivations of Operator_Type will be forced to provide an overriding definition for it.

Rather than defining a type Number_Type to represent numeric operands directly, I've defined a more general type Operand_Type so that different types of operands can be added later. The common feature of operands is that they have a value, so Operand_Type has a primitive function to return the value. This is also an abstract operation which will need to be overridden when we know what type of operand we're dealing with.

Operators come in two basic types: **binary operators** with two operands and **unary operators** with only one. We can derive further types from Operator_Type which provide primitive functions called Apply to apply the operator to its operands:

```
type Binary_Operator_Type is
                abstract new Operator_Type with null record;

function Apply (Operator    : Binary_Operator_Type;
                Left, Right : Integer)
                            return Integer is abstract;
type Unary_Operator_Type is
                abstract new Operator_Type with null record;
```

```
function Apply (Operator : Unary_Operator_Type;
               Right     : Integer)
                              return Integer is abstract;
```

Some operators can be either binary or unary; unfortunately Ada does not allow **multiple inheritance** where a derived type can have more than one parent (although it's possible to use workarounds involving generics or access discriminants), but in this case we can achieve something close to the desired effect by rederiving from Binary_Operator_Type:

```
type Variadic_Operator_Type is
                abstract new Binary_Operator_Type
                with null record;
function Unary_Priority (Operator : Variadic_Operator_Type)
                return Operator_Priority_Type is abstract;
function Apply (Operator    : Variadic_Operator_Type;
               Left, Right : Integer)
                return Integer is abstract;
function Apply (Operator : Variadic_Operator_Type;
               Right    : Integer)
                return Integer is abstract;
```

This has two versions of Apply: the first is inherited from Binary_Operator_Type to deal with the case where the operator is used in its binary form and the second is a new one introduced to deal with the case where it is used in its unary form. There is also a separate function Unary_Priority to return the priority of the unary form of the operator. For now we'll have two main categories of operator: adding operators (+ and −) and multiplication operators (* and /). Here are the declarations we need for these:

```
type Multiplying_Operator_Type is
                abstract new Binary_Operator_Type
                with null record;
function Priority (Operator : Multiplying_Operator_Type)
                return Operator_Priority_Type;


type Adding_Operator_Type is
                abstract new Variadic_Operator_Type
                with null record;
function Priority (Operator : Adding_Operator_Type)
                return Operator_Priority_Type;
function Unary_Priority (Operator : Adding_Operator_Type)
                return Operator_Priority_Type;
```

Priority is no longer an abstract operation since we know what the priorities of multiplication and addition operators are:

```
function Priority (Operator : Multiplying_Operator_Type)
                     return Operator_Priority_Type is
begin
  return 5;
end Priority;

function Priority (Operator : Adding_Operator_Type)
                     return Operator_Priority_Type is
begin
  return 6;
end Priority;

function Unary_Priority (Operator : Adding_Operator_Type)
                     return Operator_Priority_Type is
begin
  return 2;
end Unary_Priority;
```

The priorities 5 and 6 have been chosen to allow other operators to have even lower priorities if necessary; the unary priority for the adding operators is the second highest to allow for one higher level. Now we can derive the final concrete types. Here is the definition of a type to represent '−':

```
type Minus_Operator is new Adding_Operator_Type
                                 with null record;
function Apply (Operator    : Minus_Operator;
               Left, Right : Integer) return Integer;
function Apply (Operator    : Minus_Operator;
               Right       : Integer) return Integer;
```

The other operators are similar; I'll leave it to you to come up with their declarations. Here are the bodies of the Apply primitives for Minus_Operator:

```
function Apply (Operator    : Minus_Operator;
               Left, Right : Integer) return Integer is
begin
  return Left - Right;
end Apply;

function Apply (Operator : Minus_Operator;
               Right    : Integer) return Integer is
begin
  return -Right;
end Apply;
```

It may seem strange to have a data type that contains no data, but in fact there is one item of data that these types all have: their **tag**. The tags are the reason that we need these types at all, so that we can dispatch to the correct operation. Once again, you can think of these data types as collections of operations rather than as collections of data.

We can derive a type to represent numeric operands by derivation from Operand_Type:

```
type Number_Type (Value : Integer) is
                    abstract new Operand_Type with null record;
function Value (Operand : Number_Type) return Integer;
```

Unlike the other types, this does contain one item of data apart from the tag, namely the value of the number. This is supplied as a discriminant so that the value of a Number_Type object must be set when it is declared. The primitive function Value simply returns the value of the discriminant:

```
function Value (Operand : Number_Type) return Integer is
begin
   return Operand.Value;
end Value;
```

17.3   Token extraction

Extracting successive tokens from the string contained in an Expression_Type value can be done by a primitive operation of Expression which I'll call Next_Token. Next_Token can use its knowledge about the expected format of an expression to create specific types of token based on the characters it reads from a string. Here's how it can be declared:

```
type Token_Access is access Token_Type'Class;

package Token_Pointers is
        new JE.Pointers (Token_Type'Class, Token_Access);

subtype Token_Pointer is Token_Pointers.Pointer_Type;

procedure Next_Token (Syntax : in Expression_Type;
                      Expr   : in String;
                      From   : in out Positive;
                      Token  : in out Token_Pointer);
```

Next_Token needs to start at the position in Expr specified by From, skip over any spaces and then use the character it's found to determine the actual token type. It will then need to create a token of the appropriate type and return a class-wide pointer using the Token parameter. The package JE.Pointers from the previous chapter is used to ensure that all pointers are automatically destroyed after use. It's also possible that Next_Token will go past the end of the expression buffer, so it needs to check for this and return an End_Of_Expression token if it happens. Here's the implementation of Next_Token:

```
procedure Next_Token (Syntax : in Expression_Type;
                      Expr   : in String;
                      From   : in out Positive;
                      Token  : in out Token_Pointer) is
begin
   -- Find start of next token
   while From <= Expr'Last and then Expr(From) = ' ' loop
      From := From + 1;
   end loop;

   -- Check for end of expression
   if From > Expr'Last then
      Token := Pointer(new End_Of_Expression);
   else
      Fetch_Token (Expression_Type'Class(Syntax),
               Expr, From, Token);
   end if;
end Next_Token;
```

This begins by skipping over any spaces and then checking if the current position is beyond the end of the string. If so, it creates a new End_Of_Expression token to be the result of the procedure. If not it calls another primitive function Fetch_Token to extract the next token from the string.

⇒   *Using **new** to create tokens like End_Of_Expression is somewhat wasteful since all objects of this type are identical. Try to modify the design so that there would only be one token of each type that operations like Next_Token would return pointers to.*

Note that Syntax is converted to a class-wide value so that the call to Fetch_Token will be a dispatching call; if you forget to do this, overriding Fetch_Token will have no effect since Next_Token will still be calling the Expression_Type version of the procedure. Fetch_Token is declared like this:

```
procedure Fetch_Token (Syntax : in Expression_Type;
                       Expr   : in String;
                       From   : in out Positive;
                       Token  : in out Token_Pointer);
```

Here's how Fetch_Token can be implemented:

```
procedure Fetch_Token (Syntax : in Expression_Type;
                       Expr    : in String;
                       From    : in out Positive;
                       Token   : in out Token_Pointer) is
begin
  case Expr(From) is
    when '+' =>
      Token := Pointer(new Plus_Operator);
    when '-' =>
      Token := Pointer(new Minus_Operator);
    when '*' =>
      Token := Pointer(new Times_Operator);
    when '/' =>
      Token := Pointer(new Over_Operator);
    when '(' =>
      Token := Pointer(new Left_Parenthesis);
    when ')' =>
      Token := Pointer(new Right_Parenthesis);
    when '0'..'9' =>
      declare
        Value : Integer;
      begin
        Ada.Integer_Text_IO.Get (Expr(From..Expr'Last),
                                  Value, From);
        Token := Pointer(new Number_Type(Value));
      end;
    when others =>
      Ada.Exceptions.Raise_Exception (Syntax_Error'Identity,
            "Illegal character '" & Expr(From) & "'");
  end case;
  From := From + 1;
end Fetch_Token;
```

A **case** statement is used to select amongst alternatives based on the first character of the token. I've assumed that there are descendants of Token_Type called Plus_Operator, Times_Operator and Over_Operator which have been defined by a similar process to Minus_Operator. Numbers are dealt with using yet another version of Get defined in Ada.Integer_Text_IO which reads a value from a string. The first parameter is the string to read from (in this case, everything from the current position to the end of the string), the second is the variable to store the result in, and the third is an output which is set to the position of the last character that was read. At the end of Fetch_Token, the current position is incremented to get past the last character of the token. In the case where the character that's been read in isn't recognised at all, Ada.Exceptions.Raise_Exception is used to raise a Syntax_Error exception. I've done it this way instead of using a **raise** statement because Raise_Exception provides the ability to specify a message which will be associated with the exception.

17.4 Expression evaluation

Now it's time to look at the implementation of Evaluate. All it needs to do is to call another primitive function called Parse to parse the expression and then check that the final token is an End_Of_Expression token. Here's how it can be implemented:

```
function Evaluate (Syntax : Expression_Type;
                   Expr   : String) return Integer is
   Token  : Token_Pointer;
   From   : Positive := Expr'First;
   Result : Integer;
begin
   Parse (Expression_Type'Class(Syntax), Expr, From,
          Priority_Type'Last, Result, Token);
   if Value(Token).all not in End_Of_Expression'Class then
      Ada.Exceptions.Raise_Exception (Syntax_Error'Identity,
            "Missing operator or left parenthesis");
   end if;
   return Result;
end Evaluate;
```

Parse will do the actual expression evaluation, storing the result in Value as well as returning the terminating token. If the terminating token is not an End_Of_Expression token, there is either an operator missing or too many right parentheses (i.e. a missing left parenthesis) so a Syntax_Error exception is reported.

Parse is declared like this:

```
procedure Parse (Syntax : in Expression_Type;
                 Expr   : in String;
                 From   : in out Positive;
                 Prio   : in Priority_Type;
                 Result : out Integer;
                 Next   : in out Token_Pointer);
```

The intention here is to do recursive descent parsing as described in chapter 13. The reason for the Prio parameter is that an expression can be considered to be a sequence of **terms** separated by low-priority (priority 9) operators; each term is a sequence of terms separated by priority 8 operators, each of which is a sequence of terms separated by priority 7 operators, and so on. This can be represented as a set of syntax rules using the same notation as was used in chapter 13:

```
Expression    = Term_8  { Op_9 Term_8 }
Term_8        = Term_7  { Op_8 Term_7 }
Term_7        = Term_6  { Op_7 Term_6 }
...
Term_1        = Term_0  { Op_1 Term_0 }
Term_0        = Operand
```

Note that in general, Term_N can be defined as

```
Term_N        = Term_(N-1)  { Op_N Term_(N-1) }
```

You can see the sense in this if you consider how similar the functions Expression and Term were in chapter 13. Parse can simply call itself recursively with the value of N (the operator priority) as the value of the parameter Prio. The recursion will end when the highest operator priority is reached; each term will then be an operand (i.e. a number, a unary operator followed by a subexpression or a subexpression in parentheses). A priority of zero can be used to indicate that we need to read an operand. This is the reason why Priority_Type has a wider range than Operator_Priority_Type. Parse can therefore be implemented like this:

```
procedure Parse (Syntax : in Expression_Type;
                 Expr   : in String;
                 From   : in out Positive;
                 Prio   : in Priority_Type;
                 Result : out Integer;
                 Next   : in out Token_Pointer) is
begin
  if Prio = Priority_Type'First then     -- Term_0
    Get_Operand (Expression_Type'Class(Syntax),
                 Expr, From, Result, Next);
  else                                   -- Term_N for N > 0
    declare
      Right : Integer;
      Op    : Token_Pointer;
    begin
      Parse (Syntax, Expr, From, Prio-1, Result, Op);
      while Value(Op).all in Binary_Operator_Type'Class
            and then
        Priority(Binary_Operator_Type'Class(Value(Op).all))
            = Prio
      loop
        Parse (Syntax, Expr, From, Prio-1, Right, Next);
        Result :=
          Apply (Binary_Operator_Type'Class(Value(Op).all),
```

```
                    Result, Right);
            Op := Next;
        end loop;
        Next := Op;
      end;
   end if;
end Parse;
```

If the supplied priority is zero, we need to get an operand. This is done by calling Get_Operand (which is another dispatching call, thanks to the conversion to Expression_Type'Class). If the priority is non-zero, Parse is called recursively to get a term involving operators at the next higher priority (i.e. Prio–1). The value of the term will be stored in Value, and the token which terminated it will be stored in Op. The terminating token might be a binary operator of the required priority, in which case we need to get the next term by calling Parse again. This time the value is stored in Right and the terminating token is stored in Next. The operator in Op is then applied to the two operands in Value and Right, and Next is then copied into Op to be used as the operator the next time around the loop. When the loop exits, the token in Op (the final terminating token) is copied back into Next before returning.

⇒ *Why didn't I need to convert the Syntax parameter to a class-wide type in the recursive calls to Parse?*

All that's left to do now is to define Get_Operand. An operand can be a number, an expression enclosed in parentheses or a unary operator followed by an expression involving operators with a higher priority than the unary operator. The syntax of operands can therefore be written like this:

```
Operand = Number
        | ( Expression )
        | Unary_Operator_N  Term_(N-1)
```

This uses 'Unary_Operator_N' to symbolise a unary operator with priority 'N'. Here's the implementation:

```
procedure Get_Operand (Syntax : in Expression_Type;
                        Expr   : in String;
                        From   : in out Positive;
                        Result : out Integer;
                        Next   : in out Token_Pointer) is
   Op : Token_Pointer;
begin
   Next_Token (Expression_Type'Class(Syntax),
               Expr, From, Next);
```

```
if Value(Next).all in Operand_Type'Class then
   -- Operand
   Result := Value (Operand_Type'Class(Value(Next).all));
   Next_Token (Expression_Type'Class(Syntax),
               Expr, From, Next);

elsif Value(Next).all in Left_Parenthesis'Class then
   -- Left parenthesis
   Parse (Expression_Type'Class(Syntax),
          Expr, From, Priority_Type'Last, Result, Next);
   if Value(Next).all in Right_Parenthesis'Class then
      Next_Token (Expression_Type'Class(Syntax),
                  Expr, From, Next);
   else
      Ada.Exceptions.Raise_Exception (Syntax_Error'Identity,
            "Missing right parenthesis");
   end if;

elsif Value(Next).all in Unary_Operator_Type'Class then
   -- Unary operator
   Op := Next;
   Parse (Expression_Type'Class(Syntax), Expr, From,
          Priority(Unary_Operator_Type'Class
                                    (Value(Op).all)),
          Result, Next);
   Result := Apply (Unary_Operator_Type'Class
                                    (Value(Op).all),
                    Result);

elsif Value(Next).all in Variadic_Operator_Type'Class then
   -- Variadic operator
   Op := Next;
   Parse (Expression_Type'Class(Syntax), Expr, From,
          Unary_Priority (Variadic_Operator_Type'Class
                                    (Value(Op).all),
          Result, Next);
   Result := Apply (Variadic_Operator_Type'Class
                                    (Value(Op).all),
                    Result);

elsif Value(Next).all in End_Of_Expression'Class then
   -- End of expression
   Ada.Exceptions.Raise_Exception (Syntax_Error'Identity,
         "Expression incomplete");
```

```
      else
         -- Unknown token
         Ada.Exceptions.Raise_Exception (Syntax_Error'Identity,
               "Illegal token");
      end if;
   end Get_Operand;
```

If the next token is an operand, its Value operation is used to set the value of the Result parameter and the next token is returned. If it's a left parenthesis, an expression is processed using Parse to get its value into Result and a check is then made that the token returned by Parse is a right parenthesis. If it is, the token after the right parenthesis is read; otherwise, a syntax error is reported. If the token is a unary operator, Parse is called to process the term that follows; thanks to the lack of multiple inheritance this code has to be replicated for Variadic_Operator_Type as well. If the token is none of these, it's an error: either an unexpected end of expression or an invalid token.

17.5   Was it worth it?

What we've got now is a lot more complex than the calculator program in chapter 13. It's tempting to dismiss the extra complexity as gimmickry, but as you'll see in the next chapter it serves a useful purpose. What we've got now is an expression evaluator that can be adapted for use in any other program we write that needs to be able to evaluate expressions. The whole thing is now extensible in various ways: extra operators can be added without disturbing the existing code by deriving from Operator_Type, and extra operands can be added by deriving from Operand_Type. The token handling procedures will need updating to deal with the new tokens, but this can be done by deriving from Expression_Type and overriding Fetch_Token. The overridden version of Fetch_Token can call the old version of Fetch_Token to deal with the existing types of token, so there's no duplication of code. The complexity is there for a purpose; without everything you've seen in this chapter it will be necessary to modify all the existing code whenever you need to be able to cope with a small variation on the form that an expression can take. It's complex because it's completely universal, and in the next chapter you'll see how it can be adapted for use in a spreadsheet.

Exercises

17.1   Modify the calculator to support an exponentiation operator represented by '^' with the same precedence as the Ada operator '**', i.e. with a higher priority than any other operator.

17.2   Modify the calculator to allow expressions to contain hexadecimal values which are indicated by a prefix of '$', e.g. $03FF for 16#03FF#.

17.3   Modify the calculator to allow postfix operators (i.e. operators which appear *after* their operands), and provide a factorial operator '!' (see chapter 13) so that, for example, '5!' evaluates to 120.

17.4   Modify the program in this chapter to convert an arithmetic expression into 'reverse Polish' notation. The reverse Polish form of an expression consists of the operands of an operator followed by the operator itself, so that '5+3' is translated to '5 3 +', and '(1+2)*(3+4)' is translated to '1 2 + 3 4 + *'. This can be done by modifying Get_Operand to display operands as they are read and modifying Term to display operators after the operands have been dealt with, rather than using Apply to evaluate the result of the operation as at present.

CHAPTER 18

Designing a spreadsheet

Write the vision, and make it plain upon tables.
— Habakkuk, 2:2

18.1 Spreadsheets

Now that the principal features of tagged types have been covered, it's time to take another look at the design process and see how all this fits in. In the first part of the book I described how top-down design could be used to break problems down into a number of smaller problems; in the second part I described how the design process should revolve around the types of data that the program is intended to model using a combination of top-down and bottom-up design. The object-oriented design process also involves identifying type classes. As I mentioned in connection with abstract data types in chapter 10, nouns in a specification often correspond to data types and verbs to the operations on those types. Adjectives also provide a useful clue for identifying type classes by their inheritance relationships; for example, an *urgent* appointment is clearly a form of appointment so there will presumably be an inheritance relationship between Appointment_Type and Urgent_Appointment_Type (or between these and some common parent type). Also, as I showed you in the last chapter, not all type classes contain data; sometimes classes which just encapsulate a set of operations are a useful abstraction.

The design process is therefore similar to the approach I described for use with abstract data types except that there are a few more questions you need to ask. If two types are similar, is there an inheritance relationship between them or should there be a common parent type which encapsulates the features they share? In either case, you want to use tagged types. Then you need to consider what operations of the types are primitive, which should be class-wide, which should *not* be primitive. Might any of the types need extending at some point in the future? If so, you need to use tagged types again. This case requires some foresight and a feeling for possible maintenance scenarios in order to decide what sort of provision to make for future extensions.

In this chapter I'm going to illustrate this by developing a **spreadsheet**. Spreadsheets are among the most widely used applications for computers, and I've chosen it as an example because it's one I expect most people to be familiar with. A spreadsheet consists of a grid of **cells**; the rows are numbered from 1 upwards and the columns are named A, B, C and so on. To allow for more than 26 columns, columns after Z are named AA, AB,

AC and so on up to AZ, then BA, BB, BC and so on. Individual cells are referred to by their grid coordinate, e.g. A1 or BC100.

There are several possible different types of cell. Initially all cells are empty; the user can enter an expression to be stored in a cell (a **formula cell**) or a literal string that is displayed as it is (a **string cell**) for use as table headings and so on. Other types of cell are also possible. Naturally, the expression evaluator developed in the previous chapter will be a useful component for implementing formula cells.

Whenever the spreadsheet changes it is **recalculated** and redisplayed. Recalculation involves evaluating the expression in each formula cell. Expressions can refer to the values in other formula cells, so a change to a single cell might affect the values of several other cells. Empty cells and string cells have no value (they are **undefined**); if a formula refers to an empty cell or string cell its value is also undefined. Cells can't refer to their own value, directly or indirectly; for example, if cell A1 was defined to be A2+1 and A2 was defined as A1–1 it would be impossible to work out the values of A1 or A2. If this happens it's an error; the value of any cell whose definition is circular is undefined.

Looking at this specification, we can start work on it by identifying the classes that will be needed. We will obviously need types for spreadsheets and cells. Should these be tagged or untagged? Making a spreadsheet a tagged type will allow it to be extended in the future, so this seems to be a good idea. The specification above mentions several types of cell, so a cell should definitely be a tagged type and specific types of cell can then be derived from it (string cells and formula cells, for now). The spreadsheet can deal with a grid of class-wide pointers to cells to allow different cell types to be used within a single spreadsheet. As an implementation detail, empty cells can be dealt with by the spreadsheet itself; any cell that isn't in use is empty. This will avoid having to store empty cells in memory.

What operations are needed on these types? The specification tells us that spreadsheets can be recalculated and displayed, and cell values can be changed. Changing an existing cell might involve changing its type, so this will have to be done by deleting the existing cell (if any) and creating a new one. Since expressions in formula cells can refer to other cells, we need some way of locating a particular cell as well. Recalculation is needed if a cell is changed, so it would probably be a good idea to have a procedure that a cell can call to notify the spreadsheet that a change has taken place. Doing it this way rather than recalculating every time a cell changes allows the spreadsheet to decide when recalculation is necessary (e.g. just before redisplaying the spreadsheet) to minimise the number of times that it gets recalculated. These considerations also imply that a cell must be able to identify the spreadsheet it belongs to.

We'll also need a procedure to be called to cancel the change notification after the spreadsheet has been recalculated and a function to test if the spreadsheet has changed; these should only be called from within Recalculate, so they can go in the private part of the package. Although the only thing they'll do will be to access a Boolean variable, it's still a good idea to provide primitive operations to do this rather than just accessing the variable directly so that any future derived types can override them to provide different behaviour if necessary. This is an application of the sort of foresight I mentioned earlier. Finally, the problem of circular definitions for cells can be reported with an exception;

syntax errors in expressions will also be reported by an exception. Here's a first stab at a spreadsheet type:

```
type Spreadsheet_Type is abstract tagged limited private;

type Cell_Type (Sheet : access Spreadsheet_Type'Class) is
                abstract tagged limited private;
type Cell_Access is access Cell_Type'Class;

procedure Recalculate (Sheet : in out Spreadsheet_Type);
procedure Display     (Sheet : in out Spreadsheet_Type)
                                        is abstract;
procedure Change      (Sheet : in out Spreadsheet_Type);
procedure Updated     (Sheet : in out Spreadsheet_Type);
function  Changed     (Sheet : Spreadsheet_Type)
                                        return Boolean;
function  Cell        (Sheet : Spreadsheet_Type;
                       Where : String)  return Cell_Access;

procedure Insert      (Sheet : in out Spreadsheet_Type;
                       Where : in String;
                       What  : in Cell_Access);
procedure Delete      (Sheet : in out Spreadsheet_Type;
                       Where : in String);

Circularity_Error : exception;
```

The Display procedure is abstract since this is view dependent; a program using a spreadsheet will need to derive a concrete type which displays the spreadsheet in an appropriate way. The spreadsheet type is limited to prevent assignment of one spreadsheet to another (since the effect would be to copy the pointers to the cells rather than the cells themselves). Each cell needs to know which spreadsheet it belongs to (so it can notify the spreadsheet whenever it changes) so I've used an **access discriminant** as described in chapter 11 to act as a pointer to the spreadsheet it's part of. As explained in chapter 11, access discriminants are only allowed for limited types, so Cell_Type has to be limited; they can't be null, so it isn't possible to create cells without reference to a specific spreadsheet, and the accessibility checks used on named access types don't apply. Cell_Type will be derived from Limited_Controlled since destroying a cell might well involve some clean-up action; for example, the cell could notify the spreadsheet that it had changed as the result of a cell being destroyed. Again, I'm applying some foresight to the design.

Cells have a number of common properties. They have a value that can be displayed on the screen; the value can also be accessed as an integer if it isn't undefined. If the value is undefined, we can raise an exception to report it. Cells need to be evaluated as part of the spreadsheet recalculation, so a procedure to re-evaluate a cell will be needed. It might also be useful to be able to inspect the actual cell contents rather than just the evaluated result of the expression. Here's a list of some plausible primitive operations for Cell_Type:

```
procedure Evaluate   (Cell : in out Cell_Type) is abstract;
function  Text_Value (Cell : Cell_Type) return String
                                          is abstract;
function  Num_Value  (Cell : Cell_Type) return Integer
                                          is abstract;
function  Contents   (Cell : Cell_Type) return String
                                          is abstract;

Undefined_Cell_Error : exception;
```

The operations declared here are all abstract, so derived cell types will need to override them in an appropriate way. Formula cells can be derived from Cell_Type by adding an extra discriminant and overriding the abstract operations:

```
type Formula_Cell_Type (Sheet : access Spreadsheet_Type'Class;
                         Size  : Natural) is
             new Cell_Type(Sheet) with private;

procedure Evaluate   (Cell : in out Formula_Cell_Type);
function  Text_Value (Cell : Formula_Cell_Type) return String;
function  Num_Value  (Cell : Formula_Cell_Type) return Integer;
function  Contents   (Cell : Formula_Cell_Type) return String;
```

You can't inherit from a discriminated type without providing the necessary discriminants, so Formula_Cell_Type has an access discriminant called Sheet which is then used as the constraint for Cell_Type in the type declaration. Formula_Cell_Type also has a Natural as a discriminant which will be used for the length of the expression associated with the cell. String cells will also need a similar set of discriminants:

```
type String_Cell_Type (Sheet : access Spreadsheet_Type'Class;
                        Size  : Natural) is
             new Cell_Type(Sheet) with private;

procedure Evaluate   (Cell : in out String_Cell_Type);
function  Text_Value (Cell : String_Cell_Type) return String;
function  Num_Value  (Cell : String_Cell_Type) return Integer;
function  Contents   (Cell : String_Cell_Type) return String;
```

The extra discriminant in this case is the size of the string in the cell. Constructor functions can be declared to construct a cell from a spreadsheet pointer and a string:

```
function String_Cell (Sheet : access Spreadsheet_Type'Class;
                      Value : String) return Cell_Access;
function Formula_Cell (Sheet : access Spreadsheet_Type'Class;
                      Value : String) return Cell_Access;
```

Notice that these are not primitive operations of the cell types, so the inheritance problems related to constructors that I described earlier will be avoided.

18.2   Defining the program

Now that we've got this much of the design in place, we can start writing a program to use a spreadsheet before coming back to looking at the implementation of the spreadsheet abstraction. As usual I'll define a view package:

```
with JE.Spreadsheets;
procedure JE.Views.Spreadsheet is
   type Command_Type is (Modify, Display, Quit);
   function Next_Command return Command_Type;

   type Sheet_Type is limited private;
   procedure Display (Sheet : in out Sheet_Type);
   procedure Modify  (Sheet : in out Sheet_Type);

private
   type Sheet_Extension is
         new JE.Spreadsheets.Spreadsheet_Type with null record;
   procedure Display (Sheet : in out Sheet_Extension);

   type Sheet_Type is
      limited record
         Innards : aliased Sheet_Extension;
      end record;
end JE.Views.Spreadsheet;
```

Sheet_Type is a limited private type; it's actually a record containing a single Sheet_Extension component, where Sheet_Extension is derived from Spreadsheet_Type. The reason for this is that we need to be able to supply cells with a discriminant value which points to the spreadsheet they're part of, so the spreadsheet is made into an aliased component of Sheet_Type. Since the component is aliased, the 'Access attribute can be used to get a pointer to it which can then be used when creating new cells.

The commands are Modify, Display and Quit. The intention is that Modify will ask the user to select a cell, display its current contents and then ask for a new value. The main program will use the view package to process commands from the user:

```
with JE.Views.Spreadsheet;
procedure Spreadsheet is
   Sheet : JE.Views.Spreadsheet.Sheet_Type;
begin
   JE.Views.Spreadsheet.Display (Sheet);
   loop
      case JE.Views.Spreadsheet.Next_Command is
         when JE.Views.Spreadsheet.Modify =>
            JE.Views.Spreadsheet.Modify (Sheet);
         when JE.Views.Spreadsheet.Display =>
            JE.Views.Spreadsheet.Display (Sheet);
         when JE.Views.Spreadsheet.Quit =>
            exit;
      end case;
   end loop;
end Spreadsheet;
```

Now we'll need to implement the package body. This version will just use Ada.Text_IO; it's a lowest-common-denominator interface that could easily be improved:

```
with Ada.Text_IO; use Ada.Text_IO;
package body JE.Views.Spreadsheet is
   function  Next_Command return Command_Type
                          is ... end Next_Command;
   procedure Display (Sheet : in Sheet_Extension)
                          is ... end Display;
   procedure Display (Sheet : in Sheet_Type)
                          is ... end Display;
   procedure Modify  (Sheet : in out Sheet_Type)
                          is ... end Modify;
end JE.Views.Spreadsheet;
```

Next_Command just needs to display a short menu and command prompt:

```
function Next_Command return Command_Type is
   Command : Character;
begin
   loop
      New_Line;
      Put ("(M)odify, (D)isplay or (Q)uit: ");
      Get (Command);
      Skip_Line;
      case Command is
         when 'M' | 'm' =>
```

```
         return Modify;
      when 'D' | 'd' =>
         return Display;
      when 'Q' | 'q' =>
         return Quit;
      when others =>
         Put_Line ("Invalid command -- " &
                     "please enter M, D or Q.");
      end case;
   end loop;
exception
   when End_Error =>
      return Quit;
end Next_Command;
```

The version of Display for Sheet_Type will just call the version of Display for Sheet_Extensions to display its Innards component:

```
procedure Display (Sheet : in out Sheet_Type) is
begin
   Display (Sheet.Innards);
end Display;
```

I'll assume that this program will be run on a standard 80-column text screen with 25 lines of text. I'll use a couple of constants for this which you can change if you need to:

```
Screen_Width  : constant := 80;
Screen_Length : constant := 25;
```

I'll display the cells in columns which are 12 columns wide; this will allow for six columns (A to F) with a seven-character left margin for the row number and a one-character right margin (to prevent the cursor 'wrapping' to a new line if text is displayed in the last column of the screen). I'll leave one row for the column headings and another four for the menu and user responses, which leaves 20 rows. The spreadsheet itself might be bigger than 20 rows of six columns each, but if so the extra cells won't get displayed. I'll need some more constants for the rows and columns:

```
Right_Margin  : constant := 1;
Column_Width  : constant := 12;
Column_Count  : constant :=
                   (Screen_Width - Right_Margin) / Column_Width;
Left_Margin   : constant :=
                   Screen_Width - Right_Margin
                              - (Column_Count * Column_Width);
```

```
Top_Margin      : constant := 1;
Bottom_Margin : constant := 4;
Row_Count       : constant :=
                     Screen_Length - Top_Margin - Bottom_Margin;
```

Here's how the version of Display for a Sheet_Extension can be implemented:

```
procedure Display (Sheet : in out Sheet_Extension) is
   Column   : Character;
   Cell_Ptr : Cell_Access;
   Width    : Integer;
begin
   Recalculate (Sheet);
   New_Line (Screen_Length);      -- clear screen by scrolling up
   Set_Col (Left_Margin);
   Column := 'A';
   for I in 0 .. Column_Count-1 loop
     Set_Col (Positive_Count(Left_Margin +
                         I*Column_Width + 1));
     Put (Column);
     Column := Character'Succ(Column);
   end loop;
   for R in 1 .. Row_Count loop
     Put (R, Width => Left_Margin-2);
     Put (":");
     Column := 'A';
     for C in 0 .. Column_Count-1 loop
       declare
          Row : String := Integer'Image(R);
       begin
          Set_Col (Positive_Count(Left_Margin +
                            C*Column_Width + 1));
          Cell_Ptr := Cell (Sheet, Column & Row(2..Row'Last));
          if Cell_Ptr /= null then
            Width := Integer'Min (Column_Width - 1,
                            Text_Value(Cell_Ptr.all)'Length);
            Put (Text_Value(Cell_Ptr.all)(1..Width));
          end if;
          Column := Character'Succ(Column);
       end;
     end loop;
     New_Line;
   end loop;
end Display;
```

The spreadsheet is recalculated before it's displayed in case anything's changed recently. Notice that the code above assumes that we'll never have more than 26 columns (A to Z); multicharacter column names aren't catered for. It uses a procedure called Set_Col from Ada.Text_IO; Set_Col moves the cursor to the specified column (character position) of the current screen line. The screen layout constants are used to calculate where each item being displayed should go. Note that the innermost loop which displays the actual values uses the character in Col together with the row number to construct a string which is the coordinate of the required cell; the row number is converted to a string using Integer'Image and the second character onwards is used in the name of the cell coordinate (the first character is the sign, either a space or a minus sign). If the text to be displayed is wider than one character less than the column width it will be truncated. This is the purpose of the variable Width; it is set to the minimum of Column_Width–1 and the width of the cell's value, and the result is used to slice out the appropriate number of characters from the cell's value.

Modifying the current cell will involve getting the cell coordinates, displaying the current cell contents and inviting the user to type in a new value. I'll use the convention that string cells are created by typing a value beginning with a quote, empty cells are created by typing in a full stop, and formula cells are created for any other input. Entering a blank line will leave the current value unchanged. Here's how it's done:

```
procedure Modify (Sheet : in out Sheet_Type) is
   Name         : String(1..10);
   Name_Size    : Natural
   Line         : String(1..50);
   Line_Size    : Natural;
   Which        : Cell_Access;
begin
   Put ("Cell coordinate: ");
   Get_Line (Name, Name_Size);
   Which := Cell (Sheet.Innards, Name(1..Name_Size));

   Put ("Current value of " & Name(1..Name_Size) & ": ");
   if Which = null then               -- empty cell
      Put ("<empty>");
   else
      if Which.all in String_Cell_Type'Class then
         Put ('"');                    -- string cell
      end if;
      Put (Contents(Which.all));
   end if;
   New_Line;

   Put ("Enter new value: ");
   Get_Line (Line, Line_Size);
```

```
          if Line_Size > 0 then              -- new value entered
             case Line(1) is
                when '.' =>                   -- empty cell
                   Delete (Sheet.Innards, Name(1..Name_Size));
                when '"' =>                   -- string cell
                   Insert (Sheet.Innards, Name(1..Name_Size),
                           String_Cell (Sheet.Innards'Access,
                                        Line(2..Line_Size)) );
                when others =>                -- formula cell
                   Insert (Sheet.Innards, Name(1..Name_Size),
                           Formula_Cell (Sheet.Innards'Access,
                                         Line(1..Line_Size)) );
             end case;
             Display (Sheet);
          end if;
       end Modify;
```

18.3 The spreadsheet class

Now that the main program is written (and of course tested using stubs for the missing
spreadsheet and cell operations as described in chapter 8) we can move on to the
spreadsheet class itself. The first thing to do is to consider what the full declaration of
Spreadsheet_Type will look like. Here's one approach:

```
with JE.Lists;
package Spreadsheets is
   type Spreadsheet_Type is abstract tagged limited private;
   type Cell_Type (Sheet : access Spreadsheet_Type'Class) is
                     abstract tagged limited private;
   type Cell_Access is access Cell_Type'Class;
   ...    -- etc.


private
   Cell_Name_Length : constant := 6;
   subtype Cell_Size is Integer range 0..Cell_Name_Length;

   package Cell_Pointers is
              new JE.Pointers (Cell_Type'Class, Cell_Access);

   type Cell_Record is
      record
         Where : String(1..Cell_Name_Length);
         Size  : Cell_Size;
```

```
         Cell   : Cell_Pointers.Pointer_Type;
       end record;
    package Cell_Lists is new JE.Lists (Cell_Record);

    type Spreadsheet_Type is
       abstract tagged limited record
         Cells : Cell_Lists.List_Type;
         Dirty : Boolean := False;
       end record;
 end Spreadsheets;
```

⇒ *I've used a constant so that cell names are limited to a maximum of six characters.*
   See if you can devise a method which will allow names to be unlimited in length, or
   a method which will allow the maximum length to be changed without recompiling
   the package and all its clients.

The spreadsheet consists of a list of (non-empty) cells and a 'dirty' flag. Despite the fact
that the spreadsheet is theoretically a grid of cells, there's no reason why a linked list can't
be used to implement it. After all, a spreadsheet is really just a collection of cells which
happens to be presented as a rectangular grid; the external representation needn't have
anything to do with the internal representation. Each Cell_Record in the list contains the
cell's coordinate and a 'smart pointer' to the cell itself (as described in chapter 16). Using
a smart pointer ensures that the cell will be destroyed automatically when it's removed
from the list.

Finding a cell with a given coordinate is just a matter of searching the list for a cell
with that coordinate. If you can't find it, it's an empty cell. The Dirty flag is set whenever
any cell has changed; this indicates when a recalculation is necessary. The primitive
procedure Change sets the dirty flag, Updated clears it and the primitive function Changed
tests it:

```
procedure Change (Sheet : in out Spreadsheet_Type) is
begin
   Sheet.Dirty := True;
end Change;

procedure Updated (Sheet : in out Spreadsheet_Type) is
begin
   Sheet.Dirty := False;
end Updated;

function Changed (Sheet : Spreadsheet_Type) return Boolean is
begin
   return Sheet.Dirty;
end Changed;
```

Cell needs to scan through the linked list looking for a Cell_Record whose coordinate (the Where component) matches the coordinate given as its parameter. As I mentioned earlier, if the cell isn't found Cell will just return a null pointer to indicate that it's an empty cell:

```
function Cell (Sheet : Spreadsheet_Type;
                  Where : String) return Cell_Access is
  Iter : List_Iterator := First(Sheet.Cells);
  Cell : Cell_Record;
begin
  while Iter /= Last(Sheet.Cells) loop
    Cell := Value(Iter);
    exit when To_Upper(Cell.Where(1..Cell.Size)) =
                                    To_Upper(Where);
    Iter := Succ(Iter);
  end loop;

  if Iter /= Last(Sheet.Cells) then
    return Value(Value(Iter).Cell);
  else
    return null;
  end if;
end Cell;
```

This uses the function To_Upper from Ada.Characters.Handling to ignore case differences when comparing cell coordinates so that 'a1' will be recognised as referring to the same cell as 'A1'.

Delete searches for the named cell and deletes it from the list if it's there, or does nothing if it isn't :

```
procedure Delete (Sheet : in out Spreadsheet_Type;
                  Where : in String) is
  Iter : List_Iterator;
  Cell : Cell_Record;
begin
  Iter := First (Sheet.Cells);
  while Iter /= Last (Sheet.Cells) loop
    Cell := Value(Iter);
    if To_Upper(Cell.Where(1..Cell.Size)) =
                                    To_Upper(Where) then
      Delete (Iter);
      Change (Spreadsheet_Type'Class(Sheet));
      exit;
    end if;
    Iter := Succ(Iter);
```

```
      end loop;
    end Delete;
```

Deleting a cell will cause the smart pointer inside it to finalise itself, so the Cell_Type it points to will be deallocated properly.

Insert deletes the cell with the given coordinates if it already exists and then creates a new Cell_Record using the coordinate and cell pointer supplied as parameters (but if the cell pointer is null there's nothing to insert, so this needs checking for) and then adds it to the end of the list:

```
    procedure Insert (Sheet : in out Spreadsheet_Type;
                       Where : in String;
                       What  : in Cell_Access) is
      New_Cell : Cell_Record;
    begin
      Delete (Sheet, Where);
      if What /= null then
        New_Cell.Size := Integer'Min (Cell_Name_Length,
                                      Where'Length);
        New_Cell.Where (1..New_Cell.Size) :=
            Where (Where'First .. Where'First+New_Cell.Size-1);
        New_Cell.Cell := Pointer(What);
        Insert (Last(Sheet.Cells), New_Cell);
      end if;
      Change (Spreadsheet_Type'Class(Sheet));
    end Insert;
```

Recalculate checks if the spreadsheet has changed by calling Changed, and then goes through the list asking each cell to evaluate itself if it has:

```
    procedure Recalculate (Sheet : in out Spreadsheet_Type) is
      Iter : List_Iterator;
      Cell : Cell_Pointers.Pointer_Type;
    begin
      if Changed(Spreadsheet_Type'Class(Sheet)) then
        Iter := First(Sheet.Cells);
        while Iter /= Last(Sheet.Cells) loop
          Cell := Value(Iter).Cell;
          Evaluate (Value(Cell).all);
          Iter := Succ(Iter);
        end loop;
        Updated (Spreadsheet_Type'Class(Sheet));
      end if;
    end Recalculate;
```

This is not going to be terribly efficient; the expression in a formula cell can refer to the names of other formula cells, so evaluating a formula cell will involve evaluating any other formula cells that it refers to. This means that individual cells can end up being evaluated several times. One way to overcome this is to get cells to remember when they were last evaluated. If we keep an 'evaluation number' in the spreadsheet which is updated on each call to Recalculate, each cell can copy the evaluation number when it's evaluated and then just return the current value without re-evaluating it if the spreadsheet's current evaluation number is the same as the copy in the cell. Only two evaluation numbers are needed to distinguish between two successive calls to Recalculate. Here's how the declaration of Spreadsheet_Type will need to change:

```
type Evaluation_Number is mod 2;

type Spreadsheet_Type is
  tagged limited record
    Cells : Cell_Lists.List_Type;
    Dirty : Boolean := False;
    Eval  : Evaluation_Number := Evaluation_Number'First;
  end record;
```

There'll also need to be another primitive function to enable cells to access the current evaluation number:

```
function Evaluation (Sheet : Spreadsheet_Type)
                              return Evaluation_Number;
```

All this will need to do is to return a copy of the Eval component:

```
function Evaluation (Sheet : Spreadsheet_Type)
                              return Evaluation_Number is
begin
  return Sheet.Eval;
end Evaluation;
```

Recalculate will need to increment the evaluation number at the very beginning:

```
procedure Recalculate (Sheet : in out Spreadsheet_Type) is
  -- as before
begin
  if Changed(Spreadsheet_Type'Class(Sheet)) then
    Sheet.Eval := Sheet.Eval + 1;
    -- as before
  end if;
end Recalculate;
```

Since the evaluation number is modular, it will go 0, 1, 0, 1 and so on on successive calls to Recalculate.

18.4 Cell implementation

The next piece of the jigsaw is how cells are implemented. Looking through what we've already got, we can immediately identify the data components that Cell_Type will need to contain:

- A pointer to the enclosing spreadsheet. This is already there in the form of an access discriminant.
- The current evaluation number, as explained above.
- A flag to record if it is currently being evaluated. If this flag is set and the cell is asked to evaluate itself it indicates that there's a circular reference, and we can use this to detect circular definitions and raise a Circularity_Error.
- A flag to record if an error occurred during evaluation.
- A flag to record if the cell's value is undefined or not.

The last three can be combined into a **state variable** based on an enumerated type since they're mutually exclusive; a cell is either being evaluated, or it's erroneous, or it's either defined or undefined. I'll also have another value for when its state is unknown:

```
type Cell_State_Type is (Unknown, Evaluating, Defined,
                         Undefined, Error);
```

The Unknown state can be used as an initial value before the cell has been evaluated for the first time:

```
type Cell_Type (Sheet : access Spreadsheet_Type'Class) is
               abstract new Limited_Controlled with
   record
     State : Cell_State_Type := Unknown;
     Eval  : Evaluation_Number;
   end record;
```

During evaluation the cell will be in the Evaluating state; at the end of evaluation it will end up as Defined, Undefined or Error.

Now we need to consider the derived types String_Cell_Type and Formula_Cell_Type. Here's the full declaration for these types:

```
type String_Cell_Type (Sheet : access Spreadsheet_Type'Class;
                        Size  : Natural) is
               new Cell_Type(Sheet) with
```

```
record
   Text : String(1..Size);
end record;

type Formula_Cell_Type (Sheet : access Spreadsheet_Type'Class;
                        Size  : Natural) is
   new Cell_Type(Sheet) with
   record
      Text  : String(1..Size);
      Value : Integer;
   end record;
```

Both have a string to hold the cell contents, the size of which is given by their Size discriminants; Formula_Cell_Type also has an Integer component to record the result of evaluating the cell. The constructor functions for the two types can be defined like this:

```
function String_Cell (Sheet : access Spreadsheet_Type'Class;
                       Value : String)
                            return Cell_Access is
   Cell : Cell_Access :=
               new String_Cell_Type (Sheet, Value'Length);
begin
   String_Cell_Type(Cell.all).Text := Value;
   return Cell;
end String_Cell;

function Formula_Cell (Sheet : access Spreadsheet_Type'Class;
                       Value : String) return Cell_Access is
   Cell : Cell_Access :=
               new Formula_Cell_Type (Sheet, Value'Length);
begin
   Formula_Cell_Type(Cell.all).Text := Value;
   return Cell;
end String_Cell;
```

Now we need to override the abstract operations inherited from Cell_Type. I'll deal with String_Cell_Type first of all since it's going to be simpler than Formula_Cell_Type.

The Text_Value and Contents operations just need to return the value of the string contained in the cell:

```
function Text_Value (Cell : String_Cell_Type) return String is
begin
   return Cell.Value;
end Text_Value;
```

```
function Contents (Cell : String_Cell_Type) return String is
begin
   return Cell.Value;
end Contents;
```

The value of a string cell is always undefined, so Evaluate just needs to set the state to Undefined and Num_Value just needs to raise Undefined_Cell_Error:

```
procedure Evaluate (Cell : in out String_Cell_Type) is
begin
   Cell.State := Undefined;
end Evaluate;
function Num_Value (Cell : String_Cell_Type) return Integer is
begin
   raise Undefined_Cell_Error;
end Num_Value;
```

18.5 Formula cells

Formula cells will need to use a derivation of Expression_Type as defined in the previous chapter to evaluate the expressions they contain; I'll call it Formula_Type but I won't consider how it's going to be implemented just yet.

As with String_Cell_Type, Contents just needs to return the string discriminant:

```
function Contents (Cell : Formula_Cell_Type) return String is
begin
   return Cell.Expr;
end Contents;
```

Text_Value needs to return the current value as a String if the state of the cell is Defined. If the state of the cell is Error then it should return an error message. Otherwise, the cell value is unknown so it should just return a null string:

```
function Text_Value (Cell : Formula_Cell_Type) return String is
begin
   if Cell.State = Defined then
      return Integer'Image(Cell.Value);
   elsif Cell.State = Error then
      return "*ERROR*";
   else
      return "";
   end if;
end Text_Value;
```

Num_Value needs to return the current value as an Integer. If the value isn't defined it can just raise an Undefined_Cell_Error exception:

```
function Num_Value (Cell : Formula_Cell_Type) return Integer is
begin
  if Cell.State = Defined then
    return Cell.Value;
  else
    raise Undefined_Cell_Error;
  end if;
end Num_Value;
```

This only leaves us with Evaluate to be defined. If the cell is already being evaluated, it needs to raise a Circularity_Error. If the state is unknown or the evaluation number is out of date, the cell needs to be evaluated; otherwise, it's already been evaluated and nothing needs to be done. If it does need evaluating, the evaluation number needs to be updated and the formula needs to be evaluated. The cell state must be set to Evaluating while the formula is being evaluated; afterwards the state can be set to Defined if all is well, or Undefined if a reference to an undefined cell occurs (which will be reported by Value as an Undefined_Cell_Error), or Error if an error occurs. The error can be a Syntax_Error from the expression evaluation, a Constraint_Error because the result is out of range, or a Circularity_Error as described above:

```
procedure Evaluate (Cell : in out Formula_Cell_Type) is
  Expr : Formula_Type (Cell.Sheet);
begin
  if Cell.State = Evaluating then
    raise Circularity_Error;
  elsif Cell.State = Unknown or
              Cell.Eval /= Evaluation(Cell.Sheet.all) then
    Cell.Eval  := Evaluation(Cell.Sheet.all);
    Cell.State := Evaluating;
    Cell.Value := Evaluate (Expr, Cell.Text);
    Cell.State := Defined;
  end if;

exception
  when Undefined_Cell_Error =>
    if Cell.State /= Error then      -- don't change state if
      Cell.State := Undefined;       -- there's already been an
    end if;                          -- error reported
  when Syntax_Error | Constraint_Error | Circularity_Error =>
    Cell.State := Error;
end Evaluate;
```

The formula will need to be supplied with a pointer to the spreadsheet it's associated with so that cells referenced in the expression can be looked up. This is done by providing Formula_Type with an access discriminant, which means that Formula_Type will need to be a limited type.

As I've mentioned before, handling errors inside a package is generally a bad idea. It leads to a lack of flexibility, and providing flexibility is what object-oriented programming is all about. Another type of spreadsheet derived in the future might want to report errors to the user as they arise and give the option of carrying on or aborting the recalculation, but this isn't possible with the current design. A better idea would be to provide a primitive operation of Spreadsheet called Handle_Error and call this from the exception handler above, like this:

```
when Fault : Syntax_Error | Constraint_Error
                         | Circularity_Error =>
  Cell.State := Error;
  Handle_Error (Cell.Sheet, Fault);
```

Since Sheet is a class-wide access discriminant, the call to Handle_Error will be a dispatching call. This means that Handle_Error will need to be declared like this:

```
procedure Handle_Error
          (Sheet : access Spreadsheet_Type;
           Error : in Ada.Exceptions.Exception_Occurrence);
```

The **access parameter** Sheet allows any access-to-Spreadsheet value to be used to call Handle_Error; also, as mentioned in chapter 14, an access parameter is treated as a controlling parameter so that Handle_Error will be a primitive operation of Spreadsheet_Type. The Error parameter allows Handle_Error to use the operations in Ada.Exceptions to get more information about the exception.

The default action can just be to do nothing, but making it a primitive operation of Spreadsheet means that derived spreadsheets can override it. Parent types in class hierarchies quite often end up with primitive operations which do nothing to act as 'hooks' to allow extra processing to be added in later by derived classes if it's needed. You should always look carefully at 'do-nothing' bits of your code (null clauses in **case** statements, missing **else** parts in **if** statements and so on) and consider whether there will ever be a need to change it to do *something*. If so, add a primitive operation to do nothing for you. However, it takes some experience to be able to spot these things, because there's nothing there to make you notice them!

Returning from Handle_Error will effectively mean that the error has been ignored, but an overridden version of Handle_Error could raise another exception (or the same one) in which case it will be raised at the point where Evaluate was called from (remember that if an exception is raised inside an exception handler, you immediately exit from the block containing the handler and you then look for an exception handler in the block you've returned to).

18.6 Deriving a new expression type

The final step to complete the program is to derive Formula_Type from the type Expression_Type defined in the previous chapter. This can go in a child package of JE.Expressions:

```
with JE.Spreadsheets;
package JE.Expressions.Spreadsheet is
   type Formula_Type (Sheet : access Spreadsheet_Type'Class) is
               new Expression_Type with private;
private
   type Formula_Type (Sheet : access Spreadsheet_Type'Class) is
               new Expression_Type with null record;
   ...    -- other declarations
end JE.Expressions.Spreadsheet;
```

The only difference between Formula_Type and Expression_Type is that Formula_Type needs to recognise cell coordinates as a new type of operand. This means we need a new type derived from Operand_Type together with an overriding declaration for the primitive operation Value:

```
type Cell_Operand_Type (Cell : Cell_Access) is
                        new Operand_Type with null record;
function Value (Operand : Cell_Operand_Type) return Integer;
```

These declarations will need to go in the private part of the package. This type has a Cell_Access value as a discriminant which points to the cell being referenced as an operand. The Value operation will involve evaluating the cell (in case it hasn't been evaluated yet) and then returning its value:

```
function Value (Operand : Cell_Operand_Type) return Integer is
begin
   if Operand.Cell = null then
     raise Undefined_Cell_Error;
   else
     Evaluate (Operand.Cell.all);
   end if;
   return Value (Operand.Cell.all);
end Value;
```

The only other thing that's necessary is to recognise cell coordinates as a new type of token within the expression. This can be done by overriding the Fetch_Token primitive inherited from Expression_Type. Here's the declaration for an overridden Fetch_Token procedure for Formula_Type:

```
procedure Fetch_Token (Syntax : in Formula_Type;
                       Expr   : in String;
                       From   : in out Positive;
                       Token  : in out Token_Pointer);
```

Cell coordinates always begin with a letter and consist entirely of letters and digits. Fetch_Token will need to check that the current character is a letter and then search for the end of the token. The characters making up the token can then be used to obtain a pointer to the corresponding cell, and this can be used to create a Cell_Operand_Type to be returned as the value of the function. To make things easier I'll use some more functions from Ada.Characters.Handling: Is_Letter, which tests if its parameter is a letter, and Is_Alphanumeric, which tests if its parameter is a letter or a digit:

```
procedure Fetch_Token (Syntax : in Formula_Type;
                       Expr   : in String;
                       From   : in out Positive;
                       Token  : in out Token_Pointer) is
begin
   if Is_Letter(Expr(From)) then
      declare
         First : Integer := From;
      begin
         while From <= Expr'Last and then
                          Is_Alphanumeric(Expr(From)) loop
            From := From + 1;
         end loop;
         Cell_Ptr := Cell (Syntax.Sheet.all,
                           Expr(First..From-1));
         Token := Pointer(new Cell_Operand_Type(Cell_Ptr));
      end;
   else
      Fetch_Token (Expression_Type(Syntax), Expr, From, Token);
   end if;
end Fetch_Token;
```

If the token doesn't start with a letter, the Formula_Type parameter is converted to an Expression_Type value. The original Expression_Type version of Fetch_Token will then be used to extract the token, so this will deal with numbers, operators and so on.

Exercises

18.1   Modify the existing spreadsheet design so that the cell coordinates are stored in the cells themselves, rather than in a separate Cell_Record structure.

18.2   At the moment you can't save a spreadsheet to a file or load a spreadsheet from a file. Provide primitive operations to load and save the spreadsheet. These should each take a String parameter representing the name of the file to load from or save to.

18.3   Modify the spreadsheet to support a new cell type which is like a formula cell except that its value represents a student's percentage grade (which should be between 0 and 100) and displays it as a letter grade: A for 80 or above, B for 65 to 79, C for 55 to 64, D for 40 to 54, E for 20 to 39 or F for below 20.

18.4   Modify the spreadsheet to support a new cell type which is like a formula cell except that it has a second discriminant called Base, which is a value between 2 and 16 specifying the number base to be used for the text value of the cell; for example, when Base = 2 the cell's value will be displayed in binary.

CHAPTER 19

Multitasking

Tell me your tasks in order.
— Dylan Thomas, *Under Milk Wood*

19.1 Active objects

The objects you've met so far (spreadsheet cells, diary appointments and so on) are all essentially **passive** objects. They are acted upon by subprograms called (ultimately) by the main program; they don't do anything of their own accord, only when asked to do so. However, **active objects** are often useful as well. Consider a type of spreadsheet cell that continually updates itself with constantly changing prices obtained online from the stock market. The current design would require the cell to obtain the latest prices whenever the spreadsheet was recalculated. The main program could recalculate the spreadsheet repeatedly if it was otherwise idle, but that puts the responsibility for recalculating on the program rather than on the object which requires it, in this case a particular type of spreadsheet cell. In a spreadsheet with no cells of this type, the continuous recalculating is a waste of resources. An active spreadsheet cell would resolve the problem by operating at the same time as (in parallel with) the rest of the program and requesting the spreadsheet to do a recalculation whenever its value changed. That way the program needn't know anything about how the spreadsheet works or what type of cells it might contain and would have no extra responsibilities for managing the spreadsheet.

Ada allows you to define **tasks** which are executed independently. The program itself is executed by an **environment task**, and this is allowed to create further tasks which are executed in parallel with all the other tasks in the program. You could define a new type of spreadsheet cell which contained a task. As soon as such a cell was created, the task associated with it would begin executing in parallel with the rest of the program. **Active cells** like this would be able to change their values in response to external conditions and then call on the spreadsheet to recalculate itself. The spreadsheet itself could be an active object which waits for recalculation requests and then recalculates and displays itself, in parallel with everything else that's happening.

Note that this feature of Ada is heavily dependent on the underlying operating system; an operating system like MS-DOS has no multitasking capabilities (and, indeed, is positively hostile to multitasking) so that implementations of Ada for MS-DOS systems can only provide multitasking capabilities poorly, if at all. Fortunately the situation is changing, and 'real' operating systems like Unix, OS/2 and Windows/NT are driving out the 'toy' systems which sprang up in the infancy of microcomputers and have stayed with us like some debilitating disease ever since.

19.2   Task types

Like packages, Ada tasks are defined in two parts, a specification part and a body part. Unlike packages, they are not compilation units; they cannot be compiled independently and added to the library. Instead, they must be declared inside a package or subprogram. When declared in a package, the specification goes in the package specification and the body goes in the package body; when declared in a subprogram, both specification and body must be defined in the subprogram.

The task specification defines a **task type**. The simplest form that this can take looks like this:

```
task type Repeat;
```

This defines a type called Repeat; you can then declare as many tasks of this type as you require:

```
A, B : Repeat;              -- two tasks
C : array (1..100) of Repeat;    -- an array of 100 tasks
```

These tasks will be started at the end of the declaration section where they were created, i.e. immediately before the first statement in the block where they are declared:

```
declare
   A, B : Repeat;
   C : array (1..100) of Repeat;
begin            -- all 102 tasks are started at this point
   ...
end;             -- wait here for all 102 tasks to end
```

When they are started, they will each execute a copy of the task body in parallel with everything else that's happening. The tasks are local to the block, so they cease to exist at the end of the block. When the task executing the block reaches the end of the block, it will have to wait for all 102 tasks to end before it can proceed. The task executing the block is said to be the **master** of the tasks created within it, and the tasks within the block are known as the **dependents** of their master task.

The task body will normally contain a loop. Here's a simple example:

```
task body Repeat is
begin
   for I in 1..5 loop
```

```
      Put_Line ("Hello!");
      delay 2.0;
   end loop;
end Repeat;
```

This will display the message 'Hello!' five times before terminating. After the message is displayed, the task will be delayed for two seconds before continuing by the **delay statement**:

```
delay 2.0;
```

Here 2.0 is a value of the standard fixed point type Duration which specifies the length of the delay in seconds. You can also delay until a particular time like this:

```
delay until Ada.Calendar.Time_Of (Day=>25, Month=>12,
                                  Year=>1999);
```

This statement will cause the task which executes it to wait until Christmas 1999. The time is specified as a value of type Ada.Calendar.Time.

Task types are limited types, so you can't assign tasks to one another or compare them; this also means that any type which contains a task as a component must also be a limited type. If you only want a single task of a particular type, you can declare the task specification like this:

```
task Repeat;
```

The task type is now anonymous, and Repeat is the only object belonging to this anonymous type. In other words, this is effectively like writing the following:

```
task type ???;  -- ??? is the "name" of the anonymous task type
Repeat : ???;   -- declare one object of this type
```

Tasks can also have discriminants, which can be a useful feature for providing initial values:

```
task type Repeat (Count : Natural);

task body Repeat is
begin
   for I in 1..Count loop   -- discriminant controls loop length
      Put_Line (Integer'Image(Count) & " Hello!");
      delay 2.0;
   end loop;
end Repeat;
```

```
A : Repeat (Count => 10);    -- this task says hello 10 times
```

Notice that the discriminant is only specified in the task specification and not in the body, but it can still be referred to from within the body. Also, since task types are limited types, access discriminants are perfectly acceptable.

19.3   Communicating with tasks

Usually a task will be expected to do something more complex than just displaying a message over and over. It will normally be necessary for tasks to communicate with each other; for example, a task in a spreadsheet cell will need to be asked what the cell value is from time to time, or a spreadsheet may need to be asked to recalculate itself. In such cases the task specification needs to be expanded to list the services that a task can provide. Here's the specification of a spreadsheet task which allows other tasks to ask it to do a recalculation:

```
task type Spreadsheet_Task is
   entry Recalculate;
end Spreadsheet_Task;

Sheet : Spreadsheet_Task;    -- declare a Spreadsheet_Task
```

This task type provides an **entry specification** which another task can call just like a procedure; for example, a task can ask Sheet to recalculate with an **entry call** like this:

```
Sheet.Recalculate;
```

The task body has to provide a way of servicing calls to its entries. This is done using an **accept** statement:

```
task body Spreadsheet_Task is
begin
  loop
    accept Recalculate;
    Do_Recalculation;
  end loop;
end Spreadsheet_Task;
```

When the task body starts executing, it will wait at the **accept** statement until an entry call to Recalculate is made. It will then call a procedure Do_Recalculation to perform the recalculation and go round the loop again to wait for the next call to Recalculate. If another task calls Recalculate before the spreadsheet task has got back to the **accept** statement again, the calling task is forced to wait. Thus the calling task and the one being called will wait for each other until they are both ready, which is when the caller is waiting for its entry call to be accepted and the one being called is waiting at the **accept** statement. This synchronisation of the two tasks is known as a **rendezvous**.

The task body above has one major problem; since it's an infinite loop there's no way to get it to terminate, so the master task won't be able to terminate either; it'll end up waiting forever at the end of the block where the spreadsheet task was declared. One way to get around this is to abort the task with an **abort** statement:

```
abort Sheet;
```

This will force the task and any dependent tasks it might have to terminate. However, this is rather drastic since the spreadsheet might be halfway through a recalculation at the time. A better way would be to add another entry to allow the master task to ask it to shut down in an orderly manner:

```
task type Spreadsheet_Task is
   entry Recalculate;
   entry Shutdown;
end Spreadsheet_Task;
```

Now the task body needs to be able to respond to calls to either entry. It's no good accepting them one after the other in a loop since this will force the entries to be called alternately. One solution would be to test if any calls are pending before accepting them. You can do this using the 'Count attribute for an entry which gives the number of pending calls for that entry:

```
task body Spreadsheet_Task is
begin
   loop
      if Recalculate'Count > 0 then
         accept Recalculate;
         Do_Recalculation;
      elsif Shutdown'Count > 0 then
         accept Shutdown;
         exit;
      end if;
   end loop;
end Spreadsheet_Task;
```

However, this isn't particularly reliable. As you'll see later, tasks can choose to abandon entry calls if they aren't responded to within a certain time period, and this means that even if Recalculate'Count is non-zero, by the time you execute the **accept** statement for Recalculate the calling task might have timed out and abandoned its call, in which case you'll be stuck at the **accept** statement until some other task calls Recalculate. And if that never happens, you'll never be able to accept a call to Shutdown. The correct solution to this is to put the calls inside a **select** statement:

```
task body Spreadsheet_Task is
begin
  loop
    select
      accept Recalculate;
      Do_Recalculation;
    or
      accept Shutdown;
      exit;
    end select;
  end loop;
end Spreadsheet_Task;
```

This **select** statement contains two **accept alternatives** which must each be headed by an **accept** statement. It will wait until one of the entries named in the **accept** statements is called, and it will then execute the appropriate alternative. If calls to both entries are already pending, one will be accepted non-deterministically. The **select** statement ends after the chosen alternative has been executed; if Recalculate was called, the task will then go around the loop again and wait for another entry call, but if Shutdown was called it will exit from the loop and terminate. Note that the task will not respond to calls to Shutdown if a recalculation is in progress; it will only respond when it's waiting for an entry call in the **select** statement, which will happen after the call to Recalculate finishes and the loop is repeated.

This solution requires the master task to call Shutdown explicitly when it wants to terminate the task. The disadvantage with this approach is that it's possible to forget to call Shutdown. A better solution is to add a **terminate alternative** to the **select** statement:

```
task body Spreadsheet_Task is
begin
  loop
    select
      accept Recalculate;
      Do_Recalculation;
    or
      accept Shutdown;
      exit;
    or
      terminate;
    end select;
  end loop;
end Spreadsheet_Task;
```

The terminate alternative must be the last one in a **select** statement, and it can't contain anything except a **terminate** statement like the one shown above. When the master task gets to the end of the block where the spreadsheet was declared, the spreadsheet task will terminate the next time that the **select** statement is executed (or immediately, if the task is already waiting in the **select** statement). This means that the master doesn't have to do anything special to terminate the task, but it can still call Shutdown if it wants to terminate the task before the end of the block where it was declared. Note that once a task has terminated, you'll be rewarded with a Tasking_Error exception if you try to call any of its entries.

19.4   More about select statements

Select statements can also be used for entry calls. If a calling task isn't prepared to wait for a rendezvous, it can use a **select** statement with an **else** alternative like this:

```
select
   Sheet.Recalculate;
else
   Put_Line ("Sheet is busy -- giving up");
end select;
```

In this case, if Sheet is not able to accept the entry call to Recalculate immediately, the entry call will be abandoned and the **else** alternative will be executed. If the calling task is willing to wait for a limited time, it can use a **select** statement with a **delay alternative** like this:

```
select
   Sheet.Recalculate;
or
   delay 5.0;
   Put_Line ("Sheet has been busy for 5 seconds -- giving up");
end select;
```

If the entry call is not accepted within the time specified in the **delay** statement (five seconds in this case), it's abandoned and the **delay alternative** is executed instead. A **delay until** statement can always be used instead of a **delay** statement:

```
select
   Sheet.Recalculate;
or
   delay until Christmas;
   Put_Line ("Sheet has been busy for ages -- giving up");
end select;
```

You can also set an upper limit on the time it takes to process an entry call:

```
select
  delay 5.0;
  Put_Line ("Sheet not recalculated yet -- " &
           "recalculation abandoned");
then abort
  Sheet.Recalculate;
end select;
```

This starts evaluating the statements between **then abort** and **end select**, which in this case is a call to Sheet.Recalculate. If the delay specified by the **delay** (or **delay until**) statement after **select** expires before this completes, the call to Sheet.Recalculate is aborted (as if by an **abort** statement) and the message 'Sheet not recalculated yet -- recalculation abandoned' will be displayed. You aren't restricted to using this in connection with multitasking; for example, you could use it to abort lengthy calculations where the total execution time is important (or where the calculation might diverge to give potentially infinite execution times):

```
select
  delay 5.0;
  Put_Line ("Horribly long calculation abandoned");
then abort
  Horribly_Long_And_Possibly_Divergent_Calculation;
end select;
```

A **select** statement inside a task body can also have an **else** alternative or one or more **delay** alternatives instead of a **terminate** alternative. You must also have at least one **accept** alternative. An **else** alternative is activated if none of the **accept** statements have a pending entry call; a **delay** alternative is activated if none of the **accept** statements accept an entry call within the time specified in the **delay** statement. These three possibilities (**else**, **delay** and **terminate**) are mutually exclusive; you cannot have a **delay** alternative as well as a **terminate** alternative, for example.

19.5 Transferring data during a rendezvous

It may also be necessary to transfer data between tasks during a rendezvous. For example, a spreadsheet cell might need an entry to allow other tasks to get its value. To allow this to happen, task entries can also have parameters just like procedures:

```
task type Counter_Task is
  entry Get (Value : out Integer);
end Counter_Task;
```

```
task body Counter_Task is
  V : Integer := 0;
begin
  loop
    select
      accept Get (Value : out Integer) do
        Value := V;
        V := V + 1;
      end Get;
    or
      terminate;
    end select;
  end loop;
end Counter_Task;
```

The **accept** statement in this task body acts basically like a procedure which is invoked by the entry call. It can even contain **return** statements just like a procedure. When the entry call is accepted, any **in** parameters are transferred from the caller. The body of the **accept** statement is then executed, and at the end any **out** parameters are transferred back to the caller. The rendezvous is then complete, and the caller is allowed to continue. In this case the task will generate ever-increasing integer values each time Get is called.

You might not always be willing to accept an entry call. Consider this task which contains a stack which other tasks can push data onto or pop items off:

```
task type Stack_Manager is
  entry Push (Item : in Integer);
  entry Pop  (Item : out Integer);
end Stack_Manager;

task body Stack_Manager is
  package Int_Stacks is new JE.Stacks (Integer);
  Stack : Int_Stacks.Stack_Type;
begin
  loop
    select
      accept Push (Item : in Integer) do
        Int_Stacks.Push (Stack,Item);
      end Push;
    or
      accept Pop (Item : out Integer) do
        Int_Stacks.Pop (Stack,Item);
      end Pop;
    or
      terminate;
```

```
      end select;
   end loop;
end Stack_Manager;
```

An exception will be raised if an attempt is made to call Pop on an empty stack. Note that if an exception occurs during a rendezvous, the exception will be raised in the calling task as well as the one being called. To prevent this happening, we can add a **guard** to the **accept** statement for Pop like this:

```
when not Int_Stacks.Empty (Stack) =>
   accept Pop (Item : out Integer) do ...
```

A **guarded accept statement** can only be activated when the condition specified in the guard is True, which in this case means that Pop can only be called when the stack is not empty. Any task which calls Pop when the stack is empty will be forced to wait until another task calls Push. As soon as Push has been called, the stack will no longer be empty so that the next time the **select** statement is executed the pending call to Pop will immediately be accepted.

Guarded entries can also be useful for aborting actions in a **select** ... **then abort** construct. A **select** ... **then abort** construct is governed by a **triggering alternative** (the first statement after **select**) which must be an entry call or a **delay** statement. When the triggering alternative is activated (the entry call is accepted or the delay expires) the **abortable part** between **then abort** and **end select** is aborted as if by an **abort** statement:

```
select
   User.Interrupt;
   Put_Line ("Horribly long calculation interrupted by user");
then abort
   Horribly_Long_And_Possibly_Divergent_Calculation;
end select;
```

In this case, if the call to User.Interrupt (the Interrupt entry of the task User) is ever accepted, the horribly long calculation will be aborted. If User.Interrupt has a guard, this means that when the guard condition becomes True the horribly long calculation between **then abort** and **end select** will be aborted.

19.6   Sharing data between tasks

Using a task to allow multiple tasks to access a common stack like the example above is a very elaborate and expensive way of sharing data. It means there has to be an extra task to manage the stack on behalf of the other tasks which want to use it, and a rendezvous is required to access the stack. A rendezvous is a relatively lengthy operation, so it adds quite a large overhead to what would otherwise be a fairly simple procedure call.

The stack could of course be declared in the same scope as the task types that need to access it, but this is extremely risky. Consider the following section of code from chapter 13:

```
procedure Pop (Stack : in out Stack_Type;
               Item  : out Item_Type) is
begin
  Item := Stack.Body(Stack.Top);      -- 1
  Stack.Top := Stack.Top - 1;         -- 2
exception
  when Constraint_Error =>
    raise Stack_Underflow;
end Pop;
```

This shows how Pop is implemented using an array. In an environment where only one task is executing this code, it's perfectly safe. If more than one task is executing it simultaneously, both tasks might execute statement 1 at the same time so that they will both be given a copy of the same item. When they execute statement 2, Stack.Top might be decremented twice or both tasks might retrieve the same value for Stack.Top, subtract 1 from it and then store the result in Stack.Top so that Stack.Top will appear to have been decremented only once.

In other words, the result will be completely unpredictable since it depends on the precise timing relationship between the two tasks. Unpredictability on this scale is rarely a good property for computer systems to have. The moral of the story is that tasks should never access external data; they should only ever access their own local objects.

To get around this problem, Ada allows data to be encapsulated in a **protected record** which guarantees that this sort of situation can't arise. A protected record is a passive data type rather than an active type like a task, so the costs of a rendezvous and the scheduling of an extra task are avoided. Protected records are divided into a specification and a body, just like tasks. The specification contains a visible part which declares a set of functions, procedures and entries that tasks are allowed to call as well as a private part which contains the data to be protected. Here's a protected record which encapsulates a stack of integers:

```
protected type Shared_Stack_Type is
   procedure Push  (Item : in Integer);
   entry      Pop   (Item : out Integer);
   function   Top    return Integer;
   function   Size   return Natural;
   function   Empty return Boolean;
private
   package Int_Stacks is new JE.Stacks (Integer);
   Stack : Int_Stacks.Stack_Type;
end Shared_Stack_Type;
```

```
Stack : Shared_Stack_Type;       -- declare an instance
                                 -- of Shared_Stack_Type
```

As with tasks, you can declare a single protected record of an anonymous type by leaving out the word **type**:

```
protected Shared_Stack_Type is ... ;
                   -- same as: protected type ???;
                   --               Shared_Stack_Type : ???;
```

The body provides the implementations of the functions, procedures and entries declared in the specification. The difference between the three types of operation is that functions are only allowed to read the values of private data items; such items appear to a function as if they were constants and the function is unable to alter them. Since it's safe for several tasks to read the same data at the same time, multiple tasks are allowed to execute functions in a protected object at the same time. Procedures and entries are allowed to alter the private data, so a task can't call any protected operations while another task is executing a procedure or entry call. The difference between a procedure and an entry is that entries have guards which act like the guards on **accept** statements; an entry can only be executed when its guard is True, and any task which calls an entry whose guard is False will be suspended until the guard becomes True (at which point the entry call can then be executed).

In the protected type Shared_Stack_Type, there are three functions (Top, Size and Empty) which don't affect the private stack it contains. Tasks will be able to call these functions as long as no procedure or entry call is in progress; if there is already a procedure or entry call in progress, the task calling the function will not be allowed to proceed until the active call finishes executing. There is one procedure (Push); any task calling Push will have to wait until any other active calls have finished executing. There is one entry (Pop); any task calling Pop will have to wait, not only until any other active calls have finished executing, but also until the entry guard is True.

Here's the protected body. The guard condition for the entry Pop is specified after the parameter list between **when** and **is**:

```
protected body Shared_Stack_Type is
   procedure Push (Item : in Integer) is
   begin
      Int_Stacks.Push (Stack,Item);
   end Push;

   entry Pop (Item : out Integer)
      when not Int_Stacks.Empty (Stack) is
   begin
      Int_Stacks.Pop (Stack,Item);
   end Pop;
```

```
function Top return Integer is
begin
   return Int_Stacks.Top (Stack);
end Top;

 function Size return Natural is
begin
   return Int_Stacks.Size (Stack);
end Size;

 function Empty return Boolean is
begin
   return Int_Stacks.Empty (Stack);
end Empty;
end Shared_Stack_Type;
```

So, as many tasks as want to can simultaneously inspect the top item on the stack, find out the size of the stack or test if it's empty as long as no-one's pushing an item onto the stack or popping one off it. Popping an item off the stack is only allowed if the stack isn't empty; if it is empty the caller task will have to wait until another task calls Push. Calls to Push and Pop will only go ahead when the protected record isn't in use by any other task.

19.7   An active spreadsheet

To illustrate all this in action, let's consider a modification of the spreadsheet in the previous chapter which will allow active cells to be included in the spreadsheet. A simple example will be a cell containing a task which changes its value every five seconds:

```
task type Counter_Task
            (Sheet : access Speadsheet_Type'Class) is
   entry Get (Value : out Integer);
   entry Stop;
end Counter_Task;
```

This task has an access discriminant which will be set to point to the spreadsheet containing the task. The body of this task will look like this:

```
task body Counter_Task is
   type Count_Type is mod 10000;
   Count       : Count_Type := Count_Type'First;
   Update_Time : Ada.Calendar.Time := Ada.Calendar.Clock + 5.0;
begin
   loop
```

```
      select
        accept Get (Value : out Integer) do
          Value := Integer(Count);
        end Get;
      or
        accept Stop;
        exit;
      or
        delay until Update_Time;
        Update_Time := Update_Time + 5.0;
        Count := Count + 1;
        Change (Sheet.all);
      end select;
    end loop;
  end Counter_Task;
```

All this does is to sit in a loop accepting entry calls to Get or Stop or delaying until the update time is reached. Note that a **delay** statement which said 'delay 5.0' wouldn't be any good; the delay would then be five seconds plus the time it took to get around the loop and back to the **delay** statement again; although the time it takes to get around the loop may be very small it will gradually accumulate. This would be unacceptable in a time-critical application.

Get returns the current counter value and Stop terminates the task. If neither of these is called before the update time is reached, the delay will expire with the result that the update time and the count are both updated and the spreadsheet is notified that a change has taken place. A modular type is used for Count so that when it reaches its maximum value it will go back to zero rather than raising a Constraint_Error.

A problem with this is that calling Change will update an unprotected data item (the Dirty flag in the spreadsheet); we could derive a new type of spreadsheet which incorporates a protected record to get around this if it's a problem:

```
  protected type Shared_Flag_Type is
    function  State return Boolean;
    procedure Set;
    procedure Clear;
  private
    State_Flag : Boolean := False;
  end Shared_Flag_Type;

  protected body Shared_Flag_Type is
    function State return Boolean is
    begin
      return State_Flag;
    end State;
```

```
      procedure Set is
      begin
        State_Flag := True;
      end Set;

      procedure Clear is
      begin
        State_Flag := False;
      end Clear;
  end Shared_Flag_Type;

  type Active_Spreadsheet_Type is
    abstract new Spreadsheet_Type with
    record
      Modified : Shared_Flag_Type;
    end record;
```

The primitive operations Change, Updated and Changed will need overriding to use the operations of Shared_Flag_Type:

```
  procedure Change (Sheet : in out Active_Spreadsheet_Type) is
  begin
    Sheet.Modified.Set;
  end Change;

  procedure Updated (Sheet : in out Active_Spreadsheet_Type) is
  begin
    Sheet.Modified.Clear;
  end Updated;

  function Changed (Sheet : Active_Spreadsheet_Type)
                   return Boolean is
  begin
    return Sheet.Modified.State;
  end Changed;
```

The next thing we need is a derived Cell_Type to hold an instance of the counter task:

```
  type Counting_Cell_Type
                   (Sheet : access Spreadsheet_Type'Class) is
    new Cell_Type(Sheet) with
    record
      Counter : Counter_Task(Sheet);
    end record;
```

Since the parent type Cell_Type is derived from Limited_Controlled, we can override Finalize to stop the counter task:

```
procedure Finalize (Object : in out Counting_Cell_Type) is
begin
  Object.Counter.Stop;
end Finalize;
```

The primitive operations Contents, Cell_Value and Num_Value and Evalute which were inherited from Cell_Type will all need to be overridden. Contents can be defined to return a string identifying the cell as a five-second counter:

```
function Contents (Cell : Counting_Cell_Type)
            return String is
begin
  return "<5-second counter>";
end Contents;
```

Text_Value can be implemented by returning the current value of the cell as a string. The current value can be got by calling Num_Value:

```
function Text_Value (Cell : Counting_Cell_Type)
            return String is
begin
  return Integer'Image(Num_Value(Cell));
end Text_Value;
```

Num_Value needs to rendezvous with the task to get the current value of the counter:

```
function Num_Value (Cell : Counting_Cell_Type)
            return Integer is
  I : Integer;
begin
  Cell.Counter.Get (I);
  return I;
end Value;
```

Evaluate just needs to set the cell state to Defined since the value of a counting cell is always well-defined:

```
procedure Evaluate (Cell : in out Counting_Cell_Type) is
begin
  Cell.State := Defined;
end Evaluate;
```

Finally, a constructor function is needed, just like the constructors for String_Cell_Type and Formula_Cell_Type:

```
function Counting_Cell (Sheet : access Spreadsheet_Type'Class)
                            return Cell_Access is
  Cell : Cell_Access := new Counting_Cell_Type (Sheet);
begin
  return Cell;
end Counting_Cell;
```

The view package will also need some modification. Obviously the declaration of Sheet_Type must be changed to use an Active_Spreadsheet_Type instead of an ordinary Spreadsheet_Type. If you're waiting for a command and the spreadsheet gets updated, you'll need to redisplay the spreadsheet. One way to do this is to supply the spreadsheet as a parameter to Next_Command and get Next_Command to redisplay it if it's been updated. You can use the procedure Get_Immediate from Ada.Text_IO to do this:

```
procedure Get_Immediate (Item      : out Character;
                         Available : out Boolean);
```

This procedure doesn't wait for a key to be pressed; if a key has been pressed it returns it in Item and sets Available to True, but if not it just returns immediately with Available set to False. Here's how it could be used:

```
function Next_Command return Command_Type is
  Command   : Character;
  Available : Boolean;
begin
  loop
    New_Line;
    Put ("(M)odify, (D)isplay or (Q)uit: ");
    loop
      Get_Immediate (Command, Available);
      exit when Available;
      if Changed(Sheet.Innards) then
        Display (Sheet.Innards);
        New_Line;
        Put ("(M)odify, (D)isplay or (Q)uit: ");
      end if;
    end loop;
    Skip_Line;
    case Command is
      ...    -- as before
    end case;
```

```
   end loop;
end Next_Command;
```

As long as no key is pressed, the inner loop will keep checking the state of the spreadsheet and redisplay it if necessary, but as soon as a key is pressed it'll cause the inner loop to exit and command processing will then be done as normal.

This isn't an ideal solution; probably the best thing would be to put the spreadsheet inside a task in the view package and get the task to monitor the spreadsheet for changes and redraw it whenever necessary, rather than depending on Next_Command to do all the work. However, this depends on your ability to write to particular places on the screen without affecting the input cursor, so this would be a very system-dependent solution.

The final step is to change Modify so that it can create counting cells. I'll use the character '#' to create counting cells:

```
procedure Modify (Sheet : in out Sheet_Type) is
   Name         : String(1..10);
   Name_Size    : Natural
   Line         : String(1..50);
   Line_Size    : Natural;
   Which        : Cell_Access;
begin
   ...    -- as before
   Put ("Enter new value: ");
   Get_Line (Line, Line_Size);
   if Line_Size > 0 then                -- new value entered
      case Line(1) is
         when '#' =>                     -- counting cell
            Insert (Sheet.Innards, Name(1..Name_Size),
                     Counting_Cell (Sheet.Innards'Access));
         when '.' =>                     -- empty cell
            ...    -- as before
         when '"' =>                     -- string cell
            ...    -- as before
         when others =>                  -- formula cell
            ...    -- as before
      end case;
      Display (Sheet);
   end if;
end Modify;
```

Apart from anything else, this shows how easy it can be to modify the existing spreadsheet. The object-oriented approach accommodates new types of cells since the spreadsheet can handle any type derived from Cell_Type, so as long as the services provided by Cell_Type are adequate we can override them to provide whatever behaviour we want without affecting the spreadsheet itself; similarly the spreadsheet itself can be modified by overriding any operations whose implementation needs to change. In this case I've added a protected record; since all that it's used for is to protect a single Boolean variable it's unlikely to make any practical difference, but it shows how important it is that the original spreadsheet provided a set of primitive operations for manipulating its own internal state rather than assuming that the internal state would always be managed in the same way.

Exercises

19.1   Modify Counting_Cell_Type so that you can specify the delay rather than having a fixed five-second delay.

19.2   Modify the spreadsheet program in this chapter to use an abortable **select** statement instead of calling Get_Immediate to get commands from the user. The **select** statement should call Get or Get_Line and abort the call if it has not completed within one second, redisplaying the spreadsheet if it has changed.

19.3   Modify the guessing game program from exercise 5.1 to impose a maximum time limit within which the user must guess the secret value.

19.4   Define a bank account type similar to that described in exercise 14.2 which is based on a protected record to make it safe for use in a multitasking program (so that multiple tasks can 'simultaneously' deposit and withdraw money). Test it using two tasks which deposit and withdraw amounts of money at random intervals; check that the totals deposited and withdrawn by each task match up with the final balance of the account.

CHAPTER 20

Loose ends

> *I thought at first that you had done something clever,*
> *but I see there was nothing in it, after all.*
> — Sir Arthur Conan Doyle, *The Red-Headed League*

20.1   Other features of Ada

As I said in the preface, this book does not pretend to provide a complete coverage of Ada
95. Ada's a big language, and it would take a much bigger book than this to do it justice.
Many of the features I've omitted have been omitted because you shouldn't use them, or
because you're unlikely to need to use them, or a combination of both. Others have simply
been the victims of a lack of space. Here's a list of the major omissions and the reasons
why I left them out:

- **The goto statement**. Ever since the 1960s the **goto** statement has been denounced
  as the root of all unstructured evil in programming, the source from which
  'spaghetti code' is created. It's so bad I won't even discuss it here. Suffice it to
  say that three decades after this heresy was exposed, Ada still has a **goto** statement.
  It's really not something you want to know about.
- **Pragmas and representation clauses**. Pragmas are clauses which provide hints to
  the compiler about possible optimisations and other compilation-related issues.
  Compilers are allowed to ignore pragmas or to add extra pragmas to the ones
  recommended by the language definition, so I've avoided mentioning them on the
  grounds that they're implementation dependent. Representation clauses allow you
  to control details of the internal representation of parts of your program such as the
  physical memory layout of record components and the physical location of
  individual objects. This again is such an implementation-dependent issue that I've
  ignored it entirely.
- **The standard packages**. These haven't been described in full simply because of
  lack of space; there are a lot of them, and it would be very difficult to think up
  examples to illustrate everything in them. You should nevertheless make the effort
  to familiarise yourself with what's available if you want to be a serious Ada
  programmer; the standard environment is described in detail in Annex A of the Ada
  95 Reference Manual. Unless you're familiar with what's available you'll end up
  wasting time reinventing the wheel; for example, I used the To_Upper function
  from Ada.Characters.Handling in a couple of examples rather than write an upper

case conversion function. It would have been easy enough to write one, but I've got better things to do with my time. Also, To_Upper deals correctly with accented and other non-English characters like à, é and ñ whereas I might easily have overlooked that sort of detail. There are also packages for direct access input/output, command line processing, variable-length string handling, character-to-character translation, random number generation, mathematical functions, complex numbers and more. Some day you're likely to need to use at least some of these things, so you need at least to know that they exist.

Some features have only been mentioned briefly:

- **Loop labels and multilevel exit statements**. These are a lesser heresy than **goto** statements; they enable you to exit from multiple levels of loop at once ('in a single bound Jack was free!'). Although some people find them acceptable, my experience is that there is usually a better way to do the same thing; a lot of the time it's better to consider returning from a subprogram, or possibly raising an exception if the reason you want to get out is that an error has occurred.
- **Variant records**. Tagged types can generally be used more easily instead of variant records to achieve the same effect. Variant records are a feature inherited (ahem!) from Ada 83, which didn't have tagged types. If you ever feel the urge to use a variant record, think about using a family of tagged types instead.
- **Decimal types**. These are new in Ada 95 but compilers are not required to support them. For this reason I didn't feel that it was worth spending very much time on them.
- **Multitasking**. Although I devoted a chapter to this, it's a complex enough topic that it's impossible to do more than to scratch the surface of it in a book this size. Some features (e.g the **requeue** statement and entry families) weren't mentioned at all. Rather than aim for complete coverage, I felt it would be better to concentrate on a brief description of the essential features of multitasking in Ada 95 and content myself with illustrating its use and interaction with object-oriented design.

20.2 Other sources of information

A lot of documentation about Ada is freely available, usually electronically via the Internet (either on the World-Wide Web or by FTP). This includes the Ada 95 Reference Manual and the accompanying Rationale as well as the Annotated Reference Manual and Style Guide. Another useful document is the Ada Programming FAQ (Frequently Asked Questions list). A lot of software is also available in the same way, including the GNAT compiler system (which is available for most development platforms) and a variety of other development tools, as well as an ever-growing library of useful packages.

Here's a list of good places to start looking if you're interested in online resources. For your convenience, there are links to the resources listed below at the website for this book (*http://www.comp.it.brighton.ac.uk/je/adacraft*):

- **Home of the Brave Ada Programmers** (*http://lglwww.epfl.ch/Ada*) — a website with links to most of the other sites listed here as well as many other places. The Ada FAQs and reference manuals are available from here, and there's also a hypertext version of the Ada Reference Manual. This is your best starting point for any web browsing.
- **Ada Internet Resource List** (*http://www.cera.com/ada.htm*) — another website with links to lots of Ada-related material around the world.
- **The Public Ada Library** (*http://wuarchive.wustl.edu/languages/ada/pal.html*) — a web front-end to the Public Ada Library, an FTP archive of Ada software and other material. The PAL is also mirrored at many sites around the world (e.g. at *http://www.cnam.fr/Languages/Ada/PAL*)
- **The Ada Information Clearinghouse** (*http://sw-eng.falls-church.va.us/AdaIC*) — another important Ada archive providing a variety of Ada-related documents.

The Public Ada Library and the Ada Information Clearinghouse can be accessed by anonymous FTP rather than going via the World-Wide Web. The Public Ada Library is at *wuarchive.wustl.edu* in the directory */languages/ada* and there is a European mirror at *ftp.cnam.fr* in the directory */pub/Ada*. The Ada Information Clearinghouse can be found at *sw-eng.falls-church.va.us* in the directory */public/AdaIC*. The GNAT compiler can also be obtained by anonymous FTP from *cs.nyu.edu* in the directory */pub/gnat* or a number of mirror sites (e.g. *snowwhite.it.brighton.ac.uk* in */gnat*).

Paper copies of some documents can be had for the asking, and most online resources are available on CD if you don't have convenient access to the Internet. Here are some sources:

- **Ada 95 Reference Manual and Rationale** — paper copies of these are available on request from the National Technical Information Service at 5285 Port Royal Road, Springfield, VA 22151, USA. You'll need to quote the correct order number for the document you want: for the Ada 95 Reference Manual it's AD A293760, for the Rationale it's AD A293708 and for the Annotated Reference Manual it's AD A298367.
- **Walnut Creek** — this company is a major archive site and CD publisher; they mirror the Public Ada Library and publish it as a two-disk CD set. For details, contact Walnut Creek at 1547 Palos Verdes Mall, Suite 260, Walnut Creek, CA 94596, USA; you can also get their latest catalogue and ordering information from their website at *http://www.cdrom.com* or by fingering *info@cdrom.com*.

There is a Usenet newsgroup which discusses Ada-related issues:

- **comp.lang.ada** — if you have problems understanding some of the trickier bits of Ada or you want information about getting hold of particular resources, this is a good place to ask. However, you're advised to read the Ada FAQ (see above) and think carefully before you post in accordance with the standard 'netiquette'; what you write will be seen by people all over the world.

There are also a number of Ada-related special interest groups around the world:

- **ACM SIGAda** — a special interest group of the Association for Computing Machinery. SIGAda publishes a quarterly journal called SIGAda Notes. There is also a SIGAda website at *http://www.acm.org/sigada*. For more information contact the ACM at 1515 Broadway, New York, NY 10036, USA, or at Avenue Marcel Thiry 204, 1200 Brussels, Belgium, or by e-mail to *acmhelp@acm.org*.
- **Ada-UK** — a British Ada special interest group. Ada-UK publishes a bimonthly journal called Ada User and hosts an annual conference every October. There is a website at *http://www.adauk.org.uk*. For more information contact Ada-UK at PO Box 322, York YO1 3GY, England.
- **Ada-Europe** — a European Ada special interest group which hosts an annual conference and publishes a quarterly journal called Ada-Europe News. Ada-Europe can be contacted at ATM Computer GmbH, Bücklestrasse 1–5, D-78467 Konstanz, Germany, or by e-mail to *ada-euro@atm.aeg.kn.DaimlerBenz.com*.

Appendices

Language summary

This appendix gives an informal summary of the syntax of Ada 95. I've deliberately tried to keep it informal to make it easier to understand at a glance, but because of its informality it is incomplete and not everything is spelled out in full. You should consult the Ada 95 Reference Manual if you need a more detailed syntax of the language.

In the descriptions below, items in *italics* refer to syntactic categories, items in **bold** must be entered as shown and items enclosed in square brackets [like this] are optional and may be omitted. Unless otherwise noted, *sequence-of-X* means one or more *X*s (so *sequence-of-statements* means one or more statements) while *list-of-X* means one or more *X*s separated by commas (so *list-of-names* means one or more names separated by commas).

A.1 Compilation units

A.1.1 Compilation units (chapter 2, chapter 4)

```
[sequence-of-context-clauses]
[private] package-or-subprogram-declaration
```

The *package-or-subprogram-declaration* can be a package specification, a package body, a procedure declaration or a function declaration. Only child packages and child subprograms can be specified as **private**.

A.1.2 Separate units (chapter 4)

```
[sequence-of-context-clauses]
separate ( parent-unit-name )
body-declaration
```

The *body-declaration* can be the body of a subprogram, package, task or protected record.

A.1.3   Context clauses (chapter 2, chapter 9)

```
with list-of-library-units ;
use list-of-packages ;
                    -- packages in use clauses can't be generic
use type list-of-types ;
```

A.1.4   Subprograms (chapter 2, chapter 4)

```
procedure name [( parameter-list )] is
                               -- see below for parameter-list
   [sequence-of-declarations]
begin
   sequence-of-statements
[exception
   sequence-of-exception-handlers]
end name ;


function name [( parameter-list )] return type-name is
   [sequence-of-declarations]
begin
   sequence-of-statements
                 -- must include at least one return statement
[exception
   sequence-of-exception-handlers]
end name ;
```

A *parameter-list* consists of one or more parameter declarations separated by semicolons. Each parameter declaration looks like this:

```
list-of-names : [mode] type-name [:= default-value]
```

For a procedure, *mode* is either **in**, **out**, **in out** or **access**. For a function, *mode* is either **in** or **access**. If it is omitted, **in** is assumed.

A.1.5   Subprogram specifications (chapter 2, chapter 4)

```
procedure name [( parameter-list )] ;
function  name [( parameter-list )] return type-name ;
```

A.1.6   Separate subunits (chapter 4, chapter 10)

```
procedure name [( parameter-list )] is separate;
function  name [( parameter-list )] return type-name
                                    is separate;

package body name   is separate;
task body name      is separate;
protected body name is separate;
```

A.1.7   Abstract subprograms (chapter 15)

```
procedure name [( parameter-list )] is abstract;
function  name [( parameter-list )] return type-name
                                    is abstract;
```

Abstract subprograms must be primitive operations of abstract types.

A.1.8   Package specifications (chapter 4, chapter 9)

```
package name is
    sequence-of-declarations
[private
    sequence-of-declarations]
end name ;
```

A.1.9   Package bodies (chapter 4, chapter 9)

```
package body name is
    sequence-of-declarations
[begin
    sequence-of-statements
[exception
    sequence-of-exception-handlers]]
end name ;
```

A.2   Statements

A.2.1   The null statement (chapter 3)

```
null;
```

A.2.2   Assignment statements (chapter 3)

```
variable-name := expression ;
```

A.2.3   Procedure call statements (chapter 2)

```
procedure-name [( list-of-parameters )] ;
```

Each parameter in the *list-of-parameters* takes the following form:

```
[parameter-name =>] expression
```

Named parameters must come after any parameters which do not specify a name.

A.2.4   If statements (chapter 3)

```
if condition then
    sequence-of-statements
[sequence-of-elsif-parts]
[else
    sequence-of-statements]
end if;
```

An elsif-*part* looks like this:

```
elsif condition then
    sequence-of-statements
```

A.2.5   Case statements (chapter 3)

```
case expression is
    sequence-of-alternatives
end case;
```

Each alternative in the *sequence-of-alternatives* looks like this:

```
when choice-list =>
    sequence-of-statements
when others =>                  -- if present, must come last
    sequence-of-statements
```

A *choice-list* is a list of one or more choices separated by vertical bars ('|'). Choices can take either of the following forms:

```
expression          -- execute this choice if the controlling
                    -- expression is equal to expression
expression .. expression
                    -- execute this choice if the controlling
                    -- expression is in the specified range
```

The expressions must be able to be evaluated at compile time. There must be a choice for every possible value of the type of the controlling expression (or an **others** choice).

A.2.6 Loop statements (chapter 3)

```
[loop-name :]      -- if present, must be given after end loop
loop
     sequence-of-statements          -- exit statement required!
end loop [loop-name] ;
```

If a *loop-name* is specified at the beginning of the loop, it must also be repeated after **end loop**.

A.2.7 Exit statements (chapter 3)

```
exit [loop-name] ;                  -- unconditional
exit [loop-name] when condition ;   -- when condition is true
```

A.2.8 While loops (chapter 3)

```
[loop-name :]
while condition loop        -- repeat while condition is true
     sequence-of-statements
end loop [loop-name] ;
```

A.2.9 For loops (chapter 6)

```
[loop-name :]
for name in [reverse] subtype-specification loop
     sequence-of-statements
end loop [loop-name] ;
```

A *subtype-specification* takes either of the following forms:

```
expression .. expression     -- treated as a subtype of Integer
type-name [range expression .. expression]
```

A.2.10   Return statements (chapter 4)

```
return;               -- in procedures and accept statements
return expression ;   -- in functions; result is expression
```

A.2.11   Blocks (chapter 3, chapter 4, chapter 7)

```
[declare
    sequence-of-declarations]
begin
    sequence-of-statements
[exception
    sequence-of-exception-handlers]
end;
```

A.3   Declarations

A.3.1   Object declarations (chapter 2, chapter 3)

```
list-of-names : [aliased] [constant] type-name
                            [:= initial-value] ;
list-of-names : [aliased] [constant] array
                    ( list-of-index-subtypes )
                    of type-name [:= initial-value] ;
```

The *initial-value* is any expression of the appropriate type and is assigned to all the variables defined in the *list-of-names*.

A.3.2   Named numbers (chapter 4)

```
list-of-names : constant := numeric-value;
```

The *numeric-value* is any expression with a real or integer value which must be static (i.e. it must be able to be evaluated at compile time). The *list-of-names* will be defined as universal values (*universal real* or *universal integer*).

A.3.3   Renaming declarations (chapter 4, chapter 7)

```
name : type-name renames object-name ;
name : exception renames exception-name ;


[generic] package name renames package-name ;
[generic] procedure name [( parameter-list )]
                                    renames procedure-name ;
[generic] function  name [( parameter-list )] return type-name
                              renames function-name ;
```

A.3.4   Type declarations (chapter 4)

```
type name is type-specification ;
```

See A.4 below for more details about type declarations.

A.3.5   Subtype declarations (chapter 4)

```
subtype name is type-name [range expression .. expression] ;
```

A.4   Type declarations

A.4.1   Signed integer types (chapter 5)

```
type name is range expression .. expression ;
```

A.4.2   Modular integer types (chapter 5)

```
type name is mod expression ;
```

A.4.3   Floating point types (chapter 5)

```
type name is digits expression
                         [range expression .. expression] ;
```

A.4.4   Fixed point types (chapter 5)

```
type name is delta expression range expression .. expression;
                         -- note that range is required
```

A.4.5   Decimal types (chapter 5)

```
type name is delta expression digits expression
                        [range expression .. expression] ;
```

A.4.6   Enumeration types (chapter 5)

```
type name is ( list-of-enumeration-literals );
```

An *enumeration-literal* can be either a name or a character literal.

A.4.7   Record types (chapter 6, chapter 14)

```
type name [(discriminant-part)] is
    [[abstract] tagged] [limited] record
        sequence-of-component-declarations
    end record;
```

A *sequence-of-component-declarations* which does not contain any components must be specified as **null**.

```
type name [(discriminant-part)] is
        [[abstract] tagged] [limited] null record;

type name (discriminant-part) is
    [[abstract] tagged] [limited]
    record
        [sequence-of-component-declarations]
        case discriminant-name is
            variant-part
        end case;
    end record;
```

A *component-declaration* looks like an object declaration (but may not be a constant or an anonymous array).

A *discriminant-part* has the same format as the parameter list in a subprogram declaration except that the mode must be either **access** or omitted, and the type of a discriminant must be either a discrete type or an access type.

A *variant-part* looks like this:

```
when choice-list =>
    sequence-of-component-declarations
```

A.4.8   Array types (chapter 6)

```
type name is array ( list-of-index-subtypes ) of type-name ;
```

An *index-subtype* takes either of the following forms:

```
expression .. expression    -- treated as a subtype of Integer
type-name [range expression .. expression]
```

A.4.9   Private types (chapter 9)

```
type name is [[abstract] tagged] [limited] private;
type name (discriminant-part) is
           [[abstract] tagged] [limited] private;
type name (<>) is [[abstract] tagged] [limited] private;
```

A.4.10   Access types (chapter 11)

```
type name is access name ;        -- pool-specific access type
type name is access all name ;    -- general access type
type name is access constant name ;
                                  -- access-to-constant type
```

A.4.11   Incomplete declarations (chapter 11)

```
type name ;
type name (discriminant-part) ;
type name (<>);
```

A.4.12   Derived types (chapter 5, chapter 14)

```
type name is new type-name [range expression .. expression];
type name is [abstract] new tagged-type-name with private;
type name is [abstract] new tagged-type-name
                                        with null record;

type name is [abstract] new tagged-type-name with
   record
     sequence-of-components
   end record;
```

A.5   Exceptions

A.5.1   Exception handlers (chapter 3, chapter 7)

```
when [name :] exception-list =>
    sequence-of-statements
when [name :] others =>
    sequence-of-statements
```

The *exception-list* is a list of one or more exception names separated by bars ('|'). If there is an **others** choice it must come last. If there a *name* is specified, it declares an object of the type Ada.Exceptions.Exception_Occurrence which is initialised with details of the exception that was raised.

A.5.2   Exception declarations (chapter 7)

```
list-of-names : exception;
```

A.5.3   Raise statements (chapter 7)

```
raise [exception-name] ;
```

The *exception-name* can only be omitted inside an exception handler, in which case the original exception is reraised.

A.6   Expressions

A.6.1   Expressions (chapter 2, chapter 3)

An expression is a sequence of one or more terms separated by operators. The operators are applied to the operands (highest-priority operators first) to yield a value of a specific type.

Terms within an expression can be object names or literal values, or can take any of the following forms:

```
unary-operator expression              -- unary subexpression
[type-name '] ( expression )           -- subexpression
[type-name '] ( aggregate )            -- aggregate
type-name ( expression )               -- type conversion
type-name ' attribute-name [( list-of-parameters )]
                                       -- type attribute
```

```
new type-name ['( initial-value )]      -- storage allocator
array-name ( list-of-subscripts )       -- array element/slice
record-name . component-name            -- record component
function-name [( list-of-parameters )]  -- function call
```

A.6.2 Membership operators (chapter 5)

```
expression [not] in expression .. expression
expression [not] in subtype-name
```

A.6.3 Array aggregates (chapter 6)

An array aggregate is a comma-separated list of one or more values for specifying the components of an array. Values in an array aggregate take the following form:

```
[component-selector-list =>] expression
```

A *component-selector-list* consists of one or more component selectors separated by vertical bars ('|'). Component selectors are as follows:

```
expression
expression .. expression
others            -- must be used by itself as the last selector
```

A.6.4 Subscripts (chapter 6)

```
expression                   -- select a single array element
expression .. expression     -- select a slice (subarray) of
                             -- an array
```

A.6.5 Record aggregates (chapter 6)

A record aggregate is either a comma-separated list of one or more values for specifying the components of a record, or **null record**. Values in an aggregate other than a **null record** take the following form:

```
[component-selector-list =>] expression
```

A *component-selector-list* consists of one or more component names separated by vertical bars ('|').

A.6.6   Extension aggregates (chapter 14)

```
parent-value with record-aggregate
parent-value with null record
```

A.7   Generics

A.7.1   Generic units (chapter 12)

```
generic
    [sequence-of-generic-parameters]
subprogram-or-package-specification
```

A.7.2   Generic type parameters (chapter 12)

```
type name is [[abstract] tagged] [limited] private;
type name is (<>);
type name is range <>;
type name is mod <>;
type name is digits <>;
type name is delta <>;
type name is delta <> digits <>;
type name is access [all] type-name;
type name is access constant type-name;
type name is array (type-name [range <>]) of type-name;
type name is [abstract] new type-name [with private] ;
```

A.7.3   Generic subprogram and package parameters (chapter 12)

```
with procedure procedure-specification [is <>] ;
with procedure procedure-specification is name ;
with function function-specification [is <>] ;
with function function-specification is name ;
with package name is new generic-package-name [(<>)] ;
with package name is new generic-package-name
                          [( list-of-generic-parameters )] ;
```

A.7.4   Generic object parameters (chapter 12)

```
list-of-names : [mode] type-name [:= default-value] ;
```

The *mode* must be **in** or **in out**. If it is omitted, **in** is assumed.

A.7.5 Generic instantiations (chapter 5, chapter 12)

```
package name is new generic-package-name
                 [( list-of-generic-parameters )] ;
procedure name is new generic-procedure-name
                 [( list-of-generic-parameters )] ;
function name is new generic-function-name
                 [( list-of-generic-parameters )] ;
```

Generic parameters have the following form:

```
[parameter-name =>] value
```

A.8 Multitasking features

A.8.1 Task specifications (chapter 19)

```
task [type] name [( list-of-discriminants )] ;

task [type] name is
    sequence-of-entry-declarations
[private
    sequence-of-entry-declarations]
end name ;
```

A.8.2 Entry declarations (chapter 19)

```
entry name [( parameter-list )] ;
```

A.8.3 Task bodies (chapter 19)

```
task body name is
    [sequence-of-declarations]
begin
    sequence-of-statements
[exception
    sequence-of-exception-handlers]
end name ;
```

A.8.4 Delay statements (chapter 19)

```
delay expression ;          -- expression is of type Duration
delay until expression ;    -- expression is of type
                            -- Ada.Calendar.Time
```

A.8.5 Accept statements (chapter 19)

```
accept entry-name ;

accept entry-name [( parameter-list )] do
    sequence-of-statements
end entry-name ;
```

A.8.6 Selective accept statements (chapter 19)

```
select
    sequence-of-accept-alternatives
[or
    delay-or-terminate-alternatives]
[else
    sequence-of-statements]
end select;
```

You cannot have both a *delay-or-terminate-alternative* and an **else** part. The *sequence-of-accept-alternatives* consists of one or more *accept-alternatives* separated from each other by **or**. The *delay-or-terminate-alternatives* consist of either a single terminate alternative, or one or more delay alternatives separated by **or**.

A.8.7 Accept alternatives (chapter 19)

```
[when condition =>]
    accept-statement
    [sequence-of-statements]
```

A.8.8 Delay alternatives (chapter 19)

```
[when condition =>]
    delay-statement
    [sequence-of-statements]
```

A.8.9 Terminate alternatives (chapter 19)

```
[when condition =>]
    terminate;
```

A select statement may not contain more than one terminate alternative.

A.8.10 Selective entry calls (chapter 19)

```
select
    entry-call
    [sequence-of-statements]
[or
    delay-alternative]
[else
    sequence-of-statements]
end select;
```

You can have either a *delay-alternative* or an **else** part, but not both.

A.8.11 Abortable select statements (chapter 19)

```
select
    entry-call-or-delay-statement
    [sequence-of-statements]
then abort
    sequence-of-statements
end select;
```

A.8.12 Abort statements (chapter 19)

```
abort list-of-task-names ;
```

A.8.13 Protected record specifications (chapter 19)

```
protected [type] name [( list-of-discriminants )] is
    sequence-of-subprogram-or-entry-declarations
[private
    sequence-of-declarations]
end name ;
```

A.8.14   Protected record bodies (chapter 19)

```
protected body name is
    sequence-of-subprogram-or-entry-bodies
end name ;
```

A.8.15   Entry body (chapter 19)

```
entry name [( parameter-list )]
    when condition is
    [sequence-of-declarations]
begin
    sequence-of-statements
[exception
    sequence-of-exception-handlers]
end name ;
```

A.9   The Ada type hierarchy

```
Elementary types
    - scalar types
        - discrete types
            - enumerations
            - integers                      \
                - signed integers           |
                - modular integers          |
        - real types                        | numeric types
            - floating point                |
            - fixed point                   |
                - ordinary fixed point      |
                - decimal fixed point       /
    - access types
        - access-to-object
        - access-to-subprogram


Composite types
    - array types
    - record types
        - untagged records
        - tagged records
    - tasks
    - protected records
```

Selected standard packages

This appendix gives the specifications of the standard Ada library packages used in this book. For full details of the packages available, refer to Annex A of the Ada 95 Language Reference Manual, which is where the packages described in this appendix were copied from (with minor formatting changes). The following copyright notice applies:

In addition to the packages listed here, chapter 9 gives the declaration of the package Ada.Calendar (section 9.10).

B.1 The hierarchy of the standard packages

All the packages in the standard library are descended from one of the parent packages Ada, System or Interfaces. The child packages of Ada are as follows:

Asynchronous_Task_Control	Direct_IO
Calendar	Dynamic_Priorities
Characters	Exceptions
Handling	Finalisation
Latin_1	Interrupts
Command_Line	Names
Decimal	IO_Exceptions

Numerics	Strings (continued)
Complex_Elementary_Functions	Wide_Bounded
Complex_Types	Wide_Fixed
Discrete_Random	Wide_Maps
Elementary_Functions	Wide_Constants
Float_Random	Wide_Unbounded
Generic_Complex_Elementary_Functions	Synchronous_Task_Control
Generic_Complex_Types	Tags
Generic_Elementary_Functions	Task_Attributes
Real_Time	Task_Identification
Sequential_IO	Text_IO
Storage_IO	Complex_IO
Streams	Editing
Stream_IO	Text_Streams
Strings	Unchecked_Conversion
Bounded	Unchecked_Deallocation
Fixed	Wide_Text_IO
Maps	Complex_IO
Constants	Editing
Unbounded	Text_Streams

B.2   The package Standard

Note: Some of the contents of this package are not expressible in Ada. These parts are shown in *italics* to emphasise that they are given for explanatory purposes rather than being part of the language. For example, there are no types called *root_integer* or *universal_integer*; these are just conceptual types which are used in the language definition to formulate the rules for the way integer types work in Ada. For further information see section A.1 of the Ada 95 Reference Manual.

```
package Standard is
   pragma Pure(Standard);

   type Boolean is (False, True);

   -- The predefined relational operators for this type
   -- are as follows:

   -- function "="   (Left, Right : Boolean) return Boolean;
   -- function "/="  (Left, Right : Boolean) return Boolean;
   -- function "<"   (Left, Right : Boolean) return Boolean;
   -- function "<="  (Left, Right : Boolean) return Boolean;
   -- function ">"   (Left, Right : Boolean) return Boolean;
```

```
-- function ">="   (Left, Right : Boolean) return Boolean;


-- The predefined logical operators and the predefined
-- logical negation operator are as follows:

-- function "and" (Left, Right : Boolean) return Boolean;
-- function "or"  (Left, Right : Boolean) return Boolean;
-- function "xor" (Left, Right : Boolean) return Boolean;

-- function "not" (Right : Boolean) return Boolean;

-- The integer type root_integer is predefined.
-- The corresponding universal type is universal_integer.

type Integer is range implementation-defined;

subtype Natural  is Integer range 0 .. Integer'Last;
subtype Positive is Integer range 1 .. Integer'Last;

-- The predefined operators for type Integer are as follows:

-- function "="  (Left, Right : Integer'Base) return Boolean;
-- function "/=" (Left, Right : Integer'Base) return Boolean;
-- function "<"  (Left, Right : Integer'Base) return Boolean;
-- function "<=" (Left, Right : Integer'Base) return Boolean;
-- function ">"  (Left, Right : Integer'Base) return Boolean;
-- function ">=" (Left, Right : Integer'Base) return Boolean;

-- function "+"   (Right : Integer'Base) return Integer'Base;
-- function "-"   (Right : Integer'Base) return Integer'Base;
-- function "abs" (Right : Integer'Base) return Integer'Base;

-- function "+"   (Left, Right : Integer'Base) return Integer'Base;
-- function "-"   (Left, Right : Integer'Base) return Integer'Base;

-- function "*"   (Left, Right : Integer'Base) return Integer'Base;
-- function "/"   (Left, Right : Integer'Base) return Integer'Base;
-- function "rem" (Left, Right : Integer'Base) return Integer'Base;
-- function "mod" (Left, Right : Integer'Base) return Integer'Base;

-- function "**"  (Left : Integer'Base; Right : Natural)
--        return Integer'Base;

-- The specification of each operator for the type root_integer,
```

```
-- or for any additional predefined integer type, is obtained by
-- replacing Integer by the name of the type in the specification
-- of the corresponding operator of the type Integer.  The right
-- operand of the exponentiation operator remains as subtype Natural.

-- The floating point type root_real is predefined.
-- The corresponding universal type is universal_real.

type Float is digits implementation-defined;

-- The predefined operators for this type are as follows:

-- function "="   (Left, Right : Float) return Boolean;
-- function "/="  (Left, Right : Float) return Boolean;
-- function "<"   (Left, Right : Float) return Boolean;
-- function "<="  (Left, Right : Float) return Boolean;
-- function ">"   (Left, Right : Float) return Boolean;
-- function ">="  (Left, Right : Float) return Boolean;

-- function "+"   (Right : Float) return Float;
-- function "-"   (Right : Float) return Float;
-- function "abs" (Right : Float) return Float;

-- function "+"   (Left, Right : Float) return Float;
-- function "-"   (Left, Right : Float) return Float;
-- function "*"   (Left, Right : Float) return Float;
-- function "/"   (Left, Right : Float) return Float;

-- function "**"  (Left : Float; Right : Integer'Base)
--      return Float;

-- The specification of each operator for the type root_real, or for
-- any additional predefined floating point type, is obtained by
-- replacing Float by the name of the type in the specification of
-- the corresponding operator of the type Float.

-- In addition, the following operators are predefined for
-- the root numeric types:

function "*" (Left : root_integer; Right : root_real)
  return root_real;

function "*" (Left : root_real;    Right : root_integer)
  return root_real;
```

```
function "/" (Left : root_real;    Right : root_integer)
  return root_real;
-- The type universal_fixed is predefined.
-- The only multiplying operators defined between fixed point types
-- are:

function "*" (Left  : universal_fixed;
              Right : universal_fixed)
  return universal_fixed;

function "/" (Left  : universal_fixed;
              Right : universal_fixed)
  return universal_fixed;


-- The declaration of type Character is based on the
-- standard ISO 8859-1 character set.
-- There are no character literals corresponding to the
-- positions for control characters.
-- They are indicated in italics in this definition.

type Character is
  (nul,    soh,    stx,    etx,       eot,    enq,    ack,    bel,
   bs,     ht,     lf,     vt,        ff,     cr,     so,     si,
   dle,    dc1,    dc2,    dc3,       dc4,    nak,    syn,    etb,
   can,    em,     sub,    esc,       fs,     gs,     rs,     us,

   ' ',    '!',    '"',    '#',       '$',    '%',    '&',    ''',
   '(',    ')',    '*',    '+',       ',',    '-',    '.',    '/',

   '0',    '1',    '2',    '3',       '4',    '5',    '6',    '7',
   '8',    '9',    ':',    ';',       '<',    '=',    '>',    '?',

   '@',    'A',    'B',    'C',       'D',    'E',    'F',    'G',
   'H',    'I',    'J',    'K',       'L',    'M',    'N',    'O',

   'P',    'Q',    'R',    'S',       'T',    'U',    'V',    'W',
   'X',    'Y',    'Z',    '[',       '\',    ']',    '^',    '_',

   '`',    'a',    'b',    'c',       'd',    'e',    'f',    'g',
   'h',    'i',    'j',    'k',       'l',    'm',    'n',    'o',

   'p',    'q',    'r',    's',       't',    'u',    'v',    'w',
   'x',    'y',    'z',    '{',       '|',    '}',    '~',    del,
```

```
        reserved_128,   reserved_129,    bph,     nbh,
        reserved_132,   rel,      ssa,   esa,

        hts,     htj,     vts,    pld,    plu,   ri,    ss2,    ss3,

        dcs,     pu1,     pu2,    sts,    cch,   mw,    spa,    epa,

        sos,     reserved_153,    sci,    csi,
        st,      osc,     pm,     apc,

        ' ',     '¡',     '¢',    '£',    '¤',   '¥',   '¦',    '§',
        '¨',     '©',     'ª',    '«',    '¬',   '',   '®',    '¯',

        '°',     '±',     '²',    '³',    '´',   'µ',   '¶',    '·',
        '¸',     '¹',     'º',    '»',    '¼',   '½',   '¾',    '¿',

        'À',     'Á',     'Â',    'Ã',    'Ä',   'Å',   'Æ',    'Ç',
        'È',     'É',     'Ê',    'Ë',    'Ì',   'Í',   'Î',    'Ï',

        'Ð',     'Ñ',     'Ò',    'Ó',    'Ô',   'Õ',   'Ö',    '×',
        'Ø',     'Ù',     'Ú',    'Û',    'Ü',   'Ý',   'Þ',    'ß',

        'à',     'á',     'â',    'ã',    'ä',   'å',   'æ',    'ç',
        'è',     'é',     'ê',    'ë',    'ì',   'í',   'î',    'ï',

        'ð',     'ñ',     'ò',    'ó',    'ô',   'õ',   'ö',    '÷',
        'ø',     'ù',     'ú',    'û',    'ü',   'ý',   'þ',    'ÿ');


-- The predefined operators for the type Character are the
-- same as for any enumeration type.

-- The declaration of type Wide_Character is based on the standard
-- ISO 10646 BMP character set.
-- The first 256 positions have the same contents as type Character.

type Wide_Character is (nul, soh ... FFFE, FFFF);

package ASCII is ... end ASCII;   -- Obsolescent


-- Predefined string types:

type String is array(Positive range <>) of Character;
pragma Pack(String);
```

```
-- The predefined operators for this type are as follows:

-- function "="  (Left, Right: String) return Boolean;
-- function "/=" (Left, Right: String) return Boolean;
-- function "<"  (Left, Right: String) return Boolean;
-- function "<=" (Left, Right: String) return Boolean;
-- function ">"  (Left, Right: String) return Boolean;
-- function ">=" (Left, Right: String) return Boolean;

-- function "&" (Left: String;    Right: String)
--    return String;
-- function "&" (Left: Character; Right: String)
--    return String;
-- function "&" (Left: String;    Right: Character)
--    return String;
-- function "&" (Left: Character; Right: Character)
--    return String;

type Wide_String is
   array (Positive range <>) of Wide_Character;
pragma Pack(Wide_String);
-- The predefined operators for this type correspond to
-- those for String

type Duration is delta implementation-defined
              range implementation-defined;
-- The predefined operators for the type Duration are the
-- same as for any fixed point type.

-- The predefined exceptions:
Constraint_Error : exception;
Program_Error    : exception;
Storage_Error    : exception;
Tasking_Error    : exception;

end Standard;
```

B.3 The package Ada.Text_IO

Note: The package Ada.Integer_Text_IO is functionally identical to an instantiation of Ada.Text_IO.Integer_IO for the standard type Integer, and similarly Ada.Float_Text_IO is functionally identical to an instantiation of Ada.Text_IO.Float_IO for the standard type Float. For further information see section A.10 of the Ada 95 Reference Manual.

```ada
with Ada.IO_Exceptions;
package Ada.Text_IO is
   type File_Type is limited private;
   type File_Mode is (In_File, Out_File, Append_File);

   type Count is range 0 .. implementation-defined;
   subtype Positive_Count is Count range 1 .. Count'Last;

   Unbounded : constant Count := 0;        -- line and page length

   subtype Field is Integer range 0 .. implementation-defined;

   subtype Number_Base is Integer range 2 .. 16;

   type Type_Set is (Lower_Case, Upper_Case);

   -- File Management
   procedure Create (File : in out File_Type;
                     Mode : in File_Mode := Out_File;
                     Name : in String    := "";
                     Form : in String    := "");

   procedure Open    (File : in out File_Type;
                      Mode : in File_Mode;
                      Name : in String;
                      Form : in String := "");

   procedure Close   (File : in out File_Type);
   procedure Delete  (File : in out File_Type);

   procedure Reset   (File : in out File_Type;
                      Mode : in File_Mode);
   procedure Reset   (File : in out File_Type);

   function  Mode    (File : in File_Type) return File_Mode;
   function  Name    (File : in File_Type) return String;
   function  Form    (File : in File_Type) return String;

   function  Is_Open(File : in File_Type) return Boolean;

   -- Control of default input and output files
   procedure Set_Input (File : in File_Type);
   procedure Set_Output(File : in File_Type);
   procedure Set_Error (File : in File_Type);
```

```
function Standard_Input   return File_Type;
function Standard_Output  return File_Type;
function Standard_Error   return File_Type;

function Current_Input    return File_Type;
function Current_Output   return File_Type;
function Current_Error    return File_Type;

type File_Access is access constant File_Type;

function Standard_Input   return File_Access;
function Standard_Output  return File_Access;
function Standard_Error   return File_Access;

function Current_Input    return File_Access;
function Current_Output   return File_Access;
function Current_Error    return File_Access;

-- Buffer control
procedure Flush (File : in out File_Type);
procedure Flush;

-- Specification of line and page lengths
procedure Set_Line_Length (File : in File_Type;
                           To   : in Count);
procedure Set_Line_Length (To   : in Count);

procedure Set_Page_Length (File : in File_Type;
                           To   : in Count);
procedure Set_Page_Length (To   : in Count);

function  Line_Length(File : in File_Type) return Count;
function  Line_Length  return Count;

function  Page_Length (File : in File_Type) return Count;
function  Page_Length  return Count;

-- Column, Line, and Page Control
procedure New_Line    (File    : in File_Type;
                       Spacing : in Positive_Count := 1);
procedure New_Line    (Spacing : in Positive_Count := 1);
procedure Skip_Line   (File    : in File_Type;
                       Spacing : in Positive_Count := 1);
procedure Skip_Line   (Spacing : in Positive_Count := 1);
```

```
function  End_Of_Line (File : in File_Type) return Boolean;
function  End_Of_Line  return Boolean;

procedure New_Page    (File : in File_Type);
procedure New_Page;

procedure Skip_Page   (File : in File_Type);
procedure Skip_Page;

function  End_Of_Page (File : in File_Type) return Boolean;
function  End_Of_Page  return Boolean;

function  End_Of_File (File : in File_Type) return Boolean;
function  End_Of_File  return Boolean;

procedure Set_Col (File : in File_Type;
                   To   : in Positive_Count);
procedure Set_Col (To   : in Positive_Count);

procedure Set_Line(File : in File_Type;
                   To   : in Positive_Count);
procedure Set_Line(To   : in Positive_Count);

function Col  (File : in File_Type) return Positive_Count;
function Col   return Positive_Count;

function Line (File : in File_Type) return Positive_Count;
function Line  return Positive_Count;

function Page (File : in File_Type) return Positive_Count;
function Page  return Positive_Count;

-- Character Input-Output
procedure Get (File : in  File_Type; Item : out Character);
procedure Get (Item : out Character);

procedure Put (File : in  File_Type; Item : in Character);
procedure Put (Item : in  Character);

procedure Look_Ahead (File       : in  File_Type;
                      Item       : out Character;
                      End_Of_Line : out Boolean);
procedure Look_Ahead (Item       : out Character;
                      End_Of_Line : out Boolean);
```

```
procedure Get_Immediate (File       : in  File_Type;
                          Item       : out Character);
procedure Get_Immediate (Item       : out Character);

procedure Get_Immediate (File       : in  File_Type;
                          Item       : out Character;
                          Available : out Boolean);
procedure Get_Immediate (Item       : out Character;
                          Available : out Boolean);


-- String Input-Output
procedure Get (File : in  File_Type; Item : out String);
procedure Get (Item : out String);

procedure Put (File : in  File_Type; Item : in String);
procedure Put (Item : in  String);

procedure Get_Line (File : in  File_Type;
                    Item : out String;
                    Last : out Natural);
procedure Get_Line (Item : out String; Last : out Natural);

procedure Put_Line (File : in  File_Type; Item : in String);
procedure Put_Line (Item : in  String);

-- Generic packages for Input-Output of Integer Types
generic
   type Num is range <>;
package Integer_IO is
   Default_Width : Field := Num'Width;
   Default_Base  : Number_Base := 10;

   procedure Get (File  : in  File_Type;
                  Item  : out Num;
                  Width : in Field := 0);
   procedure Get (Item  : out Num;
                  Width : in  Field := 0);
   procedure Put (File  : in File_Type;
                  Item  : in Num;
                  Width : in Field := Default_Width;
                  Base  : in Number_Base := Default_Base);
   procedure Put (Item  : in Num;
                  Width : in Field := Default_Width;
                  Base  : in Number_Base := Default_Base);
```

```
    procedure Get (From : in  String;
                   Item : out Num;
                   Last : out Positive);

    procedure Put (To   : out String;
                   Item : in Num;
                   Base : in Number_Base := Default_Base);
end Integer_IO;

generic
   type Num is mod <>;
package Modular_IO is
   Default_Width : Field := Num'Width;
   Default_Base  : Number_Base := 10;

   procedure Get (File : in  File_Type;
                  Item : out Num;
                  Width : in Field := 0);
   procedure Get (Item : out Num;
                  Width : in  Field := 0);

   procedure Put (File : in File_Type;
                  Item : in Num;
                  Width : in Field := Default_Width;
                  Base : in Number_Base := Default_Base);
   procedure Put (Item : in Num;
                  Width : in Field := Default_Width;
                  Base  : in Number_Base := Default_Base);

   procedure Get (From : in  String;
                  Item : out Num;
                  Last : out Positive);
   procedure Put (To   : out String;
                  Item : in Num;
                  Base : in Number_Base := Default_Base);
end Modular_IO;

-- Generic packages for Input-Output of Real Types
generic
   type Num is digits <>;
package Float_IO is
   Default_Fore : Field := 2;
   Default_Aft  : Field := Num'Digits-1;
   Default_Exp  : Field := 3;
```

```
      procedure Get (File  : in  File_Type;
                     Item  : out Num;
                     Width : in  Field := 0);
      procedure Get (Item  : out Num;
                     Width : in  Field := 0);

      procedure Put (File : in File_Type;
                     Item : in Num;
                     Fore : in Field := Default_Fore;
                     Aft  : in Field := Default_Aft;
                     Exp  : in Field := Default_Exp);
      procedure Put (Item : in Num;
                     Fore : in Field := Default_Fore;
                     Aft  : in Field := Default_Aft;
                     Exp  : in Field := Default_Exp);

      procedure Get (From : in String;
                     Item : out Num;
                     Last : out Positive);

      procedure Put (To   : out String;
                     Item : in Num;
                     Aft  : in Field := Default_Aft;
                     Exp  : in Field := Default_Exp);
   end Float_IO;

   generic
      type Num is delta <>;
   package Fixed_IO is
      Default_Fore : Field := Num'Fore;
      Default_Aft  : Field := Num'Aft;
      Default_Exp  : Field := 0;

      procedure Get (File  : in  File_Type;
                     Item  : out Num;
                     Width : in  Field := 0);
      procedure Get (Item  : out Num;
                     Width : in  Field := 0);

      procedure Put (File : in File_Type;
                     Item : in Num;
                     Fore : in Field := Default_Fore;
                     Aft  : in Field := Default_Aft;
                     Exp  : in Field := Default_Exp);
```

```
      procedure Put (Item : in Num;
                     Fore : in Field := Default_Fore;
                     Aft  : in Field := Default_Aft;
                     Exp  : in Field := Default_Exp);

      procedure Get (From : in  String;
                     Item : out Num;
                     Last : out Positive);
      procedure Put (To   : out String;
                     Item : in Num;
                     Aft  : in Field := Default_Aft;
                     Exp  : in Field := Default_Exp);
   end Fixed_IO;

generic
   type Num is delta <> digits <>;
package Decimal_IO is
   Default_Fore : Field := Num'Fore;
   Default_Aft  : Field := Num'Aft;
   Default_Exp  : Field := 0;

      procedure Get (File  : in  File_Type;
                     Item  : out Num;
                     Width : in  Field := 0);
      procedure Get (Item  : out Num;
                     Width : in  Field := 0);

      procedure Put (File : in File_Type;
                     Item : in Num;
                     Fore : in Field := Default_Fore;
                     Aft  : in Field := Default_Aft;
                     Exp  : in Field := Default_Exp);

      procedure Put (Item : in Num;
                     Fore : in Field := Default_Fore;
                     Aft  : in Field := Default_Aft;
                     Exp  : in Field := Default_Exp);

      procedure Get (From : in  String;
                     Item : out Num;
                     Last : out Positive);

      procedure Put (To   : out String;
                     Item : in Num;
```

```ada
                    Aft  : in Field := Default_Aft;
                    Exp  : in Field := Default_Exp);
   end Decimal_IO;


   -- Generic package for Input-Output of Enumeration Types
   generic
      type Enum is (<>);
   package Enumeration_IO is
      Default_Width   : Field := 0;
      Default_Setting : Type_Set := Upper_Case;

      procedure Get (File : in  File_Type;
                     Item : out Enum);
      procedure Get (Item : out Enum);

      procedure Put (File  : in File_Type;
                     Item  : in Enum;
                     Width : in Field    := Default_Width;
                     Set   : in Type_Set := Default_Setting);
      procedure Put (Item  : in Enum;
                     Width : in Field    := Default_Width;
                     Set   : in Type_Set := Default_Setting);

      procedure Get (From : in  String;
                     Item : out Enum;
                     Last : out Positive);
      procedure Put (To   : out String;
                     Item : in  Enum;
                     Set  : in  Type_Set := Default_Setting);
   end Enumeration_IO;


   -- Exceptions
   Status_Error : exception renames IO_Exceptions.Status_Error;
   Mode_Error   : exception renames IO_Exceptions.Mode_Error;
   Name_Error   : exception renames IO_Exceptions.Name_Error;
   Use_Error    : exception renames IO_Exceptions.Use_Error;
   Device_Error : exception renames IO_Exceptions.Device_Error;
   End_Error    : exception renames IO_Exceptions.End_Error;
   Data_Error   : exception renames IO_Exceptions.Data_Error;
   Layout_Error : exception renames IO_Exceptions.Layout_Error;

private
   ... -- not specified by the language
end Ada.Text_IO;
```

B.4   The package Ada.Sequential_IO

For further information see section A.8 of the Ada 95 Reference Manual.

```
with Ada.IO_Exceptions;
generic
   type Element_Type(<>) is private;
package Ada.Sequential_IO is
   type File_Type is limited private;
   type File_Mode is (In_File, Out_File, Append_File);

   -- File management

   procedure Create (File : in out File_Type;
                     Mode : in File_Mode := Out_File;
                     Name : in String := "";
                     Form : in String := "");

   procedure Open   (File : in out File_Type;
                     Mode : in File_Mode;
                     Name : in String;
                     Form : in String := "");

   procedure Close  (File : in out File_Type);
   procedure Delete (File : in out File_Type);

   procedure Reset  (File : in out File_Type;
                     Mode : in File_Mode);
   procedure Reset  (File : in out File_Type);

   function  Mode   (File : in File_Type) return File_Mode;
   function  Name   (File : in File_Type) return String;
   function  Form   (File : in File_Type) return String;

   function Is_Open (File : in File_Type) return Boolean;

   -- Input and output operations

   procedure Read   (File : in File_Type;
                     Item : out Element_Type);
   procedure Write  (File : in File_Type;
                     Item : in Element_Type);

   function End_Of_File (File : in File_Type) return Boolean;
```

```
   -- Exceptions

   Status_Error : exception renames IO_Exceptions.Status_Error;
   Mode_Error   : exception renames IO_Exceptions.Mode_Error;
   Name_Error   : exception renames IO_Exceptions.Name_Error;
   Use_Error    : exception renames IO_Exceptions.Use_Error;
   Device_Error : exception renames IO_Exceptions.Device_Error;
   End_Error    : exception renames IO_Exceptions.End_Error;
   Data_Error   : exception renames IO_Exceptions.Data_Error;

private
   ... -- not specified by the language
end Ada.Sequential_IO;
```

B.5   The package Ada.Streams.Stream_IO

For further information see section A.12.1 of the Ada 95 Reference Manual.

```
with Ada.IO_Exceptions;
package Ada.Streams.Stream_IO is
   type Stream_Access is access all Root_Stream_Type'Class;

   type File_Type is limited private;
   type File_Mode is (In_File, Out_File, Append_File);

   type    Count        is range 0 .. implementation-defined;
   subtype Positive_Count is Count range 1 .. Count'Last;
                        -- Index into file, in stream elements.

   procedure Create (File : in out File_Type;
                     Mode : in File_Mode := Out_File;
                     Name : in String    := "";
                     Form : in String    := "");

   procedure Open (File : in out File_Type;
                   Mode : in File_Mode;
                   Name : in String;
                   Form : in String := "");

   procedure Close  (File : in out File_Type);
   procedure Delete (File : in out File_Type);
   procedure Reset  (File : in out File_Type;
                     Mode : in File_Mode);
```

```
procedure Reset   (File : in out File_Type);

function Mode (File : in File_Type) return File_Mode;
function Name (File : in File_Type) return String;
function Form (File : in File_Type) return String;

function Is_Open     (File : in File_Type) return Boolean;
function End_Of_File (File : in File_Type) return Boolean;

function Stream (File : in File_Type) return Stream_Access;
      -- Return stream access for use with T'Input and T'Output

-- Read array of stream elements from file

procedure Read (File : in  File_Type;
                Item : out Stream_Element_Array;
                Last : out Stream_Element_Offset;
                From : in  Positive_Count);

procedure Read (File : in  File_Type;
                Item : out Stream_Element_Array;
                Last : out Stream_Element_Offset);

-- Write array of stream elements into file

procedure Write (File : in File_Type;
                 Item : in Stream_Element_Array;
                 To   : in Positive_Count);

procedure Write (File : in File_Type;
                 Item : in Stream_Element_Array);

-- Operations on position within file

procedure Set_Index(File : in File_Type;
                    To   : in Positive_Count);

function Index(File : in File_Type) return Positive_Count;
function Size (File : in File_Type) return Count;

procedure Set_Mode(File : in out File_Type;
                   Mode : in File_Mode);

procedure Flush(File : in out File_Type);
```

```
-- Exceptions
Status_Error : exception renames IO_Exceptions.Status_Error;
Mode_Error   : exception renames IO_Exceptions.Mode_Error;
Name_Error   : exception renames IO_Exceptions.Name_Error;
Use_Error    : exception renames IO_Exceptions.Use_Error;
Device_Error : exception renames IO_Exceptions.Device_Error;
End_Error    : exception renames IO_Exceptions.End_Error;
Data_Error   : exception renames IO_Exceptions.Data_Error;

private
    ... -- not specified by the language
end Ada.Streams.Stream_IO;
```

B.6   The package Ada.Characters.Handling

For further information see section A.3.2 of the Ada 95 Reference Manual.

```
package Ada.Characters.Handling is
   pragma Preelaborate(Handling);

   -- Character classification functions

   function Is_Control  (Item : in Character) return Boolean;
   function Is_Graphic  (Item : in Character) return Boolean;
   function Is_Letter   (Item : in Character) return Boolean;
   function Is_Lower    (Item : in Character) return Boolean;
   function Is_Upper    (Item : in Character) return Boolean;
   function Is_Basic    (Item : in Character) return Boolean;
   function Is_Digit    (Item : in Character) return Boolean;
   function Is_Decimal_Digit
                       (Item : in Character) return Boolean
                                          renames Is_Digit;
   function Is_Hexadecimal_Digit
                       (Item : in Character) return Boolean;
   function Is_Alphanumeric
                       (Item : in Character) return Boolean;
   function Is_Special  (Item : in Character) return Boolean;

   -- Conversion functions for Character and String

   function To_Lower (Item : in Character) return Character;
   function To_Upper (Item : in Character) return Character;
   function To_Basic (Item : in Character) return Character;
```

```
function To_Lower (Item : in String) return String;
function To_Upper (Item : in String) return String;
function To_Basic (Item : in String) return String;

-- Classifications of and conversions between Character and
-- ISO 646

subtype ISO_646 is
     Character range Character'Val(0) .. Character'Val(127);

function Is_ISO_646 (Item : in Character) return Boolean;
function Is_ISO_646 (Item : in String)    return Boolean;

function To_ISO_646 (Item      : in Character;
                     Substitute : in ISO_646 := ' ')
     return ISO_646;

function To_ISO_646 (Item      : in String;
                     Substitute : in ISO_646 := ' ')
     return String;

-- Classifications of and conversions between Wide_Character
-- and Character

function Is_Character (Item : in Wide_Character)
     return Boolean;
function Is_String    (Item : in Wide_String)
     return Boolean;

function To_Character (Item      : in Wide_Character;
                       Substitute : in Character := ' ')
     return Character;

function To_String    (Item      : in Wide_String;
                       Substitute : in Character := ' ')
     return String;

function To_Wide_Character (Item : in Character)
     return Wide_Character;

function To_Wide_String    (Item : in String)
     return Wide_String;

end Ada.Characters.Handling;
```

B.7 The package Ada.Characters.Latin_1

For further information see section A.3.3 of the Ada 95 Reference Manual.

```
package Ada.Characters.Latin_1 is
   pragma Pure(Latin_1);

   -- Control characters:

   NUL                : constant Character := Character'Val(0);
   SOH                : constant Character := Character'Val(1);
   STX                : constant Character := Character'Val(2);
   ETX                : constant Character := Character'Val(3);
   EOT                : constant Character := Character'Val(4);
   ENQ                : constant Character := Character'Val(5);
   ACK                : constant Character := Character'Val(6);
   BEL                : constant Character := Character'Val(7);

   BS                 : constant Character := Character'Val(8);
   HT                 : constant Character := Character'Val(9);
   LF                 : constant Character := Character'Val(10);
   VT                 : constant Character := Character'Val(11);
   FF                 : constant Character := Character'Val(12);
   CR                 : constant Character := Character'Val(13);
   SO                 : constant Character := Character'Val(14);
   SI                 : constant Character := Character'Val(15);

   DLE                : constant Character := Character'Val(16);
   DC1                : constant Character := Character'Val(17);
   DC2                : constant Character := Character'Val(18);
   DC3                : constant Character := Character'Val(19);
   DC4                : constant Character := Character'Val(20);
   NAK                : constant Character := Character'Val(21);
   SYN                : constant Character := Character'Val(22);
   ETB                : constant Character := Character'Val(23);

   CAN                : constant Character := Character'Val(24);
   EM                 : constant Character := Character'Val(25);
   SUB                : constant Character := Character'Val(26);
   ESC                : constant Character := Character'Val(27);
   FS                 : constant Character := Character'Val(28);
   GS                 : constant Character := Character'Val(29);
   RS                 : constant Character := Character'Val(30);
   US                 : constant Character := Character'Val(31);
```

```
-- ISO 646 graphic characters:

Space                : constant Character := ' ';   --Character'Val(32)
Exclamation          : constant Character := '!';   --Character'Val(33)
Quotation            : constant Character := '"';   --Character'Val(34)
Number_Sign          : constant Character := '#';   --Character'Val(35)
Dollar_Sign          : constant Character := '$';   --Character'Val(36)
Percent_Sign         : constant Character := '%';   --Character'Val(37)
Ampersand            : constant Character := '&';   --Character'Val(38)
Apostrophe           : constant Character := ''';   --Character'Val(39)
Left_Parenthesis     : constant Character := '(';   --Character'Val(40)
Right_Parenthesis    : constant Character := ')';   --Character'Val(41)
Asterisk             : constant Character := '*';   --Character'Val(42)
Plus_Sign            : constant Character := '+';   --Character'Val(43)
Comma                : constant Character := ',';   --Character'Val(44)
Hyphen               : constant Character := '-';   --Character'Val(45)
Minus_Sign           : Character renames Hyphen;
Full_Stop            : constant Character := '.';   --Character'Val(46)
Solidus              : constant Character := '/';   --Character'Val(47)

-- Decimal digits '0' through '9' are at positions 48 through 57

Colon                : constant Character := ':';   --Character'Val(58)
Semicolon            : constant Character := ';';   --Character'Val(59)
Less_Than_Sign       : constant Character := '<';   --Character'Val(60)
Equals_Sign          : constant Character := '=';   --Character'Val(61)
Greater_Than_Sign    : constant Character := '>';   --Character'Val(62)
Question             : constant Character := '?';   --Character'Val(63)
Commercial_At        : constant Character := '@';   --Character'Val(64)

-- Letters 'A' through 'Z' are at positions 65 through 90

Left_Square_Bracket  : constant Character := '[';   --Character'Val(91)
Reverse_Solidus      : constant Character := '\';   --Character'Val(92)
Right_Square_Bracket : constant Character := ']';   --Character'Val(93)
Circumflex           : constant Character := '^';   --Character'Val(94)
Low_Line             : constant Character := '_';   --Character'Val(95)

Grave                : constant Character := '`';   --Character'Val(96)
LC_A                 : constant Character := 'a';   --Character'Val(97)
LC_B                 : constant Character := 'b';   --Character'Val(98)
LC_C                 : constant Character := 'c';   --Character'Val(99)
LC_D                 : constant Character := 'd';   --Character'Val(100)
LC_E                 : constant Character := 'e';   --Character'Val(101)
```

```
LC_F                   : constant Character := 'f';   --Character'Val(102)
LC_G                   : constant Character := 'g';   --Character'Val(103)
LC_H                   : constant Character := 'h';   --Character'Val(104)
LC_I                   : constant Character := 'i';   --Character'Val(105)
LC_J                   : constant Character := 'j';   --Character'Val(106)
LC_K                   : constant Character := 'k';   --Character'Val(107)
LC_L                   : constant Character := 'l';   --Character'Val(108)
LC_M                   : constant Character := 'm';   --Character'Val(109)
LC_N                   : constant Character := 'n';   --Character'Val(110)
LC_O                   : constant Character := 'o';   --Character'Val(111)

LC_P                   : constant Character := 'p';   --Character'Val(112)
LC_Q                   : constant Character := 'q';   --Character'Val(113)
LC_R                   : constant Character := 'r';   --Character'Val(114)
LC_S                   : constant Character := 's';   --Character'Val(115)
LC_T                   : constant Character := 't';   --Character'Val(116)
LC_U                   : constant Character := 'u';   --Character'Val(117)
LC_V                   : constant Character := 'v';   --Character'Val(118)
LC_W                   : constant Character := 'w';   --Character'Val(119)
LC_X                   : constant Character := 'x';   --Character'Val(120)
LC_Y                   : constant Character := 'y';   --Character'Val(121)
LC_Z                   : constant Character := 'z';   --Character'Val(122)
Left_Curly_Bracket     : constant Character := '{';   --Character'Val(123)
Vertical_Line          : constant Character := '|';   --Character'Val(124)
Right_Curly_Bracket    : constant Character := '}';   --Character'Val(125)
Tilde                  : constant Character := '~';   --Character'Val(126)

DEL                    : constant Character := Character'Val(127);

-- ISO 6429 control characters:

IS4                    : Character renames FS;
IS3                    : Character renames GS;
IS2                    : Character renames RS;
IS1                    : Character renames US;

Reserved_128           : constant Character := Character'Val(128);
Reserved_129           : constant Character := Character'Val(129);
BPH                    : constant Character := Character'Val(130);
NBH                    : constant Character := Character'Val(131);
Reserved_132           : constant Character := Character'Val(132);
NEL                    : constant Character := Character'Val(133);
SSA                    : constant Character := Character'Val(134);
ESA                    : constant Character := Character'Val(135);
```

```
HTS                       : constant Character := Character'Val(136);
HTJ                       : constant Character := Character'Val(137);
VTS                       : constant Character := Character'Val(138);
PLD                       : constant Character := Character'Val(139);
PLU                       : constant Character := Character'Val(140);
RI                        : constant Character := Character'Val(141);
SS2                       : constant Character := Character'Val(142);
SS3                       : constant Character := Character'Val(143);

DCS                       : constant Character := Character'Val(144);
PU1                       : constant Character := Character'Val(145);
PU2                       : constant Character := Character'Val(146);
STS                       : constant Character := Character'Val(147);
CCH                       : constant Character := Character'Val(148);
MW                        : constant Character := Character'Val(149);
SPA                       : constant Character := Character'Val(150);
EPA                       : constant Character := Character'Val(151);

SOS                       : constant Character := Character'Val(152);
Reserved_153              : constant Character := Character'Val(153);
SCI                       : constant Character := Character'Val(154);
CSI                       : constant Character := Character'Val(155);
ST                        : constant Character := Character'Val(156);
OSC                       : constant Character := Character'Val(157);
PM                        : constant Character := Character'Val(158);
APC                       : constant Character := Character'Val(159);

-- Other graphic characters:
-- Character positions 160 (16#A0#) .. 175 (16#AF#):
No_Break_Space            : constant Character := Character'Val(160)
NBSP                      : Character renames No_Break_Space;
Inverted_Exclamation      : constant Character := Character'Val(161);
Cent_Sign                 : constant Character := Character'Val(162);
Pound_Sign                : constant Character := Character'Val(163);
Currency_Sign             : constant Character := Character'Val(164);
Yen_Sign                  : constant Character := Character'Val(165);
Broken_Bar                : constant Character := Character'Val(166);
Section_Sign              : constant Character := Character'Val(167);
Diaeresis                 : constant Character := Character'Val(168);
Copyright_Sign            : constant Character := Character'Val(169);
Feminine_Ordinal_Indicator : constant Character := Character'Val(170);
Left_Angle_Quotation      : constant Character := Character'Val(171);
Not_Sign                  : constant Character := Character'Val(172);
Soft_Hyphen               : constant Character := Character'Val(173);
```

```
Registered_Trade_Mark_Sign  : constant Character := Character'Val(174);
Macron                      : constant Character := Character'Val(175);


-- Character positions 176 (16#B0#) .. 191 (16#BF#):
Degree_Sign                 : constant Character := Character'Val(176);
Ring_Above                  : Character renames Degree_Sign;
Plus_Minus_Sign             : constant Character := Character'Val(177);
Superscript_Two             : constant Character := Character'Val(178);
Superscript_Three           : constant Character := Character'Val(179);
Acute                       : constant Character := Character'Val(180);
Micro_Sign                  : constant Character := Character'Val(181);
Pilcrow_Sign                : constant Character := Character'Val(182);
Paragraph_Sign              : Character renames Pilcrow_Sign;
Middle_Dot                  : constant Character := Character'Val(183);
Cedilla                     : constant Character := Character'Val(184);
Superscript_One             : constant Character := Character'Val(185);
Masculine_Ordinal_Indicator : constant Character := Character'Val(186);
Right_Angle_Quotation       : constant Character := Character'Val(187);
Fraction_One_Quarter        : constant Character := Character'Val(188);
Fraction_One_Half           : constant Character := Character'Val(189);
Fraction_Three_Quarters     : constant Character := Character'Val(190);
Inverted_Question           : constant Character := Character'Val(191);


-- Character positions 192 (16#C0#) .. 207 (16#CF#):
UC_A_Grave                  : constant Character := Character'Val(192);
UC_A_Acute                  : constant Character := Character'Val(193);
UC_A_Circumflex             : constant Character := Character'Val(194);
UC_A_Tilde                  : constant Character := Character'Val(195);
UC_A_Diaeresis              : constant Character := Character'Val(196);
UC_A_Ring                   : constant Character := Character'Val(197);
UC_AE_Diphthong             : constant Character := Character'Val(198);
UC_C_Cedilla                : constant Character := Character'Val(199);
UC_E_Grave                  : constant Character := Character'Val(200);
UC_E_Acute                  : constant Character := Character'Val(201);
UC_E_Circumflex             : constant Character := Character'Val(202);
UC_E_Diaeresis              : constant Character := Character'Val(203);
UC_I_Grave                  : constant Character := Character'Val(204);
UC_I_Acute                  : constant Character := Character'Val(205);
UC_I_Circumflex             : constant Character := Character'Val(206);
UC_I_Diaeresis              : constant Character := Character'Val(207);


-- Character positions 208 (16#D0#) .. 223 (16#DF#):
UC_Icelandic_Eth            : constant Character := Character'Val(208);
UC_N_Tilde                  : constant Character := Character'Val(209);
```

```
UC_O_Grave                : constant Character := Character'Val(210);
UC_O_Acute                : constant Character := Character'Val(211);
UC_O_Circumflex           : constant Character := Character'Val(212);
UC_O_Tilde                : constant Character := Character'Val(213);
UC_O_Diaeresis            : constant Character := Character'Val(214);
Multiplication_Sign       : constant Character := Character'Val(215);
UC_O_Oblique_Stroke       : constant Character := Character'Val(216);
UC_U_Grave                : constant Character := Character'Val(217);
UC_U_Acute                : constant Character := Character'Val(218);
UC_U_Circumflex           : constant Character := Character'Val(219);
UC_U_Diaeresis            : constant Character := Character'Val(220);
UC_Y_Acute                : constant Character := Character'Val(221);
UC_Icelandic_Thorn        : constant Character := Character'Val(222);
LC_German_Sharp_S         : constant Character := Character'Val(223);

-- Character positions 224 (16#E0#) .. 239 (16#EF#):
LC_A_Grave                : constant Character := Character'Val(224);
LC_A_Acute                : constant Character := Character'Val(225);
LC_A_Circumflex           : constant Character := Character'Val(226);
LC_A_Tilde                : constant Character := Character'Val(227);
LC_A_Diaeresis            : constant Character := Character'Val(228);
LC_A_Ring                 : constant Character := Character'Val(229);
LC_AE_Diphthong           : constant Character := Character'Val(230);
LC_C_Cedilla              : constant Character := Character'Val(231);
LC_E_Grave                : constant Character := Character'Val(232);
LC_E_Acute                : constant Character := Character'Val(233);
LC_E_Circumflex           : constant Character := Character'Val(234);
LC_E_Diaeresis            : constant Character := Character'Val(235);
LC_I_Grave                : constant Character := Character'Val(236);
LC_I_Acute                : constant Character := Character'Val(237);
LC_I_Circumflex           : constant Character := Character'Val(238);
LC_I_Diaeresis            : constant Character := Character'Val(239);

-- Character positions 240 (16#F0#) .. 255 (16#FF#):
LC_Icelandic_Eth          : constant Character := Character'Val(240);
LC_N_Tilde                : constant Character := Character'Val(241);
LC_O_Grave                : constant Character := Character'Val(242);
LC_O_Acute                : constant Character := Character'Val(243);
LC_O_Circumflex           : constant Character := Character'Val(244);
LC_O_Tilde                : constant Character := Character'Val(245);
LC_O_Diaeresis            : constant Character := Character'Val(246);
Division_Sign             : constant Character := Character'Val(247);
LC_O_Oblique_Stroke       : constant Character := Character'Val(248);
LC_U_Grave                : constant Character := Character'Val(249);
```

```
LC_U_Acute                     : constant Character := Character'Val(250);
LC_U_Circumflex                : constant Character := Character'Val(251);
LC_U_Diaeresis                 : constant Character := Character'Val(252);
LC_Y_Acute                     : constant Character := Character'Val(253);
LC_Icelandic_Thorn             : constant Character := Character'Val(254);
LC_Y_Diaeresis                 : constant Character := Character'Val(255);

end Ada.Characters.Latin_1;
```

Language-defined attributes

This appendix is fairly lax with its terminology. In particular I use the term 'type' instead of 'subtype' for simplicity, but this is not entirely accurate, particularly for floating point types. Treat this as an outline guide, and see annex K of the Ada 95 Reference Manual for the full story. The language-defined attributes are as follows:

P'Access	(*P: any subprogram*) An access value for the subprogram P.
X'Access	(*X: any aliased object*) An access value for X.
X'Address	(*X: any object or program unit*) The address of the first of the storage elements allocated to X as a value of type System.Address.
S'Adjacent	(*S: any floating point type*) A function which returns the adjacent machine number to the first parameter in the direction of the value of the second parameter.
S'Aft	(*S: any fixed point type*) The number of decimal digits needed after the decimal point to accommodate the delta of S as a *universal_integer*.
X'Alignment	(*X: any type or object*) The alignment of X in memory as a *universal_integer*.
S'Base	(*S: any scalar type*) The unconstrained base type of S.
S'Bit_Order	(*S: any record type*) The bit ordering for S as a value of type System.Bit_Order.
P'Body_Version	(*P: any program unit*) A String that identifies the version of the body of the compilation unit containing P.
T'Callable	(*T: any task*) True when T is callable.
E'Caller	(*E: an entry name*) A value of the type Task_ID that identifies the task whose call to E is now being serviced.
S'Ceiling	(*S: any floating point type*) A function which returns the smallest integral value greater than or equal to its parameter.

S'Class	(*S: any tagged type*) The class-wide type for the class rooted at S.
X'Component_Size	(*X: any array type or object*) The size in bits of the components of X as a *universal_integer*.
S'Compose	(*S: any floating point type*) A function which combines a fraction given as its first parameter and an exponent given as its second parameter into a floating point value.
A'Constrained	(*A: any discriminated* type) True if A is constrained.
S'Copy_Sign	(*S: any floating point type*) A function which returns a value whose magnitude is that of its first parameter but with the same sign as its second parameter.
E'Count	(*E: any entry name*) The number of calls presently queued on E as a *universal_integer*.
S'Definite	(*S: any formal indefinite type*) True if the actual type of S is definite.
S'Delta	(*S: any fixed point type*) The delta of S as a *universal_real*.
S'Denorm	(*S: any floating point type*) True if denormalised values of S are machine numbers.
S'Digits	(*S: any decimal or floating point type*) The number of digits for S as a *universal_integer*.
S'Exponent	(*S: any floating point type*) A function which returns the normalised exponent of its parameter as a *universal_integer*.
S'External_Tag	(*S: any tagged type*) A representation of S'Tag as a String.
A'First(N)	(*A: any array*) The lower bound of the N-th index range of A.
A'First	(*A: any array*) The lower bound of the first index range of the array A.
S'First	(*S: any scalar type*) The lower bound of the range of S.
R.C'First_Bit	(*R.C: any component C of a record type R*) The number of bits to the first bit of C within R as a *universal_integer*.
S'Floor	(*S: any floating point type*) A function which returns the largest integral value less than or equal to its parameter.
S'Fore	(*S: any fixed point type*) The minimum number of characters needed before the decimal point for the decimal representation of any value of S as a *universal_integer*.
S'Fraction	(*S: any floating point type*) A function which returns the fractional part of its parameter.
E'Identity	(*E: any exception*) The unique identity of E as a value of type Exception_Id.

`T'Identity`	(*T: any task*) A value of the type Task_ID that identifies T.
`S'Image`	(*S: any scalar type*) A function which returns an image of its parameter as a String.
`S'Input`	(*S: any type*) A function which reads and returns a value of type S from the stream given as its parameter.
`S'Class'Input`	(*S'Class: any class-wide type*) A function which reads a tag from the stream given as its parameter, dispatches to the subprogram denoted by the Input attribute of the specific type identified by the tag and returns that result.
`A'Last(N)`	(*A: any array*) The upper bound of the N-th index range of A.
`A'Last`	(*A: any array*) The upper bound of the first index range of A.
`S'Last`	(*S: any scalar type*) The upper bound of the range of S.
`R.C'Last_Bit`	(*R.C: any component C of a record type R*) The number of bits to the last bit of C within R as a *universal_integer*.
`S'Leading_Part`	(*S: any floating point type*) A function which returns the leading part of its first parameter with the number of radix digits given by its second parameter.
`A'Length(N)`	(*A: any array*) The length of the N-th dimension of A as a *universal_integer*.
`A'Length`	(*A: any array*) The length of the first dimension of A as a *universal_integer*.
`S'Machine`	(*S: any floating point type*) A function which returns the nearest machine-representable number to its parameter.
`S'Machine_Emax`	(*S: any floating point type*) The largest exponent of S as a *universal_integer*.
`S'Machine_Emin`	(*S: any floating point type*) The smallest exponent of the floating point type S as a *universal_integer*.
`S'Machine_Mantissa`	(*S: any floating point type*) The number of digits in the machine representation of the mantissa of S as a *universal_integer*.
`S'Machine_Overflows`	(*S: any real type*) True if overflow and divide-by-zero are detected and reported by raising Constraint_Error for every predefined operation that yields a result of type S.
`S'Machine_Radix`	(*S: any real type*) The radix of the hardware representation of S as a *universal_integer*.
`S'Machine_Rounds`	(*S: any real type*) True if rounding is performed on inexact results of every predefined operation that yields a result of type S.
`S'Max`	(*S: any scalar type*) A function which returns the greater of the values of its two parameters.

`S'Max_Size_In_Storage_Elements`
> (*S: any type*) The maximum number of storage elements of type S that will be requested via System.Storage_Pools.Allocate for an access-to-S type as a *universal_integer*.

`S'Min`
> (*S: any scalar type*) A function which returns the lesser of the values of the two parameters.

`S'Model`
> (*S: any floating point type*) A function which returns a model number which is adjacent to the value of its parameter.

`S'Model_Emin`
> (*S: any floating point type*) The model number corresponding to S'Machine_Emin.

`S'Model_Epsilon`
> (*S: any floating point type*) The absolute difference between 1.0 and the next higher model number of S as a *universal_real*.

`S'Model_Mantissa`
> (*S: any floating point type*) The model number corresponding to S'Machine_Mantissa.

`S'Model_Small`
> (*S: any floating point type*) The smallest positive model number of S as a *universal_real*.

`S'Modulus`
> (*S: any modular type*) The modulus of S as a *universal_integer*.

`S'Output`
> (*S: any type*) A procedure which writes its second parameter to the stream given by its first parameter, including any bounds or discriminants.

`S'Class'Output`
> (*S'Class: any class-wide type*) A procedure which writes the tag of its second parameter to the stream given by its first parameter and then dispatches to the subprogram denoted by the Output attribute for the specific type identified by the second parameter's tag.

`D'Partition_ID`
> (*D: any library-level declaration*) A *universal_integer* that identifies the partition in which D was elaborated.

`S'Pos`
> (*S: any discrete type*) A function which returns the position number of its parameter as a *universal_integer*.

`R.C'Position`
> (*R.C: any component C of a record type R*) The same as R.C'Address – R'Address.

`S'Pred`
> (*S: any discrete type*) A function which returns the value whose position number is one less than that of its parameter.

`A'Range(N)`
> (*A: any array type*) Equivalent to A'First(N) .. A'Last(N), except that A is only evaluated once.

`A'Range`
> (*A: any array type*) Equivalent to A'First .. A'Last, except that A is only evaluated once.

`S'Range`
> (*S: any scalar type*) Equivalent to the range S'First .. S'Last.

S'Read	(*S: any type*) A procedure which reads its second parameter from the stream given by its first parameter.
S'Class'Read	(*S'Class: any class-wide type*) A procedure which dispatches to the subprogram denoted by the Read attribute of the specific type identified by the tag of its second parameter.
S'Remainder	(*S: any floating point type*) A function which returns the remainder of dividing the first parameter by the second.
S'Round	(*S: any fixed point type*) A function which returns the rounded value of its parameter.
S'Rounding	(*S: any floating point type*) A function which returns the integral value nearest to its parameter.
S'Safe_First	(*S: any floating point type*) The lower bound of the safe range of S as a *universal_real*.
S'Safe_Last	(*S: any floating point type*) The upper bound of the safe range of S as a *universal_real*.
S'Scale	(*S: any fixed point type*) The position of the point relative to the rightmost significant digit of values of S as a *universal_integer*.
S'Scaling	(*S: any floating point type*) A function which scales its first parameter by the machine radix raised to the power of its second parameter.
S'Signed_Zeros	(*S: any floating point type*) True if the hardware representation for the S has the capability of representing both positively and negatively signed zeros.
X'Size	(*X: any type or object*) The size in bits of X as a *universal_integer*.
S'Small	(*S: any fixed point type*) The 'small' of S, i.e. the smallest value of the internal type used to represent S, as a *universal_real*.
S'Storage_Pool	(*S: any access type*) The storage pool used for S as a value of type Root_Storage_Pool'Class.
S'Storage_Size	(*S: any access type*) The result of calling Storage_Size(S'Storage_Pool).
T'Storage_Size	(*S: any task*) The number of storage elements reserved for T as a *universal_integer*.
S'Succ	(*S: any scalar type*) A function which returns the value whose position number is one more than that of the value of its parameter.
X'Tag	(*X: any tagged type or class-wide object*) The tag of X as a value of type Ada.Tags.Tag.
T'Terminated	(*T: any task*) True if T is terminated.
S'Truncation	(*S: any floating point type*) A function which truncates its parameter towards zero.

S'Unbiased_Rounding	(*S: any floating point type*) A function which returns the integral value nearest to its parameter, rounding towards the even integer if the parameter lies exactly halfway between two integers.
X'Unchecked_Access	(*X: any aliased object*) The same as X'Access except that accessibility checks are not performed.
S'Val	(*S: any discrete type*) A function which returns a value of type S whose position number equals the value of its parameter.
X'Valid	(*X: any scalar object*) True if X is normal and has a valid representation.
S'Value	(*S: any scalar type*) A function which returns a value of type S given an image of the value as a String, ignoring any leading or trailing spaces.
P'Version	(*P: any program unit*) A String that identifies the version of the compilation unit that contains the declaration of P.
S'Wide_Image	(*S: any scalar type*) A function which returns an image of its parameter as a Wide_String.
S'Wide_Value	(*S: any scalar type*) A function which returns a value of type S given an image of the value as a Wide_String, ignoring any leading or trailing spaces.
S'Wide_Width	(*S: any scalar type*) The maximum length of a Wide_String returned by S'Wide_Image as a *universal_integer*.
S'Width	(*S: any scalar type*) The maximum length of a String returned by S'Image as a *universal_integer*.
S'Write	(*S: any type*) A procedure which writes the value of its second parameter to the stream given by its first parameter.
S'Class'Write	(*S'Class: any class-wide type*) A procedure which dispatches to the subprogram denoted by the Write attribute of the specific type identified by the tag of its second parameter.

Package listings

This appendix gives the final versions of the packages developed in this book. There are minor differences between the forms of the packages shown here and those in the main text; apart from some changes in layout, all **with** clauses are now shown in full and **use** and **use type** clauses are sometimes placed differently. In some cases, **use** clauses that were assumed for the sake of clarity of exposition in the main text are omitted in favour of fully qualified names. These changes do not affect the meaning or the behaviour of the code.

D.1 JE

(See chapter 4)

```
package JE is
   -- an empty package!
end JE;
```

D.2 JE.Appointments

(See chapters 10, 14 and 15)

```
with JE.Times;
use  JE.Times;
package JE.Appointments is

   type Appointment_Type is abstract tagged private;

   function Date    (Appt : Appointment_Type) return Time_Type;
   function Details (Appt : Appointment_Type) return String;
```

```
      procedure Appointment (Date    : in Time_Type;
                             Details : in String;
                             Result  : out Appointment_Type);
      procedure Put (Appt : in Appointment_Type) is abstract;
   private
      type Appointment_Type is
         abstract tagged record
            Time    : Time_Type;
            Details : String (1..50);
            Length  : Natural := 0;
         end record;
   end JE.Appointments;
```

---------------- *Package body* -----------------

```
package body JE.Appointments is

   function Date (Appt : Appointment_Type) return Time_Type is
   begin
      return Appt.Time;
   end Date;

   function Details (Appt : Appointment_Type) return String is
   begin
      return Appt.Details (1..Appt.Length);
   end Details;

   procedure Appointment (Date    : in Time_Type;
                          Details : in String;
                          Result  : out Appointment_Type) is
   begin
      Result.Time := Date;
      if Details'Length > Result.Details'Length then
         Result.Details :=
               Details(Details'First ..
                        Details'First+Result.Details'Length-1);
         Result.Length := Result.Details'Length;
      else
         Result.Details(1..Details'Length) := Details;
         Result.Length := Details'Length;
      end if;
   end Appointment;

end JE.Appointments;
```

D.3 JE.Appointments.Meetings

(See chapters 14 and 15)

```
package JE.Appointments.Meetings is
   subtype Room_Type is Integer range 100 .. 999;
   type Meeting_Type is abstract new Appointment_Type with private;

   procedure Meeting (Date    : in Time_Type;
                      Details : in String;
                      Room    : in Room_Type;
                      Result  : out Meeting_Type);

   function  Room (Appt : Meeting_Type) return Room_Type;

   -- Date, Details and Put inherited unchanged from Appointment_Type;
   -- so is Appointment, but don't use it!

private
   type Meeting_Type is abstract new Appointment_Type with
      record
         Room : Room_Type;
      end record;
end JE.Appointments.Meetings;
```

---------------- *Package body* -----------------

```
package body JE.Appointments.Meetings is

   procedure Meeting (Date    : in Time_Type;
                      Details : in String;
                      Room    : in Room_Type;
                      Result  : out Meeting_Type) is
   begin
      Appointment (Date, Details, Result);
      Result.Room := Room;
   end Meeting;

   function Room (Appt : Meeting_Type) return Room_Type is
   begin
      return Appt.Room;
   end Room;

end JE.Appointments.Meetings;
```

D.4   JE.Appointments.Deadlines

(See chapter 15)

```
package JE.Appointments.Deadlines is
   type Deadline_Type is
            abstract new Appointment_Type with null record;
   procedure Put (Appt : in Deadline_Type) is abstract;

   -- Date, Details and Appointment inherited unchanged
   -- from Appointment_Type
end JE.Appointments.Deadlines;
```

D.5   JE.Diaries

(See chapters 10, 11, 12 and 15)

```
with JE.Appointments, JE.Lists;
use  JE.Appointments;
package JE.Diaries is
   type Diary_Type is limited private;

   procedure Load   (Diary : in out Diary_Type;
                     From  : in String);
   procedure Save   (Diary : in Diary_Type;
                     To    : in String);
   procedure Add    (Diary : in out Diary_Type;
                     Appt  : in Appointment_Type'Class);
   function  Choose (Diary : Diary_Type;
                     Appt  : Positive) return Appointment_Type'Class;
   procedure Delete (Diary : in out Diary_Type;
                     Appt  : in Positive);
   function  Size   (Diary : Diary_Type) return Natural;

   Diary_Error : exception;
private
   type Appointment_Access is access Appointment_Type'Class;
   package Lists is new JE.Lists (Item_Type => Appointment_Access);
   type Diary_Type is
      limited record
         List : Lists.List_Type;
      end record;
end JE.Diaries;
```

```
----------------- Package body -----------------

with Ada.Streams.Stream_IO, JE.Times;
package body JE.Diaries is

   use type JE.Times.Time_Type;        -- to allow use of ">"
   use type Lists.List_Iterator;       -- to allow use of "/="

   function Size (Diary : Diary_Type) return Natural is
   begin
      return Lists.Size(Diary.List);
   end Size;

   function Choose (Diary : Diary_Type;
                    Appt  : Positive) return Appointment_Type'Class is
      Iterator : Lists.List_Iterator;

   begin
      if Appt not in 1 .. Lists.Size(Diary.List) then
         raise Diary_Error;
      else
         Iterator := Lists.First(Diary.List);
         for I in 2 .. Appt loop
            Iterator := Lists.Succ(Iterator);
         end loop;
         return Lists.Value(Iterator).all;
      end if;
   end Choose;

   procedure Delete (Diary : in out Diary_Type;
                     Appt  : in Positive) is
      Iterator : Lists.List_Iterator;

   begin
      if Appt not in 1 .. Lists.Size(Diary.List) then
         raise Diary_Error;
      else
         Iterator := Lists.First(Diary.List);
         for I in 2 .. Appt loop
            Iterator := Lists.Succ(Iterator);
         end loop;
         Lists.Delete (Iterator);
      end if;
   end Delete;
```

```ada
procedure Add (Diary : in out Diary_Type;
               Appt  : in Appointment_Type'Class) is
   Iterator : Lists.List_Iterator;
begin
   Iterator := Lists.First(Diary.List);
   while Iterator /= Lists.Last(Diary.List) loop
      exit when Date(Lists.Value(Iterator).all) > Date(Appt);
      Iterator := Lists.Succ(Iterator);
   end loop;
   Lists.Insert (Iterator, new Appointment_Type'Class'(Appt));
exception
   when Storage_Error =>
      raise Diary_Error;
end Add;

procedure Save (Diary : in Diary_Type;
                To    : in String) is
   File   : Ada.Streams.Stream_IO.File_Type;
   Stream : Ada.Streams.Stream_IO.Stream_Access;
   I : Lists.List_Iterator := Lists.First(Diary.List);
begin
   Ada.Streams.Stream_IO.Create (File, Name => To);
   Stream := Ada.Streams.Stream_IO.Stream(File);

   while I /= Lists.Last(Diary.List) loop
      Appointment_Type'Class'Output (Stream, Lists.Value(I).all);
      I := Lists.Succ(I);
   end loop;

   Ada.Streams.Stream_IO.Close (File);
end Save;

procedure Load (Diary : in out JE.Diaries.Diary_Type;
                From  : in String) is
   File   : Ada.Streams.Stream_IO.File_Type;
   Stream : Ada.Streams.Stream_IO.Stream_Access;
begin
   while Size(Diary) > 0 loop
      Lists.Delete (Lists.First(Diary.List));
   end loop;

   Ada.Streams.Stream_IO.Open (File, Name => From,
                               Mode => Ada.Streams.Stream_IO.In_File);
   Stream := Ada.Streams.Stream_IO.Stream(File);
```

```
      while not Ada.Streams.Stream_IO.End_Of_File(File) loop
         Add (Diary, Appointment_Type'Class'Input (Stream));
      end loop;
      Ada.Streams.Stream_IO.Close (File);

   exception
      when Ada.Streams.Stream_IO.Name_Error =>
         raise Diary_Error;
   end Load;
end JE.Diaries;
```

D.6 JE.Expressions

(See chapter 17)

```
with JE.Pointers;
package JE.Expressions is

   type Expression_Type is tagged limited private;

   function Evaluate (Syntax : Expression_Type;
                      Expr   : String) return Integer;

   Syntax_Error : exception;

private
   type    Priority_Type  is range 0..9;
   subtype Operator_Priority_Type
                        is Priority_Type range 1..Priority_Type'Last;

   type Expression_Type   is tagged limited null record;

   type Token_Type        is abstract tagged null record;
   type Token_Access      is access Token_Type'Class;

   package Token_Pointers is new JE.Pointers (Token_Type'Class,
                                              Token_Access);
   subtype Token_Pointer  is Token_Pointers.Pointer_Type;

   procedure Next_Token  (Syntax : in Expression_Type;
                          Expr   : in String;
                          From   : in out Positive;
                          Token  : in out Token_Pointer);
```

```
procedure Fetch_Token (Syntax : in Expression_Type;
                       Expr   : in String;
                       From   : in out Positive;
                       Token  : in out Token_Pointer);
procedure Parse        (Syntax : in Expression_Type;
                        Expr   : in String;
                        From   : in out Positive;
                        Prio   : in Priority_Type;
                        Result : out Integer;
                        Next   : in out Token_Pointer);
procedure Get_Operand (Syntax : in Expression_Type;
                       Expr   : in String;
                       From   : in out Positive;
                       Result : out Integer;
                       Next   : in out Token_Pointer);
type Left_Parenthesis  is new Token_Type with null record;
type Right_Parenthesis is new Token_Type with null record;
type End_Of_Expression is new Token_Type with null record;

type Operand_Type is abstract new Token_Type with null record;
function Value (Operand : Operand_Type) return Integer is abstract;

type Number_Type (Value : Integer) is new Operand_Type
                                     with null record;
function Value (Operand : Number_Type) return Integer;

type Operator_Type is abstract new Token_Type with null record;
function Priority (Operator : Operator_Type)
          return Operator_Priority_Type is abstract;

type Unary_Operator_Type is abstract new Operator_Type
                               with null record;
function Apply (Operator : Unary_Operator_Type;
               Right     : Integer) return Integer is abstract;

type Binary_Operator_Type is abstract new Operator_Type
                               with null record;
function Apply (Operator    : Binary_Operator_Type;
               Left, Right : Integer) return Integer is abstract;

type Variadic_Operator_Type is abstract new Binary_Operator_Type
                                 with null record;
function Apply (Operator : Variadic_Operator_Type;
               Right     : Integer) return Integer is abstract;
```

```
    type Multiplying_Operator_Type is abstract new Binary_Operator_Type
                                 with null record;

    function Priority (Operator : Multiplying_Operator_Type)
                                     return Operator_Priority_Type;

    type Adding_Operator_Type is abstract new Variadic_Operator_Type
                              with null record;
    function Priority (Operator : Adding_Operator_Type)
                                     return Operator_Priority_Type;
    function Unary_Priority (Operator : Adding_Operator_Type)
                                     return Operator_Priority_Type;

    type Times_Operator is new Multiplying_Operator_Type with null record;
    function Apply (Operator    : Times_Operator;
                    Left, Right : Integer) return Integer;

    type Over_Operator is new Multiplying_Operator_Type with null record;
    function Apply (Operator    : Over_Operator;
                    Left, Right : Integer) return Integer;

    type Plus_Operator is new Adding_Operator_Type with null record;
    function Apply (Operator    : Plus_Operator;
                    Left, Right : Integer) return Integer;
    function Apply (Operator    : Plus_Operator;
                    Right       : Integer) return Integer;

    type Minus_Operator is new Adding_Operator_Type with null record;
    function Apply (Operator    : Minus_Operator;
                    Left, Right : Integer) return Integer;
    function Apply (Operator    : Minus_Operator;
                    Right       : Integer) return Integer;

end JE.Expressions;

----------------- Package body -----------------

with Ada.Exceptions, Ada.Integer_Text_IO;
package body JE.Expressions is
   use Token_Pointers;

   function Evaluate (Syntax : Expression_Type;
                      Expr   : String) return Integer is
     Token  : Token_Pointer;
```

```
   From    : Positive := Expr'First;
   Result : Integer;
begin
   Parse (Expression_Type'Class(Syntax), Expr, From,
          Priority_Type'Last, Result, Token);
   if Value(Token).all not in End_Of_Expression'Class then
      Ada.Exceptions.Raise_Exception (Syntax_Error'Identity,
             "Missing operator or left parenthesis");
   end if;
   return Result;
end Evaluate;

function Priority (Operator : Multiplying_Operator_Type)
                                  return Operator_Priority_Type is
begin
   return 5;
end Priority;

function Priority (Operator : Adding_Operator_Type)
                                  return Operator_Priority_Type is
begin
   return 6;
end Priority;

function Unary_Priority (Operator : Adding_Operator_Type)
                                  return Operator_Priority_Type is
begin
   return 2;
end Unary_Priority;

function Apply (Operator    : Times_Operator;
                Left, Right : Integer) return Integer is
begin
   return Left * Right;
end Apply;

function Apply (Operator    : Over_Operator;
                Left, Right : Integer) return Integer is
begin
   return Left / Right;
end Apply;

function Apply (Operator    : Plus_Operator;
                Left, Right : Integer) return Integer is
```

```ada
begin
   return Left + Right;
end Apply;

function Apply (Operator : Plus_Operator;
               Right     : Integer) return Integer is
begin
   return Right;
end Apply;

function Apply (Operator    : Minus_Operator;
               Left, Right : Integer) return Integer is
begin
   return Left - Right;
end Apply;

function Apply (Operator : Minus_Operator;
               Right     : Integer) return Integer is
begin
   return -Right;
end Apply;

function Value (Operand : Number_Type) return Integer is
begin
   return Operand.Value;
end Value;

procedure Next_Token (Syntax : in Expression_Type;
                      Expr    : in String;
                      From    : in out Positive;
                      Token   : in out Token_Pointer) is
begin
   -- Find start of next token
   while From <= Expr'Last and then Expr(From) = ' ' loop
      From := From + 1;
   end loop;

   -- Check for end of expression
   if From > Expr'Last then
      Token := Pointer(new End_Of_Expression);
   else
      Fetch_Token (Expression_Type'Class(Syntax), Expr, From, Token);
   end if;
end Next_Token;
```

```ada
procedure Fetch_Token (Syntax : in Expression_Type;
                       Expr   : in String;
                       From   : in out Positive;
                       Token  : in out Token_Pointer) is
begin
   case Expr(From) is
      when '+' =>
         Token := Pointer(new Plus_Operator);
      when '-' =>
         Token := Pointer(new Minus_Operator);
      when '*' =>
         Token := Pointer(new Times_Operator);
      when '/' =>
         Token := Pointer(new Over_Operator);
      when '(' =>
         Token := Pointer(new Left_Parenthesis);
      when ')' =>
         Token := Pointer(new Right_Parenthesis);
      when '0'..'9' =>
         declare
            Value : Integer;
         begin
            Ada.Integer_Text_IO.Get (Expr(From..Expr'Last),
                                     Value, From);
            Token := Pointer(new Number_Type(Value));
         end;
      when others =>
         Ada.Exceptions.Raise_Exception (Syntax_Error'Identity,
            "Illegal character '" & Expr(From) & "'");
   end case;
   From := From + 1;
end Fetch_Token;


procedure Parse (Syntax : in Expression_Type;
                 Expr   : in String;
                 From   : in out Positive;
                 Prio   : in Priority_Type;
                 Result : out Integer;
                 Next   : in out Token_Pointer) is
begin
   if Prio = Priority_Type'First then
      Get_Operand (Expression_Type'Class(Syntax),
                   Expr, From, Result, Next);
   else
```

```
      declare
         Right : Integer;
         Op    : Token_Pointer;
      begin
         Parse (Syntax, Expr, From, Prio-1, Result, Op);
         while Value(Op).all in Binary_Operator_Type'Class and then
               Priority(Binary_Operator_Type'Class(Value(Op).all)) = Prio
         loop
             Parse (Syntax, Expr, From, Prio-1, Right, Next);
             Result := Apply (Binary_Operator_Type'Class(Value(Op).all),
                              Result, Right);
             Op := Next;
         end loop;
         Next := Op;
      end;
   end if;
end Parse;


procedure Get_Operand (Syntax : in Expression_Type;
                       Expr   : in String;
                       From   : in out Positive;
                       Result : out Integer;
                       Next   : in out Token_Pointer) is
   Op : Token_Pointer;

begin
   Next_Token (Expression_Type'Class(Syntax), Expr, From, Next);

   if Value(Next).all in Operand_Type'Class then
      Result := Value (Operand_Type'Class(Value(Next).all));
      Next_Token (Expression_Type'Class(Syntax), Expr, From, Next);

   elsif Value(Next).all in Left_Parenthesis'Class then
      Parse (Expression_Type'Class(Syntax),
             Expr, From, Priority_Type'Last, Result, Next);
      if Value(Next).all in Right_Parenthesis'Class then
         Next_Token (Expression_Type'Class(Syntax), Expr, From, Next);
      else
         Ada.Exceptions.Raise_Exception (Syntax_Error'Identity,
                    "Missing right parenthesis");
      end if;

   elsif Value(Next).all in Unary_Operator_Type'Class then
      Op := Next;
```

```
       Parse (Expression_Type'Class(Syntax), Expr, From,
              Priority (Unary_Operator_Type'Class(Value(Op).all)),
              Result, Next);
       Result := Apply (Unary_Operator_Type'Class(Value(Op).all),
                        Result);

     elsif Value(Next).all in Variadic_Operator_Type'Class then
       Op := Next;
       Parse (Expression_Type'Class(Syntax), Expr, From,
              Priority (Variadic_Operator_Type'Class(Value(Op).all)),
              Result, Next);
       Result := Apply (Variadic_Operator_Type'Class(Value(Op).all),
                        Result);

     elsif Value(Next).all in End_Of_Expression'Class then
       Ada.Exceptions.Raise_Exception (Syntax_Error'Identity,
               "Expression incomplete");

     else
       Ada.Exceptions.Raise_Exception (Syntax_Error'Identity,
               "Illegal token");
     end if;
   end Get_Operand;

end JE.Expressions;
```

D.7   JE.Expressions.Spreadsheet

(See chapter 18)

```
with JE.Spreadsheets;
use  JE.Spreadsheets;
package JE.Expressions.Spreadsheet is
   type Formula_Type (Sheet : access Spreadsheet_Type'Class) is
                    new Expression_Type with private;
private
   type Cell_Operand_Type (Cell : Cell_Access) is new Operand_Type
       with null record;

   function Value (Operand : Cell_Operand_Type) return Integer;

   type Formula_Type (Sheet : access Spreadsheet_Type'Class) is
                      new Expression_Type with null record;
```

```ada
   procedure Fetch_Token (Syntax : in Formula_Type;
                          Expr   : in String;
                          From   : in out Positive;
                          Token  : in out Token_Pointer);
end JE.Expressions.Spreadsheet;
```

---------------- *Package body* ----------------

```ada
with JE.Spreadsheets;  use JE.Spreadsheets;
package body JE.Expressions.Spreadsheet is

   use JE.Expressions.Token_Pointers;

   function Value (Operand : Cell_Operand_Type) return Integer is
   begin
      if Operand.Cell = null then
         raise Undefined_Cell_Error;
      else
         Evaluate (Operand.Cell.all);
      end if;
      return Num_Value (Operand.Cell.all);
   end Value;

   procedure Fetch_Token (Syntax : in Formula_Type;
                          Expr   : in String;
                          From   : in out Positive;
                          Token  : in out Token_Pointer) is
   begin
      case Expr(From) is
         when 'A'..'Z' | 'a'..'z' =>
            declare
               First    : Integer := From;
               Cell_Ptr : Cell_Access;
            begin
               while (From <= Expr'Length) and then
                              (Expr(From) in 'A'..'Z' or
                               Expr(From) in 'a'..'z' or
                               Expr(From) in '0'..'9')
               loop
                  From := From + 1;
               end loop;
               Cell_Ptr := Cell (Syntax.Sheet.all, Expr(First..From-1));
               Token := Pointer(new Cell_Operand_Type(Cell_Ptr));
            end;
```

```
            when others =>
                Fetch_Token(Expression_Type(Syntax), Expr, From, Token);
         end case;
      end Fetch_Token;

end JE.Expressions.Spreadsheet;
```

D.8   JE.Lists

(See chapters 12 and 16)

```
with Ada.Finalization;
use  Ada.Finalization;
generic
   type Item_Type is private;
package JE.Lists is
   type List_Type is new Limited_Controlled with private;
   type List_Iterator is private;

   function  Size   (List     : List_Type)       return Natural;
   function  First  (List     : List_Type)       return List_Iterator;
   function  Last   (List     : List_Type)       return List_Iterator;

   function  Succ   (Iterator : List_Iterator) return List_Iterator;
   function  Pred   (Iterator : List_Iterator) return List_Iterator;
   function  Value  (Iterator : List_Iterator) return Item_Type;

   procedure Insert (Iterator : in List_Iterator;
                     Item     : in Item_Type);
   procedure Delete (Iterator : in List_Iterator);

   List_Error : exception;

private
   type Item_Record;
   type Item_Access is access Item_Record;

   type Item_Record is
     record
       Item : Item_Type;
       Next : Item_Access;
       Pred : Item_Access;
     end record;
```

```ada
      type List_Header is
         record
            First : Item_Access;
            Last  : Item_Access;
            Count : Natural := 0;
         end record;
      type List_Access is access List_Header;

      type List_Type is new Limited_Controlled with
         record
            List : List_Access := new List_Header;
         end record;

      procedure Finalize (Object : in out List_Type);

      type List_Iterator is
         record
            List    : List_Access;
            Current : Item_Access;
         end record;

end JE.Lists;
```

```
----------------- Package body -----------------
```

```ada
with Ada.Unchecked_Deallocation;
package body JE.Lists is
   procedure Delete_Item is new Ada.Unchecked_Deallocation
                                 (Item_Record, Item_Access);

   function Size (List : List_Type) return Natural is
   begin
      return List.List.Count;
   end Size;

   function First (List : List_Type) return List_Iterator is
   begin
      return (List => List.List, Current => List.List.First);
   end First;

   function Last (List : List_Type) return List_Iterator is
   begin
      return (List => List.List, Current => null);
   end Last;
```

```
function Succ (Iterator : List_Iterator) return List_Iterator is
begin
   if Iterator.List = null or else Iterator.Current = null then
      raise List_Error;
   else
      return (List => Iterator.List, Current => Iterator.Current.Next);
   end if;
end Succ;

function Pred (Iterator : List_Iterator) return List_Iterator is
begin
   if Iterator.List = null or else
      Iterator.Current = Iterator.List.First then
      raise List_Error;
   elsif Iterator.Current = null then
      return (List => Iterator.List, Current => Iterator.List.Last);
   else
      return (List => Iterator.List, Current => Iterator.Current.Pred);
   end if;
end Pred;

function Value (Iterator : List_Iterator) return Item_Type is
begin
   if Iterator.List = null or else Iterator.Current = null then
      raise List_Error;
   else
      return Iterator.Current.Item;
   end if;
end Value;

procedure Delete (Iterator : in List_Iterator) is
   Item : Item_Access := Iterator.Current;
begin
   if Iterator.List = null or else Iterator.Current = null then
      raise List_Error;
   else
      if Iterator.Current.Next = null then
         Iterator.List.Last := Iterator.Current.Pred;
      else
         Iterator.Current.Next.Pred := Iterator.Current.Pred;
      end if;

      if Iterator.Current.Pred = null then
         Iterator.List.First := Iterator.Current.Next;
```

```
      else
         Iterator.Current.Pred.Next := Iterator.Current.Next;
      end if;
      Delete_Item (Item);
      Iterator.List.Count := Iterator.List.Count - 1;
   end if;
end Delete;

procedure Insert (Iterator : in List_Iterator;
                  Item     : in Item_Type) is
   New_Item : Item_Access;
begin
   if Iterator.List = null then
      raise List_Error;
   else
      New_Item := new Item_Record;
      New_Item.Next := Iterator.Current;
      New_Item.Item := Item;

      if Iterator.Current = null then
         New_Item.Pred := Iterator.List.Last;
         Iterator.List.Last := New_Item;
      else
         New_Item.Pred := Iterator.Current.Pred;
         Iterator.Current.Pred := New_Item;
      end if;

      if Iterator.Current = Iterator.List.First then
         Iterator.List.First := New_Item;
      else
         New_Item.Pred.Next := New_Item;
      end if;

      Iterator.List.Count := Iterator.List.Count + 1;
   end if;
end Insert;

procedure Finalize (Object : in out List_Type) is
   procedure Delete_Header is
      new Ada.Unchecked_Deallocation (List_Header, List_Access);
begin
   while First(Object) /= Last(Object) loop
      Delete (First(Object));
   end loop;
```

```
      Delete_Header (Object.List);
   end Finalize;

end JE.Lists;
```

D.9   JE.Menus

(See chapter 12)

```
with JE.Lists;
generic
package JE.Menus is
   type Action_Type is access procedure;
   type Menu_Type   is limited private;

   procedure Add      (Menu   : in out Menu_Type;
                       Title  : in String;
                       Key    : in Character;
                       Action : in Action_Type);
   function  Execute (Menu    : Menu_Type) return Boolean;

private
   type Menu_Item_Type is
     record
        Title  : String (1..40);
        Length : Natural;
        Choice : Character;
        Action : Action_Type;
     end record;

   package Menu_Lists is new JE.Lists (Menu_Item_Type);

   type Menu_Type is
     limited record
        Menu_List : Menu_Lists.List_Type;
     end record;
end JE.Menus;
```

---------------- *Package body* -----------------

```
with Ada.Text_IO, Ada.Characters.Handling;
use  Ada.Text_IO;
package body JE.Menus is
```

```ada
procedure Add (Menu    : in out Menu_Type;
               Title   : in String;
               Key     : in Character;
               Action  : in Action_Type) is
   Item : Menu_Item_Type;
   use Menu_Lists;
begin
   if Title'Length > Item.Title'Length then
      Item.Title  :=
               Title (Title'First .. Item.Title'Length-Title'First+1);
      Item.Length := Item.Title'Length;
   else
      Item.Title (Item.Title'First .. Title'Length-Item.Title'First+1)
               := Title;
      Item.Length := Title'Length;
   end if;
   Item.Choice := Ada.Characters.Handling.To_Upper(Key);
   Item.Action := Action;
   Insert( Last(Menu.Menu_List), Item );
end Add;

function Execute (Menu : Menu_Type) return Boolean is
   Item    : Menu_Item_Type;
   Choice  : Character;
   use Menu_Lists;
   I : List_Iterator;
begin
   loop
      New_Line (3);

      -- Display the menu
      I := First(Menu.Menu_List);
      while I /= Last(Menu.Menu_List) loop
         Item := Value(I);
         Put ("   [");
         Put (Item.Choice);
         Put ("] ");
         Put_Line (Item.Title(1..Item.Length));
         I := Succ(I);
      end loop;

      -- Display the Quit option and prompt
      Put_Line ("   [Q] Quit");
      Put ("Enter your choice: ");
```

```
            -- Get user's choice in upper case
            Get (Choice);
            Choice := Ada.Characters.Handling.To_Upper(Choice);
            if Choice = 'Q' then
               -- Quit chosen, so return
               return False;
            else
               -- Search menu for choice
               I := First(Menu.Menu_List);
               while I /= Last(Menu.Menu_List) loop
                  if Choice = Value(I).Choice then
                     -- Choice found, so call procedure and return
                     Value(I).Action.all;
                     return True;
                  end if;
                  I := Succ(I);
               end loop;
            end if;

            -- Choice wasn't found, so display error message and loop
            Put_Line ("Invalid choice -- please try again.");
         end loop;
      end Execute;
end JE.Menus;
```

D.10   JE.Pointers

(See chapter 16)

```
with Ada.Finalization;
generic
   type Item_Type(<>) is limited private;
   type Access_Type   is access Item_Type;
package JE.Pointers is
   type Pointer_Type is private;
   function Pointer (Value   : Access_Type)  return Pointer_Type;
   function Value    (Pointer : Pointer_Type) return Access_Type;
private
   type Reference_Counted_Object is
      record
         Value : Access_Type;
         Count : Natural;
      end record;
```

```
    type Reference_Counted_Pointer is access Reference_Counted_Object;

    type Pointer_Type is new Ada.Finalization.Controlled with
       record
          Pointer : Reference_Counted_Pointer;
       end record;

    procedure Finalize (Object : in out Pointer_Type);
    procedure Adjust   (Object : in out Pointer_Type);
end JE.Pointers;
```

---------------- *Package body* -----------------

```
with Ada.Unchecked_Deallocation;
package body JE.Pointers is

    procedure Delete_Item is
          new Ada.Unchecked_Deallocation (Item_Type, Access_Type);
    procedure Delete_Pointer is
          new Ada.Unchecked_Deallocation (Reference_Counted_Object,
                                          Reference_Counted_Pointer);

    function Pointer (Value : Access_Type) return Pointer_Type is
       Object : Pointer_Type;
    begin
       if Object.Pointer /= null then
          Delete_Item (Object.Pointer.Value);
       else
          Object.Pointer := new Reference_Counted_Object;
       end if;

       Object.Pointer.all := (Value => Value, Count => 1);
       return Object;
    end Pointer;

    function Value (Pointer : Pointer_Type) return Access_Type is
    begin
       if Pointer.Pointer = null then
          return null;

       else
          return Pointer.Pointer.Value;
       end if;
    end Value;
```

```ada
   procedure Finalize (Object : in out Pointer_Type) is
   begin
      if Object.Pointer /= null then
         Object.Pointer.Count := Object.Pointer.Count - 1;
         if Object.Pointer.Count = 0 then
            Delete_Item (Object.Pointer.Value);
            Delete_Pointer (Object.Pointer);
         end if;
      end if;
   end Finalize;

   procedure Adjust (Object : in out Pointer_Type) is
   begin
      if Object.Pointer /= null then
         Object.Pointer.Count := Object.Pointer.Count + 1;
      end if;
   end Adjust;
end JE.Pointers;
```

D.11   JE.Spreadsheets

(See chapter 18)

```ada
with Ada.Finalization, Ada.Exceptions, JE.Lists, JE.Pointers;
use  Ada.Finalization;
package JE.Spreadsheets is
   type Spreadsheet_Type   is abstract tagged limited private;

   type Cell_Type (Sheet : access Spreadsheet_Type'Class)
                 is abstract tagged limited private;

   type Formula_Cell_Type (Sheet : access Spreadsheet_Type'Class;
                           Size  : Natural)
                 is new Cell_Type(Sheet) with private;

   type String_Cell_Type  (Sheet : access Spreadsheet_Type'Class;
                           Size  : Natural)
                 is new Cell_Type(Sheet) with private;

   type Cell_Access is access Cell_Type'Class;

   function  Formula_Cell (Sheet : access Spreadsheet_Type;
                           Value : String) return Cell_Access;
```

```
function  String_Cell  (Sheet : access Spreadsheet_Type;
                        Value : String) return Cell_Access;
procedure Evaluate     (Cell  : in out Cell_Type) is abstract;
function  Text_Value   (Cell  : Cell_Type) return String is abstract;
function  Contents     (Cell  : Cell_Type) return String is abstract;
function  Num_Value    (Cell  : Cell_Type) return Integer is abstract;

procedure Recalculate  (Sheet : in out Spreadsheet_Type);
procedure Display      (Sheet : in out Spreadsheet_Type) is abstract;
procedure Change       (Sheet : in out Spreadsheet_Type);
function  Changed      (Sheet : Spreadsheet_Type) return Boolean;
function  Cell         (Sheet : Spreadsheet_Type;
                        Where : String) return Cell_Access;
procedure Delete       (Sheet : in out Spreadsheet_Type;
                        Where : in String);
procedure Insert       (Sheet : in out Spreadsheet_Type;
                        Where : in String;
                        What  : in Cell_Access);

Cell_Name_Length     : constant := 6;
Circularity_Error    : exception;
Undefined_Cell_Error : exception;

private
   type Cell_State_Type  is (Unknown, Defined, Undefined,
                             Evaluating, Error);
   type Evaluation_Number is mod 2;

   type Cell_Type (Sheet : access Spreadsheet_Type'Class) is
      abstract new Limited_Controlled with
      record
        State : Cell_State_Type := Unknown;
        Eval  : Evaluation_Number;
      end record;

   type Formula_Cell_Type (Sheet : access Spreadsheet_Type'Class;
                           Size  : Natural) is new Cell_Type(Sheet) with
      record
        Text  : String(1..Size);
        Value : Integer;
      end record;

   procedure Evaluate    (Cell : in out Formula_Cell_Type);
   function  Text_Value  (Cell : Formula_Cell_Type) return String;
```

```
function  Contents   (Cell : Formula_Cell_Type) return String;
function  Num_Value  (Cell : Formula_Cell_Type) return Integer;

type String_Cell_Type (Sheet : access Spreadsheet_Type'Class;
                        Size  : Natural) is
                new Cell_Type(Sheet) with
  record
    Text  : String(1..Size);
  end record;

procedure Evaluate   (Cell : in out String_Cell_Type);
function  Text_Value (Cell : String_Cell_Type) return String;
function  Contents   (Cell : String_Cell_Type) return String;
function  Num_Value  (Cell : String_Cell_Type) return Integer;

subtype Cell_Size    is Natural range 0 .. Cell_Name_Length;
package Cell_Pointers is new JE.Pointers (Cell_Type'Class,
                                          Cell_Access);

type Cell_Record is
  record
    Where : String (1..Cell_Name_Length);
    Size  : Cell_Size;
    Cell  : Cell_Pointers.Pointer_Type;
  end record;

package Cell_Lists is new JE.Lists (Cell_Record);

type Spreadsheet_Type is
  abstract tagged limited record
    Cells : Cell_Lists.List_Type;
    Dirty : Boolean := False;
    Eval  : Evaluation_Number := Evaluation_Number'First;
  end record;

procedure Updated  (Sheet : in out Spreadsheet_Type);
procedure Handle_Error
          (Sheet : access Spreadsheet_Type;
           Error : in Ada.Exceptions.Exception_Occurrence);

function  Evaluation (Sheet : Spreadsheet_Type)
                                return Evaluation_Number;

end JE.Spreadsheets;
```

```
---------------- Package body ----------------

with JE.Expressions.Spreadsheet, Ada.Characters.Handling;
use  JE.Expressions.Spreadsheet, Ada.Characters.Handling;
package body JE.Spreadsheets is

   use Cell_Lists, Cell_Pointers;

   function Formula_Cell (Sheet : access Spreadsheet_Type'Class;
                          Value : String) return Cell_Access is
      Cell : Cell_Access := new Formula_Cell_Type(Sheet, Value'Length);
   begin
      Formula_Cell_Type(Cell.all).Text := Value;
      return Cell;
   end Formula_Cell;

   function String_Cell (Sheet : access Spreadsheet_Type;
                         Value : String) return Cell_Access is
      Cell : Cell_Access := new String_Cell_Type(Sheet, Value'Length);
   begin
      String_Cell_Type(Cell.all).Text := Value;
      return Cell;
   end String_Cell;

   procedure Recalculate (Sheet : in out Spreadsheet_Type) is
      Iter : Cell_Lists.List_Iterator;
      Cell : Cell_Pointers.Pointer_Type;
   begin
      Sheet.Eval := Sheet.Eval + 1;         -- increment evaluation number
      if Changed(Spreadsheet_Type'Class(Sheet)) then
         Iter := First(Sheet.Cells);
         while Iter /= Last(Sheet.Cells) loop
            Cell := Value(Iter).Cell;
            Evaluate (Value(Cell).all);
            Iter := Succ(Iter);
         end loop;
         Updated (Spreadsheet_Type'Class(Sheet));
      end if;
   end Recalculate;

   procedure Change (Sheet : in out Spreadsheet_Type) is
   begin
      Sheet.Dirty := True;
   end Change;
```

```ada
procedure Updated (Sheet : in out Spreadsheet_Type) is
begin
   Sheet.Dirty := False;
end Updated;

function Changed (Sheet : Spreadsheet_Type) return Boolean is
begin
   return Sheet.Dirty;
end Changed;

function Cell (Sheet : Spreadsheet_Type;
               Where : String) return Cell_Access is
   Iter : Cell_Lists.List_Iterator := Cell_Lists.First(Sheet.Cells);
   Cell : Cell_Record;
begin
   while Iter /= Cell_Lists.Last(Sheet.Cells) loop
      Cell := Cell_Lists.Value(Iter);
      exit when To_Upper(Cell.Where(1..Cell.Size)) = To_Upper(Where);
      Iter := Cell_Lists.Succ(Iter);
   end loop;

   if Iter /= Cell_Lists.Last(Sheet.Cells) then
      return Value(Cell_Lists.Value(Iter).Cell);
   else
      return null;
   end if;
end Cell;

procedure Delete (Sheet : in out Spreadsheet_Type;
                  Where : in String) is
   Iter : Cell_Lists.List_Iterator;
   Cell : Cell_Record;
begin
   Iter := Cell_Lists.First (Sheet.Cells);
   while Iter /= Cell_Lists.Last (Sheet.Cells) loop
      Cell := Cell_Lists.Value(Iter);
      if To_Upper(Cell.Where(1..Cell.Size)) = To_Upper(Where) then
         Delete (Iter);
         Change (Spreadsheet_Type'Class(Sheet));
         exit;
      end if;
      Iter := Cell_Lists.Succ(Iter);
   end loop;
end Delete;
```

```
procedure Insert (Sheet : in out Spreadsheet_Type;
                  Where : in String;
                  What  : in Cell_Access) is
   New_Cell : Cell_Record;
begin
   Delete (Sheet, Where);

   if What /= null then
      New_Cell.Size := Integer'Min(Cell_Name_Length,Where'Length);
      New_Cell.Where (1..New_Cell.Size) :=
            Where (Where'First .. Where'First+New_Cell.Size-1);
      New_Cell.Cell := Pointer(What);
      Cell_Lists.Insert (Last(Sheet.Cells), New_Cell);
   end if;

   Change (Spreadsheet_Type'Class(Sheet));
end Insert;


function Evaluation (Sheet : Spreadsheet_Type)
                              return Evaluation_Number is
begin
   return Sheet.Eval;
end Evaluation;


function Text_Value (Cell : String_Cell_Type) return String is
begin
   return Cell.Text;
end Text_Value;


function Contents (Cell : String_Cell_Type) return String is
begin
   return Cell.Text;
end Contents;


procedure Evaluate (Cell : in out String_Cell_Type) is
begin
   Cell.State := Undefined;
end Evaluate;


function Num_Value (Cell : String_Cell_Type) return Integer is
begin
   raise Undefined_Cell_Error;
   return 0;                 -- to keep some compilers happy!
end Num_Value;
```

```ada
function Text_Value (Cell : Formula_Cell_Type) return String is
begin
   if Cell.State = Defined then
      return Integer'Image(Cell.Value);
   elsif Cell.State = Error then
      return "*ERROR*";
   else
      return "";
   end if;
end Text_Value;

function Contents (Cell : Formula_Cell_Type) return String is
begin
   return Cell.Text;
end Contents;

function Num_Value (Cell : Formula_Cell_Type) return Integer is
begin
   if Cell.State = Defined then
      return Cell.Value;
   else
      raise Undefined_Cell_Error;
   end if;
end Num_Value;

procedure Evaluate (Cell : in out Formula_Cell_Type) is
   Expr : Formula_Type (Cell.Sheet);
begin
   if Cell.State = Evaluating then
      raise Circularity_Error;
   elsif Cell.State = Unknown or
         Cell.Eval /= Evaluation(Cell.Sheet.all) then

      Cell.Eval  := Evaluation(Cell.Sheet.all);
      Cell.State := Evaluating;
      Cell.Value := Evaluate (Expr, Cell.Text);
      Cell.State := Defined;
   end if;

exception
   when Undefined_Cell_Error =>
      if Cell.State /= Error then
         Cell.State := Undefined;
      end if;
```

```
      when Fault : Circularity_Error | JE.Expressions.Syntax_Error
                                      | Constraint_Error =>
         Cell.State := Error;
         Handle_Error (Cell.Sheet, Fault);
      end Evaluate;

      procedure Handle_Error (Sheet : access Spreadsheet_Type;
                              Error : Ada.Exceptions.Exception_Occurrence) is
      begin
         null;      -- do nothing, but allow for future overriding
      end Handle_Error;

end JE.Spreadsheets;
```

D.12   JE.Spreadsheets.Active

(See chapter 19)

```
package JE.Spreadsheets.Active is
   use JE.Spreadsheets;
   type Active_Spreadsheet_Type is abstract new Spreadsheet_Type
                                 with private;
   procedure Change   (Sheet : in out Active_Spreadsheet_Type);
   function  Changed (Sheet : Active_Spreadsheet_Type) return Boolean;

   type Counting_Cell_Type (Sheet : access Spreadsheet_Type'Class) is
                            new Cell_Type(Sheet) with private;
   function Counting_Cell (Sheet : access Spreadsheet_Type'Class)
                           return Cell_Access;

   procedure Evaluate    (Cell : in out Counting_Cell_Type);
   function  Contents    (Cell : Counting_Cell_Type) return String;
   function  Text_Value (Cell : Counting_Cell_Type) return String;
   function  Num_Value  (Cell : Counting_Cell_Type) return Integer;

private
   protected type Shared_Flag_Type is
      function  State return Boolean;
      procedure Set;
      procedure Clear;
   private
      State_Flag : Boolean := False;
   end Shared_Flag_Type;
```

```
   type Active_Spreadsheet_Type is abstract new Spreadsheet_Type with
      record
         Modified : Shared_Flag_Type;
      end record;


   procedure Updated (Sheet : in out Active_Spreadsheet_Type);


   task type Counter_Task (Sheet : access Spreadsheet_Type'Class) is
      entry Get (Value : out Integer);
      entry Stop;
   end Counter_Task;


   type Counting_Cell_Type (Sheet : access Spreadsheet_Type'Class) is
      new Cell_Type(Sheet) with
      record
         Counter : Counter_Task(Sheet);
      end record;


   procedure Finalize (Object : in out Counting_Cell_Type);

end JE.Spreadsheets.Active;
```

---------------- *Package body* ----------------

```
with Ada.Calendar;
package body JE.Spreadsheets.Active is
   use type Ada.Calendar.Time;                 -- to allow use of "+"

   task body Counter_Task is
      type Count_Type is mod 10000;
      Count       : Count_Type           := Count_Type'First;
      Update_Time : Ada.Calendar.Time := Ada.Calendar.Clock + 5.0;
   begin
      loop
         select
            accept Get (Value : out Integer) do
               Value := Integer(Count);
            end Get;
         or
            accept Stop;
            exit;
         or
            delay until Update_Time;
            Update_Time := Update_Time + 5.0;
```

```
         Count := Count + 1;
         Change (Sheet.all);
      end select;
   end loop;
end Counter_Task;

protected body Shared_Flag_Type is

   function State return Boolean is
   begin
      return State_Flag;
   end State;

   procedure Set is
   begin
      State_Flag := True;
   end Set;

   procedure Clear is
   begin
      State_Flag := False;
   end Clear;

end Shared_Flag_Type;

procedure Change (Sheet : in out Active_Spreadsheet_Type) is
begin
   Sheet.Modified.Set;
end Change;

procedure Updated (Sheet : in out Active_Spreadsheet_Type) is
begin
   Sheet.Modified.Clear;
end Updated;

function Changed (Sheet : Active_Spreadsheet_Type) return Boolean is
begin
   return Sheet.Modified.State;
end Changed;

procedure Finalize (Object : in out Counting_Cell_Type) is
begin
   Object.Counter.Stop;
end Finalize;
```

```
   function Contents (Cell : Counting_Cell_Type) return String is
   begin
      return "<5-second counter>";
   end Contents;


   function Text_Value (Cell : Counting_Cell_Type) return String is
   begin
      return Integer'Image(Num_Value(Cell));
   end Text_Value;


   function Num_Value (Cell : Counting_Cell_Type) return Integer is
      I : Integer;
   begin
      Cell.Counter.Get (I);
      return I;
   end Num_Value;


   procedure Evaluate (Cell : in out Counting_Cell_Type) is
   begin
      Cell.State := Defined;
   end Evaluate;


   function Counting_Cell (Sheet : access Spreadsheet_Type'Class)
                           return Cell_Access is
      Cell : Cell_Access := new Counting_Cell_Type (Sheet);
   begin
      return Cell;
   end Counting_Cell;
end JE.Spreadsheets.Active;
```

D.13   JE.Stacks

(See chapter 13)

```
generic
   type Item_Type is private;
package JE.Stacks is
   type Stack_Type is limited private;

   procedure Push  (Stack : in out Stack_Type;
                    Item  : in Item_Type);
   procedure Pop   (Stack : in out Stack_Type;
                    Item  : out Item_Type);
```

```
function  Top   (Stack : Stack_Type) return Item_Type;
function  Size  (Stack : Stack_Type) return Natural;
function  Empty (Stack : Stack_Type) return Boolean;

Stack_Overflow, Stack_Underflow : exception;

private
   type Stack_Item;
   type Stack_Type is access Stack_Item;
end JE.Stacks;
```

----------------- *Package body* -----------------

```
with JE.Lists;
package body JE.Stacks is

   package Lists is new JE.Lists (Item_Type);

   type Stack_Item is
      record
         L : Lists.List_Type;
      end record;

   procedure Push (Stack : in out Stack_Type;
                   Item  : in Item_Type) is
   begin
      if Stack = null then
         Stack := new Stack_Item;
      end if;
      Lists.Insert (Lists.First(Stack.L), Item);
   exception
      when Storage_Error =>
         raise Stack_Overflow;
   end Push;

   procedure Pop (Stack : in out Stack_Type;
                  Item  : out Item_Type) is
   begin
      Item := Top(Stack);
      Lists.Delete (Lists.First(Stack.L));
   exception
      when Lists.List_Error =>
         raise Stack_Underflow;
   end Pop;
```

```ada
   function Top (Stack : Stack_Type) return Item_Type is
   begin
      return Lists.Value(Lists.First(Stack.L));
   exception
      when Lists.List_Error =>
         raise Stack_Underflow;
   end Top;

   function Size (Stack : Stack_Type) return Natural is
   begin
      if Stack = null then
         return 0;
      else
         return Lists.Size (Stack.L);
      end if;
   end Size;

   function Empty (Stack : Stack_Type) return Boolean is
   begin
      return Size(Stack) = 0;
   end Empty;

end JE.Stacks;
```

D.14   JE.Times

(See chapter 9)

```ada
with Ada.Calendar;
package JE.Times is
   subtype Time_Type    is Ada.Calendar.Time;

   subtype Year_Type    is Ada.Calendar.Year_Number;
   type    Month_Type   is (Jan, Feb, Mar, Apr, May, Jun,
                            Jul, Aug, Sep, Oct, Nov, Dec);
   subtype Day_Type     is Ada.Calendar.Day_Number;
   subtype Hour_Type    is Integer range 0..23;
   subtype Minute_Type  is Integer range 0..59;
   subtype Second_Type  is Integer range 0..59;

   subtype Day_Duration is Ada.Calendar.Day_Duration;

   function Clock return Ada.Calendar.Time   renames Ada.Calendar.Clock;
```

```
function Interval (Days    : Natural := 0;
                   Hours   : Natural := 0;
                   Minutes : Natural := 0;
                   Seconds : Natural := 0) return Duration;
function Year    (Date : Ada.Calendar.Time) return Year_Type
                                     renames Ada.Calendar.Year;
function Month   (Date : Time_Type) return Month_Type;
function Day     (Date : Ada.Calendar.Time) return Day_Type
                                     renames Ada.Calendar.Day;
function Hour    (Date : Time_Type) return Hour_Type;
function Minute  (Date : Time_Type) return Minute_Type;
function Second  (Date : Time_Type) return Second_Type;

function Time    (Year   : Year_Type;
                  Month  : Month_Type;
                  Day    : Day_Type;
                  Hour   : Hour_Type   := 0;
                  Minute : Minute_Type := 0;
                  Second : Second_Type := 0)    return Time_Type;

function "+" (Left  : Ada.Calendar.Time;
             Right : Duration)           return Ada.Calendar.Time
                                         renames Ada.Calendar."+";
function "+" (Left  : Duration;
             Right : Ada.Calendar.Time) return Ada.Calendar.Time
                                         renames Ada.Calendar."+";
function "-" (Left  : Ada.Calendar.Time;
             Right : Duration)           return Ada.Calendar.Time
                                         renames Ada.Calendar."-";
function "-" (Left  : Ada.Calendar.Time;
             Right : Ada.Calendar.Time) return Duration
                                         renames Ada.Calendar."-";

function "<" (Left, Right : Ada.Calendar.Time) return Boolean
                                         renames Ada.Calendar."<";
function "<="(Left, Right : Ada.Calendar.Time) return Boolean
                                         renames Ada.Calendar."<=";
function ">" (Left, Right : Ada.Calendar.Time) return Boolean
                                         renames Ada.Calendar.">";
function ">="(Left, Right : Ada.Calendar.Time) return Boolean
                                         renames Ada.Calendar.">=";

Time_Error : exception renames Ada.Calendar.Time_Error;
end JE.Times;
```

---------------- *Package body* ----------------

```
package body JE.Times is

   Seconds_Per_Minute : constant := 60;
   Minutes_Per_Hour   : constant := 60;
   Hours_Per_Day      : constant := 24;
   Seconds_Per_Hour   : constant := Minutes_Per_Hour * Seconds_Per_Minute;
   Seconds_Per_Day    : constant := Hours_Per_Day * Seconds_Per_Hour;
   type Integer_Time is range 0 .. Seconds_Per_Day;

   function Convert_Time (Time : Day_Duration) return Integer_Time is
      T : Integer_Time := Integer_Time (Time);
   begin
      return T mod Integer_Time'Last;
   end Convert_Time;

   function Interval (Days    : Natural := 0;
                      Hours   : Natural := 0;
                      Minutes : Natural := 0;
                      Seconds : Natural := 0) return Duration is
   begin
      return Duration( (Days * Seconds_Per_Day) +
                       (Hours * Seconds_Per_Hour) +
                       (Minutes * Seconds_Per_Minute) + Seconds );
   end Interval;

   function Month  (Date : Ada.Calendar.Time) return Month_Type is
   begin
      return Month_Type'Val (Ada.Calendar.Month(Date) - 1);
   end Month;

   function Hour (Date : Time_Type) return Hour_Type is
      S : Ada.Calendar.Day_Duration := Ada.Calendar.Seconds (Date);
   begin
      return Hour_Type( Convert_Time(S) / Seconds_Per_Hour );
   end Hour;

   function Minute (Date : Time_Type) return Minute_Type is
      S : Ada.Calendar.Day_Duration := Ada.Calendar.Seconds (Date);
   begin
      return Minute_Type( (Convert_Time(S) / Seconds_Per_Minute)
                                       mod Minutes_Per_Hour );
   end Minute;
```

```
   function Second (Date : Time_Type) return Second_Type is
      S : Ada.Calendar.Day_Duration := Ada.Calendar.Seconds (Date);
   begin
      return Second_Type( Convert_Time(S) mod Seconds_Per_Minute );
   end Second;


   function Time (Year    : Year_Type;
                  Month   : Month_Type;
                  Day     : Day_Type;
                  Hour    : Hour_Type    := 0;
                  Minute  : Minute_Type  := 0;
                  Second  : Second_Type  := 0) return Time_Type is
      Seconds : Day_Duration :=
                  Day_Duration( (Hour * Seconds_Per_Hour) +
                                (Minute * Seconds_Per_Minute) + Second );
   begin
      return Ada.Calendar.Time_Of (Year, Month_Type'Pos(Month) + 1,
                                   Day, Seconds);
   end Time;

end JE.Times;
```

Glossary

*(**Note**: Some of the terms included here are technical terms which I've defined loosely and informally. Such definitions are for your guidance only, and are not necessarily complete or entirely accurate.)*

Abstract operation: An operation for which no implementation can be provided. Only **abstract types** can have abstract operations. Derived **concrete types** must override any inherited abstract operations.

Abstract data type: A type whose implementation details are hidden and can only be handled using the publicly accessible operations provided for it. Not to be confused with **abstract type**.

Abstract type: A type declared using the reserved word **abstract**. Only abstract types can have **abstract operations**. You cannot declare objects belonging to an abstract type; the purpose of an abstract type is to act as the parent for a class of derived types.

Access discriminant: A discriminant whose type is an **anonymous general access type**. Access discriminants can only be given for limited types; the values supplied for them cannot be null and they cannot be copied or altered.

Access parameter: A form of **input parameter** which is an **anonymous general access type**. Access parameters cannot be null and they cannot be copied or altered.

Access type: A type whose values are **access values**. **Pool-specific access types** can only refer to objects created using **new**, while **general access types** can also refer to **aliased objects**.

Access value: A value which refers to ('points to') other objects defined elsewhere, commonly referred to as a **pointer**.

Accessor: A **function** which accesses an internal component of a **private type**.

471

Actual parameter: The **parameter** value supplied in a **subprogram call** (often referred to as an **argument**) or a **generic instantiation**.

ADT: An acronym for **abstract data type**.

Algorithm: A method for solving a particular problem which is guaranteed to terminate in a finite time.

Aliased object: An object declared using the reserved word **aliased** which can be accessed by a general access value, so that the same object might be referred to by more than one 'alias'.

Anonymous type: A type whose name is not known so that objects of that type cannot be declared explicitly.

Argument: Often used as a synonym for **parameter**. Technically speaking, arguments are the 'actual parameters' supplied when calling a subprogram (or instantiating a generic unit) to match the 'formal parameters' given in its specification.

Array: A collection of objects of the same type which can be selected by an index belonging to the **index subtype** of the array.

Attribute: A characteristic of a type which can be used to access various details of the type and its implementation.

Block: A section of a program incorporating an optional set of **declarations** valid within the block, a set of **statements** defining the processing to be carried out, and an optional set of **exception handlers**.

Body: The portion of a package, subprogram, task or protected record which contains the statements which define its implementation.

Bottom Up: The opposite of **top down**; an approach which builds simple low-level objects into more complex higher-level objects.

Bug: An error in a program.

Call: The invocation of a subprogram which causes **in** parameters to be transferred into the subprogram, followed by execution of the subprogram body and the transfer of **out** parameters back to the surrounding environment.

Child: A **package** or **subprogram** which acts as an extension of a **parent** package, thus allowing packages to be extended without modifying the original specifications.

Class: A family of **derived types** with a common **parent type**.

Class-wide type: A type which can refer to an object of any type within a **class**. Class-wide types are created by applying the 'Class **attribute** to a **tagged type**.

Client: A program unit which makes use of the services provided by a particular **package**.

Compilation unit: A portion of a program which can be submitted to the compiler independently; a **package** specification or body, a **subprogram** body or a **generic instantiation**.

Compiler:	A program which translates the **source code** for a **library unit** into an **object module** in a **program library**.
Component:	An element of a **composite type**.
Composite type:	An **array** or **record** type which represents a collection of smaller components.
Concrete type:	A non-abstract type (see **abstract type**).
Constant:	An **object** whose value cannot be changed.
Constrained type:	A type whose **constraints** have all been specified so that the compiler knows exactly how it should be represented in memory.
Constraint:	A **discriminant** for a record or a range for a subtype or array index subtype which usually determines the amount of memory the compiler must allocate for objects of the type.
Constructor:	A subprogram which constructs a value of a private type from its component parts.
Container:	A type which contains a number of simpler elements. Array types are provided as a built-in container type in Ada.
Context clause:	A **with** or **use** clause at the start of a **compilation unit** which specifies the context within which a program unit should be compiled (i.e. which names should be recognised as being valid).
Controlled type:	A type which provides for user-defined initialisation and finalisation procedures.
Controlling operand:	A parameter of a primitive operation of a tagged type (or a result in the case of a function) which belongs to that tagged type.
Coupling:	A linkage between two parts of a program such that if one part of the program is modified, the behaviour of the other part may also be affected. This can lead to maintenance problems.
Crash:	What happens when something goes wrong and your program (or worse, its operating environment) ceases to function.
Dangling pointer:	A **pointer** (**access value**) which points to an object that no longer exists.
Debugger:	A tool for tracing program execution to help track down **bugs**.
Debugging:	The process of discovering and correcting **bugs** in a program.
Declaration:	The definition of a name and its meaning.
Dependents:	For a particular unit of a program, all those parts of the program which depend on it (e.g. via a **with** clause) and which will need recompiling as a result of any changes.
Derivation:	The definition of a new type in terms of an existing one.
Derived type:	A type created from an existing **parent type** which inherits the primitive operations of its parent. Objects of a derived type can always be converted to a parent type and vice versa.

Discrete type:	An **integer** or **enumeration type**.
Discriminant:	A 'parameter' to a **record type** whose value may be used in array index constraints for record components, as an initial value for components, or to select between record **variants**.
Dispatching:	The selection of the correct **primitive operation** to be executed based on the actual tag of a **class-wide** value.
Entry:	The means by which one **task** can request a service from another task or from a **protected record**.
Enumeration type:	A type whose possible values are enumerated (i.e. listed) as part of its declaration.
Exception:	An error indication which can be 'raised' when an error is detected and which can be handled by an **exception handler** elsewhere in the program.
Exception handler:	A section of code at the end of a **block** which defines the recovery actions to be performed in response to **exceptions** raised within that block.
Executable program:	A **subprogram** which has been compiled into the program **library** and then linked with any other library units it depends on.
Expression:	Something which can be evaluated to produce a value which can be stored or otherwise processed.
Extensibility:	The ability to add new features to an existing program without disturbing any existing code.
Field:	A synonym for 'component'.
Finalisation:	The actions which take place immediately before an object is destroyed.
Fixed point:	A variety of **real number** whose value is accurate to within a given magnitude.
Flag:	A Boolean value which can be 'set' to True or 'reset' to False.
Floating point:	A variety of **real number** which is represented to a specified number of significant figures regardless of how big or small it is.
Formal parameter:	The definition of a **parameter** in a **specification**.
Full view:	The unrestricted view of a **private type** available from the package body where the type is declared, or from the body of a child package or from the private parts of any of the associated specifications.
Function:	A **subprogram** which returns a value of a specified type which is invoked as part of an **expression**.
Garbage collection:	The automatic reclamation of dynamically allocated objects that are no longer accessible. Garbage collection is not usually provided in Ada.
General access type:	A type which can refer to **aliased** objects as well as objects created using **new**.

Generic unit:	A unit defined in terms of generalised types or subprograms and which can be **instantiated** to use any compatible types or subprograms in their place.
Global object:	An **object** declared outside the current **block** (especially one declared at **library level**) so that the current block is not the only place where it can be referenced.
GNAT:	The GNU Ada Translator, a free Ada 95 compiler available for a range of platforms. See Chapter 20 for more details.
Guard:	A condition used with an **accept** statement or a **protected entry** that specifies when it can be invoked.
Heap:	A synonym for what Ada refers to as a **storage pool**.
Identifier:	A name given to a program entity that can be used to refer to it. Identifiers must begin with a letter and must consist entirely of letters, digits and underline characters. The last character must not be an underline character.
Indefinite type:	A type with unknown discriminants; a **class-wide type** or a type whose discriminants are specified as '(<>)'.
Index subtype:	A **subtype** specifying the range of possible **subscripts** for an **array**.
Inheritance:	The automatic definition of the characteristics of a type based on the characteristics of its **parent type**.
Initialisation:	The actions which are performed immediately after an object is created to prepare it for use.
Instantiation:	The act of creating an 'instance' of a generic unit by replacing its **formal parameters** by a set of matching **actual parameters**.
Integer type:	A type capable of holding any whole number from a specified range of values. In Ada these can be signed integer types or modular types.
Iteration:	A synonym for 'repetition', as in a **loop**.
Iterator:	A data type used to mark a position in a collection of data (e.g. a **linked list**) and to move from item to item within the collection.
Library:	A repository managed by the **compiler** which is used to hold information about units which have been compiled.
Library level:	The outermost level of **scope** in a program. Only the names of **library units** and names declared in a library-level **package** are at library level.
Library unit:	A **subprogram** or **package** compiled as a stand-alone unit (i.e. not embedded within any other unit) and added to the program **library**.
Limited type:	A type which cannot be copied by assignment and for which the standard equality tests are not provided (although you can overload "=" and "/=" to provide these yourself).

Linked list:	A data collection where each item in the collection points to its neighbours using **access values**.
Linker:	A program which binds a library subprogram together with any other **library units** it refers to into an **executable program**.
Literal:	A representation of a value of a particular type, as with integer literals (e.g. 123) or string literals (e.g. "xyzzy").
Loop:	A section of code which is repeated ('iterated').
Magic number:	A number appearing in a program whose appearance tells you nothing about its intended purpose or meaning.
Maintenance:	The process of fixing **bugs** in, and adding new features to, existing software.
Model:	A representation of some aspect of external reality in a program.
Multitasking:	The ability to execute several parts of a **program** in parallel (or apparently in parallel).
Namespace:	The set of names accessible at a given point in a program.
Null pointer:	An **access value** which does not refer to any object.
Object:	A **constant** or **variable** of a specified type.
Opaque type:	A **private type** whose implementation details are made completely invisible by moving them into the package body and using an **access value** for an incompletely declared type in the package specification.
Overloading:	Giving multiple meanings to the same name, but making them distinguishable by context. For example, two procedures with the same name are overloading that name as long as the compiler can determine which one you mean from contextual information such as the type and number of parameters that you supply when you call it.
Overriding:	Providing a **declaration** which matches another declaration of the same name, thereby hiding the existing declaration.
Package:	A collection of logically related **declarations** (both public and **private**); typically, the declaration of a **type** together with the operations of that type. Implementation details are concealed within the corresponding package **body**.
Parameter:	A value or object which is used to transfer information to or from **subprograms**. Input parameters can be thought of as being copied into the subprogram when it is called, and output parameters can be thought of as having their values copied back to the caller when the subprogram returns.
Parent type:	The type from which a **derived type** was created.
Partial view:	The view of a **private type** to a client where not all characteristics of the type are visible.
Pointer:	A common synonym for what Ada calls an **access value**.

Pool-specific access type: An **access type** which can only refer to objects allocated by **new** from a **storage pool** specific to the object's type.

Portability: A measure of system independence; portable programs can be moved to a new system by recompiling without having to make any other changes.

Precedence: The order in which arithmetic operations are performed.

Prettyprinter: A tool for automatically formatting Ada **source code**.

Primitive operation: An operation of a type which is **inherited** by all types derived from it. The primitive operations of a type are those operations with a controlling operand or result of that type declared in the same package specification as the type itself.

Private type: A type whose internal implementation is inaccessible outside the **package** where it is declared.

Procedure: A **subprogram** which is invoked by a procedure call **statement**.

Program: A **subprogram** (usually a parameterless **procedure**) which has been linked to produce an executable file.

Protected record: A data structure which provides synchronised access to the data it contains for use in **multitasking** situations.

Real type: A type representing numeric values which include a fractional part. In Ada these can be **floating point** or **fixed point** types.

Record: A composite type consisting of a collection of named components, not necessarily all of the same type.

Recursion: The definition of an operation in terms of itself.

Rendezvous: A form of intertask communication and synchronisation, where one **task** calls an entry of another task and the called task executes an **accept** statement for the entry being called.

Reusability: The ability of a package or subprogram to be used again without modification as a building block in a different program from the one it was originally written for.

Scalar type: A type representing single values which cannot be broken down into smaller components, namely a **discrete type** or a **real type**.

Scope: The region of a program where a name is visible, extending from its declaration to the end of the block which contains the declaration.

Slice: A section of an **array** selected by specifying its lower and upper limits.

Source code: The original textual form of a program.

Specification: A description of the interface provided by a subprogram, package, task or protected record. The implementation details are hidden in the corresponding **body**.

Statement: An instruction to carry out some action; a single step within a program.

Stepwise refinement:	The development of a program by breaking the original problem into smaller subproblems and then applying the same process to each subproblem.
Storage pool:	A block of unused memory, often referred to as a **heap**, which can be used to allocate objects dynamically using **new** for use with **access types**.
String:	A sequence of characters.
Stub:	A temporary implementaion of part of a program for **debugging** purposes.
Subprogram:	A set of statements which can be executed by calling the subprogram by name.
Subscript:	An index into an **array** which is used to specify an individual array component.
Subtype:	A **type** together with a **constraint** which possibly restricts the allowed range of values. Strictly speaking, all types in Ada are actually subtypes of anonymous unconstrained types.
Syntax:	The rules of a language which determine what is and is not acceptable to the compiler.
Syntax analysis:	The process of checking that something conforms to the rules of a given **syntax** and analysing its structure according to those rules.
Tagged type:	A type which can be extended by **derivation** to add new components or operations.
Task:	A construct consisting of a **specification** and a **body** whose body is executed in parallel with other tasks in the program.
Token:	Anything treated as a single symbol during **syntax analysis** such as a name, a literal or an operator.
Top-down:	An approach which starts from a high (generalised) level and works towards lower (more specific) levels.
Top-down design:	A synonym for **stepwise refinement**.
Type:	Every **object** has a type which specifies the set of values allowed and the **primitive operations** which it provides. Types are grouped into **classes** which share the same primitive operations.
Unconstrained type:	A type which is not fully specified, e.g. an **array** whose index subtype is incompletely specified or a type with **discriminants** whose values are not known. You cannot declare objects of an unconstrained type without supplying the missing **constraints** (although you can supply them by providing an initial value as part of the declaration).
Undefined:	Having an unpredicatable (and not necessarily valid) value.
Variable:	An **object** of a specified type whose value can be changed.
Variant record:	A record which can take different forms depending on the value of a **discriminant**.

View: An external representation of an internal processing **model** which is used to interact with the internal model.

Wrapper: A **package** which changes the interface to an existing package without substantially increasing its functionality.

Index